BEYOND THE STEPPE FRONTIER

STUDIES OF THE WEATHERHEAD EAST ASIAN INSTITUTE, COLUMBIA UNIVERSITY

The Studies of the Weatherhead East Asian Institute of Columbia University were inaugurated in 1962 to bring to a wider public the results of significant new research on modern and contemporary East Asia.

Beyond the Steppe Frontier

A HISTORY OF THE SINO-RUSSIAN BORDER

SÖREN URBANSKY

PRINCETON UNIVERSITY PRESS

PRINCETON & OXFORD

Copyright © 2020 by Princeton University Press

Published by Princeton University Press
41 William Street, Princeton, New Jersey 08540
6 Oxford Street, Woodstock, Oxfordshire OX20 1TR

press.princeton.edu

Library of Congress Cataloging-in-Publication Data

Names: Urbansky, Sören, author.
Title: Beyond the steppe frontier : a history of the Sino-Russian border /
  Sören Urbansky.
Description: Princeton : Princeton University Press, [2020] | Series: Studies
  of the Weatherhead East Asian Institute, Columbia University | Includes
  bibliographical references and index.
Identifiers: LCCN 2019022974 (print) | LCCN 2019022975 (ebook) |
  ISBN 9780691181684 (hardcover) | ISBN 9780691195445 (ebook)
Subjects: LCSH: China—Boundaries—Russia. | Russia—Boundaries—China. |
  China—Boundaries—Soviet Union. | Soviet Union—Boundaries—China. |
  Borderlands—China—History—20th century. | Borderlands—Russia—
  History. | Borderlands—Soviet Union—History.
Classification: LCC DS740.5.R8 U73 2020 (print) | LCC DS740.5.R8 (ebook) |
  DDC 957/.7—dc23
LC record available at https://lccn.loc.gov/2019022974
LC ebook record available at https://lccn.loc.gov/2019022975

British Library Cataloging-in-Publication Data is available

Editorial: Eric Crahan and Thalia Leaf
Production Editorial: Karen Carter
Jacket/Cover Design: Layla Mac Rory
Production: Danielle Amatucci
Publicity: Alyssa Sanford and Julia Hall
Copyeditor: Joseph Dahm

Jacket/Cover Credit: Detail from cover of *Granitsa na zamke* by Nikolai Kostarev
  (Moscow: Molodaia gvardiia, 1930), artist unknown

This book has been composed in Arno

Printed on acid-free paper. ∞

Printed in the United States of America

10 9 8 7 6 5 4 3 2 1

Für 静茹

CONTENTS

ACKNOWLEDGMENTS

MY CHILDHOOD MEMORIES of life near the Iron Curtain sparked my curiosity about the subject. A long train ride from Berlin to Beijing in the summer of 2002 opened my eyes. When I got off the train at Zabaikalsk, the last Russian station, to cross the border into China, I realized that this dusty outpost would be the subject of my research. This book is therefore a project that, overall, has taken many years to mature and complete. Along the way I have received enormous amounts of help and advice.

I owe my deepest gratitude to my two academic advisors. The intellectual guidance and support of Jürgen Osterhammel in Konstanz have been invaluable and helped expand my thinking beyond the Eurasian horizon. Karl Schlögel, my mentor and a source of inspiration since my undergraduate days in Frankfurt on the Polish border, has taught me to always stay curious about the details and think about how they relate to make the big picture. I am very grateful to four other scholars who have provided me with insightful counsel, constant encouragement, and continual personal support. Sabine Dabringhaus offered me a lectureship in Chinese history at the University of Freiburg early on my way and gave me all the freedom to disappear for fieldwork or in the library nonetheless. Frank Grüner inspired many of the ideas in this book, and I owe a great deal to our *Kharbinskii kruzhok* in Heidelberg. By hiring me for a lectureship in Russian history at the Ludwig Maximilian University of Munich, Andreas Renner gave me the opportunity to return to my Slavic roots and think about what comes next. Last but not the least, Caroline Humphrey's extensive knowledge of the region and anthropological outlook on the subject enabled me to rethink and complete the project in final book form at the University of Cambridge.

I am extremely grateful to Michel Abeßer, Lisa Furchtgott, Ashley Gonik, Willard Sunderland, my brother Henrik, and the anonymous reviewers for their close and careful reading of the manuscript during the various stages of its writing and for providing me with critical comments and suggestions. I also wish to thank a number of friends, colleagues, and fellow scholars who offered valuable insights and advice or provided support in other valuable ways: Felix Ackermann, Nadine Amsler, Jörg Baberowski, Olga Bakich, Franck Billé,

Sebastian Conrad, Viktor I. Diatlov, Elisabeth Engel, Victoria Frede, Arunabh Ghosh, Jörn Happel, Susanne Hohler, Mikko Huotari, Akihiro Iwashita, Jan C. Jansen, Robert Kindler, Thomas Lahusen, David Lazar, Heinz-Dietrich Löwe, Lorenz Lüthi, Silke Martini, Norihiro Naganawa, Julia Obertreis, Sergey Radchenko, Anne Clara Schenderlein, Wang Shuo, Mirjam Sprau, Richard Wetzell, David Wolff, and Ross Yelsey. Over the years research for the book took me to three dozen archives and libraries in seven countries, where staff members made my research much easier than it would otherwise have been. I also wish to express heartfelt thanks to my colleagues and friends in China and Russia for sharing their information, unique perspectives, access to their networks, and time, making my fieldwork not only interesting but also enjoyable. I particularly wish to express my sincere gratitude to Elena E. Aurilene, Natal'ia A. Beliaeva, Chen Kaike, Vladimir G. Datsyshen, Evgenii V. Dobrotushenko, Andrei V. Doronin, Tat'iana P. Filobok, Aleksandr V. Frolov, Huang Dingtian, Liubov A. Kuvardina, Aleksandr G. Larin, Viktor L. Larin, Li Tielun, Aleksandr V. Popenko, Shen Zhihua, Ivan V. Stavrov, Su Fenglin (+), Aleksandr P. Tarasov, Anatolii V. Taukhelov, Wu Tieying, Xu Zhanxin, Yang Cheng, Ol'ga V. Zalesskaia, and Igor' G. Balashov, a local Zabaikalsk citizen for the stroll across one of the minefields near the border, from which the explosives apparently had been removed a few years previous.

I had the good fortune of presenting portions of this work at various lectures, workshops, and conferences in Heidelberg, Freiburg, Vladivostok, Harbin, Bielefeld, Stockholm, Munich, Kolkata, Marburg, Leipzig, Tübingen, Sapporo, Bremen, Beijing, Basel, Washington, D.C., Berlin, New Orleans, Konstanz, Cambridge, Vilnius, Hamburg, Frankfurt an der Oder, Seoul, New Haven, Shanghai, Krasnoiarsk, and Oxford, and in a train compartment on the Trans-Siberian Railroad somewhere near Erofei Pavlovich. I have benefited enormously from the discussions that have helped to shape my ideas. It goes without saying that all remaining shortcomings of the pages that follow are irrevocably my own.

Work on this book was graciously funded by the German Academic Scholarship Foundation, the German Academic Exchange Service, the German Historical Institute in Moscow, the Asia and Europe in a Global Context Research Cluster at Heidelberg University, and the Economic and Social Research Council of the United Kingdom. I am most grateful to these institutions for their generous support of my research.

It has been a great pleasure working with Princeton University Press commissioning editor Brigitta van Rheinberg, whose enthusiasm and support have made this book possible. I would like to also thank Eric Crahan, Thalia Leaf, Amanda Peery, Karen Carter, and Merli Guerra for their work in turning the manuscript into a book and bringing it to publication, and Joseph Dahm for his stellar editorial work. Finally, I would like to thank David Cox for making the maps, Layla Mac Rory for the cover design, and Max Brunner and Emily Woessner for compiling the index.

My greatest personal debts are to my family. My parents, Wolfgang and Sonja, have always been proud of me and my research, even though they know little about that faraway corner of the earth. My thanks equally to my parents-in-law, Hailiang and Cuixia, for treating me like one of their own. My deepest appreciation goes to my wife, Jingru, who is from somewhere near that distant place and has been more central to this enterprise than she can ever know. Our two wonderful children, Alma and Golo, who were born during this exciting journey, have brought unprecedented joy to my life. Without them and their mother, everything would be nothing.

A NOTE ON TRANSLATION, ROMANIZATION, AND DATES

RUSSIAN, CHINESE, AND JAPANESE calendar systems have been converted to the Gregorian calendar. Names, places, and terms that have entered into the common mode of expression appear in their more prevalent Western spellings. Generally, places that have changed national affiliations over time are referred to in their present forms; but in describing rivers under shared Chinese and Russian ownership, and that have been given dual names, I have settled on the Russian versions. Chinese terms in Russian sources are often opaque. Whenever I was unable to identify the original, I have used the transliteration of the Russian. All translations are my own unless otherwise indicated.

BEYOND THE STEPPE FRONTIER

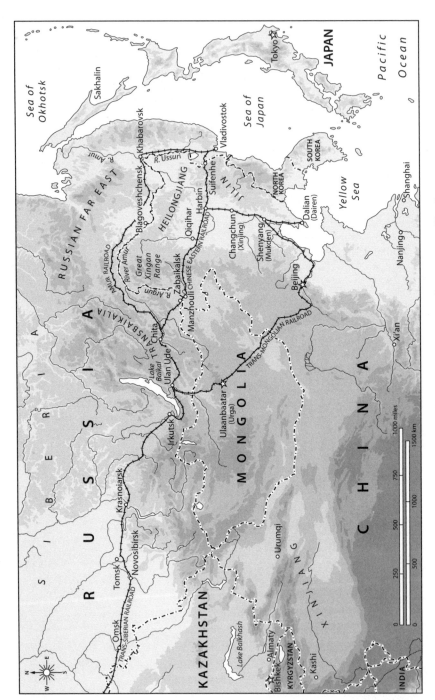

FIGURE 0.1. Inner and Northeast Asia with present-day international borders.

Introduction

MANY RIVERS UNITE rather than divide, even if they represent borders between states. For a long time the Argun, a river marking the boundary between Russia and China, was no exception. Until well into the twentieth century nomadic peoples crisscrossed the river to let their animals graze on summer and winter pastures in the rolling steppe. To sedentary borderland peoples the river had an equally uniting quality, as it provided a living for settlers on both sides, regardless of nationality. Cossacks residing near the Argun visited Chinese territory to hunt game and to lease land from the Mongols for raising hay. Others bartered in the stalls of Chinese petty traders. Chinese migrants from provinces south of the Great Wall worked as hunters and gold miners on both shores of the river. Many were fluent in Russian and dressed in Russian style, wearing short black fur coats and hats with flaps covering the head and ears. Some settled in Russian villages, were baptized, and married Russian women. Those who had not assimilated through marriage or religion nonetheless came into contact with people from across the river, often communicating in pidgin.

This overlapping and mingling of distinct nomadic and sedentary cultures and European and Asian civilizations along the Argun came to an end only when the border gained geopolitical significance in the late nineteenth century. During the following decades the imperial interests of Russia, followed by the Soviet Union, would clash with those of Qing (later Republican) China and Japan. Subsequently, the world's two large leviathans of communism would hail their friendship and stage their enmity. At that juncture the centers of power strove to seal national limits, a protracted process resulting in the disintegration of transborder relations between different peoples. Within less than a century the states had by and large succeeded in suppressing traditional borderland cultures by halting existing cross-border networks of kinship and friendship and destroying cross-border land use and economy through rule of law, physical force, deportation, reeducation, and propaganda. Only after the disintegration of the Soviet Union would China and Russia reopen their common border.

This oscillation of the rigidity of the Russia-China border—soft, hard, soft—contradicts teleological assumptions of borders' irreversible evolutionary movement from indefinite zones toward precise lines of demarcation. However, in this case, the image of a common, functional boundary is not completely obsolete. Even more than a quarter of a century on, artifacts such as abandoned observation towers and rusted barbed-wire fences remind the visitor that the states' military power was once a formidable physical presence on the soil of the borderlands. Today, despite emerging transborder entanglements, such as trade, tourism, and overlapping Russian and Chinese cellular telephone networks, the boundary is not completely fossilized. The Argun demarcates two distinct regions on its opposite banks—one in Russia, another in China. The majority of the people living in the Russian borderland are Russian: they speak Russian, live in Soviet or old Russian-style houses, watch *Vremia* news, and dress similarly to people in other parts of rural Russia. On the Chinese side of the border, passports identify the majority of settlers as being ethnically Han. People on the right bank speak Mandarin, watch the evening Beijing-time *Xinwen Lianbo*, and wear Chinese-style garments. Beyond phenotype, language, and culture, however, many additional borders exist. No statistics on food consumption are available for this particular borderland. Yet it seems safe to assume that potato and rice consumption preferences would, most likely, accord with the red line on the map. These contemporary differences point to deep-rooted structures that define the culture and language of the people who populate the borderland today. Presently the Sino-Russian state border coincides with cultural and linguistic limits. How, then, did the red line come to be such a stark line of separation? And how did it become possible for so arbitrary a division to permeate almost every part of the typical border dweller's life?

In searching for answers to these questions, this book traces the transformation of the Sino-Russian border from an open interimperial frontier into a division of bordered lands in the modern sense—that is, a landscape divided by congruent lines of economic, political, social, cultural, ethnic, and psychological differences. The evolution of the border dividing the two largest Eurasian empires entailed a gradual process of brokering: between diverse groups of the local borderland society, between the different political powers claiming sovereignty over the boundary and adjoining territories, and between political metropoles and peripheral borderland populations. The central argument put forward in this book is that both people *and* states were responsible for the making of the Sino-Russian border. This creation evolved as a complex set of successive and yet often overlapping and interlinked government policies. The ultimate goal of these programs was to eliminate ambivalence and extend the metropoles' control over the periphery to the very boundary of the state (and often further afield). But the mixed local population played a significant role in both supporting and undermining processes of border making. The present work thus examines how central authorities tried to establish control at the state boundary and in the frontier zone and borderland, how local people strove to subvert such efforts, and how, sometimes, they became agents of state power themselves or fell victim to its abuses. By doing so—and by combining a history from above with a history from below—this book examines the policies implemented by the metropoles and recovers the flexibility of the strategies and practices pursued by ordinary people in coping with the border's remakings.

Empires and Peoples, Frontiers and Borderlands

The study of the multiple ways in which the Sino-Russian border was negotiated on the ground remains a lacuna in the scholarship. Such neglect is all the more striking in light of the landmark's geopolitical significance and pivotal role in world history, its unique and radical changes over time, and the growth of general academic interest in borders. When it is a focus of research, the borderland has been analyzed within conventional vertical, centrist, macro perspectives of diplomatic, economic, or military history, in which power flows only from the metropoles to the periphery, uninfluenced by any interactions around the border itself.[1]

Therefore, this book puts forth a radically new perspective: by focusing on the lives of people on both sides of a closely defined area, it follows the formation and transformation of this extensive Eurasian land border over the *longue durée*. Beginning in the late seventeenth century, when both empires first attempted to demarcate their common frontier, this work traces the border's history until the collapse of the Soviet Union in 1991, when it was finally reopened. Over this extended time span, but particularly during the last century, multiple new border regimes followed one another rapidly, with each shift bearing profound effects on residents throughout the border world. Quite often, the frontier and borderland had their own timeline. Changes occurred there earlier or later than in the metropolitan centers of China and Russia. The borderland underwent radical changes, from a vaguely demarcated interimperial frontier, roamed by nomads, Cossacks, savvy contrabandists, and other highly mobile people, passing it via barge or on horseback, to a tightly patrolled borderland, where most locals accepted the idea of national territorial sovereignty, knowing their neighbors across the river only from state propaganda—although they could still gaze across the border from peaks atop the steppe hills.

Recent debates on old notions of frontiers and borderlands have influenced this work.[2] While distinctions between frontiers and borderlands are becoming more nuanced, the emphasis of current research has shifted toward the concept of borderlands, urging recognition of cross-cultural perspectives and interpretations of developments across peripheries. Borderlands are indeed seen as crossroads where interactions between the local populace and the state are frequently overtly visible. In borderlands, where the power of rivaling empires or nation-states is still fragmented and mechanisms of control are still weak, local societies are able to challenge, subvert, and negotiate hegemony. Precisely this discrepancy between the power aspirations of the political centers and realities on the periphery shaped the gradual evolution of modern state borders, in all their surprisingly persistent ambiguity and unpredictability.[3]

In this book "frontier" refers to a remote, sparsely populated, and vaguely defined territory lying beyond the periphery of two or more core powers. Metropoles expand culturally, economically, and politically over time into this intermediate zone of contact. They are contested by rivaling imperial powers and local populations and characterized by permanent negotiation and compromise. A frontier becomes a borderland when it is incorporated into the expanding core of one or more nation-states or empires through a prolonged process marked by changes in the form of centralizing policies. "Borderland" thus denotes the territorial entity emerging from the frontier on the periphery of a polity during the competition of empires or nation-states and the creation of a rigid, well-defined, linear boundary by substantive, state-imposed changes to economic, political, military, ethnic, social, and cultural environments, processes often shaped by violence, forced population movements, and subjugation of outsiders. While borderland describes a clearly defined broader ambit with inner and outer limits—in which the international border shapes social and economic networks directly, a distinct set of laws operates, and the access of ordinary people is restricted by dint of state policy—"border" refers to the area immediately adjoining the boundary. The "boundary" is thus the line— the dash on the map, rock marker, fence, or guard post—that indicates the territorial limits of state sovereignty.[4] In the end, however, any overly rigid definitions make the complex story of a gradually consolidated frontier too simple. An orthodox terminology with clear distinctions entails the danger of deception and must fall short of explaining the complex nature of a borderland where some locally rooted and contingent characteristics of the frontier continue to coexist.

In contrast to insular Britain, which *had* an empire overseas, Russia and China *were* land-based empires.[5] Together they both divided Inner Asia— Manchuria, Mongolia, and Xinjiang—into separate spheres of interest by the end of the eighteenth century. In spite of their different social and economic structures, both powers displayed some similarities in imperial practices on their shared frontier: as continental empires, they conquered territories on their margins.[6] To incorporate these areas, which Owen Lattimore called defensive "inward-facing frontiers," into increasingly multicultural systems of rule, both imperial powers relied on co-opting indigenous elites, most importantly by preserving some of their privileges.[7]

In the nineteenth century the world witnessed the formation of modern nation-states.[8] Drawing precise state boundaries to define and defend the national territory as "decision space" was a major component of this process. Territorial orthodoxy found its strongest form, perhaps, in the fascist and communist regimes of the twentieth century. Only with the end of the bipolar world, the rise of global capitalism, and the growing importance of supranational structures and the renaissance of regionalism have inscriptions of territorial identity and unique social formations declined.[9]

The global tendency toward territorial state formation also developed in the Qing (1644–1912) and Romanov (1613–1917) imperial states. Despite many of their fringes still being inhabited predominantly by indigenous pastoralists, hunters, or fishing people, the territorial boundaries of the Romanov and Qing empires were simultaneously colored by the idea of a homogeneous sovereignty, one increasingly intolerant of competing authorities, alternative meanings, and uncontrolled passage.[10] Attempts to eliminate ambiguity at the peripheries outlived the old regimes and intensified when their successors (the Soviet Union, Manchukuo-Japan, and the People's Republic of China) introduced even more extreme forms of territorialization, capable of profoundly altering social dynamics in the borderlands. While the communist governments in Moscow and Beijing were not qualitatively different in their closed border regimes, their coercive monopolies were far more sweeping than those of many other states. As a consequence, within just a few decades' time, a complex amalgam of geostrategic aspirations, competing ideologies, and radical plans to alter the life of each and every person living in the contested regions resulted in the leapfrogging transformation from a premodern, interimperial Eurasian frontier into a borderland between two centralized regimes possessing clearly coded, demarcated spaces.[11]

In that process, borders provided crucial state-building functions by helping to prevent secession, perform external security duties, surveil society, and control the domestic economy. They formed separate national identities for the same ethnolinguistic groups and, as highly politicized symbols, became sites of social change. While, for example, the historian Peter Sahlins has shown how localism formed national identities on the Franco-Spanish border in the Pyrenees, processes of local co-optation and compromise took place to a much lesser degree in Inner Asia.[12] When the borderland was incorporated into the periphery of the postrevolutionary state—the successor to a former multicultural empire—as a distinctive administrative unit it gradually ceased to be a hybrid place of mutual accommodation between empires and the non-state world of local populations.

This reorganization of social, economic, political, and cultural space through the projection of centralized state power into the borderland did not stop conflicts over political or cultural belonging among the local populations. Quite to the contrary, such struggles persisted, played out among the competing imperial entities, both in the metropoles and among the borderland peoples who sought ways to fight against assimilation and conversion and to preserve independence or at least autonomy and mobile forms of life.[13]

The relationship between core and periphery thus remained dynamic and fluid, marked by strong influences moving in both directions, prompting questions regarding the role of the locals at the outermost periphery of the state. For how long did social actors below the level of decision-making elites have a say in how the border was run? In what ways did they support or undermine policies of border formation enacted by the state? By narrating a comprehensive history of the Sino-Russian border through a regional lens and making use of a long perspective, this book uncovers the complex interplay of people *and* states. It demonstrates that the local population, far from living at the end of the world, played a more significant role in the story of territorialization of the state than has been previously acknowledged.

First, historical work of this scale occupies a vital role in defining zonal and lineal notions of borders. Concepts of borders held both by different generations of state agents in the metropole and by different cohorts of locals in the borderland changed over time. Rather than being divided by state boundaries, the traditional frontier society maintained ties of kinship, economy, language, and religion stretching across it and had a distinct character of its own. In many cases internal boundaries between banners or tribes were often more strictly enforced than the essentially permeable international boundary. But—unable to cross the locked international border any longer, lacking interest and sufficient language skills—later cohorts of border dwellers stand in stark contrast to earlier generations, often implicitly supporting national territorial sovereignty claims.

Second, this study shows how formal command wielded by a centralizing power does not inevitably result in the establishment of territorial control over a borderland and its subjects. Due to the porous nature of a vast continental border, insufficient resources of overextended empires, conflicting objectives of adjacent regimes, and the absence of modern infrastructure to connect peripheral regions with imperial capitals, centralizing powers were often unable to invigilate their shared outward-facing border, even if they grew increasingly intolerant of any local exchanges across the boundary. This inability was rooted in traditional practices and fluid forms of interaction among different groups in the borderland. Even those who had originally been sent by the state to staff sentry posts would not necessarily follow the government's agenda.

Third, this work illustrates the circumstances under which old frontiers and modern state borders have existed simultaneously. With the introduction of railroads, the metropoles authorized a particular form of border crossing through a narrow corridor and in doing so fostered new processes of border making. Modern means of government control were not, however, introduced all at once along the entire state border. And—however or wherever introduced—these did not perfectly serve the state. In fact, they were used to counter central aims quite often, as they served to ground novel zones of contact between the native and the global worlds and to create a very different social fabric. Along with these, a new form of border was built.

Fourth, this approach exemplifies circumstances under which command over the borderlands can tighten. Particularly during military confrontations and internal struggles, metropoles allocated significant resources to monitor the state border more efficiently, implemented new regimes of border maintenance to isolate the borderland from inside and outside, and gradually replaced disloyal people with those deemed reliable citizens. The reciprocity between the power center and its brokers on one side and a partially remade borderland population on the other not only increased the legitimacy of a coherent bounded space but welded subjects and ruler together in more complementary ways.

Finally, it is instructive to study how open borders are closed and closed borders are opened. While a border of friendship between ally states may be depicted officially as open to everyone, it still can be impassable to most locals. A guarded border of conflict, by contrast, may remain surmountable for certain privileged individuals and groups. The discrepancy between rhetoric and reality is also an indicator of how the power of the metropole over its periphery has grown stronger or became weakened.

These five contrasting but complementary topics indicate the main themes treated in this book. They serve as an array of lenses focusing attention on distinct but interrelated ways in which borders are shifted and relocated over time.

The Argun Basin

The steppes and taiga forests of Inner Asia have rarely favored sedentary powers since humans began to populate the great Eurasian landmass. Extreme climate, difficult topography, and untraversable distances between the Sea of Japan in the east and the Altai and Tianshan mountains in the west kept the

settled civilizations of Asia and Europe at bay. In fact, Inner Asia is more re-
membered for nomadic conquerors, most notably Chinggis Khan, the great
Mongol ruler, who created the largest land empire of all time in the thirteenth
century.

Some boundary relics of earlier cultures remind us, however, that demarcation and territorial defense are not a Russian or Chinese innovation in this
region. The so-called Wall of Chinggis Khan, a historic fortification curving
some five hundred kilometers gently from present-day eastern Mongolia into
China and Russia, is still visible on aerial photographs. Its name is misleading
as, in fact, it was the Jurchen rulers of the Jin dynasty (1115–1234) who established this earthen berm in an unsuccessful attempt to insulate themselves
from the Mongolian and Tatar tribes. Flattened by centuries of erosion, the
wall is in some places still recognizable from the ground as well, for instance,
at the southern edge of Zabaikalsk, a small settlement on the China-Russia
border just footsteps away from the corroded fence.[14]

Initially, Ming and Muscovite rulers took little interest in colonizing the
immense territories or erecting new fortifications. Another four hundred years
or so would pass until Inner Asia became the zone of direct contact between
the Russians and Chinese in the seventeenth century and their rulers slowly
began to consolidate their respective frontiers. In the mid-nineteenth century
it became the longest international land border the world has ever known,
stretching roughly 12,000 kilometers from the Central Asian mountain ranges
through the Inner Asian steppes and along meandering river valleys up to the
Sea of Japan. Today, following the independence of Mongolia and the disintegration of the Soviet Union, China and Russia still share a common border of
about 4,200 kilometers along the Argun, Amur, and Ussuri rivers and a small
strip of land measuring a mere fifty-five kilometers in the Altai Mountains—
the world's sixth-longest international border.[15]

The Sino-Russian frontier remained scarcely populated well into the twentieth century. While today Han Chinese and ethnic Russians together form
the overwhelming majority of the population along the three great border
rivers, these areas have been home to a number of highly distinctive indigenous people. By far the largest ethnic minority groups are the agricultural Koreans and the Buriat and other mobile livestock-raising Mongolic-speaking
people.[16] Much smaller in numbers are the Tungusic-speaking hunting, gathering, and fishing tribes.

Just as the autochthonous people of the Qing-Russian frontier, the Russians
and Han Chinese who live in the provinces adjacent to the Ussuri, Amur, and
Argun rivers are by no means culturally and ethnically homogenous. Old set-
tler peasants and Cossacks arrived in the territories between Lake Baikal and
the Argun River beginning in the seventeenth century. Cossacks settled on

separated lands as horse-raising farmer-soldiers on the outer edges of this frontier with the Chinese Empire. These women and men adapted to local conditions and native customs to survive in this inhospitable world. Over time they mixed with the indigenous inhabitants of the region. Only the Old Believers, who were forcibly resettled to the region in the eighteenth century, would live a life in nearly complete isolation having rejected the reform of the Russian Church by Patriarch Nikon. At the turn of the twentieth century different kinds of migrants, far greater in number, were pouring into the Russian territories adjacent to China from European Russia. Encouraged by agrarian reforms and the construction of the Trans-Siberian Railroad, these new settlers were competing with the earlier peasants and herdsmen for the best pastures.[17] New voluntary and involuntary waves of migration occurred during Soviet times, among them townsfolk, mine and forestry workers, agricultural workers on state farms, military personnel, and railroad employees. These various groups of Russians are to be understood here as *rossiane*—a community most easily defined by its use of the Russian language.

Chinese migration to the Sino-Russian frontier increased in the late nineteenth century, once restrictions against Han migration into Manchuria had been lifted.[18] Seasonal laborers, temporary refugees, as well as poor farmers and other settlers who had the intention of staying permanently flooded the Chinese Northeast. Immigration from provinces south of the Great Wall accelerated with the introduction of modern and efficient transportation during the early twentieth century. In the second half of the twentieth century the movement of people to China's northern frontier was the result of clear strategic, economic, and political motivations formulated in Beijing, driven by land reclamation, national security interests, and the assimilation of minority peoples. Today Han Chinese in the border areas far outnumber the ethnic Russians across the Argun, Amur, and Ussuri.[19]

Situated at the very heart of the vast Inner Asian frontier, the Argun marks the boundary between Russia and China for 944 kilometers. The resulting area constitutes the oldest boundary section between the two powers to survive subsequent territorial changes. Moreover, the area stands for two different sorts of borders. The river is generally crossed and the rural Russian, Chinese, and native worlds are intricately interwoven. Only a short ride away, however, a railroad town represents a very different social fabric, and along with it a new form of border. These different realms make the Argun basin a powerful lens through which to view the history of the Sino-Russian frontier and borderland.[20]

The core area to which we will confine our attention is the upper basin of the river located between the Great Xingan Range in the north and east and the Gobi Plateau in the south and west in today's Sino-Russian-Mongolian

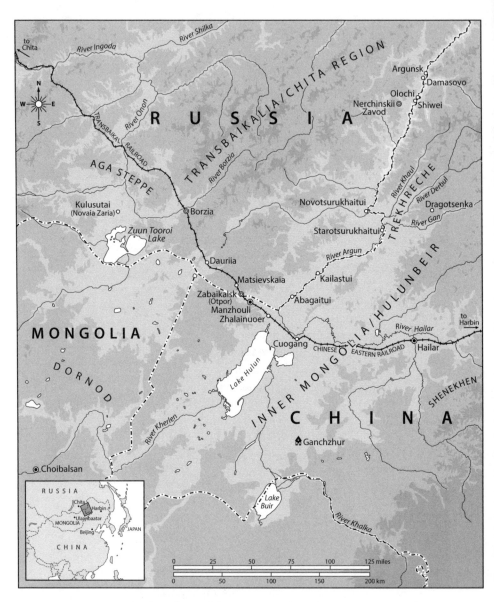

FIGURE 0.2. Time-collapsed map of the Argun borderland, showing important settlements from the eighteenth century to the present.

border triangle. It comprises about seventy thousand square kilometers—approximately the size of the Republic of Georgia. The edges of this region roughly represent the outer limits of the free trade zone introduced in 1862 and the separate administrative structure of the border districts that were established from the late 1920s onward. They can be roughly demarcated as follows: The gently sloping plain of the Aga Steppe where the Borzia River flows into the Onon defines its limits in the West. Olochi, a Cossack village on the middle reaches of the Argun, marks the northern fringe. The foothills of the forested slopes of the Great Xingan, separating the Hulunbeir Plateau from the Manchurian Plain, signal its limits in the east. The Hailar River, a tributary of the Argun and by some considered as simply its upper course, and the shallow Lake Hulun (or Dalai) represent its southern edge.

The Argun constitutes a number of wandering channels running through swamps in a wide valley that gave the river its name.[21] Often separating into two or more distinct arms, the waterway runs relatively slowly north-northeastward through to its joining with the Amur. Because of its winding nature it often covers three times its linear distance. Its main stream has frequently changed in the past, sparking conflicts over the sovereignty of its hundreds of islands, some of them mere sand bars while others are very large pristine pastures. Along its upper reaches the Argun meanders through a slightly rolling and grass-covered steppe that is linked to the Mongolian plains. A boreal taiga forest belt blankets the riverbanks along its middle and lower reaches. Today the Russian territory on the left bank belongs to the Chita region in Transbaikalia.[22] The Chinese bank to the right is part of Hulunbeir,[23] the northeastern tip of the Inner Mongolian Autonomous Region in China, named after the two lakes that are located in the south of this region (Hulun and Buir). Russians call this region "Barga," a term adopted from an old Mongol tribal name.[24]

Extreme continental climate was pivotal in the formation of this frontier region, perhaps more so than the impact of colonists, soldiers, and railroad men. The climate ranges from humid taiga forest in the north to semiarid steppe in the south. Weather patterns are harsh everywhere, with extremely cold but clear and windless winters and short but hot summers. Temperatures can fall as low as fifty degrees Celsius below zero in January. Rivers and lakes usually freeze in late October, and their ice cover melts before May. In July the thermometer goes up to thirty-five degrees Celsius, though absolute maximum temperatures are often higher. Heavy summer rains regularly cause the Argun and its tributaries to flood.

A great diversity of ecosystems characterizes the region. While rivers and lakes abound with sturgeon, Manchurian trout, Amur grayling, pike, and catfish, the stony and poor-quality soils of the floodplains, wetlands, steppes, and mountains are rarely suitable for farming. The broad valleys of the Trekhreche (Three Rivers) triangle on the Chinese bank of the Argun, drained by the Derbul, the Gan, and the Khaul, represent the most fertile areas in the region. But even in this delta plowing and harvesting are possible only during the short four- to five-month vegetation period. The temperate grassland steppes are home to Mongolian gazelles, roe deer, red foxes, gray wolves, and Siberian marmots. The grasslands are used as pastures and hayfields. While the rolling foothills rising gently above its shores are often barren, the slopes of the Great Xingan to the east are thickly forested with larch, birch, and pine. The mountains, with peaks between one thousand and fifteen hundred meters, are home to fur-bearing animals such as reindeer, sable, and squirrels.

Climate and topography posed challenges to overland travel and communication between sparsely populated areas of the indigenous people and early Russian and Chinese settlers. Rivers were often the preferred means of transportation as dirt roads and random tracks were easily passable only during the cold and dry season. People navigated the waterways in barges, dugout canoes, or rafts to transport people, livestock, and goods. When winters turned the Argun into a frozen road for sledges or carts pulled by horses, the scattered outposts came within easier reach of each other, thereby refuting the geodeterminist idea of a river as a natural border.

Until the late nineteenth century there were no significant settlements in this vast and thinly populated territory on the Argun. The only nearby town was Hailar, founded as a garrisoned outpost of Manchu banner troops in the eighteenth century. Established around the same time, Abagaitui was one of the few Cossack villages to dot the Russian bank of the Argun. In 1903 the construction of the Chinese Eastern Railroad, the last leg of the Trans-Siberian Railroad, finally linked Chita and Vladivostok through Manchuria, stimulating the establishment of new settlements and replacing rivers as the main means of communication. Of these, the border town of Manzhouli at the very center of the region under study became the most important. The railroad transformed the frontier from a remote no-man's-land into a center of cross-border economic exchange, with Manzhouli emerging as the major economic hub for Sino-Russian commerce. On Russian territory, just across the international boundary, Railroad Siding 86 developed into a small border station called Otpor, later renamed Zabaikalsk when it was upgraded to an urban-type village during the 1950s.

These bustling twin communities and the yurts dotting the steppe and sleepy villages nestled on the river surrounding them make for an excellent prism through which to view the different kinds of borders and to study the various phenomena of border making and border breaking in the numerous waxing and waning zones of contact between diverse groups of borderlanders.

As a territorial unit, the Argun borderland was (and is) a space in which many different kinds of interactions between Russians, Chinese, and autochthonous borderlanders were possible—some fostered by the states, others by geographic position. The lush grasslands, sparkling rivers and forested hills on the Argun were places where people ventured inside and out and traveled on foot or by animal carts, barges, and trains, bringing along different things and ideas. People went into this space partly because they wanted to pass from China into Russia and vice versa. Others lived on the Argun because they wanted to trade things with each other or because they needed access to the pastures for their animals or proximity to the river to fish. It was this complex setting of interactions that the states wanted to control and ultimately shut down, making such movements impossible.

Looking beyond the big politics that formed this border to focus instead on the everyday life of the locals, practices in the borderland, and entanglements of local communities with the wider world is a difficult endeavor. Nomads with mobile lifestyles and contrabandists with secret trade networks were illiterate or had no interest in writing proprietary documents. The same holds true for train conductors and border guards. This limitation must be kept in mind while tackling the project of narrating everyday encounters in remote contact zones. Yet writing about this border has proven to be more challenging than penetrating the subaltern spheres of the local people, as we also have to deal with a range of archival cultures. In China more than in Russia, borderlands and minority issues remain sensitive topics in national historiography and the politics of history. Many collections of primary sources for the region and period under study are incomplete or classified at present. The Russo-centric imbalance of the archival sources was reduced in our case for two reasons: Archival records bearing on shared state borders are of course based in at least two countries and, luckily, some Chinese correspondence ended up in foreign archives.[25] In addition, newspapers, ethnographic surveys, local gazetteers, and the field notes of travelers located in libraries and private collections offer a bottom-up perspective for writing borderlanders back into history. Finally, oral history has been a valuable source of information. The interviewees featured in this book, locals from both sides of the steppe hills, worked as train engineers, clerks, farmers, and teachers. Their commonplace professions and other facets of their life stories make their narratives indispensable to the task of deepening our insight into everyday social practices characterizing the Argun basin.

A few final words on the structure of the book: the chapters progress from the seventeenth century to the late twentieth century, privileging thematic coherence over strict chronology. Chapter 1 reviews the affairs of frontier people from the first direct but sporadic encounters between Russians and

Chinese, as they took place during the seventeenth century—when both empires first attempted to demarcate a common frontier—to the end of the nineteenth century, when railroads and other elements of modernity began to alter life on the Argun, intensifying and regulating exchanges across the border. Chapter 2 covers the introduction of more assertive policies to govern the international border at the turn of the twentieth century that were replacing long-pursued laissez-faire practices. It examines the framing of local disputes over territorial boundaries in national terms as well as the reorganization of customs and sanitary borders as part of a general evolution toward a territorial boundary. By focusing on the distinct social and ethnic fabrics of Manzhouli and its pastoral surroundings, chapter 3 studies the revolutionary political struggles and indigenous secessionist movements following the collapse of imperial rule in China and Russia in 1911 and 1917, respectively. Chapter 4 introduces collectivization and other radical early Soviet programs of domestication that prohibited rather than regulated cross-border contacts and shows how they altered the political, ethnic, economic, and social landscapes in the upper Argun basin. Chapter 5 explores impacts of the Sino-Soviet conflict of 1929 and the 1931 Japanese occupation of Manchuria that affected the Argun borderland, compelling the regimes to considerably increase their peripheral power. Chapter 6 examines the period between the late 1940s and the early 1960s. Despite being marked by an increasingly ubiquitous rhetoric of friendship and bilateral cooperation, the period's border connections were no longer established informally but overseen by Moscow and Beijing. The Sino-Soviet split in the 1960s and 1970s, discussed in chapter 7, had a lasting influence on the situation along their border, with dire consequences for the economy and demography of the Argun borderland. While the Beijing-Moscow trains were filled no longer with Soviet or Chinese citizens but with passengers from North Korea and Vietnam, propaganda campaigns resuscitated old motifs of infiltration, sabotage, espionage, and disinformation, imbuing the border with new legitimacy as a space of enmity. Chapter 8 traces developments during the 1980s. It explores how the border between the two communist states became permeable again, through both policies adopted by the central governments and local populations' strategies.

1

Cossacks and Bannermen on the Argun Frontier

IN 1867, Agaton Giller, a Pole exiled to Transbaikalia from 1851 until 1856 as a prisoner of the Russian state for his role in the Polish independence movement, wrote the following observations of Olochi, a Cossack village in the middle reaches of the Argun about twenty kilometers from Nerchinskii Zavod:

> A Sino-Siberian fair took place . . . in Olochi a few days ago. . . . In addition to Olochi there are similar markets in Tsurukhaitui, in Aksha on the Onon River, and in Gorbitsa on the Shilka River. The markets are held every year, usually during the first days of July. Siberians offer glass, sheepskin, furs, antlers, lead, and various metals, and the Mongols barter millet, rice, Chinese vodka, pipes, cigar holders made of glass, statues and trinkets, silk and semi-silk fabrics, tobacco, tea, and so forth. Unable to talk to each other, both point to the subject they wish to purchase, and the thing that they will offer for it.[1]

When the Pole, who would later become a notable historian, lived out his exile in the mid-nineteenth century, the Sino-Russian border on the Argun was quite open: the river united the peoples on both shores rather than dividing them. The image of exile in Siberia conjures remote and isolated areas offering no outside contact, but the lively exchange there between the Chinese, Mongols, and Russians, trading with virtually no interference from state control, suggests otherwise. Russians, be they convicts or members of the self-governing and semi-military communities of Cossacks, were relatively new to this place, and the commodities that the indigenous reindeer herders and nomads bartered had been sold to them by Chinese traders previously.

In fact, these fairs often coincided with regular review visits carried out by Chinese border inspectors every summer. A contemporary of Giller, Nikolai I. Kashin, a graduate of the Medical Faculty of Moscow University, spent seven years working as a physician in Olochi during the 1850s. He witnessed those Russo-Chinese gatherings every summer. By then the Chinese border

FIGURE 1.1. A Cossack village on the lower reaches of the Argun, late nineteenth century. People, animals, and goods were shipped on barges and rafts along the river and across it.

expeditions could already look back at a tradition of more than a century and a half. These followed a ritualized set of customs, beginning with a formal exchange of border delegates, followed by barter trade, before the Chinese inspectors would then return in small boats to their border control duties.

After three weeks of overland travel from Mergen (now Nenjiang), the Chinese border expedition corps, comprising 130 to 150 men, usually alighted in the early summer at the border camp on the Argun. Meetings began with an exchange of gifts, such as a cow or several sheep proffered by the Russians in return for poor-quality liquor, cases of confections, tea of inferior value, and the like from the Chinese. On a day agreed upon in advance, the Russians would host a reception for the entire Chinese group from noon until late into the evening. At Olochi, Kashin observed the conduct of the Chinese:

> At the table, they behave quite sedately, unless any one of them is strongly drunk. They are always curious to inspect our table linen, but most inquisitive toward the bottles of raspberry wine. Often we invited to this celebration some musicians from Nerchinskii Zavod, who usually played music while we sat at the table. The music they play, I can say, is pretty decent. . . . It is obvious that [Chinese] ears are not used to a harmonious and melodic

sound of the accordion. They are not entertained unless the sound is terrific: a quavering broken horn, drum, or even, perhaps, only the rattle.

The next day the Russians were typically invited to a similar feast on the Chinese bank, again lasting until the late evening. The Chinese had the habit of giving gun salutes to say goodbye to their guests. Following the mutual visits the usual barter began, hosted alternately on the Russian and the Chinese banks.[2] Kashin's and Giller's recollections paint an evocative picture of cultural zones of encounter between Russians, Chinese, and autochthonous frontiersmen ranging beyond barter, to reveal such incommensurable moments as divergent musical accompaniments to dinner.

This chapter reviews the affairs of frontier people in the years between the first contacts of Russians and Chinese on the Argun in the early seventeenth century, when a clear state boundary was not recognizable yet, to the end of the nineteenth century, a time when railroads, telegraphs, customs surveillance structures, and other elements of modernity began to alter life on the frontier.

Relations between the Russian and Chinese empires on their shared steppe frontier during that stage can be divided into three phases. The first phase lasted through the late seventeenth century. During this time Cossacks entered Transbaikalia and came in contact with Mongol nobles while the Qing established rule over Hulunbeir. Both parties struggled over supremacy of the Amur basin. Only the treaties of Nerchinsk and Kiakhta, concluded in 1689 and 1728, respectively, drew a boundary between the two empires. The second phase, from roughly 1728 to 1851, was characterized by a balance of power between Beijing and Saint Petersburg, the establishment of permanent yet deficient border surveillance by both polities, and intensifying contacts on the border, in particular routed through Kiakhta, the year-round location for border trade. The third and final phase lasted from 1851 to the end of the nineteenth century. This period was marked by a shift of power in favor of Russia. With backing from the newly founded Transbaikal Cossack Host, Russia incorporated the territories north of the Amur and east of the Ussuri rivers. Simultaneously, Transbaikalia was fully integrated into the provincial system of the Russian Empire, and Russian Cossack forces began to expand their indirect influence onto the Chinese bank of the river Argun.

The Beginnings of Sino-Russian Contact: Establishing a Balance of Power

Russia and China first initiated indirect contact during the *pax mongolica*. At the time of Ivan the Terrible, Cossacks were probably the earliest Russian visitors to China, but they received no audience with the emperor.[3] The Russian expansion toward Siberia and the territories east of Lake Baikal made possible regular contact between the two metropoles: Russian forts in Siberia were established in Tiumen (1586), Tomsk (1604), Eniseisk (1619), and Irkutsk (1654). Among the various elements moving eastward, Cossacks formed the backbone of the conquest.[4]

The north- and westward expansion of the rising Manchus, Tungusic people who lived in Manchuria, which occurred contemporaneously with Russian colonization of Eastern Siberia, created a common, overlapping frontier forcing the two expansionist forces onto a collision course. Shortly before the Manchus came to power in China in 1644, they formed alliances with the neighboring Mongol tribes. As a result, Inner Mongolia came under their control in 1636. Between 1655 and 1691, Khalkha, the eastern part of Outer Mongolia, was brought under Qing rule, and the Western Mongol Oriats who inhabited Dzungaria were conquered in 1750. Whereas Ming China (1368–1644) was arguably a nation-state, its borders roughly following the settlement areas of the Han ethnic group, Qing China was a multiethnic empire in which the Manchus were rulers by conquest.[5]

The first direct contact between China and Russia occurred somewhat later, with the departure of an inaugural Russian mission to Beijing in 1618 and 1619, headed by the envoy Cossack Ivan Petlin. It took more than three decades to send another mission, this time led by Fedor I. Baikov from 1653 to 1657. Afterward the contacts continued sporadically and were partly overshadowed by clashes between China and Russia at their overlapping imperial peripheries. These missions often had dual economic and diplomatic objectives.[6]

Meanwhile, Cossack explorers had arrived in the territories east of Lake Baikal and along the Amur River in the mid-seventeenth century. In Eastern Transbaikalia, Russians had established their first permanent and fortified frontier outposts in the 1650s. These *ostrogi* soon became centers of economic and diplomatic exchange with the indigenous frontier tribes, in particular the Nerchinsk fort (1654) on the Shilka River. Though the Russians began to subjugate autochthonous Tungisic and Mongol peoples, forcing them to pay tribute, known as *iasak*, their presence remained diffuse and weak. Additionally, the ensuing decades saw a number of conflicts with the natives of the forests and steppes of Transbaikalia.[7]

Hulunbeir, the territory to the east of the Argun River, entered into the Russian domain when Tungus chieftain Gantimur of Hulunbeir proved unwilling to surrender to Manchu rule and became a Russian citizen in 1675. The Russians made him commander of a Tungus Cossack regiment responsible for patrolling the Nerchinsk section of the Qing-Russian frontier. Yet to the disappointment of the Russian explorers, they soon discovered that the Manchus regarded the entire Amur basin and the territories west of the Great Xingan Mountain range as their own preserve. The superior Manchu military impeded the construction of Russian forts and villages along the Amur and Argun, a conflict culminating in sieges of the Russian Albazin ostrog on the Amur in 1685 and 1686.[8]

Forty years of hostilities between Russian Cossacks and Chinese banner forces and the struggle for Albazin underscored the need for an amicable delimitation and demarcation of boundaries within the known territories between Beijing and Moscow. The demonstration of Qing's strength marshaled by the emperor Kangxi brought the Russians to the negotiation table. Looking to forge an amicable solution, Moscow appointed Fedor A. Golovin as its first ambassador plenipotentiary to China, sending him to the Chinese emperor, which marked the beginning of a new period of encounter characterized by accommodation rather than conflict.

In August 1689, returning from Beijing, Golovin convened with his Manchu counterpart Grand Secretary Songgotu (Suo Etu), head of the Chinese emperor's Chamber of Foreign Affairs, at the Russian frontier outpost of Nerchinsk to negotiate the first substantive agreement between the two powers. The outcome, the Treaty of Nerchinsk, was thus the first to delineate the frontier between Russia and China. It was also the earliest agreement ever signed between China and a European power and formed the foundation for a rather peaceful accord between the two powers for more than one and a half centuries.

The first of the six short articles constituting the treaty delimited a boundary in the overlapping imperial frontier. It stipulated that the western boundary section be the mainstream of the Argun, thus excluding Russia from Hulunbeir. The northern section of the boundary was to begin at the Gorbitsa (now Amazar) River, a left bank tributary of the Shilka River, and to run irregularly to the Sea of Okhotsk. Further, all the northern slopes of the Stanovoi Mountains and the rivers flowing north to the Lena River were to belong to Russia and the rivers flowing southward to the Amur to China. The agreement thus closed the Amur outlet to the Pacific to Russia. In terms of territorial sovereignty, China had undoubtedly won. In another sense, however, the Treaty of Nerchinsk gave a limited number of Russian merchants trading privileges into China, as it provided Moscow with direct marketing rights in Beijing.[9]

At the time of the Treaty of Nerchinsk, the Manchus had not yet fully established control over the nomadic tribes in their northern imperial periphery. As the Manchus pushed the opposing Oriats further westward, they lobbied for another agreement with the Russians. The Chinese imperial court was anxious about possible Russian support for the Oirats, fearing that disobedient subjects might flee to the Russians. At the same time, Qing command over new territories opened possibilities for trade on the frontier. Therefore, in 1728 Russian and Qing officials concluded the Treaty of Kiakhta—the second crucial agreement between the two powers. By and large it constituted a specification of the Treaty of Nerchinsk, delimitating the border more or less precisely. To accomplish this, a joint commission inspected and formally demarcated the border by erecting sixty-three stone markers or cairns whose exact location was stipulated in two supplementary protocols. Demarcation work was carried out with the help of Khori Buriats in the western area. The local people thus had a preexisting idea of where their tribal lands ended and those of neighboring tribes began.[10]

The remaining provisions of the Treaty of Kiakhta for the most part dealt with the cross-border flow of people and commodities. The autochthonous nomadic hunters and livestock herders had to limit their seasonal migrations. At least in theory, these could now be controlled by the states, thanks to now-precise boundary demarcation. Finally, several articles defined what would soon become a unique relationship between the two countries: the Russian court in Saint Petersburg gained permission to station representatives in Beijing by establishing an ecclesiastical mission, a quasi-diplomatic embassy, and a language school in the Qing capital.[11]

With the new treaty trade became limited to Kiakhta and Tsurukhaitui on the border. After signing the Treaty of Nerchinsk, Russian caravans to Beijing emerged as having been the crucial form of commercial and political exchange. But caravan trade was a dangerous venture, as roaming Mongol bandits plundered trade convoys and extreme weather posed further challenges to their safety. A particularly difficult leg of those journeys usually spanned the sparsely populated Argun basin. In the case of the caravan led by Adam Brand and Isbrand Ides, the first official caravan to arrive at Beijing after the Treaty of Nerchinsk had been signed, intense summer rainfalls in 1692 led the Argun tributaries in the Trekhreche delta to overflow, rendering the crossing with camels and horses difficult. And although the Argun boundary had been mapped three years earlier, real surveillance existed only in theory: the caravan at last encountered a Chinese sentry post after nearly one month on Chinese territory. In the years between the treaties of Nerchinsk and Kiakhta, a total of fourteen caravans reached Beijing—many experiencing similar perils.[12]

It was understandable, then, that both powers were eager to regulate trade. With the Treaty of Kiakhta, Beijing and Saint Petersburg had created the so-called the Kiakhta system—which, in opposition to China's trade with the Western powers (the Kanton system), instantiated a new form of legitimate overland caravan trade directly at two officially recognized links on the

FIGURE 1.2. Street scene in Maimaicheng (1885 or 1886), China's trading outpost just across the border from Kiakhta. For over a century and a half, the barter-based trading system on the border dominated the bilateral exchange of tea, fur, and other commodities.

frontier, gradually replacing informal Russian caravan trade to the Chinese capital.[13]

In this new schema, Kiakhta emerged as the principal trading point and perhaps, due to its significance, the only relatively well-guarded area of the Russia-China frontier.[14] Perched on the Mongolian frontier, the town prospered from cross-border trade with Maimaicheng (Altanbulag) on Chinese territory, despite numerous setbacks caused by Chinese moratoriums on trade. The barter-based Kiakhta system dominated the bilateral exchange for more than a hundred fifty years, brick and fine teas being its principal Chinese commodities. In addition, the Chinese offered yellow tobacco, silks, and cottons, in exchange for Russian bulls, horses, sheep, and other live animals, as well as skins and fox and sable pelts. Only with the rise of merchant shipping in the mid-nineteenth century did the Kiakhta trade begin to wane. At the turn of the twentieth century, the Trans-Siberian Railroad finally deprived Kiakhta of its former economic significance as a continental entrepôt, as will be shown in chapter 2.[15]

Starotsurukhaitui on the Argun had been the second exclusive frontier trading post established in 1728. It had been charted previously because it was located on the initial main trade route between Russia and China. Caravans had regularly passed through in the late seventeenth century. The physical setting was, however, unfavorable: it featured poor grazing grounds, distant sources of firewood, and regular flooding by the uncontrolled Argun. It was also a miserable location for commerce, as it was remote from trade hubs in Siberia and Mongolia. Not surprisingly, the trading post on the Argun could hardly compete with the bustling twin communities of Kiakhta and Maimaicheng. For a long time its trade volume was so small and the post so distant from the administrative centers that the Russians collected no customs duties at all there. There was simply nothing available at Starotsurukhaitui that was not available at Kiakhta.[16]

For the Russians, in fact, the impetus to restrict trade to limited places on the Russo-Chinese frontier had been the collection of taxes on the frontier. Therefore, the origins of Russian customs control in its Asian domains go back to trade agreements between Russia and the Qing Empire, codified in the Treaty of Kiakhta in 1728. The Russian customs compound at Kiakhta was to become the largest of its kind in Siberia.[17] In China, where the Qing court maintained tribute relations with many of its neighbors, no such custom controls existed on the northern frontier.[18] Despite its regulations, however, the Kiakhta trading system failed to prevent cross-border barter of goods beyond the two exclusive trading outposts on the Qing-Russian frontier.[19]

Frontier Colonization: Tungus, Buriats, Solons, and Russians on the Argun

After the demarcation of the Argun border the Romanov court began to populate its newly incorporated territories in Transbaikalia with loyal subjects more vigorously than had the Qing government in Hulunbeir, although Russian colonization in Transbaikalia was relatively small compared to adjacent Russian provinces. Russian migration began in the mid-seventeenth century and gained momentum after a decree for agricultural colonization of Transbaikalia was passed in 1799.[20] Significant factors in the population increase were the resettlement of ethnic Russians from the European parts of the empire and the emigration of Mongols from Khalkha and Hulunbeir to Transbaikalia. Though this Russian province housed many ethnic groups, two remained dominant until the middle of the nineteenth century.

The first group was the *inorodtsy* (literally "those of different descent," and in fact a catchall used for the various ethnic minorities of the empire), tribute-paying people who pursued their traditional way of life. State bureaucracy divided those autochthonous people into several subgroups, of which two were represented in Transbaikalia: the Khori Buriats, a nomadic people consisting of a great variety of Mongol-speaking clans in the southern and western parts of the province, and the Tungus, itinerants who subsisted practicing hunting and gathering and reindeer herding farther to the north and east. House-dwelling Russians who, with the exception of Cossacks and some Old Believers, predominantly made their homes in regions away from the Argun frontier belong to the second group. The Old Believers, who had been forcibly resettled to the region during the eighteenth century, were jealous of the good land held by Cossacks, deeply hostile to the Buriats and Tungus, and shunned by other Orthodox Russian settlers for religious reasons. Earlier peasants were also resettled to the Nerchinsk mining area on the Shilka River after large deposits of silver and other metals had been discovered in that region at the end of the seventeenth century. In the early eighteenth century a growing army of forced labor exiles (*katorga*) gradually replaced those established peasants in the mines. The Nerchinsk peasants were turned into Cossacks and became the founding cornerstone of the Transbaikal Cossack Host in 1851.[21]

Compared with the early peasants and the inorodtsy, Transbaikalia's other population groups were negligible until the mid-nineteenth century. For instance, in 1784, just 4,790 (or 8 percent) of the overall population of 57,518 were Cossacks, of whom only a small portion lived along the Qing-Russian frontier.[22] By 1897, when the first and only census was carried out in the Russian Empire, the structure of the rural population of Transbaikalia had changed considerably and consisted of three groups, each accounting for about one-third of the population: established peasants (31.8 percent), natives (inorodtsy), mainly nomadic Buriats but also Tungusic peoples living in the north (30.5 percent), and Cossacks (29.7 percent), of which every fifth was a native Buriat and Tungus Cossacks from the region. The remaining 8 percent were predominantly exiles and newly arrived migrant farmers. In the territories adjacent to China, in particular on the shores of the Onon, Ingoda, Shilka, and Argun rivers, the population composition differed from the central regions of Transbaikalia. The majority of inhabitants comprised native and ethnic Russian Cossacks: their share was 99 percent in the Aksha district and 57 percent in the Nerchinskii Zavod district. In contrast, only 7 percent of the population in the centrally located Chita district belonged to the Cossacks. Even in 1910 the population in the two districts of Aksha and Nerchinskii Zavod that bordered with China remained mainly Cossack. The population density in both districts combined was only slightly above one person per square kilometer, and about 63 percent of the area, mostly lands used by wandering people, was practically classified as "uninhabited."[23]

Despite government incentives, which had already existed since the early 1800s, voluntary migration had far less of a purchase on the regions east of Lake Baikal than in other parts of Siberia. After Nikolai N. Murav'ev, governor-general of Eastern Siberia, took the Amur, the stream of settlers moved further eastward, but not to Transbaikalia. Thus for many decades Transbaikalia remained merely a corridor or a land in between.[24] Also the land reforms initiated by Prime Minister Petr A. Stolypin barely affected rural life on the Argun frontier. In November 1906, the conservative statesman issued a decree that enabled each peasant household to claim individual ownership of its land allotment and to withdraw from the commune.[25] In the areas east of Lake Baikal, this policy was not only aimed at creating a class of small farmers who would exert a stabilizing influence in the countryside and support the autocracy but also meant to help assemble a colonial shield against a demographic "yellow peril" through increased migration from the central black-earth, land-poor provinces to Siberia and the Far East. Despite the opening of new settlement lands in Transbaikalia, however, the reform was only a moderate success and Russian colonization remained an erratic and uneven process. The reform was of little significance for the eastern part of the province as the share of newly arrived settlers in rural parts of the region was negligible. Transbaikalia was among the least popular destinations (the greatest share of new settlement was taking place in Western Siberia), and Russian peasants hardly constituted a presence on the Argun border with China.[26]

The Buriats in Transbaikalia still largely retained their old way of life. The most numerous and culturally prominent tribes in Eastern Transbaikalia were the Khori Buriats. By the nineteenth century several Khori Buriat clans occupied the Aga Steppe, a gently sloping plain stretching about one hundred kilometers in the southeastern Transbaikala region between the Onon and Ingoda rivers, while most of the Khori still lived to the west of Aga in valleys closer to Lake Baikal.[27] In 1908, about 38,584 Buriats lived in the two districts of Aginsk and Tsugal'sk (formerly belonging to the autonomous council of the Aga Steppe Duma).[28] Until the early twentieth century the Khori Buriats of the Aga Steppe remained nomads who bred horses, domestic cattle, camels, goats, and sheep. The Russian term "nomad" (*kochevnik*) was still more than a purely legal term, denoting a distinctive way of life. Relative to the Mongols in Hulunbeir and Khalkha and their exposure to the Han Chinese, relations between the Khori Buriats in Transbaikalia and the Russians of the empire were of an older vintage, as they had sworn loyalty to the tsar from the time their regiments were founded in the mid-eighteenth century. Yet compared to the Buriats west of Lake Baikal, few of the Transbaikal nomads had undergone cultural assimilation. The Aga Steppe Buriats retained the highest level of mobility of all tribes in the province. By the turn of the century, nine out of ten Buriat families in the Aga Steppe still lived in yurts.[29]

Summarized statistically, the number of inhabitants in Transbaikalia between the late eighteenth and late nineteenth centuries increased from 57,518 people in 1784 to 672,072 in 1897. By then almost two-thirds of the population was ethnic Russian (442,744). On the other hand, the share of the two major indigenous groups, the Buriats and Evenks (whom Russians referred to by the common name *tungusy*), had declined to less than a third of the overall population, in other words to 177,970 and 34,403 people, respectively.[30] The number of Chinese in the province, working mostly as traders or miners, was still quite low. Significant communities could, rather, be found in Chita (517 people) or in the gold mines. But there were no permanent Chinese settlements on the Russian bank of the Argun.[31]

In Hulunbeir, the Chinese territory on the Argun frontier, the ethnic makeup was quite different and consisted of a diverse native population but literally no Han Chinese. In 1808, 29,713 people lived in this strategic area. This number increased only slightly over the next hundred years, to 32,633 people in 1912.[32] In the late nineteenth century, Hulunbeir's population composed less than one-third of the total population of the two districts in Transbaikalia that matched Hulunbeir in size and bordered it.[33] This much thinner population density was largely due to the fact that the Chinese frontier had preserved its distinct indigenous identity. The rulers in fact remained conscious of the distinct nature of the frontier areas. In Manchuria and Mongolia, the Qing state had prohibited migration of the Han Chinese up to the latter half of the nineteenth century. At the same time, the Chinese peasants had no intention of acquiring land in the forests of Manchuria or in the steppes of Mongolia. Hulunbeir, cut off from the Manchurian heartland by the Great Xingan Range, was even more isolated from immigration flows. As the following chapters will show, aside from the Chinese working in gold fields on the lower Argun River and those living in the railroad settlements, the number of settlers hailing from the Han ethnic group was insignificant and would begin to grow massively only during the later decades of the twentieth century.[34]

The tribal elements of Hulunbeir's population had their origins in the seventeenth century, when the Manchu tried to create a buffer against the advancing Russians. The Qing court installed a hybrid system of administrative divisions with features of the Manchu Eight Banners and the autonomous banner system.[35] This ethnic formation and administrative structure would remain relatively stable until the fall of the Qing dynasty, when the region was still dominated by the following tribes. First, about eight thousand members of the Solon banners formed a strongly "mongolized" Tungus ethnic conglomerate consisting of various Daur and Evenk peoples who were living as nomadic cattle breeders in the rich pasturelands to the east and south of Hailar. Chipchin Buriats, the second tribe, numbering roughly five thousand in 1912 and likewise nomadic cattle breeders, inhabited the dry steppe between the Hailar valley and the Trekhreche delta. Both Solons and Chipchins followed shamanistic customs. They were also referred to as "Old Bargut" as they had arrived with the first group of migrants, those several hundred Solon, Chipchin, and Daur troops gathered by the Yongzheng emperor in the Nen River valley and then moved westward across the Great Xingan Range to establish the garrison at Hailar. The third, and at seventeen thousand the largest ethnic contingent, were the Mongol-speaking Buriats, of the grass-covered steppes in the vicinity of Lake Hulun, in the southwest of Hulunbeir. In the seventeenth century, they had moved eastward from their native lands in Khalkha south of Lake Baikal in flight from the advancing Russians. As believers of the Lamaist Buddhist faith, they were also called "New Bargut" since they came under Manchu rule only after 1735. The Oroqen, a subgroup of the Manchu-Tungusic family, formed the fourth tribe. About two thousand Oroqen lived in northeastern Hulunbeir, close to the ridge of the Great Xingan Range, belonging neither to the "Old" nor to the "New Bargut," making a living from reindeer herding. Last, the Ölöts, a small splinter group with just several hundred people in 1912 and speakers of a Mongolian dialect, occupied the southern valleys of the Great Xingan Mountains.[36] By that time, however, the distinction between "Old" and "New Bargut" had lost much of its significance. The administration of these quite distinct groups was organized in seventeen banners along ethnic lines, following traditional Manchu administrative divisions. Mongolian-style pastoral nomadism had become the most common lifestyle among these peoples, but their written lingua franca was Manchu.[37] Thus, in addition to ethnicity and religion, administrative affiliation likewise became a decisive factor in the complex sense of belonging. For the sake of simplicity, the indigenous people of Hulunbeir were commonly known under the name Barguts.

Cossacks and Bannermen: Premodern Forms of Frontier Surveillance

Varying frontier colonization policies aside, Chinese and Russian government officials both saw benefit in sealing off the frontier and supervising movement across it ever since the treaties of Nerchinsk and Kiakhta had been concluded.

Small piles of stones serving as boundary markers hardly spelled out the kind of frontier that would enable the metropoles to control people and commodity flows as well as the loyalties of the local populace. However, protecting the nearly twenty-nine-hundred-kilometer-long Transbaikal frontier to China was anything but an easy task.[38]

Just after the Treaty of Nerchinsk in 1689, Beijing had sent troops from the garrison in Qiqihar to monitor the new border with Russia. Only after the Treaty of Kiakhta in 1728, however, did the Qing government begin to permanently secure the frontier. More generally speaking, it was during this transitional period that, for the first time in China's history, a comprehensive frontier management structure enabled the state to define recognizable boundaries and to establish a lasting frontier defense. In Manchuria this entailed the construction of garrison towns at Aigun on the Amur (1683), Mergen (1690), Qiqihar (1691), and Hailar (1732), the latter on the grass steppe of Hulunbeir. The Tungusic tribes in northern Manchuria were integrated as banner soldiers into the imperial defense system. Along the new frontier to Russia the Manchus began to erect a chain of forty-seven sentry posts known as *kalun*. Like the Russians, they marked the boundary line with small cairns of stones between two sentry posts. Along Hulunbeir's outer borders the court established twelve sentry posts: nine along the Argun and three at the land boundary with Transbaikalia. Autochthonous banner troops rotated between these posts every three months. The Qing court thus used native populations to claim these frontiers as part of its domain.[39]

To further strengthen this thin defense force, the Yongzheng court gradually increased its troops in Hulunbeir. In 1743 a lieutenant general was appointed and installed in the recently founded garrison town of Hailar to take command over all banner troops in Hulunbeir. Ten postal stations were built between Qiqihar and Hailar to speed up communication and strengthen connections with the central parts of Heilongjiang province. Indeed, physical fortification of China's frontiers with Russia in Hulunbeir continued steadily throughout the nineteenth century. The inner and outer rings of kalun were brought closer together and additional sentry posts were set up further upstream on the Argun—efforts mainly to prevent Russians from seeking gold on the Chinese bank of the Argun.[40]

This form of frontier surveillance continued until the early twentieth century, with further troop supplements and additional sentry posts added during the last years of Qing rule. The Chinese sentry post on the Argun opposite the Cossack village of Starotsurukhaitui, for instance, very much resembled the original posts established one and a half centuries earlier. In 1898 the post consisted of seven yurts and was staffed with one officer on duty, his deputy, and thirty-six soldiers, of which only eight to ten people were in fact present at any moment. The changing of guards was still carried out every three months. For their service, the sentries were provided with housing in yurts and weapons. They were paid a modest sum of money along with two tea bricks for every three months of service. No special uniform for the sentries was provided, and in the opinion of a Russian observer, "everyone dresses like he wishes."[41]

Russian frontier maintenance and defense was similar but not identical to the Chinese model. The tsarist territorial expansion on the eastern periphery demanded the emergence of institutions that would simultaneously strengthen frontier defense and allow a civilian presence for the sake of economic development in the newly annexed territories. These conditions could be successfully enforced by the Cossack troops. The main duties of Cossacks, then, were similar to those of the guards on the Chinese side: frontier protection, maintenance of the sentry posts, the capture of fugitives, safeguarding of Russian economic activities, as well as control of the indigenous population. Especially during the eighteenth century, when Cossacks were primarily non-Russians, this also meant conflict between Cossack Buriats and Buriats not in the ranks.[42]

After the signing of the treaty in 1728, thirty-one sentry posts (karaul) were established on the Transbaikal frontier,[43] facing the Mongolian and Manchurian kalun of the Qing Empire.[44] All sentry posts—each supposed to consist of five to ten yurts—were manned by native people: Khori Buriats in the western frontier sections, and Evenk (Tungus) in the east. The task of frontier patrol was placed in the hands of two newly appointed inspectors: one for the eastern section, the other for the section west of Kiakhta. Every summer both inspectors were to tour their respective sections to maintain boundary markers, examine the work of native guards, and search for fugitives.[45]

Additional sentries were subsequently established, and by the early nineteenth century the overall number had increased to seventy-five, so that the average distance between them decreased to roughly fifty kilometers. In addition to the frontier posts, fortifications were erected first along the western section and later, between 1764 and 1773, along the eastern section. The fortress of Novotsurukhaitui, located on the dirt road between Nerchinsk and Qiqihar, for instance, was meant to defend the middle reaches of the Argun. In the open steppe, however, such bulwarks could easily be bypassed.[46]

Cossack regiments grew at only a modest rate, swelled by deployments from local recruitment among indigenous tribes and by the deployment of forces from western Transbaikalia and other regions. Only from the 1770s on were Russian Cossacks transferred from fortified outposts to the sentry posts along the frontier, gradually replacing the autochthonous units.[47] Much later on the Chinese side—during the final years of Qing rule—the Qing government replaced the indigenous patrols with Han Chinese guards. The proportion of those on active frontier surveillance service among the total Cossack population remained low. In 1842, there were only 446 Russian and 499 Tungus Cossacks on duty in the two-thousand-kilometer-long Tsurukhaitui frontier section. Cossacks in this segment were assigned to the three fortresses and split among thirty-four permanent and thirteen temporary sentry posts. The permanent posts had an average population of 285 people. In each of these posts, eight to thirteen Russian Cossacks and ten to fourteen Tungus Cossacks from the Cossack regiments were on duty.[48]

On the administrative side, the Statute of 1822 introduced the rule of law to Siberia for the first time in its history. It radically changed the entire administrative system and fixed the autochthonous peoples into subordinate political statuses based on clan and territorial groupings with limited forms of self-government. The statute also altered the command structure of the Cossacks in Transbaikalia. As the Chinese polity now appeared to be stable, the statute provided a civil rather than military structure.[49]

The duties and remunerations of the Cossacks were somewhat similar to those of the Chinese guards. Ethnic Russians who signed up for twenty-five years' service received a salary of six rubles a year, weapons, and food supplies, yet a self-sustaining economy was key to survival. The state supported this subsistence, in fact, by dedicating land for the formation of villages and hamlets by the Cossacks. As a result, the typical Cossack mode of labor at the time entailed both state duties, such as frontier protection and maintenance of roads, and agriculture for sustenance. As the barren soil prevented the Cossacks from growing crops in the Tsurukhaitui section, there they made a living salting fish or breeding cattle.

State support for the indigenous Cossacks remained lower than the levels of support for ethnic Russian Cossacks, as they did not receive any food supplies. For all autochthonous Cossacks, the foremost incentive for service was an exemption from tribute payments and the allocation of land, suitable for both agriculture and herding. Non-Cossack Buriats were moved off these often fertile lands—which resulted in much resentment. Cossacks were much richer than non-Cossack Buriats and counted themselves as socially superior. Compared to the Tungus, the Khori Buriat Cossacks were better off economically. The Buriats engaged in nomadic herding in the steppe in the south, whereas the Evenk relied on hunting game in the forests further north, which yielded a less reliable food supply.[50]

Russia's Turn to the East: Frontier Barter and the Perils of a Vast State Boundary

The relatively peaceful coexistence that contributed to the economic development of the imperial frontier came to an end in the mid-nineteenth century. Compared to the territorial expansion and political conquest of the High Qing period from the mid-seventeenth to the late eighteenth century, the Manchus now faced major foreign aggression and domestic challenges, ranging from fiscal problems to discontent among certain groups of its population, culminating in armed insurrections. The Russian Empire, in turn, recovering from its defeat in the Crimean War, pushed further into Central Asia and the Far East, creating an immense frontier with the Qing Empire stretching from the Pamirs to the Pacific.

To facilitate Russian expansion in the East, Nikolai N. Murav'ev, commissioned in 1847 as the governor-general of Eastern Siberia, took advantage of Manchu involvement with English and French invasion forces during the Arrow War (Second Opium War) and in struggles with the Taiping and Nian rebellions. Such distractions made feasible the Amur expedition of 1849 to 1855, by which Russia took possession of large tracts of land north of the Amur and east of the Ussuri River. The territories were annexed on the basis of two advantageous border treaties, those of Aigun and Beijing, concluded in 1858 and 1860, and the seizure further fueled a short-lived euphoria about the Amur as the "Russian Mississippi."[51] While boundaries on maps appeared to be fixed by the middle of the nineteenth century, power structures on the ground continued to evolve.

With Russia's turn to the East in the middle of the nineteenth century the organization of Cossacks on the empire's eastern border underwent major changes. In March 1851 the Transbaikal Cossack Host (a technical term for an army subdivision) was established according to suggestions the governor-general of Eastern Siberia Murav'ev had previously formulated in his effort to pursue an expansionist policy in the Amur basin. This newly formed army consisted of Cossacks, mainly local Russian peasants but also some members of Buriat and Tungus background, with a total of 48,169 men. A significant portion of the new Cossacks were almost instantly diverted to the new Amur and Ussuri borders to populate the newly acquired territories with loyal people. The administrative nature of the Transbaikal region underwent changes too. The territories east of Lake Baikal became an ordinary Russian province in the East Siberian Governor-Generalship, headed by a military governor who supervised civil and military affairs. Later, in 1884, the Transbaikal province was incorporated into the Priamur Governor Generalship. As a result, it became part of the Russian Far East, administratively detached from

Siberia proper until 1906. As early as 1851, the *sloboda* of Chita was elevated from a fortified village to town status and became the administrative center of the province.[52]

When general military conscription in the Russian Empire was introduced in 1874, service in the Cossack hosts remained subject to its own regulations. Though many aspects came to resemble regular military service, some peculiarities continued to exist, such as the requirement for every Cossack to own a horse and a longer duration of service. In 1871 Cossack settlements gained some degree of autonomy and were granted their own local administration, a station ataman (Cossack leader), and a station court. Overall, the reforms aligned the local administration with Russia's lowest regular administrative-territorial unit, the district (*volost'*) administration.[53]

Despite those reforms, traditional customs of frontier management remained largely without modification until the end of the nineteenth century. As late as 1899, a Russian military topographer observed that "in the old days, back 20 years ago, to indicate the boundary line, Cossacks from all the sentry posts gathered and plowed the ground by angular stones. Horses, alone and in tandems, dragged the stones on belts and ropes along the ground, thereby creating a substantial furrow marking the boundary line. Even now in some places there are traces of such furrows left. But the main characters are the boundary line cairns, sketched by a pile of rocks above man-size, in pairs, one on either side of the boundary line."[54] In sum, the Chinese and Russian frontier management on the Argun underwent only minor changes—the Chinese bank was probably marked by fewer modifications. Despite all of these supplements, troops were stretched too thin to guarantee the degree of monitoring that would prevent cattle theft, smuggling, and other violations or would ensure compliance with territorial agreements, preventing locals and other trespassers from crossing the boundary for pasturing livestock, harvesting lumber, and cutting grass across the river.

Though, at first glance, the Qing and Romanov frontier surveillance policies appear to have been quite similar, with both stipulating sentry posts at intervals of roughly fifty kilometers, there was at least one striking difference. By the late nineteenth century, the Chinese sentry posts in Hulunbeir were still manned by Mongol bannermen. Their posts consisted only of yurts and the few civilians who lived with them. On the Transbaikal side, however, sentry posts had become regular Cossack villages, mainly inhabited by ethnic Russians who spoke Russian, were baptized, and remained agents of Russian culture even though they had mixed with the indigenous dwellers and adapted to their steppe environment. So even if the boundary was physically almost invisible and loosely enforced, the actual presence of people on the frontier clearly signaled Russian dominance.

Territorial acquisitions on the Amur and Ussuri rivers in the 1850s further increased the length of the already vast Sino-Russian land boundary, making frontier surveillance even more difficult. This obvious incapability forced the Russian government to reform its customs supervision in the East. In 1862 the main customs office in Siberia was moved to Irkutsk. The entire Far East (including Transbaikalia) was declared a free trade zone. Imported goods and commodities produced in the Russian Far East were now cleared to pass through customs at Lake Baikal. A key acquisition for the Russians from the Aigun and Beijing treaties was the right for Russians to trade inside the Qing Empire, enabling Russian merchants to compete at last with the Chinese, including the powerful tea trade companies. Also, this ruling enabled Russian traders in Mongolia to bring great caravans of livestock, meat, wool, and so forth to Siberia. The new system reflected specific regional characteristics: the vast territory was thinly populated and, to the metropole, economically insignificant. The new fiscal regime still entailed elements of protectionism because the Russian state had introduced a number of restrictions on the import of commodities upon which excise duty was imposed: tobacco, tea, and sugar. Alcoholic beverages were generally banned from importation.[55]

Starotsurukhaitui, the second official trade post on the frontier, gained significance only after the Russian annexation of the Amur and Ussuri territories and the declaration of free trade in that region. Russian merchants now began to traverse Hulunbeir, the Great Xingan Mountains, and the Manchurian plain, no longer limiting their trade to the Chinese and Mongols near the border. Starotsurukhaitui also became the starting point for cattle transfer from Transbaikalia to the Amur and Ussuri territories. Prince Petr A. Kropotkin, a distinguished Russian geographer, traveler, and advocate of anarchism, was one of the first to take this new route, driving livestock across Chinese territory. When his caravan reached Starotsurukhaitui in May 1864, Mongol guards from across the river inspected the livestock and goods on the Russian territory and asked the Hailar imperial resident for approval. Indeed, "the inspection on the Chinese frontier was much more indulgent than on the European borders. They believe us on our word that we do not carry any prohibited items, recorded the number of bales, inscribed with all possible details in our travel documents . . . and wrote for themselves a copy, which, as it turned out later, facilitated the travel on the road ahead."[56] The number of livestock conveyed from Eastern Transbaikalia to the Far Eastern provinces of the Russian Empire via Chinese territory increased over the years. While visiting Starotsurukhaitui in the final years of the nineteenth century, a Russian traveler counted on the river shore one barge capable of transporting a hundred passengers, two floats for twenty to thirty people, and about fifteen wooden rowboats, each seating about ten people.[57] Though the traders and escorts of horses and cattle required pas. ,orts and approval by the Chinese authorities, they were usually allowed to pass freely.[58]

The new free trade regulations of 1862 also allowed unregistered local border trade within a strip extending a width of fifty *versta* from both sides of the boundary.[59] Only products traveling beyond this zone had to be registered at Cossack posts. In the upper reaches of the Argun, three Cossack villages formed the core of the local border trade within the border zone: Abagaitui, Starotsurukhaitui, and Novotsurukhaitui. In practice, however, a substantial portion of the trade was carried out beyond these sentry posts. In the Manchu garrison town of Hailar, for instance, outside the zone, local Russians bartered their cattle against various commodities such as grain and woven fabrics. For the state, it was not even possible to estimate the volume of legally imported commodities, given the lack of documentation produced by the Cossacks in charge. As a result, the free trade zone provided a loophole for the unregistered transit of merchandise across the Sino-Russian border.[60] The free trade regime of the Russian state along its Asiatic frontiers thus offered locals ample opportunities to spin economic webs across boundaries and enabled the frontier to take on a life of its own.

At the Ganchzhur Fair (Ganjuur), a key nomadic trade hub, this premodern frontier economy was particularly visible. The fair was located about 175 kilometers away from Hailar in the southwestern corner of Hulunbeir, on the only route leading north toward Transbaikalia. Its origins go back to the early nineteenth century, when caravans of Chinese merchants from Beijing and Buir Lake made their way across Inner Mongolia to Hulunbeir. On the Buir Lake–Hailar road, they passed the famous site of the foremost Lama Temple and Monastery in Hulunbeir. Built during the reign of the Qianlong Emperor in 1784 and known as the Ganchzhur Temple, the latter rose to importance, eventually supporting several hundred resident monks.

The steppe came to life every year in the fall. Mongols left their summer pastures and moved in convoys along steppe roads to the monastery by the thousands to worship at the Ganchzhur Monastery. The spiritual site also became a lucrative center for Chinese traders. During the pilgrimage season in September, they set up their stalls next to the monastery and bustling markets sprang into existence. Taking advantage of a seemingly borderless world, caravans from northern China and the remotest corners of Mongolia and convoys from Transbaikalia, Amur, and the Maritime region would pour into the "monastery of eternal peace" to participate in the fair for five to seven days. It became a center of commerce between nomads from Khalkha, Hulunbeir, and the eastern side of the Great Xingan Mountains and, to a lesser extent, Russian and Chinese merchants. By the 1870s the monastery could no longer accommodate the growing number of merchants attending the trade fair. Therefore, it was moved about five kilometers away to a great steppe camp. The fair now covered an area of three kilometers in diameter. It was divided into Chinese and Russian trading rows as well as a horse market and surrounded by the yurts of various banners as well as those housing fair administration, dining stalls, and the like.[61]

The rise of cross-border economic ties was visible in other places of the Sino-Russian frontier as well, such as the Argun villages where, around 1900, trade was still conducted during annual summer fairs in the manner that Agaton Giller had observed in the mid-nineteenth century. These markets, like the fair at the Ganchzhur Monastery, were zones of contact between cultures: Abagaitiu's population, for instance, came in touch with people from across the river and from regions further away in the process of conducting "a decent trade in livestock and raw materials with the Chinese, who annually come from Qiqihar and Hailar to the Russian border and organize with their carts, tents, yurts and huts quite a considerable camp-fair on the right bank of the Argun."[62]

This busy exchange was possible because passage across the border at sentry posts such as Starotsurukhaitui had not changed much. For the locals, identity and luggage controls did not apply as long as they lived within the fifty-versta zone. For travelers from afar—if they encountered sentries at all—these controls were also slack but at the same time slow, as one had to wait a couple of days for approval and appointed guides from the imperial resident of Hailar.[63] Transit thus remained ponderous, bureaucratically cumbersome, and sometimes dangerous into the twentieth century. Passage was possible only at premodern frontiers, on the backs of mules, camels, horses, and other traditional means of transport, and via dirt roads once built by Cossacks. Three such roads within Chinese territory connected Hailar, leading to Starotsurukhaitui, Kailastui, and Abagaitui.[64] This antiquated transport and commodity exchange would soon come to an end, however, with the advent of the railroad age, as we will see in the next chapter.

Hailar and Abagaitui: Two Very Different Steppe Frontier Settlements

The differences of daily life on the Chinese and Russian banks of the Argun—reflecting variations in economic development, ethnic policies, and frontier maintenance—emerge most starkly in comparative portraits of settlements on their shared frontier. In this last section we pay a visit to Hailar and Abagaitui, two contrasting sites in the intermediate zone between empires.

It is difficult to speak of any form of settled community in Hulunbeir even by the late nineteenth century. The only significant exception in the otherwise nomadic environment was the Manchu garrison town of Hailar. Located on the shore of the Yimin River, a tributary of the Hailar, roughly one hundred kilometers east of the Argun border, the small and dusty town of one to one and a half thousand Chinese was the sole permanent settlement between Qiqihar and Urga (the later Ulaanbaatar). When Ivan I. Strel'bitskii, a Russian army officer and member of the Priamur section of the Russian Geographical Society, visited the town in 1894, it made quite a depressing impression:

> From outside, Hailar gives the impression of a monotonously gray mass of adobe shacks, and although at either end of the street there are big Chinese-style city gates, with their obligatory pavilions on the top, they fail to brighten up the extremely dull impression. . . . The view from inside is consistent with the first impression: a series of low, one-story walled houses on both sides of the street, embellished in two places with wooden arches. This street forms, strictly speaking, a bazaar: on both sides, through the doors, long poles are raised up on which sway all sorts of objects depicting the products traded and the shopkeeper, as elsewhere in China, replacing our signboards. . . .
>
> Suburban Hailar makes a far more attractive appearance, between the river and the heights of the left, upland shore. In this place . . . is located the brick-made Mongolian temple with its typically colorful and intricate Sino-Tibetan architecture, then comes the government office, and finally the houses of the imperial resident and his employees. Moreover, less than a versta from the town, down the river, is located a Chinese pagoda, surrounded by a graveyard giving temporary calm to those Chinese people who are waiting until their loved ones will gather their ashes to transfer them to their native China behind the Great Wall.[65]

Earlier accounts of Hailar read much the same. The horse breeder Nikolai A. Khilkovskii described the population as consisting of "temporary Han Chinese traders, almost exclusively men without their families, occupying the 53 courtyard houses . . . alongside the street," based on his visit in 1862.[66] Even with a fluid population of Chinese merchants and artisans, who returned to their native environs on a regular basis, Hailar was the only significant settlement of the Han ethnic group in Hulunbeir's predominantly nomadic environment.

The Russian side of the Argun frontier featured more settlements, yet none had as many inhabitants as Hailar. The Cossack village Abagaitui, at the southernmost point of the Argun River, had been founded soon after the boundary demarcation. In 1759 only thirty-five Tungusic residents and twenty-two horses lived in Abagaitui, sheltering in earthen huts and yurts. The number of residents reached 582 in 1883, further rising to 959 in 1912. It was still an almost purely Cossack community and, with nearly half the population under sixteen years of age, one that grew quickly.[67] The steep population increase, lasting until the 1917 Revolution, can be partly explained by the transformation of the Cossack settlements over the latter half of the nineteenth century. The formerly dual role of the residents as guards and peasants had shifted over the years, to favor the latter. This trend was reflected in impressive livestock figures: agronomic statistics listed 3,327 horses, 3,762 horned cattle, 10,254 sheep, 2,122 goats, and 94 camels for just 714 Abagaitui residents in 1895.[68]

Thus the pastoral life of the Cossacks on the Argun followed the old traditions, apparently insulated from international developments in Northeast Asia. In a series of articles in October 1903 *Kharbinskii Vestnik* (Harbin Herald), the official Russian-language newspaper of the Chinese Eastern Railroad, took its readers to the remote settlement: "Abagaitui has some 150 houses; the population engages exclusively in cattle breeding, the sale of cattle, horses, sheep, and sheep wool. Their income is supplemented to some degree by fishing and hunting. . . . The Cossack houses look very shabby, gray, and half-rotten. They are furnished with small windows without glass and with beautiful bark roofs, low, and nearly flat, with broken fences that further reinforce the sad impression."[69] Their distance from the imperial metropole had facilitated cultural blending with the indigenous surroundings despite loyalty to the tsar.[70] Thus although the tsarist government had—in contrast to the Manchu court—pursued an active immigration policy, exporting its dominant ethnic group to the Argun, Russian men and women of the frontier were not colonizers in the sense of a national or civilizational mission. Instead, they had produced hybrid ethnic and cultural "quasi-indigenous" affinities over time. Russian and native worlds had thus become thickly interwoven.[71] On his way through Abagaitui, the infantry general and military writer Nikolai A. Orlov began raising the question whether these people still constituted ideal Russian frontier people: "Cossacks, replacing the Tungus as landlords over this region, gave their village in which they are living up to this year . . . a Tungusic name. They do not notice it themselves, because almost all the Transbaikal Cossack villages, stations, lands bear Mongol, Tungus, Buriat names, they are completely mongolified, tungusified, buriatified. In any other Cossack host, as far as I know, there is no such ugly a phenomenon, conflicting with the feelings of patriotism and national pride, and carrying a cosmopolitan flavor."[72] Only when the railroad was opened for traffic would Cossack villages close to the rail line be exposed more thoroughly to "Russian" or "European" culture. One contemporary noted in 1904 that "one comes across 'civilization' in form of corsets, trendy jackets and hats, and in Abagaitui . . . girls give almost the impression of European city women."[73]

By that time, however, perceptions of the Cossack as an ideal military wing of Russian colonial formations on the frontiers of empire had already begun to fade. Cossacks often acted according to their own interests, protecting families and estates rather than securing the still thin and fragmented sovereignty of the imperial state. To overcome this perceived lack of loyalty and in an attempt to convert the open steppe frontier into a controlled borderland, the metropole would, in the not so distant future, draft plans to replace the quasi-indigenous Russians on the Argun with more reliable personnel. These would be neither stationed permanently on the border nor responsible for their own sustenance.

———

The Russian expansion toward the Amur basin and China's conquest by the Manchu allowed the first direct interactions between the Qing and Romanov empires. The treaties of Nerchinsk and Kiakhta were testament to the recognition by both metropoles of the need to formalize their encounter. All in all, despite the conflicts arising after their ratifications, those agreements secured good-natured relations between the two powers on their shared imperial periphery well into the nineteenth century.

To Saint Petersburg and Beijing the Argun River basin had little appeal either economically or strategically. It was a natural buffer territory, sparsely inhabited by autochthonous people. Despite its minor importance, both metropoles sent new settlers to the frontier. Yet significant differences became apparent in their respective policies of colonizing the region. Perceiving the Chinese Northeast as their own cultural sanctuary, the Manchus forbade Han immigration to this area. Instead, the Qing court deployed members of indigenous groups to the Argun. Over time these frontier men and women would form new, culturally distinct communities in Hulunbeir. The Russians also subjugated the nomadic Buriats and the itinerant Tungus native to Transbaikalia and incorporated some into Cossack structures, although these tribes remained far away from wholesale conversion and assimilation into Russian culture. At the same time Saint Petersburg pursued a more assertive immigration policy. Peasants, exiles, and Old Believers, many but not all of whom were ethnic Russians, were moved from other parts of the empire to this region.

As a consequence, by the end of the nineteenth century the population density on the Russian side of the Argun was higher than that on the Chinese side, with ethnic Russians outnumbering the autochthonous by a factor of three. Indigenous banner people, by contrast, still dominated the Chinese

Argun bank. Yet bare population numbers and ethnic demographics ignore the cultural contact of the frontiersmen. Members of the ethnic majorities of both empires blended with the indigenous people on each side of the boundary to some degree, but rarely across it. Russian Cossacks on the Argun in particular were isolated from their native culture. They lived in villages with Tungusic or Buriat names, intermarried, and adapted to climatic conditions that turned farmers into herders. Often it was debatable what kind of Russianness they represented. In this gradation of the frontier people, "pure" ethnic Russians, Manchus, and Han Chinese nevertheless remained at the top of the political and social hierarchy of their respective empires.

State bureaucracy was still nascent on both banks of the Argun, and a simplified administrative system existed alongside indigenous structures of self-administration. Only in the nineteenth century did the Russian state begin to implement a set of reforms that turned the Transbaikal region into a regular Russian province. Very differently, indirect rule over the native population through Hulunbeir's imperial resident remained untouched until the very last years of the Qing dynasty, as we shall see in the next chapter. Despite this weak presence of the metropoles, Russia and China both tried to secure their vast external frontiers by constructing physical barriers and stationing military administrators. Yet with sentry posts about a day's horse ride apart, the state border was characterized by a seemingly unwinnable game of numbers and geography that could hardly pose an obstacle to the passage of people, animals, and goods.

While Russians and Han Chinese came in contact with each other during the annual trading fairs in the Cossack villages on the Argun or on the bazaar street in Hailar, buying and drinking Chinese spirits did not mean the Russian purchaser became in any way Chinese. Even though their national identities may still have been nascent, their racial ones were not, as ethnic Russians and Manchu or Han Chinese were physically different. Cross-border movements thus did not imply cultural blending of ethnic Russians and Chinese, yet notions of the linear boundary held by the state collided with concepts of territoriality held by local frontier populations. In many cases they simply ignored the emerging state border and continued with the long-held ways of life of a borderless steppe world.

2

Railroads, Germs, and Gold

RAILROADS NOT only transformed the previously remote steppe economy of the interimperial margins of Inner Asia but also were crucial for empire building, as they strengthened bonds between the imperial metropole and periphery. They gave states the means to move large quantities of men and material to distant regions, acted as resources for capital accumulation, and at the same time provided the frontier with new economic opportunities. Because "the railroad reorganized space," as Wolfgang Schivelbusch has eloquently argued, it offered Russia—and soon China as well—a golden opportunity to direct national development and homogenize its dominions.[1]

For Russia, empire building beyond its international boundaries using railroad technology commenced in the last years of the nineteenth century. After the construction of the Great Siberian Railroad had begun in 1891, Russia made use of railroad diplomacy to wield imperial influence in China's Northeast—at a time when a number of powers began to compete fiercely over influence in Northeast Asia.[2] In the wake of the First Sino-Japanese War (1894–1895), Russia penned an agreement with China, the terms of which provided for the construction of the Chinese Eastern Railroad. This line was the last link of the Trans-Siberian Railroad and provided a shortcut to the Russian Far East, from Chita, across Hulunbeir and northern Manchuria via the newly founded city of Harbin to Vladivostok. In 1898 Saint Petersburg acquired, by treaty, the warm-water harbor of Port Arthur (Lüshun) at the tip of the Liaodong Peninsula in southern Manchuria, thereby extending its power to the southern parts of Manchuria. To connect the new port with the Chinese Eastern Railroad, a southern trunk line from Harbin to Port Arthur was built.[3] These changes altered the long-lasting, stable power relationships previously structuring the Sino-Russian frontier.

Behind the pragmatic justification of these measures—to wit, the need to save time and money when building the railroad link through northeastern China—lurked foreign policy anxieties and imperial dreams, fed by the heady golden era of imperialism. Russia's vehicle in this struggle for supremacy, the

Chinese Eastern Railroad, was not simply a joint Sino-Russian railroad company that happened to operate on Chinese soil, but a colonial railroad, which in its Russian (and later Soviet) comanagement represented a typical expression of informal imperialism.[4]

Perceiving Qing China and Meiji Japan as future demographic and economic competitors in Northeast Asia, Saint Petersburg followed the dictum that a vigorous offense was the best defense. The railroad concession enabled Russia to hold the potential to exert direct military domination over Manchuria, thereby creating a buffer for the vulnerable Russian Far East. The right moment arrived in 1900, when the Boxer Rebellion, a violent antiforeign and anti-Christian uprising, had spread across northern China, offering the Russian government the opportunity to occupy all of Manchuria. This Russian seizure of China's Northeast, however, united the international community in East Asia against Russian aspirations and eventually drew Japan into open conflict.[5]

In fact, Russian intentions in the region were not wholly military. Sergey Witte, the minister of finance whose brainchild the construction of the Russian railroad line through Chinese territory had been, preferred a "peaceful penetration" of foreign territories in East Asia by economic means.[6] Yet Russia's ruinous commercial policy toward Manchuria, designed to exclude other parties with whom it could not compete, undermined plans to expand Russian economic influence in China. In reality, Russia endowed Manchuria with a railroad system that would largely benefit Chinese and Japanese entrepreneurs, at its own considerable expense.[7]

At the same time, however, the construction of the railroad did further enable the tsarist state to shore up authority in its own peripheries. As will be seen in this chapter, Saint Petersburg abolished the principle of free trade in the Russian territories east of Lake Baikal and installed customs supervision along the state border in order to rake in more income from tariffs and disrupt uncontrolled and untaxed trade. More generally the new railroads transported people, capital, and ideas from the heartlands of both empires to imperial peripheries, profoundly transforming the interimperial frontier. Pioneers from Europe and Asia soon gathered in bustling steppe settlements like Manzhouli, the newly founded railroad town on the border.

Nonetheless, the Russo-Japanese War (1904–1905), a conflict in which the railroads played a key part and which was fought and lost by Russia largely on China's Manchurian soil, was a serious setback for the bold ambitions of the tsarist regime. Negotiations resulted in the Peace of Portsmouth, which stripped Saint Petersburg of Port Arthur, the southern line of the Chinese Eastern Railroad, and much of its position in Manchuria.[8] While the years between 1900 and 1905 had been the nadir of Chinese influence in the region, the Qing state gradually managed to reestablish some control over lost parts of Manchuria during and after that conflict. Then, in another reversal, a diplomatic rapprochement between Saint Petersburg and Tokyo prior to World War I yielded Japanese support for Russian interests in the leased railroad territories. This fresh Russo-Japanese alliance in the Far East offered Russia more leeway to maintain its position in the region, which, in turn, generated new conflicts with the Chinese.[9]

Mastering Imperial Space:
The Construction of the Railroad

In 1896 the Russian government initiated topographic surveys to ready land for the new trunk line of the Transbaikal Railroad from the railroad junction near Karymskoe to the Chinese border. In June of the same year a group of seven officers and fifty-eight soldiers was dispatched to explore the planned western section of the Chinese Eastern Railroad between Hailar and Qiqihar, the capital of Heilongjiang province. Near the Russian village of Starotsurukhaitui, the soldiers crossed the Argun on a primitive vessel. Opposite the Cossack village they encountered a Mongol sentry post guarding access to the Heavenly Kingdom. In their yurts, the Mongols verified travel documents, before the Russians continued their overland journey to Hailar.[10]

When railroad construction began on the Transbaikal trunk line and western section of Chinese Eastern Railroad, Russian engineers encountered great difficulties in acquiring an adequate supply of building materials in the thinly populated steppe land.[11] Further complicating construction, Buriats and Cossacks opposed installing the new line on Russian territory because it affected the grazing grounds of their livestock.[12] In Hulunbeir the Russians faced similar problems, albeit on a legal level. After negotiations between the Russian engineers and the Chinese authorities in Qiqihar and promises to the local Mongol population that "only a narrow strip was to be expropriated, not to affect their pastures at all," the Chinese provincial government gave permission to lay the railroad through Hulunbeir.[13] But another conundrum was posed by the legal status of the thousands of workers on the Chinese construction sites. They had to be equipped with special passports that would allow them to cross the border without restriction.[14]

In the summer of 1900, the anticolonial Boxer Rebellion spilled into Manchuria and interrupted work on what was to become the Chinese Eastern Railroad. Military mobilization in Transbaikalia began on 25 June 1900. The newly formed Hailar detachment went into battle with nearly five thousand men recruited from the Transbaikal Cossacks, alongside soldiers of the Transamur Border Guards, who were also in charge of security on the railroad

Для Китая

(Маньчжурія, Монголія).

№ *1.*

№ 5601

ЗАГРАНИЧНЫЙ
ПАСПОРТЪ

Предъявитель сего, подданный Россійскаго Государства *агентъ*
Общества Китайской Восточной желѣзной дороги Николай
Ганьковъ, съ женою Капитолиною Михайловной
отправля е тся въ городъ *Хулань-чэнъ*

для *жительства*

и имѣ е тъ при себѣ для самозащиты *одинъ револьверъ*
и пятьдесятъ къ нему патроновъ

Согласно существующимъ между обоими Государствами договорамъ,
благоволятъ власти Китайской Имперіи чинить *Николаю и*
Капитолинѣ Ганьковымъ

свободный пропускъ и покровительство.—Ради того и данъ сей паспортъ
~~Канцеляріею Приамурскаго~~
~~Военнымъ Губернаторомъ~~ *Генералъ*-Губернаторомъ ~~области~~, за его под-
писью и съ приложеніемъ казенной печати 18*девяносто восьмого* года

Августа 25 дня. Въ гор. *Хабаровскѣ*

~~Губернаторъ~~

Правитель Канцеляріи

Дѣлопроизводитель

~~При выдачѣ паспорта взыскано~~
~~рублей.~~

Скрѣпилъ

FIGURE 2.1. Passport of a Russian worker on the Chinese Eastern Railroad, 1898. Only with these special travel documents were they allowed unrestricted entrance into Chinese territory.

construction sites on Chinese territory. Six weeks after this mobilization the Hailar detachment had taken the Chinese positions on the western trunk line up to the Great Xingan Mountains. But relative to battles farther south, the turmoil hardly affected the Argun frontier and in particular had skirted railroad construction in Hulunbeir.[15]

As fall gave way to winter in 1900, the first military transport and construction supply trains ran along the single track of the Transbaikal trunk line up to Sibir', the final station on Russian territory.[16] To honor the contributions of Transbaikal military governor Evgenii I. Matsievskii to the construction of the railroad, the terminus was renamed Matsievskaia. In a ceremony on 23 February 1901 the first eastbound train left the station to cross the border to China. A single decorated wooden arch marked the border between railroads and nations. Matsievskii personally nailed the last missing rail linking Russia with the leased territory of the Chinese Eastern Railroad. As the engine started moving again, it severed a silk ribbon stretched under the arch, marking the beginning of a new era.[17]

Regular traffic from Saint Petersburg to Vladivostok via Manzhouli began in 1903. The Chinese Eastern Railroad, as the last link of the Great Siberian Railroad, significantly reduced the distance between the Baltic Sea and the Pacific Ocean. The long journey by sea via the Suez Canal and India was no longer required. Despite border controls and stopovers, the overland route was faster and often cheaper for passengers, and it soon enjoyed great popularity among globe-trotters and took pride of place in numerous travelogues and guidebooks.[18]

Yet the iron track remained primarily a narrow corridor through the steppes of Dauriia and Hulunbeir, hardly stimulating the areas it crossed. Most of the newly established railroad sidings and villages accommodated fewer than one hundred people. The only noteworthy Russian settlements on the line near the Chinese border were Borzia and Dauriia. The former, located some 110 kilometers northwest of the border by train, by 1910 was home to 1,469 people, mainly Cossacks from nearby who engaged in livestock farming, marmot hunting, and petty trade or were employed by the railroad. Dauriia, still about fifty kilometers away from the border, counted just 154 souls. The station, however, soon gained importance with the beginning of the construction of barracks for troops and, during the Civil War years following the Russian Revolution of 1917, as one of the main bases for the horse-borne attacks of the White commanders Baron Roman von Ungern-Sternberg (Baron Roman Fedorovich fon Ungern-Shternberg) and Ataman Grigorii M. Semenov. Matsievskaia, the final regular stop in Russia, positioned about ten kilometers from the state border, remained insignificant despite its distinguished name and position almost directly on the border.[19]

Connecting the railroad to transport on existing waterways or overland roads may have offered possibilities to overcome the limitations of the narrow railroad corridor. Such interconnections might have stimulated the economic development of Cossack settlements on the Argun. Yet because of old vehicles and poor roads, which were often impassable due to bad weather, overland transport remained stuck in the preceding century and would for decades.[20]

At first, the prospects for water transport had looked more promising. In 1901 and 1902 several Blagoveshchensk entrepreneurs with links to the Amur shipping companies saw opportunities to improve this situation. They attempted to persuade the Russian government to install a similar passenger and mail service along the long course of the Argun. According to the factory owner Semen S. Shadrin, such ferry operations would not only join the Amur steamship operations in the north to the railroad line in the south but also bring "beneficial development to the Argun region." However, the timetables, cost calculations, and technical requirements for the ships prepared by the entrepreneurs remained shut away in drawers because government bodies feared technical difficulties and doubted the respectability and credibility of the merchant and shipping companies to be involved.[21] After all, the Argun was navigable only between April and October. The shallow and often narrow riverbed on its upper course would have made the passage risky for steamers even in the summer months. During the first half of the twentieth century, the only watercraft in use on the upper Argun were small vessels made out of birch bark, used by fishermen and the Argun Cossacks for household purposes. The Russian settlement Olochi, on the middle reaches of the Argun, remained the sole terminus of the Amur river-steamer service. Unlike the Amur, the Argun as a waterway, therefore did not have any positive impact on the development of its surrounding territory.[22]

Frontier Spirit: The Birth of a Railroad Town

Apart from Harbin, Chita, and other quickly developing transportation hubs, only a few settlements along the railroad belt were to benefit from modern infrastructure. Manzhouli, eleven kilometers off the boundary on Chinese territory, was among those few and became the true border station, connecting the Transbaikal and the Chinese Eastern railroads. In a region of Cossack farmers and Mongol herdsmen, of yurts dotting the steppe and sleepy villages nestled on a river, a railroad town on the border is something anomalous. Although locals, migrants, and foreign visitors could meet one another anywhere on the steppe, Manzhouli emerged at the beginning of the twentieth century as a crucial center for Sino-Russian interactions, be these in political, economic, social, or cultural spaces.

FIGURE 2.2. View of Manzhouli, circa 1910. To the left of the shunting tracks is the Chinese
side of the village; the passenger station building is to the right. The water tower is
one of the few traces left of those early days.

Manzhouli was built by chance. Originally topographers and engineers had
projected the railroad farther north. The line was to cross the Argun about
150 kilometers north of what became the route, in the vicinity of Starotsurukhaitui. The southern route, however, proved to be more feasible. Investors
would be spared a bridge because as the Argun branches away from the state
border it turns east, to become, as Hailar, an entirely Chinese river.[23] The
border town was founded in the valley of the Kuladzhi creek at a locality called
Nagadan by local nomadic tribes. It was a place they rarely visited with their
livestock herds and was almost untouched, with wild Przewalski horses still
grazing on the open meadows.[24] The Russians named the western Chinese
Eastern Railroad terminus *stantsiia Man'churiia*. The name translates rather
neutrally as "Station Manchuria," while the Chinese version Manzhouli means
"located within Manchuria."

During the early years train passengers were still embarking on an adven-
ture reminiscent of frontier life in the outposts of the American West. People
changing at Manzhouli from Transbaikal to Chinese Eastern Railroad trains
often had to wait overnight for their connections. They had to be quick to get
a smelly, overpriced room in Metropol', Evropa, Tertumasov, or one of the
other few hotels often already occupied by "aborigines" inspecting the achievements of European culture. Other passengers spent the night in the station's
greasy waiting room or sought consolation with a beer from the overpriced
buffet—a ruble for a bottle imported from Munich. The poor slept in *plein air*
on wet soil.[25]

It took the British anthropologist Charles Hawes fifteen days to make the
trip from the Manchurian railroad's eastern terminus in Suifenhe (which the
Russians called Pogranichnaia) to the western endpoint during its trial

operations in 1902. Changing trains at the border, Hawes experienced Manzhouli in the making:

> The first thing to do was to explore the buffet, about quarter of a mile dis-
> tant. In the large outer room were crowded about 200 *mushiki* and third-
> class passengers, through whom I made my way to the one labelled first-
> class. This contained a bar and a long dining-table; and by the light of three
> candles I could see that the floor was covered with baggage and sleeping
> forms. . . . I asked, "Is there a porter here?" A jolly-faced, elderly woman
> sitting at the door, amused at such a demand, smilingly replied, "No." Such
> an institution as a porter was a thing of the future.[26]

Petr N. Krasnov, assigned by the Russian Ministry of War to conduct an inves-
tigative trip through East and South Asia, also experienced a border still pleas-
antly free from "traditional luggage inspection, customs officers, soldiers, and
money exchange." The observant traveler saw Russian traces and Russians
everywhere. "A white building with the sign 'Café Moscow' across the station
and next to it the Paramonovs, Ivanovs, Stukins in their kiosks and stalls trading all one could imagine." In his explorations around the unfinished train
station he passed Russian workers, a guard, a lady with her child, a salesman
on his bicycle, and various other Russian elements. It took Krasnov some time
to find Chinese people in Manzhouli. "There they are. Over there is a crowd
of pigtails sitting on the platform eating something, and there two Mongols
tying up their horses at a stall, chatting with a salesperson standing on a thresh-
old . . . that's it."[27] To Krasnov, the Russians were on their way to dominate and
colonize the Chinese frontier. Emitting a smell of dirty boots, *makhorka*, cheap
vodka, and onions, Russians of all four train classes united and were positioned to take over a region that many of Krasnov's contemporaries already
imagined as "Yellow Russia."

Manzhouli was not yet a town where everything was in place. Yet settlement proceeded rapidly, and the magic word "boom" was bandied about with
reference to the steppe. To many observers it was just a question of months or
maybe a few years before the border station would become a major commercial center. "Houses grow like mushrooms here after a good rainfall," exulted
one.[28] But the completion of the permanent station building with its two fa-
çades, initially scheduled to open in 1903, was delayed by the war against
Japan.[29] The public bathhouse, opening in 1905, was so overcrowded that
people had to wait for hours. A new brewery produced the first local beer for
thirsty Mongols, Russians, and Chinese. Gambling in the open air attracted
players of all nations. The disagreements and small scandals that cropped up
between quarrelsome players wherever cards were on the table were settled in
pidgin, a garbled form of Russian, native to the people of the border. A Railroad

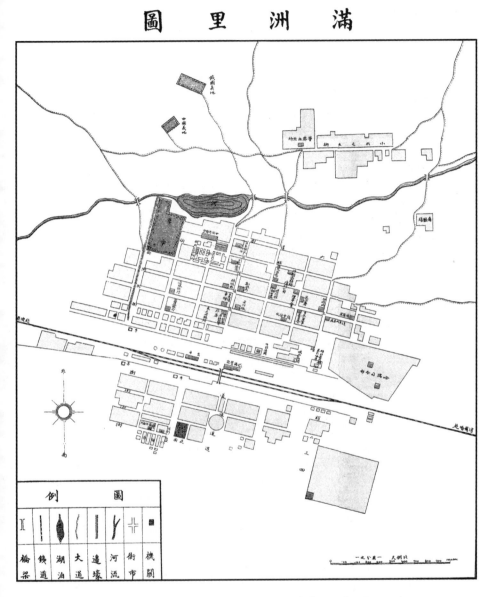

FIGURE 2.3. Projected layout of Manzhouli, 1908. Founded as a railroad town, the city is literally divided by the tracks even today.

Theater showed amateur spectacles for a selected audience. And in Mauretania, a variety theater, people could forget about their daily duties or worries for an hour or more.[30]

Manzhouli was divided by both infrastructural and semicolonial means. Like Harbin and other settlements along the Manchurian railroad, it was encircled by the boundary of the alienated corridor (*polosa otchuzhdeniia*), an extraterritorial zone on Chinese territory entirely administered and policed by Russians. Bulging at Manzhouli, the zone was 5,462 hectares in size.[31] The settlement consisted of four parts, of which three belonged to the extraterritorial zone: the Chinese side, situated south of the railroad tracks, the Transbaikal side north of them, and the bustling private village. Outside the alienated strip and extending north to the Kuladzhi creek lay only a shantytown called the "village beyond the stream" (*zarechnyi poselok*). "On the Chinese side, state-owned, mainly brick houses are built to accommodate railroad workers and servants. It is home to the Chinese Eastern Railroad's station facilities, namely: the church, hospital, school, public assembly, library . . . , police head-office and other institutions. The train station is home to the post, telegraph, and customs office. That part of the village with its broad symmetrical streets has quite original buildings . . . many of which are residential houses, small villas for 1–2 families, surrounded by gardens." The main part of town, in terms of both population and economic importance, was the private village: "Here are all the shops, businesses, and the busy bazaar. The private village hosts the following institutions: a church of the Russian-Orthodox Mission in Beijing, the municipal secondary school with four classes, a primary school, two Russian public assemblies and one Chinese, the municipal self-government, and other municipal institutions such as a fire brigade, slaughterhouse, hospital, veterinarian and library. The greater number of shops are liquor or grocery stores and those for textiles. There is also one small bookstore, two drugstores and a pharmacy."[32] The overall impression given by the border town was that of a rather aesthetic, cultivated Chinese side, with small fountains, and an uninviting Transbaikal side "covered with dust, where houses stand naked like in the steppe."[33] In late 1910 parts of the settlement under the management of the Transbaikal Railroad were handed over to the Chinese Eastern Railroad administration and unified with the railroad village. Still, the division between private and governmental districts in the settlement remained, underlining the importance of the rail company as a political agent.

Who lived in this town in the making? For quite some time Manzhouli retained a high male-to-female ratio that is characteristic of frontier settlements.[34] The accuracy of censuses taken in border settlements—with seasonal migrant workers, a floating population, and many people wishing not to be included in any statistics—must be understood as no more than fiction.

TABLE 2.1. The division into different districts is reflected in Manzhouli's population rates, 1907 to 1940

Year	Russians/Soviets	Chinese	Japanese	Others	Total
1907					1,500
1910	8,350	4,732	68	81	13,231
1921					24,990
1923					18,300
1925	8,997	2,939	41		11,977
1929	7,645	5,053	154	102	12,954
1931					3,000
1933	3,855	4,633	378		8,879
1936	1,695	3,759	837	229	6,520
1938	1,567	3,973			6,397
1940	2,976	2,986	370	14	6,346

Note: Official Russian statistics for 1907, in Glavnoe upravlenie general'nogo shtaba, Marshruty, 224; for 1910, in U.S. consular estimates for 1910, in NARA/RG 84/U.S. Consulate, Harbin, China/vol.6/307–336, 334; for 1921, in Kitaiskaia Vostochnaia zheleznaia doroga, Man'chzhuriia, appendix no. 5; for 1923 and 1925, in Kormazov, Barga, 47, 90; for 1929, in Kormazov, "Dvizhenie," 53; for 1931, in "Zakat goroda Man'chzhurii," Rupor, 20 August 1931, 3; for 1936, in Cui, Haila'er, 2:77; for 1933 and 1938 in Manzhouli shi zhi, 53; and for 1940, in Keizai Chōsakai Dai'ichibu, "Manshūri," 470–471.

Though the population estimates are doubtless inaccurate, they illustrate the truly international character of Manzhouli at the dawn of the twentieth century, despite its diminutiveness. The absence of autochthonous people in the statistics further illustrates the difference between this urban place and its pastoral surroundings.

Manzhouli had features that are prevalent in border cities, such as a population that predominantly made a living from the border. Additionally, Manzhouli was home to certain institutions the likes of which could be found only in some of the hybrid, semicolonial settlements along the railroad alienated strip in North Manchuria. Among these were the immigration post with the adjoining hospital, the Russian military barracks, the Chinese and Russian customs houses, the estates of the chief officer of the Chinese police, and the Chinese prefect, all of which were situated in the private village on the Transbaikal side north of the tracks. Furthermore, to regain control of the frontier region, Chinese authorities built their own fortified settlement, with soldiers' barracks, two kilometers south of Manzhouli in Lubin.[35]

People in Manzhouli witnessed not just boom times but severe setbacks as well since its earliest days. The border town swiftly felt the burden of its locality. Although politically the town was part of the railroad zone on Chinese territory, economically it may as well have belonged to Transbaikalia. It was built and administered by Russians, and the distance from it to Chita was about 470 kilometers by train, roughly twice as close as the 934 kilometers to Harbin. Hardly any commercial ties existed to settlements in Manchuria.

The years following the defeat by Japan in 1905 were particularly difficult. The disastrous outcome of the war reverberated in Manzhouli especially. After the Russian armies had decamped from China's Northeast, "the main customer of nearly every one of our economic endeavors . . . had gone," noted one contemporary observer.[36] The construction of the northern route of the Trans-Siberian Railroad along the Amur that began in 1907, spurred by worries that Japan might sooner or later annex Northern Manchuria, siphoned away people, money, and energy. In Manzhouli prices fell, and those who remained could buy almost everything at a discount.[37]

Yet the business people of Manzhouli still clung to hope. Many sought to emancipate the settlement from the railroad, war-related industries, and the dictates for a planned economy handed down by the Russian Ministries of Finance and War. For decades the region had been a trading center between the Russians and Mongols, and as such it could have been parlayed into a foundation for future business opportunities. But the frequency of bandit attacks targeting unarmed herders and the construction of the railroad had persuaded the Mongols to allow the settlement to lie fallow since the early 1900s. After the Russo-Japanese War, however, municipal administrators and local business elites alike rediscovered Manzhouli's strategic position between the Mongolian pastoral lands and the infrastructure that nurtured the Russian and Chinese empires. They lobbied for the formalization of secure Mongolian trade routes to be guarded by Chinese and Russian soldiers, in order to attract commerce with Mongol herdsmen once again. The establishment of a caravansary for the trade of horned cattle north of the town, where Russian and Chinese authorities would be able establish tax collection posts, as well as an international annual fair for cattle designed to compete with the traditional trade fair in Ganchzhur gave new hope.[38]

After the nomads in Hulunbeir declared independence from the Republic of China in early 1912, an issue we will discuss in chapter 3, trade with the Mongols grew at an unprecedented rate, a rate that, according to old inhabitants, "was even more extraordinary than it was during war with Japan."[39] The streets of Manzhouli were packed with camels. Numerous corporations, like the all-Russian tea company Gubkin-Kuznetsov and the fur-trading firm Batuev & Zimmerman, sent agents to grant advances to Mongols. Even foreign enterprises like the Leipzig-based Biedermann Company specializing in fur and raw materials established Manzhouli auxiliaries. In 1914 the latest rumors whispered that a new railroad link between Urga and Manzhouli would be built to further stimulate business.[40] In the long run, however, the native economy declined. Manzhouli remained a town populated by Russian and Chinese colonizers. Colonized nomadic natives to this place would remain a negligible element within the urban settlement.[41]

Some signs of growth marked the years before World War I. On the surface the border settlement developed within multiple modernities, as it took on features that hinted at concessions to twentieth-century urbanity. Telephones first appeared in the summer of 1911. Kerosene lamps illuminated parts of the Transbaikal side and were soon replaced by electric streetlights powered by a Siemens & Halske plant. In 1914 two banks opened for business and a brick church replaced the old wooden structure. Alongside the existing elementary school, teaching started at a new high school boasting seven classes.[42]

Thus high-spirited local politicians, with the chairman of the municipal council Aleksei N. Nikitin as their strongest advocate, envisioned a bright future for Manzhouli and one symbolically bound to the Russian Empire. On the occasion of the centennial of the Battle of Borodino against the French in the late summer of 1912, a bust of Alexander I was consecrated on a small, dust-covered square.[43] Such vivid praise for the tsar and the country came, certainly, not without ulterior motives. The next year Nikitin demanded a juridical city status not inferior to that of Harbin from the railroad administration, despite the fact that Manzhouli was still a dusty backwater in the steppe, lacking paved roads and a sufficient water supply and facing many other problems of basic provision. The authorities in Saint Petersburg declined the proposal. Given that their motion was composed the very year that the Russian Empire celebrated the Romanov dynasty's three hundredth anniversary, the municipal council had also suggested that Manzhouli be renamed "Romanovsk." Why Russian citizens did not wish to live any longer in a settlement called "Manzhouli" is unclear. Perhaps they at last desired a toponymic enclosure within the empire. But Saint Petersburg declined this request too. A name steeped in such honorable history was only to be bestowed upon cities, not ad hoc frontier settlements.[44]

Inspectors Lost in the Steppe:
The Dilemma of Customs Control

By the time the first trains came rumbling across steppes of Dauriia toward Manzhouli, people on the Argun still inhabited a seemingly borderless world where preexisting networks, whether social or economic, were still clearly visible. The history of customs service and smuggling, discussed in this section, analyzes state strategies of economic regulation and the corresponding responses of locals to circumvent them. The construction of the railroad went hand in hand with the establishment of economic control over the imperial periphery and international boundary and would soon challenge informal networks. However, it took decades for these controls to become sufficiently effective as to put an end to economic links and to deprive the locals of free choice of residence.

During the 1860s the entire Russian Far East (including the newly acquired territories on the Amur and Ussuri rivers but also Transbaikalia) had been declared a free trade zone, as we have seen in chapter 1—with restrictions on the import of a few items, such as tobacco, tea, and alcohol. Imported commodities and goods produced in this region were now cleared to pass through customs at Irkutsk. The Russian government saw free trade as the only way to develop the distant region because a tariff revision would have been almost impossible to implement, in addition to being fiscally pointless.

In the last decade of the nineteenth century the connection to the Russian railroad network led to the greater economic integration of the Asian imperial periphery. When Saint Petersburg revised its customs policy for its Far Eastern territories during that time, the state pursued two objectives. First, the aim was an economic homogenization of the imperial territories up to the state border, which would entail the domestication of the frontier and ultimately the end of the free trade policy. A second purpose was to further strengthen Russia's economic and geopolitical position in Northeast Asia, in part to compete against China and Japan for supremacy in Manchuria.

In 1894, years before Manzhouli appeared on the map, the Ministry of Finance deployed two expeditions to the Amur-General Government, bearing mandates to plan several sites of customs control at the Russian land border east of Kiakhta and the maritime border in the Pacific. The state bureaucracy thus abandoned the idea of establishing a tight network of customs agencies along the Chinese border similar to its European borders and confined itself rather to the creation of toll offices in major cities and transport hubs. In June 1899 temporary customs supervision was set up in Vladivostok, Nikolaevsk-on-Amur, Kiakhta, and Sretensk. On 14 January 1901 *porto franco*—the territory through which exports and imports pass without incurring duty—was a thing of the past.[45]

Despite this decision to introduce customs duties, Sergey Witte, the minister of finance whose idea the Russian settlement in Manchuria and construction of the railroad largely had been, remained skeptical of the prospects of putting an end to illicit trade on the border with China. During a journey through the Far East in 1902, Witte noted,

To this day, the regions of Transbaikalia and the Amur lived a life of their own that was completely detached from the interests of Russian trade and industry, a life beyond the imperial customs boundary. The sparse population and the lack of even rudimentary signs of a manufacturing sector made the customs protection on the borders of these vast territories fiscally and economically unenforceable and meaningless. The sheer vastness and the difficult traversability of the Transbaikal territories make the region itself an excellent barrier against the inflow of foreign products from the east to Siberia and to European Russia.

Ever a realist, Witte knew that the government had no choice but to tolerate a certain degree of uncontrolled cross-border commodity exchange:

> The protection of this extensive border by our border guards will be extremely expensive and, of course, not even a small part of the expenses will be covered by possible income from the customs revenues. Even if we abandon any of our desire of a full border control and are satisfied with the observation of the most important roads and most densely populated areas, it will be predictable that it is easy to traverse these pathways and settlements through the open sections of the Amur region to smuggle contraband. If we want to prevent its redistribution in Siberia we need to strengthen customs supervision at Lake Baikal through the customs inspection at Irkutsk. The preservation of such a second customs border, however, would further complicate the situation in the Transbaikal and Amur regions and hamper their commercial relations with Western Siberia.[46]

Despite this skepticism the state proceeded with the relocation of its customs agencies to the state border, but the implementation of the new Russian tariff policy indeed met with resistance from many locals. Fearing loss of economic significance, traders in the provincial capital Chita opposed the opening of the customs post at the western terminus of the Chinese Eastern Railroad in Manzhouli from the very beginning. In 1902 members of the municipal council petitioned the minister of finance to open the customs inspection for goods in their town rather than at the border with China.[47]

Due to an increase in contraband trade on the railroad, Saint Petersburg ignored their call and Manzhouli was among the first customs houses to be opened. In August 1901, the experienced Kiakhta customs official Stanislav N. Khmelevskii was ordered to Manzhouli to realize the difficult task of organizing the new *zastava*, which began collecting duties as of March 1902. The main tasks of the Manzhouli customs outpost were the regulation of railroad passengers, the clearance of railroad goods, and the collection of tariffs. Just as at the old customs house at Kiakhta, securing and patrolling the border was merely a subordinate task.[48]

Some travelers, such as the American missionary Marcus Lorenzo Taft, experienced painstaking inspections on the trains:

All the trunks were carried from the baggage van into a commodious room at the station, where they were opened and subjected to a rigid and rough examination. . . . The hand-baggage was examined on the train. . . . When the customs examiners came to our coupé one of them felt with his long cane under our seats, and with his hands searched beneath the mattress of our sleeping berths. Suspicious of cigar-smuggling, one inspector, noticing an outside pocket of my coat bulging a little, pointed to it, felt of it on the outside, and then requested me to show what was inside. So as soon as a red-covered "Baedecker" was produced, he seemed perfectly satisfied, promptly chalked the rest of our baggage, and speedily walked off, while the faces of the bystanders were suffused with smiles.[49]

Yet the experience of thorough luggage examination was just the impression of a single outside observer. Despite constant staff increases, their number remained too few to check all passengers and goods closely, control the border effectively, and fulfill their consular duties.[50]

Notwithstanding its growing significance—within a few years' time Manzhouli would become the key control post on the border with China—Russian customs remained housed in temporary structures, lacking buildings for proper offices, quarters for the employees, and rooms for the storage of confiscated and dutiable goods.[51] These provisional facilities reflected the contingency of Russian customs policy during the 1900s. In fact, customs control in the Russian Far East would once more be lifted from 1904 until 1909, when a free exchange of goods again became necessary to supply the eastern periphery of the Russian Empire during and after the war against Japan.[52]

In the spring of 1909, once again, with the ultimate revocation of porto franco, the Russian government reorganized customs supervision.[53] Now given substantial funding, customs agencies soared in number along the state border with China. A total of two first-level customs offices, at Manzhouli and Sretensk, operated in Transbaikalia, as well as one second-level customs office at Kiakhta. Four additional customs outposts were added to the three existing ones, and the number of lookouts shot up from just three to twenty.[54] By 1914 Manzhouli had emerged as the major land port on the border with China, and had clearly outpaced Kiakhta, the famous Sino-Russian entrepôt for the overland tea trade during the eighteenth and nineteenth centuries. Russian customs at Manzhouli now accounted for 78 percent of cleared exports and half of cleared imported commodities in Transbaikalia.[55]

The most significant change to be made to customs policy after the end of porto franco in 1909 was perhaps the gradual shift from the limited control of border sections acknowledged to be vulnerable to the full surveillance, at least on paper, of the entire land border with China. The key maneuver in this

FIGURE 2.4. The caricature "On the Occasion of the Liquidation of the 50-Vesta Free Trade Zone," which appeared in the Vladivostok newspaper *Okeanskii Vestnik* (Oceanic Herald) in October 1912, shows a newly erected Russian customs post. It mocks the Chinese who had previously benefitted from unrestricted border trade: "Gentlemen merchants and traders, please help the unemployed."

regard had been the liquidation of the fifty-versta free trade zone as of 1913, which had previously allowed unrestricted local border trade.[56] Surveillance was now relocated directly to the vast stretches of the land and river border. With additional funding the number of customs employees multiplied. In addition to the staff working at Manzhouli's railroad station, a total of seventy-five inspectors were assigned to the thirteen newly created outposts and look-outs under the vast jurisdiction of the Manzhouli customs district along the state border from Argunsk in the north to Borzia in the south.[57]

In the years before World War I, surveillance remained in the hands of these few customs employees because the military presence at the border was nearly nonexistent. Nothing more intimidating than a squadron of a hundred border guards was positioned in Dauriia, some fifty kilometers from Manzhouli, to enforce the surveillance of the entire Transbaikalian border with China. State bureaucrats and the military saw, rather, "the necessity to establish in the immediate future a border protection along the lines of Russia's western borders."[58] State forces, be they border guards or mounted customs inspectors, thus remained inadequate to deal with the many tasks of economic border surveillance in the East.

The Sino-Russian agreement on the construction of the Chinese Eastern Railroad had guaranteed China the establishment of customs houses at its two terminuses on the border with Russia.[59] But insisting that such agencies might be established only after the renegotiation of the 1881 Treaty of Saint Petersburg and the secret agreement between the Chinese government and the Russo-Chinese Bank in 1896, the Russian government successfully delayed their opening for several years.[60] Only after Russia's defeat by Japan did the United States, Japan, and other countries competing for economic influence in China's Northeast increase pressure on the Russians to accept Chinese customs control and allow international trade in the railroad concession. Since the Chinese Maritime Customs was in fact a mixed authority in which the colonial powers had a say as well, those other powers supported the Chinese position.[61] The Chinese customs house at Manzhouli began collecting duties in February 1908. By summer that year Russia and China finally agreed on provisional regulations for the conduct of the Chinese customs at Manzhouli and Suifenhe.[62] Although Saint Petersburg was forced to give in, it still exerted some indirect influence for several years afterward through the Russian nationals working in the administration of this hybrid agency.[63]

Once the Chinese began collecting duties in 1908, new problems arose. The brunt of the work of border control and customs inspections rested with the employees of the Russian customs house.[64] Russian and Chinese staff quarreled over various mundane things, such as broken customs seals on railroad cars. Sometimes the conflicts reflected hitherto unfamiliar contact between the Russian and Chinese cultures—in particular different standards of hygiene. The Russian assessors complained about the Chinese "cluttering up the rooms, throwing trash on the floor . . . and, in their spare time, gnawing sunflower seeds or dried nuts, spitting the shells on the floor." In contrast to the local Russian population, most Russian customs officials were new to the region, and Chinese culture remained foreign and, in many cases, unacceptable to them. Adopting an arrogant tone of presumed racial superiority, they professed annoyance with the Chinese customs officers' refusal to wipe down the examination hall even after inspections, thus forcing "Russian personnel to do menial work even for the lowest ranks of the Chinese Customs."[65]

While the Chinese customs authority limited its fiscal supervision to the railroad crossings where it had clustered its personnel, the Russian government continued its effort to control the entire land border.[66] Yet Witte's early doubts about the relocation of the customs border were justified. In 1909, seven years after the finance minister had inspected the situation in the Far East, his successor Vladimir N. Kokovtsov investigated the region again. Despite all the efforts made on its behalf, the fight against undercover border trade seemed virtually impossible to persecute according to Kokovtsov, due "in particular to the incredibly cheap vodka in Manchuria" consumed by the Russians on the frontier, an issue we shall turn to now.[67]

Contraband Trade: Short and Long-Distance Transborder Networks

As long as the available surveillance means were limited and profits from contraband goods were high, the illicit transfer of commodities prevailed and smuggling remained, if not the most important productive activity on the Argun, then certainly among the top few. Smuggled commodities moved in both directions across the border. Although the variety of contraband items changed over time, ranging from silk, tea, sugar, and tobacco to paper products, two commodities dominated the illicit border trade on the Argun in the late nineteenth and early twentieth centuries: gold and alcohol. As elsewhere, if one is to measure by exposed cases and by the value of the contraband, liquor was the primary contraband of the Argun frontier. In 1911, about one-quarter of all smuggling attempts discovered by the Russian customs house at Manzhouli involved liquor,[68] mainly a poor-quality millet-based spirit known by its pidgin name of *khanshin*. Within three years the number increased to about 40 percent of all cases. Calculated by value of goods, the proportion was even higher: in 1911 liquor made up two-thirds of the total value, and all but one-quarter four years later. Gold ranked second overall. Compared to gold and alcohol, the notorious opium trade was certainly a bone of contention between the Russians and the Chinese authorities on the Amur and Ussuri borders, but it was actually insignificant if one looks at the contraband statistics of the Manzhouli customs district.[69]

The analysis of alcohol and gold is useful because both were already subject to import and export restrictions during the era of porto franco. Besides their similar statistical significance, alcohol and gold are two starkly contrasting contraband commodities, in their diffusion via trafficking networks and agents. Gold, unlike alcohol, was a globally traded and smuggled item, with obvious links between translocal collaboration and world markets. Its large-scale contraband trade involved many different people in a highly complex supply chain of diggers and smugglers. Alcohol, by contrast, was a lesser, exclusively regional contraband, requiring only a network contained on the frontier for its production, distribution, and consumption.

TABLE 2.2. Smuggling prosecutions, by product and value, uncovered by Russian customs within the Manzhouli customs district between 1911 and 1915 (some smugglers carried multiple commodities at once)

Prosecutions (in rubles)	July–December 1911	July–December 1913	January–June 1914	July–November 1914	January–June 1915
Liquor	290 (10,119)	343 (13,374)	399 (12,889)	409 (15,091)	1,052 (49,753)
Gold	no data	no data	no data	269 (7,260)	291 (6,256)
Opium	0 (0)	7 (99)	10 (2,784)	26 (9,180)	24 (3,220)
Other commodities	890 (5,607)	937 (10,870)	559 (5,396)	604 (6,426)	1,279 (7,915)

Note: GAChO/107/1/83/29–30; GAChO/107/1/124/6–7; GAChO/78/1/14/172–174ob.

Beyond their economic significance, the study of these contraband commodities and their trafficking networks also unearths the processes by which locals undermined the intentions of their governments, penetrated border security, and cooperated across ethnic boundaries.[70] Additionally, the divergent social meanings of commodities in different spaces and times, which Arjun Appadurai has discussed, are important here.[71] Gold and alcohol could have entirely different social values for the Russians, Chinese, and Mongols. Persistent drunkenness, for instance, as we will see in the next section, was widespread among Cossacks and, to a lesser extent, among nomads, but it was simply not an issue among ethnic Han Chinese. Gold, by contrast, had greater cultural value among Russians than Chinese, for whom jade had higher priority.

Despite the varying contours of their networks and divergent social and cultural values, the illegal trade of gold and alcohol often intersected. Liquor was the key import commodity smuggled into Russia: the cheap khanshin was by and large produced on the Chinese side of the border and then predominantly consumed by Russians. Distilleries on the Chinese territory and in the railroad zone soon became the chief liquor suppliers of the Russian border population, in return catalyzing the illegal cross-border trade of gold since the precious metal was also a major medium of exchange. For the state, alcohol was a lucrative but dangerous commodity. On the one hand taxes on its production and sale offered a significant source of revenue. On the other consumption had a definite impact on morale and security in the border regions.

Local and Global Commodities: Alcohol and Gold

As the nineteenth century came to a close, the production, smuggling, and consumption of various forms of liquor increased dramatically on the Argun. Relatively low grain and sugar prices in China led to displacement of the

previously popular khanshin in favor of vodka among the Russian and nomadic consumers. The circulation of fake brands of liquor was widespread.
Cheap booze from Harbin was sometimes touted as mature French cognac,
aged seventeen years.[72]

Manzhouli emerged as the hub of liquor contrabanding from China to Eastern Siberia, and the production, trade, and consumption of alcohol was its
biggest business. State statistics for 1910 list 103 liquor stores in the railroad
town (i.e., one shop per 120 residents), mostly run by Russians, but also by
Chinese and Japanese proprietors. Despite Russian customs' efforts to crush
the business, the Russian-dominated municipal authorities profited from it.
They charged a one-ruble tax on every *vedro* of liquor that was produced or
traded in the village.[73] By 1910 taxes on liquor, wine, and beer businesses made
up more than two-thirds of the public administration's overall tax income.[74]
"If all the imported alcohol were imbibed by the locals, this village would
probably be the most drunk on globe," a contemporary noticed. In 1909, the
astounding quantity of 5,168 hectoliters of Chinese liquors were brought to
and then sold in Manzhouli. Only about 17 percent of this figure was consumed on the spot, however. The rest was shipped on to Russia proper.[75] Thus
municipal fiscal policy at the periphery, obliged to increase resources by taxing
liquor stores and restaurants, was utterly at odds with the efforts of central
authorities to fight illegal trade along the porous border. And as the years wore
on, the trade failed to show any sign of abating: statistics from a booklet by the
Russian Finance Ministry suggest that state restrictions on alcohol during
World War I proved largely ineffective.[76]

Open borders left loopholes for traffickers everywhere. On trains passengers often smuggled several bottles in their clothing and luggage. Some aimed
to evade the ban by fake customs endorsements on their belongings, double-
walled suitcases, or liquor bottles tied to their bodies. Larger quantities of liquor were smuggled out of China by railroad employees under the coal or in
the ceiling of a railroad carriage—orchestrated by anyone from the *chef de train*
to the lowest mechanic. Another loophole was the railroad section between
Manzhouli and the first stop on Russian territory. There the trains drove usually only at walking pace so that liquor could be handed over during the journey to passengers and conductors. The state-built railroads thus facilitated
smuggling. Overland across the steppe and on the Argun, where professional
smugglers generally tended to be bolder, liquor was often trafficked across the
practically unmanned border in horse carts or on rowboats. If one of the few
customs officers approached, the bootleggers disappeared without a trace in
the grassland or on one of the river islets.[77]

The liquor business thus increased dealings between the Chinese, Mongols,
and Russians in Manzhouli and on the Argun. Beginning in the 1900s

FIGURE 2.5. A Chinese-owned dry goods shop in Manzhouli in 1935. The Russian sign reads "wholesale-retail store," and the individual items are "haberdashery," "perfume," "liquor," "food," and "goods." With abundant stores of cheap liquor, alcoholism was a widespread social evil in the borderland.

infrastructure enabling cross-border shopping mushroomed on the Chinese riverbank. The prospect of profit attracted Han Chinese migrants who opened shops to trade with the Russians. Their steadily expanding distribution network for all kinds of goods provided a ready-made sector for the sale of alcohol.[78]

Russian authorities eyed the Chinese shopkeepers with suspicion. Yet even the British magazine *Economist* noted that customs authorities were so overwhelmed by the mass of incidents that they could "only fold their arms as they watch Russians taking excursions across to the Chinese side."[79] On an inspection tour in spring of 1908, the head of Nerchinskii Zavod district, some three hundred kilometers downstream the Argun yet still within the Manzhouli customs district, observed small houses "almost opposite every one of our villages on the right bank. Going into them I realized that they are currently set up for trade of alcohol, tobacco, and matches. Two Chinese live in each of them, one, young, who speaks Russian and the other about 45 years old not knowing any Russian." Often the houses of Chinese border guards served as storerooms for contraband. Their involvement shows clearly that it was not always in the interest of the two states to cooperate in the repression of illicit trade. What the Russians feared in addition to Chinese support of alcohol smuggling was a blending of the two distinct cultures and, obliquely related, political subversion. For Russian bureaucrats, the Chinese migrants who were "baptized and sometimes even married to Cossack women" were especially dangerous.[80] The border river was acknowledged to have failed as a dividing line, and fearful states imagined the interconnections it might facilitate between various frontier groups.

Certainly the consequences of the liquor trade were harmful for public health and morale. Entire villages were in a delirious state. Indeed, some children had already become alcoholics. Russian frontiersmen drank spirits "before, during and after the tea, basically continuously 'before,' 'during,' 'after' anything."[81] The press mocked the sad scenes that could be observed on the border: "Often you can see a Russian floating on his horse and who can barely sit in the saddle. It is a Cossack, a philistine, returning from the Chinese river bank, who had a hefty dose of 'English bitter' or just some 'bitter.'"[82]

Until World War I Russian senior government officials pondered the causes of the illegal spirit trade at the Sino-Russian border. There was a consensus that the fight against the bootlegging could be won only by closer customs supervision on the border as well as enhanced fiscal surveillance of trading and taxes on goods. Some bureaucrats, sensing a bonanza, in fact demanded that there be allowed "the importation of Manchurian alcohol and spirits of all kinds after taxation."[83]

Policing powers tried to suppress the illicit distribution of goods by means other than additional manpower and the imposition of import and export taxes. Laws and regulations were another tool wielded with the intent of seal-ing the border. With the order to liquidate the fifty-versta free trade zone in 1913, the Russian government tried to curb the trafficking of alcohol. Further-more, between 1911 and 1916 it passed a number of laws and concluded several agreements with the Chinese government on the matter. These limited sales to state monopoly stores on Russian territory and prohibited the purchase and sale of spirits in the Chinese border region and the railroad zone to Russian subjects. But, perversely, the abandonment of the spirit monopoly and the total ban of alcohol production and consumption in Russia by government legislation during the general mobilization in 1914 subverted the efforts to stop the illegal trade on the frontier.[84]

Those attempts to use legal codes to enforce the will of the imperial center in the periphery had a galvanizing effect on the illicit trade of alcohol: they further stimulated the informal economy in the border region. During World War I black market prices for alcohol in Russia amounted to as much as twenty times the prices on the Chinese shore of the Argun.[85] Cooperation between Russia and the independent Hulunbeir authorities between 1912 and 1915, which we will discuss in the following chapter, could not stop the liquor traf-ficking on the border. According to a senior Russian customs official, "Many liquor stores on the Mongol [Chinese] bank of the Argun existed under the same roof with the Hulunbeir customs, whose employees by no means prevent the owners from selling alcohol."[86]

Quite different was the career of gold, the second most notorious contra-band on the Argun frontier. During the last two decades of the nineteenth century the discovery of this precious metal triggered a rush to Eastern Trans-baikalia, the Amur basin, and other areas of the Sino-Russian frontier. In those years thousands of fortune seekers, peasants, and drifters who went to try their luck came from neighboring regions and other areas of Russia and China and some even from abroad.[87]

Gold mining became a significant economic sector on both sides of the Amur and Argun rivers. By the turn of the century dozens of mines operated in northern Heilongjiang province in the vicinity of Heihe on the Amur and in northern Hulunbeir, owned mainly by Chinese, Russian, British, and Amer-ican entrepreneurs. Gold mining loomed even more important on the Russian side. In Transbaikalia alone there were 149 gold mines, almost half of them near the lower and middle reaches of the Argun. In 1910 their annual average yield lay above 3.28 tons, compared to 1.8 tons in the Heilongjiang mines.[88]

Although the exploitation of gold in Transbaikalia had already peaked in 1901, the number of gold diggers increased over the following years. The major-ity of the 17,210 workers who would be employed in the goldfields of Transbai-kalia in 1909 came from China.[89] Russian commentators and armchair voyagers widely discussed the presence of these Chinese toilers in the Russian periphery allusively in the often-mocked catchphrase of "yellow peril," thereby shaping the imaginary of the Argun frontier.[90]

At least during the first half of the twentieth century gold was mainly trafficked from Russia to China—inverting the flow of contraband liquor. The annual contraband outflow of Russian and later Soviet gold to China was an estimated 2.46 tons through World War I and then declined to approximately 1.31 tons per year in the mid-1920s. In other words 20 to 60 percent of the region's annual gold production was smuggled out of the Far East.[91]

While gold, unlike alcohol, was a globally trafficked item, it involved similar networks of illicit traders. Chinese seasonal workers on their return home for the winter months were a major contingent. Their swelling ranks, coupled with insufficient border controls, made this smuggling channel the most promising.[92] But various other areas of contact between Russians and Chinese existed through which contrabanding activities were carried out as well. One such space was the newly established liquor and grocery stores in the Chinese Argun villages, where Cossacks purchased daily necessities and vodka, often in exchange for gold. Another significant channel was the railroad.

Until the Russian Civil War custom officers arrested train passengers at Manzhouli almost daily, among them Chinese miners, Russians officials, and Jewish merchants, whom they caught with gold, the weight of which was specified in *funt* and not in *zolotnik* in the protocols.[93] It had been purchased in Irkutsk, Chita, or the Transbaikal gold mines and, according to rumors, was often sold in one of the first major train stations on Chinese soil: Manzhouli, Zhalainuoer, or Hailar.[94] Frisked passengers and border shop customers were, no doubt, only the tip of the iceberg. Savvy contrabandists knew that they could bypass customs guards easily. If they traveled by train they disembarked at Dauriia or Matsievskaia, the last stations on Russian territory. In any of the surrounding dusty steppe villages they consigned the smuggled ware to mounted accomplices, many of whom were Russians. The border beyond the few control posts remained almost unregulated, and the gold—just as the khanshin bottles and other contraband—passed the state border smoothly on horseback or on a boat.[95]

Going Where the Grass Is Greener: Cross-Boundary Cossack Agriculture

Having explored the different ways in which economic boundaries were erected and contested up to the Russian Revolution, we now shift our focus to study how territorial demarcations, migration patterns, and quarantine regulations called traditional relations among the local populace into question and altered the nature of the frontier life of the upper Argun basin. Two rather disparate phenomena, namely border-crossing disease epidemics and territorial disputes between the Russians, Chinese, and Mongols, are illustrative for this consolidating impression of a border. These phenomena bred national identities, changed perceptions of the border, and called into question customary relations among pastoralist and agricultural frontiersmen.

Even before the experience of the great Manchurian plague of 1910–1911 a stronger awareness of the state border had taken root. It was not only the nomadic people of the frontier who traversed state borders. Argun Cossacks also crossed into the neighboring Chinese territories, often for the same reason as nomads: a lack of suitable grazing grounds for their horses, horned cattle, and camels. Yet, in contrast to the Russian government's policies toward nomads, Cossacks had official support to do so. Though Russian Cossacks had been assigned plots in Transbaikalia equal in size to those they had tended in European Russia, these proved insufficient to their economic needs. Due to climatic and topographical conditions, the particularities of economic life, and the Cossacks' culturally based sense of agricultural scale, they perceived a great shortage of land. Often they leased additional arable land and pastures from the Khori Buriats in Transbaikalia, and those who lived near the border with China sought to enlarge their pastures by tilling Chinese soil.

Since the mid-nineteenth century the Cossack population on the Argun had crossed the river to Hulunbeir to supplement their rural economy with hunting, grazing of cattle, and leasing land for wheat and winter food. In contrast to the meager soils on the Russian bank, the richly fertile land in the wide valleys of Trekhreche on the Chinese side of the border river allowed them to practice Russian-style agriculture. The birch and pine forests in the slopes of the Great Xingan Mountains in the north and east of Hulunbeir offered good conditions for forestry and hunting. Farther south, the steppe, with its lush high grassland, was ideal for the extensive breeding of sheep, cattle, and horses.[96]

The Russian commuters were undisturbed by Chinese officials or Chinese peasants and tolerated by the nomadic tribes of Hulunbeir, as the latter's collective view of land did not hamper the Cossacks. On the contrary, it gave them the opportunity to cultivate the land free of charge. In the late nineteenth century, however, the Chinese government began to strengthen its position along the border and officials tried to claim lease monies from the Russians. But China's position deteriorated in the First Sino-Japanese War of 1894–1895 and again during the Boxer Rebellion in 1900, as did its ability to collect rent.[97]

Around 1900, this creeping colonization of the Chinese frontier regions by Russians was discussed and openly supported by contemporaries in influential literary magazines such as the *Russkii Vestnik* (Russian Herald):[98] "It should be noted that in general in the life of the Transbaikal and Amur regions the land lease abroad, that is in Manchuria and Mongolia, plays a major role. . . . People in the Cossack stations on the northern Argun, such as Olochi and Argunsk, if deprived of land lease in Manchuria would become extremely poor, and many of the Cossacks would be forced to leave."[99] In this view, Russian Cossacks and farmers had the natural right to extend their habitat beyond the state's border, as this was the only way for them to make a living in their natural environment.

Yet the economic well-being of the Russian frontier population was not the only motive. When large parts of Manchuria were still occupied by the Russian army during the aftermath of the Boxer Rebellion in summer 1901, the settlement of Russians in the Chinese territories on the Argun marked an important move toward strengthening the political-strategic position of Russia in the region, or at least it appeared so to many observers. After the suppression of the Boxers and the subsequent occupation of Manchuria by Russian troops, plans for the colonization of the western Chinese Eastern Railroad section were entertained with increasing seriousness and seemed more realistic than ever before. The ultimate goal of war minister General Aleksei N. Kuropatkin and other Russian advocates was to push the international boundary line farther south to the Gobi Desert, following the southern slopes of Great Xingan Mountains to Port Arthur. The border would thus be straightened and shortened and its administration simplified.[100]

During the four years between the Boxer Rebellion and the war with Japan, Amur governor-general Nikolai I. Grodekov examined plans to populate a strip adjacent to the Russian railroad through Manchuria. To select suitable spots for Russian settlement, the government sent an experienced official and agronomist to the region.[101] By that point, initial explorations of the westernmost section of the railroad had already been undertaken, over the summer of 1902, to clarify terms for potential Russian settlers. The report characterized Hulunbeir and in particular the area along the tracks as land with "almost no population, in which agriculture is absent, but where nomadic herding is quite well developed, although at first glance it is lost in the vast expanses of the steppes."

Under the influence of the railroad line, and due to the Boxer Rebellion, traditional seasonal migration patterns had in fact been disrupted: nomads with their herds had retreated to the north, across the Argun, or south, to the Khalkha River. Only occasionally would herders appear with their cattle near the railroad line. The area in southern Hulunbeir was suitable only for animal husbandry and fishing in the Argun and its tributaries, as well as in the vicinity of Hulun Lake. The report recommended the Transbaikal Cossacks as the most appropriate group of settlers since the local climate and soil closely approximated their surroundings at home. The report, however, cautioned, "It will be difficult to compete here for the Russian people in general, and the Cossacks in particular, with the hard-working Chinese-farmer."[102]

After the Russians forced the retreat of Mongol and Chinese border posts in the wake of the Boxers in 1900, the Cossacks were no longer satisfied with temporary rights to land on the Chinese riverbank. Some began to move to Chinese lands permanently. Particularly in the Trekhreche region, Cossack settlers began to occupy vast areas of land, which they used for raising cattle and crop farming. They built dugouts and huts to use the area year-round. Soon after the Russo-Japanese War, however, the Chinese administration demanded taxes on land that the Cossack settlers now regarded as their own. Introduced as part of the broader New Policies, a subject we will return to momentarily, this assertion of power on the part of the Chinese precipitated the first disputes between the Cossacks and the Qing imperial resident (*amban*) in Hailar. In January 1906, the military governor of Heilongjiang province Cheng Dequan demanded from the Transbaikal military governor the expulsion of fifteen hundred Russian citizens allegedly involved in farming and mining on the right bank of the Argun River.

Russian authorities tried to bypass official channels, hoping to settle the question of Russian estates on the Chinese bank of the Argun with the local Mongols. As early as the spring of 1906, the Russian ambassador to China, Dmitrii D. Pokotilov, instructed Russian diplomats to negotiate land use on the Chinese banks of the Argun and Amur rivers only through private agreements with local authorities. Other agreements, he warned, could be used as evidence to underpin allegations of Russian violations of the Treaty of Portsmouth that formally ended the Russo-Japanese War.

In late 1906, local Russian authorities followed these instructions to the letter. Instead of negotiating with the governor of Heilongjiang province in Qiqihar, Popov, an interpreter at the Russian consulate general of Harbin, met in May 1907 with the Hulunbeir imperial resident in Hailar. The amban was in principle not opposed to hay making, grazing, and the construction of temporary shelters in Trekhreche on the upper Argun. He objected only to permanent Russian settlements on Chinese territory.[103]

The imperial resident invited the Russian diplomat to perform an inspection tour, accompanied by a Mongolian official, along the Argun from Hailar via Novotsurukhaitui and then up to the river Gan in Trekhreche. During the inspection, Popov negotiated with Zhou Qinli, head of China's liaison office for the Chinese miners on the Russian Argun bank, to reduce the mining fees, as requested by the Chinese. In return for this favor, Popov and Zhou agreed on a lump sum of 13,500 rubles per year for the use of pastures in Trekhreche starting in 1908, just barely an acceptable settlement to the Russian negotiator. His next challenge was then to convince the Cossacks of the fairness of that settlement, as they had formerly been accustomed to free use of the land.[104]

Another area of conflict was the roughly 130-kilometer-long road linking Starotsurukhaitui and Hailar. The Manchu garrison town boasted several features that attracted the interest of Russian fortune seekers, in particular the cheapness of commodities compared to prices prevailing on the Russian shore of the Argun and the opportunity to barter with the Chinese there. In the early 1900s, the dirt road in fact became so busy that Russian Cossacks opened seven courtyards and guest houses for travelers along the way. The owners initially received the approval from the Mongolian authorities in Hailar, but under pressure from the Chinese provincial administration of Heilongjiang the extension of this certificate was rescinded. In the eyes of Russian officials, however, such infrastructure was essential for local trade, even though it came with a few negative side effects such as alcohol trafficking. In 1907, once the administration of Hulunbeir had been incorporated into the Chinese provincial system, the Chinese authorities in Hailar closed the issue by delivering an ultimatum to the seven inn owners that gave them one week to abandon their houses and to return to Russia. Those closest to the border had already been burned down. The remaining lodges were spared while negotiations were still ongoing. For the time being, then, Russia had partly failed in its strategy to reach favorable informal agreements with local Chinese officials.[105]

Russian authorities soon realized that formal agreements with provincial government bodies were the only possible way to settle the land dispute. The first such official contract ratified between Russian diplomats and the military governor of Mukden (now Shenyang), in 1910, prohibited Russians from crossing the Argun for cattle grazing and hay making on the Chinese riverbank. The Chinese administration, however, allowed hay making on Chinese territory up to five kilometers inland in those areas, which had not yet been "opened" for the Chinese settlement. In theory, Cossacks who wished to take advantage of the arrangement had to obtain prior written permission from the Chinese colonization administration and then pay duties for the exported hay. After hay collection, the Cossacks were obliged to return to the Russian bank.[106] Yet the 1910 agreement on land use failed to bring peace to the Sino-Russian frontier. The general sentiment was tense in the summer of the following year, after an incident in which Chinese soldiers had opened fire on a Cossack who had defied their instructions. At that point it was commonplace for Chinese border guards to search Russian border crossers and ship passengers, with weapons at the ready.[107]

Thus it was Russian Cossacks who had been the first house dwelling people to farm on both shores of the Argun. Their concepts of land use were similar to those of Han Chinese farmers in that they were based on exclusive rights. The Mongols took an entirely different approach, eschewing formal owner- ship. Their pastoral areas were freely accessible and open to common use. Few disputes sparked between the Mongols and Cossacks in Hulunbeir. Pastoralist Mongols and agricultural Russians valued open dry pasture and well-watered valleys differently, so they could coexist in the same region, whereas Chinese and Russian farmers would be in direct competition. Therefore, conflicts about land use arose only after Chinese authorities began to exert direct influ- ence and to implement policies in line with their less communal concept of land use.

Land Fear: The Qing Government's New Policies

It was, however, not the farmer but the trader who would prove the most apt harbinger of Chinese colonization. Merchants were less dependent on fertile soil and mild climate. And traders, who moved with approval of the Qing court into the Mongolian steppe, settled in the neighborhood of princes or monas- teries such as Ganchzhur, offering commodities that the Mongols themselves did not produce.

By the beginning of the twentieth century, goods from mills in the Far East, distilleries, tea companies, and products of the silk and cotton industries were being traded at the exhibition near Ganchzhur. Horse and cattle trade, how- ever, dominated. Mongols came to the fair to sell their cattle to Chinese traders and to buy goods for the entire year from the revenue they earned there. Pri- vate companies, the Russian and Chinese armies, and other state organizations also purchased livestock there. During the heyday of the fair in the years just before World War I, up to fifteen thousand horned cattle, fifty thousand sheep, and two to three thousand horses changed owners annually. From Ganchzhur the animals were driven to the newly opened railroad stations of Manzhouli and Hailar and then shipped by train to Vladivostok, Chita, and Harbin. The fair was a key source of meat for the people in the Russian Far East, Transbai- kalia, and northern Manchuria. Wool, leather, and other animal raw materials were other key commodities sold by Mongols during the fair.[108]

In 1912 about fifteen hundred Chinese traders did brisk business in the fair, among them representatives from major Beijing companies selling China- made canvas, silk materials, satin jackets, shoes, metal products, saddles, snuff boxes, brick tea, and the like from their yurts and tents. At four hundred mer- chants in 1913, the Russian presence was exceptionally high due to the brief independence of Hulunbeir (1912–1915), which offered them new opportuni- ties selling everything Russian: axes, dog collars, kettles, enamelware, locks, penknives, wax candles, cloth, vodka, and Siberian millet. Exotic commodities

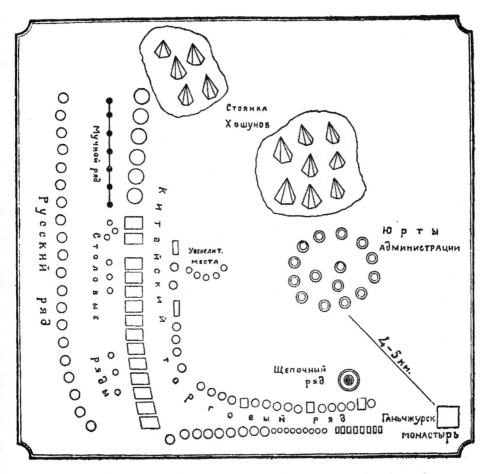

FIGURE 2.6. Scheme of the Ganchzhur Fair. Russian and Chinese merchants bartered in different sections of the fair. Banner representatives and fair administrators put up their yurts in direct proximity to the traders.

from distant regions like corals were exchanged with the Mongols for sheep, and the horsemen obsessively bought up the seashell jewelry popular among their wives and daughters. Such vigorous trade made people like the Buriat merchant Badmazhab Irdyneev rich.[109]

With World War I looming, however, the fair's total sales began to decrease. The enforcement of the border within the Khalkha region in eastern Outer Mongolia, where a significant volume of livestock was raised, made business across state borders increasingly difficult. Other factors were a rise in informal trade between the Chinese and the Mongols taking place far from the fair to

FIGURE 2.7. Chinese and Mongols trading cattle and horses at the Ganchzhur Fair in mid-September 1931. While horse carts were still common at that time, the first automobiles also made their appearance at the spectacle.

avoid taxation, the establishment of permanent trading houses with large storage capacities, and the inauguration of permanent consumer infrastructure for the nomads at Hulunbeir's main railroad stations, Manzhouli and Hailar. Over the years, too, the region's livestock trade had become more cost-effective year-round. Chinese wholesalers bought livestock in Mongolia beforehand, over the summer, to sell it during the fair. Vladimir A. Kormazov, an employee of the Economic Bureau of the Chinese Eastern Railroad, saw signs of a new way of life: "For the Mongol the need to trade in a particular place and at a certain time disappeared. He began to sell and buy when it was needed."[110]

To participate in this trade, Mongols occasionally borrowed money from the Chinese. Their shift away from traditional artisan production and development of new consumption needs led to an enormous accumulation of debts over time. Whereas the Mongol herdsman once had a higher standard of living than a Chinese peasant, the archaic Mongol economy grew anemic. Chinese officials then seized farmland from impoverished Mongols in exchange for unpaid debts. Also, Mongol princes sold or rented land to Chinese to pay off their debts that were mainly caused by exorbitant central state tax and service demands. All of this fed ethnic tensions and resentment of Qing rule.[111]

The history of this fair thus mirrors the fate of the Argun frontier and its native peoples. Since the end of the nineteenth century, the lives of the nomads and their economy underwent dramatic changes as the latter became increasingly integrated into international trade. More than ever before nomads came into contact with the outside world. At first railroads accelerated the trade, but ultimately they undermined this traditional form of commerce. The evolution and decline of the trade fair reflect both how the nomadic people originally lived and how their territories became increasingly encircled.

In the final years of Qing control, China's Manchu rulers shifted from proscription to encouragement of Han Chinese colonization of the border areas, in effect reversing their policy toward Hulunbeir and other Mongol territories. Now it was no longer just the trader but also the farmer who might make a living in the steppe. The imperial periphery was perceived no longer as a remote territory but as an object of development. Small groups of Chinese peasants, usually originating from famine-stricken regions, spread out into the fringes of the steppes. Migration accelerated in the late nineteenth century, particularly to Inner Mongolia. By the final years of the Qing, Chinese peasants far outnumbered the native population in Inner Mongolia as well as in many parts of Manchuria.[112]

The impetus behind this signal shift was to extend the Qing New Policies (*xin zheng*), the shorthand for a series of broad reforms in Chinese politics, administration, economy, military, and education, affecting the most peripheral regions of the empire. The centralizing power and extending bureaucratic control had the ultimate goal of transforming Mongolia into a regular Chinese province. The influence of the imperial center varied strongly in Inner Mongolia and Outer Mongolia. Due to Inner Mongolia's closer proximity to the Chinese heartland and the longer duration of Manchu rule there, Chinese influence had already left strong marks on the region's commerce, politics, and culture. By the late nineteenth century, the Chinese administration had already partially incorporated the region. The situation in Outer Mongolia was different. As one of the Qing Empire's ethnic frontiers, it was still ruled indirectly and feudally. In Outer Mongolia, just as in other parts of the imperial periphery, the reforms entailed a twofold policy of encouraging Han Chinese migration and administrative overhaul. The latter was intended to gradually introduce Chinese standards into Mongolian administration, working toward the aim of full subjugation to Chinese control.[113]

The Qing leadership's shift from banning to encouraging migration and their heightened focus on the periphery had one major rationale. They responded to a growing Russian threat in its border provinces. Guarding and populating the frontiers was one of the most pressing problems facing the Qing court. This difficulty was also reflected in the ethnic composition of the population of Hulunbeir. The geographic unity of this remote border region of Heilongjiang province, still dominated by seminomadic Mongols, gave it its own political weight.

Hulunbeir was incorporated into the general provincial system of China in 1906, several years before Khalkha and other parts of Outer Mongolia. Hulunbeir's transformation followed a pattern of incorporation similar to former bannerlands in Inner Mongolia. Politically, the traditional banner structures were reorganized into regular civilian administrations and transferred to Han Chinese officials. In June 1908 the office of the native imperial resident (amban), who also held the military rank of banner vice commander-in-chief of the Hulunbeir garrison (*fudutong*), was abolished. A new Han Chinese official of the rank of a circuit intendant (*daotai*), delegated by the governor of Heilongjiang province to manage prefectural administration in Hulunbeir, took on his duties as the head of Hulunbeir. In addition to this a special new civilian Han Chinese governor supervising the Chinese population was installed.[114] The region was then divided into three Chinese-style prefectures (*fu*)—Hulun in the east, Shiwei in the north, and Lubin in the west—with district administration offices in Hailar and the newly built garrisons of Jilalin and Lubin.[115]

The reforms also affected taxation and military matters. Before their implementation, the local male population would be conscripted into the banner armies whose key objective was to secure the borders with Russia. But after 1906 the Chinese military gradually took over. New garrisons were established in the three administrative centers of Hailar, Lubin, and Jilalin with Chinese soldiers stationed at these garrisons. Another issue was state finance. The Chinese administration introduced sales taxes on livestock, fish, wood, and grain products for the people in Hulunbeir. Cultural and social assimilation was promoted with the sanction of marriage between Han settlers and Mongolian women and by the granting of permission for Mongols to use Chinese names and to write documents in Chinese.[116]

Among the more controversial elements of reform, however, was the introduction of national education. Until the implementation of those reforms, only one school for Barguts, teaching twenty to thirty pupils, existed in Hailar. Children learned oral and written Manchu, but classes were taught in Mongol. From 1906 onward the Chinese administration founded a number of schools in Hulunbeir at which the indigenous offspring were to be taught in Chinese. Compared to the Russian imperial periphery and the attempts there to incorporate the Buriats of the Aga Steppe, the proportion of nomad children receiving primary education was far higher on the Chinese side of the Argun. Local elites, however, strongly opposed the introduction of compulsory education, not only on the grounds that it was to be carried out in Chinese, but also because it conflicted with the nomad way of life: herdsmen would hardly stake their felt tents in the vicinity of a school for extended periods of time. Opposition took form in open protests made by Hulunbeir leaders, ultimately scuppering some of the plans of the Chinese authorities. In line with the opposition to Chinese primary education, herdsmen and local elites hardly welcomed the new institutions, taxation, and regulation. Many of the ruling Mongol princes, who had controlled the use of pastures within their banners, were afraid that the New Policies would curtail their rights.[117]

Song Xiaolian's Dream of a Chinese Hulunbeir: Moving Peasants to the Steppe

The nomadic peoples of Hulunbeir did not welcome the restrictions of boundaries between their banners, which represented the basic military and administrative unit during the period of Manchu domination of Mongolia. In the past, bannerlands could not be sold or transferred. But like its Russian counterpart, the Chinese colonization bureau sent surveyors to the region by the turn of the century, protected by military accompaniment and tasked with producing colonization surveys and partitioning the allocated land into smaller parcels for future development. Those colonial agents pursued land expropriation by two means: they purchased areas to be used on an ongoing basis or seized some parts outright.[118]

Prior to the opening of the Chinese Eastern Railroad in 1903, the area around the western branch line slated to run through Hulunbeir remained sparsely populated. Alarmed by the Russian invasion of Manchuria during the Boxer Rebellion in 1900 and by the increasing presence of Cossack settlers, state policy shifted toward encouraging Han immigration to cultivate a strong Chinese element along the railroad and in Hulunbeir border areas. Along these lines, a project to develop Hulunbeir with Han Chinese migrants was drafted under the auspices of Heilongjiang military governor and approved in 1902. A strip of land adjacent to the Russian railroad alienated corridor with a width of about fifteen kilometers in each direction enjoyed the highest priority. Although the negotiations were still ongoing with the Mongolian banners, settlement of the Han peasants was due to begin the same year. Property was to be awarded only to "reliable" Chinese families, meaning, for the most part, natives of Shandong province.

The Hulunbeir circuit intendant Song Xiaolian, formerly the head of the Heilongjiang Foreign Relations Bureau, ranked among the strongest advocates for a hurried settlement of Hulunbeir, whose agents would be Chinese soldiers and peasants. His rallying cry invoked the principle of "return of rights and the strengthening of borders." Harboring "a deep hatred toward Russia and everything Russian," he undertook putting into place a series of reforms meant to strengthen the Chinese position in Hulunbeir.[119]

Song's first move, in line with his motto, was a reform of border control. Since the eighteenth century indigenous nomads had guarded the steppe and river border along Transbaikalia, and physical fortification in Hulunbeir had continued apace in the second half of the nineteenth century. Now, to enhance surveillance, more sentry posts were added and the outer and inner rings of these posts were brought closer together. Yet guards' yurts were still stretched thin, appointed at intervals of about fifty kilometers.[120]

Starting in 1904, the Chinese government remanned the watch posts eliminated by Russian forces during the Boxer Rebellion. Mongols were relieved of their guard duty and replaced by Han Chinese. This remobilization entailed a formal transition from a roving defense with husbandry to stationary surveillance with farming. In 1909 the government earmarked funds to build additional small military settlements. As quickly as 1910 twenty-one new Chinese border posts spaced about fifteen to sixty kilometers apart existed between the first post opposite the Russian railroad station of Sharasun and extended up to the lower reaches of the Argun. By maintaining soldiers at the border the Chinese officials sought to improve their control of the movement of people and goods, and in particular to prevent Russians from putting down roots on Chinese territory.[121]

Despite these accomplishments, the circuit intendant Song mulled ideas for a new border regime, which would by and large copy the Russian model. Migrant families were to settle in border villages to ensure permanent colonization. Aping the Russian Cossackdom, the men were to act simultaneously as peasants and guards, thereby providing a passive defense for the border as well as a vanguard for the Chinese farmer, who in the near future would transform the steppe into arable land. The state was to support this migration by providing the settlers with livestock and other essentials. Owing to the region's variable geographic and climatic conditions, settlers were to engage in animal husbandry on the upper reaches, agriculture in the middle course, and forestry on the lower reaches of the Argun. Due to recruitment difficulties, the profession of managing official (*kaguan*), who would head such a village, was to be made more attractive. In addition, those Mongols who migrated south after the railroad construction were to be forced to return to the vicinity of Manzhouli. The thorough realization of these measures was to be ensured by annual inspections by the circuit intendant.[122] Yet despite Song Xiaolian's clear desire for improvements, the program never materialized.[123]

A second element of the principle of "return of rights and the strengthening of borders," affecting areas further inland in Hulunbeir, was the allocation of land to Chinese farmers. To this end, the Chinese authorities created bureaus in Hailar and Manzhouli to seize land for cultivation in Hulunbeir. Methods of transferring the property to Chinese farmers were not always within the law. Song, for example, is said to have granted land from several banners to Chinese migrant farmers free of charge. Even when land had been acquired legally, however, there were endless disputes between the nomads and the new local house dwellers over the sums collected by the Chinese for the land.[124]

Russian observers were skeptical from the very first moment about the outcome of the new Chinese settlement policy. Veniamin F. Ladygin, a Russian explorer, explained around 1910:

> In spite of the commitment of the authorities to send Chinese to the border, to this day the region is still dominated by the Mongols, for whom agriculture plays no role and who will never accept this form of making a living. . . . Thus, despite the relatively favorable conditions for cultivation of oats, millet and the like, irrigated farming has not yet caught on the ground and land will have to wait for a long time until the first farmer will come and plow. He will come here only when all the cultivable soil in the heartland of the province is divided up to the last *shan*. Consequently, the Chinese should not harbor too many hopes in the establishment of military settlements.[125]

Even by the 1920s and 1930s, long after Song Xiaolian had implemented this settlement policy, there were still quite literally no Han Chinese farmers in Hulunbeir, as we will see in chapter 4.

Fixing the Boundary: The Treaty of Qiqihar

The situation on the Russian side of the Argun River was different. Ethnic Russians populated the river shore at the turn of the century. The Russian government formally supported the Cossacks. Simultaneously, Saint Petersburg also officially attempted to shift the boundary to the east. One key argument used by the Russian government was that waterways historically changed their course many times.

Since the Treaty of 1727, the course of the boundary between Kiakhta and the lower reaches of the Argun had remained unchanged, at least in theory. Yet the lines drawn in space that may have once satisfied diplomats no longer reflected realities on the ground. Over two centuries the topography of the area had changed considerably. The main stream of the Argun itself had altered its course, sparking disagreements over the territoriality of river islets and sand bars. Additionally, Lake Hulun had lost water and size farther south, and the river linking it to the Argun—which had served to decline the course of the boundary—had dried up.[126]

With those uncertainties in the background, and as the Russian position grew stronger in the late 1900s, the Treaty of Kiakhta suddenly came to be considered imprecise by some locals and state agents alike. They called for the fresh demarcation of the Argun boundary and a reassessment of the legal status of Manzhouli.[127] With regard to the vague topographical nature of the Argun, a new awareness of the exact boundary line had arisen gradually among the Russian local populace:

> When surveying the Argun valley, then, even at a casual glance, one can clearly see that most islands and watercourses (which mark the old course of the Argun) remain on the Chinese side, and the Argun albeit slowly but steadily pushes its riverbed for the most part toward our mountains, leaving the meadows in China. . . . If additionally there will be some massive floods, perhaps, even our generation will be deprived in the near future of all the Argun meadows. . . . This natural but uncontrollable departure of Russian territory to the Chinese is apparently not stipulated in any political agreements, as otherwise, the Chinese, in any case, would not dare to take the aforementioned lands.[128]

In 1910 the national press echoed the concerns of the people in the distant east. The progovernment paper *Novoe Vremia* (New Times) wrote,

> The Chinese have possessed themselves of about 100 islands in the Argun, comprising great tracts of meadow land which supports numbers of the Transbaikal Cossacks. . . . The settlement of this question would have great local significance for the Transbaikal Cossacks, our natural bulwark on this distant frontier. Their whole property depends on their flocks and herds which exist solely in the valley of the Argun. . . . If . . . their meadows are taken away from the Cossacks, they will be compelled to withdraw into the interior, leaving our frontier unprotected.[129]

While Cossacks feared losing territory on the Argun to China, Russian officials were mainly concerned with the land border farther south. Many criticized the vague course of the boundary and agitated to redraw the line in Russia's favor under that pretext. The head of the Russian customs house in Manzhouli complained, "Great difficulties arise while catching smugglers due to the vagueness of the boundary line and the absence of boundary markers at regular intervals. The course of the border is interpreted differently by locals by features that are only known to them, such as a virtual line from one hill to another, or from spire to spire, meaning by the latter, piles of stones, which, if necessary, can be moved thereby changing the course of the border."[130] All these complaints must be seen in the light of demarcation talks between the two governments. In March 1909 the Chinese Foreign Ministry proposed to take part in a joint examination, to which the Russians agreed. The Chinese were confident that they had ascertained the correct course of the land boundary near Manzhouli and seemed optimistic that they would be able to prove it.[131] The particular subject of these negotiations was the verification of the Transbaikalia-Hulunbeir land border between the hills of Tarbagan Dakha (border point no. 58) and Abagaitui (border point no. 63), and its contours as it moved farther along the Argun to its confluence with the Amur.[132]

Conflicts between Russians and Chinese soon overshadowed this process of boundary clarification. Owing to the increase of military outposts on the Argun, the Chinese had become more assertive. On many occasions the Russians apprehended Chinese soldiers and topographers in connection with the irregular crossing of the border. In turn, Chinese border guards repeatedly seized Cossacks horses grazing on disputed river islands and obstructed the work of Russian topographers. Scams and theft happened on both sides, and such incidents sometimes culminated in the exchange of fire across the river. Though Russian government circles knew that the Chinese forces in the region were weak, the Russian press demanded that border Cossacks be equipped with better arms and thus be enabled to respond to Chinese attacks. In fact, the above-quoted newspaper articles had been part of an anti-China campaign that had been waged in the Russian press and triggered a war scare.[133]

Despite the tense atmosphere, twenty meetings were held in Manzhouli in the summer of 1910 in an effort to settle the land and river borders, but these ended in stalemate. Finally, both sides agreed to carry out an inspection on the ground. Under the exacting scrutiny of the local population, the joint commission would have to decide the affiliation of 280 islands and sand bars. In October 1910 the Russian representative, Lieutenant Colonel Nikolai A. Zhdanov, chairman of the Border Commission of the General Staff, and General Du, senior member of the Chinese Border Commission, spent four days in Starotsurukhaitui on the middle reaches of the Argun before traveling about twenty-five kilometers by road farther downstream to Novotsurukhaitui. Their task was to locate the old silted-up riverbed to specify the precise boundary line. In this section the Russians demanded the return of several river islands with a total area of about five thousand hectares. The delegates personally inspected the disputed islands in wooden rowboats, but floods complicated the commission's effort, inundating a considerable number of islands and rendering many of them impossible to identify.

While General Du denied outright the existence of some of the disputed islands, Lieutenant Colonel Zhdanov claimed that almost all of them belonged to Russia. Local Cossacks eagerly awaited the resolution since only the possession of the lush meadows on the river guaranteed their ongoing wealth. After one day of negotiations the Russian side prevailed, and in deep gratitude and to shouts of "Hooray" from the crowd, the local Cossack head Ivan V. Kaidalov was reported to have said to Zhdanov, "Dear Mr. Lieutenant Colonel! We have followed your work in the past year as we have followed it now. Neither rain, nor bad weather, nor cold could stop you. Your work is important for our country, as it is for us Cossacks."[134]

In July 1911 negotiations began in the capital of Heilongjiang province Qiqihar with the aim of drafting a final agreement. Despite the strong interest taken in the Argun islets, the land border between the mountain Tarbagan Dakha and Abagaitui became the most contentiously disputed issue during the negotiations. Its course would decide the future national status of Manzhouli. That summer the news of the joint border commission had fueled rumors long circulating among the people of Manzhouli. Some merchants feared that if Manzhouli were to become an ordinary town on Russian territory, they would be left unable to sell duty-free goods. Others argued that with the new legal status the settlement would profit from a flourishing livestock industry.[135]

There was no consensus either among high government officials. Arguing from a military point of view, Minister of War Vladimir A. Sukhomlinov was a strong advocate of annexation of Chinese territory including the railroad terminus. He emphasized the strategic importance of Manzhouli, which "in times of war will certainly serve as a site of all kinds . . . of rear facilities." Minister of Finance Vladimir N. Kokovtsov agreed with Sukhomlinov. He insisted that Manzhouli had to be ceded to Russia and was not willing to make any compromises or deals with the Chinese. In case no solid reason could uphold this absolutist position, Kokovtsov favored the status quo: Sino-Russian agreements already guaranteed Russian domination over the railroad company for eighty years (although the Chinese retained an option to buy back the Chinese Eastern Railroad after thirty-six years). Manzhouli, as part of the railroad zone, was thus at full disposal of the Russian authorities no matter the outcome of the negotiations. But in Kokovtsov's view, an international border running through Manzhouli, dividing the railroad settlement into two parts had to be avoided at all costs. Such a division would mean a significant inconvenience, as it would affect technical and administrative matters of the Chinese Eastern Railroad and obstruct the further development of the settlement. Proper supervision of the customs border would become extremely troublesome too.[136]

While by October 1911 the border commission in Qiqihar had finished work on the Argun, the Chinese stubbornly defended their position regarding the land border at Manzhouli. They were reluctant to accept the Russian position regarding the railroad town, which they considered to be on Chinese territory.[137] That month, as the fast-spreading Wuchang Uprising left China in turmoil, the Chinese ambassador in Saint Petersburg Lu Zhengxiang informed the Russians that if they would drop their unsubstantiated claims to Man-zhouli, an agreement could be concluded immediately. Otherwise, Chinese negotiators would be compelled to postpone the negotiations dealing with the disputed border section until order was restored.[138]

The Russians accepted this compromise and dropped their claim to Man-zhouli. Accordingly, the town remained on Chinese soil within the railroad zone. Yet as a further result of the negotiations, China lost about fourteen hundred square kilometers of territory in the vicinity of Manzhouli. The actual demarcation points of the land border were shifted several kilometers south of the previous boundary line, closer to the railroad town. Of the 280 Argun islands, 160 were allotted to Russia and 120 to China.

On 8 December 1911, after nearly six months of tough negotiations in Qiqi-har, the atmosphere surrounding the signing ceremony was cordial. Though their positions had been as different as chalk and cheese, Cossack Ataman and Frontier Guard Brigade General Pavel N. Putilov, leading the Russian delega-tion, both praised the course of the diplomatic talks and the bright future ahead "with an even closer friendship for the benefit and prosperity of the two great nations." In his reply, Zhou Shumo, the governor of Heilongjiang prov-ince who headed the Chinese delegation, articulated one key desire of the Chinese: "From now on, that the boundary question is resolved the border will always and forever be respected. There will be no longer misunderstand-ings among the populations and both states in either direction, and thereby, of course, an even greater unity and truth will be achieved and will result in the same mutual proximity of neighboring nations, as between the flags of both countries in the meeting hall."[139] Such lofty rhetoric could not camou-flage the deep distrust that had evolved during the lengthy demarcation pro-cess. Locals now knew what was "ours" and "theirs." The press in both coun-tries echoed fears about expansionism of the neighboring country. The settlements emerging from the negotiations hardly amounted to a linear boundary, and what border there now was might have separated the national territorial states but not the local populace. In practice, might had made right. The Cossacks honored the new border, yet, as we saw earlier in this chapter, many would not refrain from entering Chinese territory.

The Treaty of Qiqihar came into effect just weeks before the fall of the Manchu dynasty. It soon became clear that the treaty's timing was unfortunate. Due to what was perceived to be disarray and weakness on the Chinese side, the actual demarcation of the new boundary line near Manzhouli and the land allocation to the Transbaikal Cossacks was postponed for several years, stir-ring a struggle for ownership over this now "vacant" land.

Russians in Manzhouli ignored the regulations of temporary land manage-ment enforced by the local Cossack authorities of Abagaitui, albeit from a distance of about thirty kilometers. Instead, the staff of Manzhouli's Russian police department banished the Abagaitui Cossacks from their new territories and contacted the Mongolian authorities who had come to power after the independence of Hulunbeir in early 1912, asking to rent the territories from them although they in fact now belonged to Russia. The intention of Manzhouli's police staff was to sublease them at higher rates to local Russian or Chinese residents for personal gain. In view of profits and rather by chance, the Mongols had adopted sedentary concepts of land ownership. Lieutenant General Andrei I. Kiashko, ataman of the Transbaikal Cossack Host and Transbaikal military governor, was amazed by this exercise: "This appeal came certainly entirely unexpected for the Mongols, but they were eagerly to comply: They raised their heads and began, though at a cheap price, to lease any places, which were only been requested by different Russians of Manzhouli. In their kindness the Mongols went so far as that they began to even rent out places that had never been in a dispute with China and always were in possession of the Transbaikal Cossack troops on the border."[140] Not only chieftains called for a quick settlement of Cossacks on this territory to take effective control of the border and to protect the new areas. The deputy chairman of Manzhouli's municipal council Iakov F. Shardakov, for one, professed to be tired of the constant quarreling: "For about three years Lieutenant Colonel Zhdanov worked with one hundred Cossacks on the inspection of the boundary, moving from hill to hill, spending more than 40,000 rubles without any practical result. Meanwhile, the money could have been used to dig a ditch, and then anyone could confidently say on whose land he stands."[141] Only in the summer of 1913 did the Russian vice-consul in Hailar receive orders to enter into an agreement with the Hulunbeir authorities on the installation of boundary markers, which in the event of the restoration of Chinese power would have to be reconsidered with the Chinese authorities. In early 1914, the Russian Ministry of the Interior allocated five thousand rubles for the erection of twenty-five boundary stones. On 24 October 1914 Cossack commanders from Chita and representatives of the local Cossacks jointly inspected the new boundary markers and finally settled the conflict over the disputed estates.[142]

The Qiqihar agreement set the course of the border for almost a century. New conflicts, sometimes violent, would occur in the following decades, but the Soviet Union and Manchukuo recognized the status quo in the late 1930s, as will be shown later. Though the Chinese raised these same territorial issues again during the Sino-Soviet split in the 1960s, they would be renegotiated only after the collapse of the Soviet Union.[143] Boundary agreements between states, as exemplified by the Treaty of Qiqihar, are not necessarily made for eternity. In addition, the dispute over the precise course of the international boundary between the Russians and the Chinese deepened an emerging

consciousness of the border not just among state agents but among frontiersmen too. Struggles over land encouraged processes by which people came to
be perceived and categorized along ethnic lines, promoting the formation of
national identities.

Epidemics and State Borders: The Fiction of Russian Border Quarantine

Histories of disease are illuminating because they can speak to the enmeshed
biological realities and social constructions of the past. It is a matter of fact that
microbes know no frontiers, but agencies of states sometimes expect them to.
One rather neglected aspect of the Manchurian plague in 1910–1911 was the
evolving policy of Russian border quarantine. As we will see in the following
pages, it was this epidemic that compelled Russia and China to cooperate and
to jointly enact quarantine policies on the shared border. At the same time, the
disease enabled some proponents of a stronger ethnic division to stigmatize
certain ethnic groups as inevitably "infected," thus creating notions of "us" and
"them."[144]

The Russian authorities were not caught off guard by the plague of 1910–
1911. In the 1890s the bubonic plague had swept the globe. Between 1892 and
1901 it killed more than fifteen million people worldwide.[145] As the plague
spread across China, northward toward the Russian border, authorities in
Saint Petersburg reacted quickly. As of 28 July 1894, exceptionally strict quarantine rules, comprising what were hoped to be preventive measures, were
imposed on the land border with China and within Russia's Pacific ports.
During an outbreak of the plague in Manchuria, the entire land border with
China was shuttered to any persons or goods coming from China, an edict
repealed only forty-five days after the last case of the disease was announced.
There can be little doubt that such strict quarantine rules were made on paper
only. At the turn of the twentieth century, lacking proper surveillance mechanisms along Russia's Asiatic state borders, the territory was still virtually
uncontrolled.

Yet times were changing in East Asia, less than a decade after the disease-
preventing restrictions of 1894 had been imposed. It was no longer possible,
even in theory, to keep the border sealed for weeks. The colonial expansion of
the Russian Empire to Manchuria and the construction of Russia's transcon-
tinental railroad had increased both the speed and volume of transport as well
as patterns of trade. In 1901 the Russian Ministry of Finance recognized that
the acting quarantine rules and their application on the eastern borders were
harmful to the success of the railroad's future operations as well as to shipping

traffic and commerce. There was no doubt that the old regulations needed to be replaced by new ones corresponding to local conditions and keeping in mind the likely growth of traffic, which made a complete closure of the border absolutely unthinkable.[146]

To standardize quarantine regulations at Russia's eastern borders, a committee of the Finance Ministry drafted a plan in 1900 proposing to set up twenty-one observation points along the border with China, to be tasked with monitoring the possible emergence of diseases among the local population. But the Boxer Rebellion delayed the implementation of the plan. The project also faced opposition from within the Ministry of Finance, expressed by its head, Sergey Witte, who wanted to keep costs low. Furthermore, Count Witte complained that the observation posts would not be located where they were actually needed. Rather, they were "scheduled to be set up in places like in Tsurukhaitui and Abagaitui not having any significance with respect to the movement of people and goods across the Chinese border." Instead, the minister suggested establishing medical observation points only in those four places most likely to experience the highest volume of transitory people and goods: Manzhouli, Suifenhe, the southern terminus of the Chinese Eastern Railroad, and the mouth of the Songhua River. Moreover, Witte stipulated, the observation posts should also be opened only temporarily, whenever an epidemic was reported. In the end, just the four medical observation units were set up by 1903. After reports of plague cases they were put into temporary operation the same year.[147] Thus at the beginning of the twentieth century a *cordon sanitaire* had been established: not along the state border, however, but along lines of communication and transit.

The Plague of 1910: Marmots, Profits, Diseases

The plague in its bubonic and pneumonic forms was not new to the Argun frontier. Every now and then sporadic outbreaks of the disease had been reported in Transbaikalia and Hulunbeir. The first reported case of bubonic plague in the twentieth century occurred in 1905 in the Russian settlement near the Zhalainuoer coal mines. Without considerable spread, the death toll was thirteen people in Zhalainuoer and two in nearby Manzhouli. In 1906 a Cossack died of the plague at Abagaitui, soon to be followed by five more villagers and then two residents of Manzhouli. Days before the man passed away he had skinned marmots while hunting on the steppe plains.[148]

In general the trapping of tarbagan marmots (*Marmota sibirica*), a genus of squirrels, was considered to be the primary source of infection in plague epidemics in Transbaikalia, Mongolia, and Hulunbeir.[149] As long as the hunting of marmots remained a local business, the authorities were untroubled by the fact that the disease had appeared consistently among hunters. But this was to change when marmot fur became a globally traded commodity, spurred by growing export markets in Europe within reach via the Trans-Siberian Railroad and a surge of migrant hunters on the frontier.[150] Increasing sales abroad had in return caused the price of marmot furs to shoot up over the years, from ten kopecks per pelt in 1901 to 1.15 rubles in 1910. Furthermore, the Chinese authorities constantly increased their allotment of licensed marmot hunters from just one thousand in 1909 to fifteen thousand the following year.[151] Thus, within a few years the hunting of the tarbagan marmot on the Russo-Chinese frontier created several thousand jobs for Chinese trappers during a season from August to October—contrary to the unsuccessful call for the migration of Chinese farmers—and led to growing entanglement of local and global economies as well as increased contacts between indigenous trappers, migrant hunters, and traders on the frontier. Gathering around Manzhouli's fur markets, the Chinese hunters lived, ate, and slept huddled together in poor shacks or cheap inns, thereby generating the perfect breeding ground for an epidemic. During the marmot hunting season in summer and fall about ten thousand Chinese seasonal migrants came to the border town, doubling the overall population.[152]

The epidemic that took the greatest toll was the pneumonic plague of 1910–1911. In China's Northeast the disease originated in Manzhouli. From there the plague spread at full speed across the railroad network. Although the beginning of the epidemic in Manzhouli was officially dated 25 October 1910, several facts suggest that the plague had already made its appearance by the middle of September. Local Chinese residents reported that the epidemic originated from the village of Dauriia, a railroad station on the Russian side. According to their accounts two Chinese carpenters working on a Russian military construction site had contracted the infection during their work in Dauriia and carried it to Manzhouli, where on 23 October 1910 they died spitting blood.[153]

The Russian public was less concerned with the fact that the epidemic originated in Russia than it was furious that the plague carriers had been among the "masses of Chinese coolies" working in Transbaikalia.[154] Indeed, the years prior to the epidemic saw a rapid influx of migrant workers from Shandong province and the southern regions of Manchuria to some parts of the Russian East. Yet despite embellished, xenophobic reports in the press, the number of seasonal workers in Transbaikalia stayed relatively low.[155]

Who was healthy or not was nevertheless the question of the day. The disease soon created new metaphorical borders between colonizers and colonized. In scientific circles and in Russian public discourse, the Chinese migrant workers were depicted as the major transmitter of the disease. This representation fueled first a range of discriminatory exclusions, then the wholesale expulsion of Chinese subjects from the Russian-administered rail-road zone. Social interpretations of the disease reaffirmed metaphorical bor-ders between classes as well as ethnic groups and lent a cast of inevitability to the construction of physical boundaries.[156]

But the congregation of thousands of Chinese hunters in the border settle-ments, often in poor conditions, was only one reason for the epidemic. Low hygiene standards were at least as pivotal. Just one week after the epidemic had officially erupted in Manzhouli, the municipal council was pilloried by *Novaia Zhizn'* (New Life), a popular Harbin newspaper: "Sanitation is entirely absent in Manzhouli. . . . Yards remain dirty, and even the public market has become a cesspool. The municipal representatives are mainly preoccupied with them-selves. Through the interference of the municipal council in medical matters, four doctors have been dismissed within two and a half years. Currently, the public outpatients' clinic and the hospital are under the supervision of one paramedic and one midwife. This, and only this, is the entire medical staff for a population of seven to eight-thousand people."[157] Despite its criticism of Rus-sian authorities, the paper made the Chinese responsible for the epidemic because the plague mostly appeared among the Chinese. From the Russian point of view, its rapid spread in the railroad zone was connected with an unsat-isfactory standard of hygiene permeating the area inhabited by the Chinese.[158]

Once the outbreak was known the Russian authorities responded rather quickly, in part because countermeasures had already been rehearsed in the past.[159] On 27 October 1910, two days after the official date of outbreak, the first patients were taken to the railroad hospital. The Russian garrison com-mander in Manzhouli positioned guards along the state border to prevent the passage of suspected Chinese plague carriers from Russia to the border town on Chinese soil. The Transbaikal military governor requested the inspection of all railroad passengers at Manzhouli. On 2 November 1910, the Anti-Plague Committee declared Manzhouli to be troubled by the plague. To prevent the epidemic from disseminating along the railroad, medical inspections of pas-sengers were made mandatory as a condition of permission to board. Finally, on 20 November the committee declared the entire regions of Transbaikalia and Manchuria to be afflicted by the disease.

Despite the swift response, the situation deteriorated dramatically in Man-zhouli. Within just one day the capacities of the railroad hospital became insuf-ficient. A dead-end siding of the train yard was turned into an ad hoc plague station. The number of detained Chinese was soon tallied in the hundreds. They were quartered in fifty-two primitive goods cars housing up to twenty-five inmates each. Racial segregation was strictly enforced. Europeans with suspected exposure to the plague were placed into thirteen rented houses. The further the epidemic spread, the more repressive became Russian sanitary measures against Chinese residents. Inspections were made continuously in the Chinese part of the town, and the sick and the dead were removed. The establishment of military cordons around the Chinese quarter to prevent infected people from escaping curtailed the liberty of movement of the people and thus created a de facto Chinese ghetto. On 11 November it was forbidden for Chinese residents of Manzhouli to board trains unless they had undergone a five-day observation beforehand. Many Chinese bypassed the ban by walking on foot across the border to Matsieevskaia, from there taking the train toward Harbin.

Although repressive measures were taken against Chinese migrants, Chinese authorities cooperated with the Russians. The Hulunbeir circuit intendant prepared lists of all residents of Manzhouli's Chinese quarter and appointed elders who were to report suspicious cases. On 25 November 1910 about thirty-six hundred Chinese people were interned in the plague detention camp, but "before the evacuation began, half of the population or maybe more had escaped from the Chinese village."[160] Once the Chinese village of Manzhouli had been rounded up and all remaining residents deported to the observation point, Russian authorities begun to remove all Chinese detainees who were not connected by a permanent job with the border settlement. Within two weeks five special trains had shipped 1,354 Chinese farther inland, away from the border with Russia.[161]

After Doomsday: Toward a New Border Quarantine

The epidemic quickly retreated: as of 14 December 1910 no new cases were reported. The western terminus of the Chinese Eastern Railroad was officially declared free of the plague on 7 January 1911. In Manzhouli the disease had claimed about four hundred lives, including those of fifteen Russians, some of them nurses and paramedics who had died due to insufficient preventive measures.[162]

Most likely the quarantine would not have stopped the disease as it spread from Russia to China, and definitely not in the opposite direction as it had been seen by some cautious planners within the Russian Ministry of Finance in 1901. It is all the more ironic that after the plague of 1910–1911 authorities proposed a plan of action quite similar to the one rejected a decade earlier: "If we cannot conduct plague-preventing activities in the territories of Manchuria and Mongolia, we have to protect the railroad and the Transbaikal region from bringing the plague. . . . Along the Mongolian border there could be arranged 3 to 4 medical and observation posts. Similar points with mandatory outpatient reception may be built along the Chinese Eastern Railroad, to keep an eye on the diseases of the surrounding population."[163] Instead of establishing a sanitary cordon exclusively along lines of communication, the government now aimed to immunize its own borders against germs and bacteria in a manner quite similar to the original proposal of 1901. Still, the approach of installing quarantine surveillance along the actual state boundary was rather pragmatic and implied an acceptance of open borders.

Yet quarantine inspection along the rail lines continued in a different direction after the plague. In March 1911 a Special Plague Prevention Commission within the administration of the Chinese Eastern Railroad specified strategies for combating future outbreaks. It urged the purchase of disinfection apparatuses to destroy bacteria on Russia-bound goods as well as the mandatory disinfection of clothing and luggage belonging to Chinese travelers quarantined at the four key railroad stations, in Harbin, Manzhouli, Suifenhe, and Kuanchengzi. Furthermore, it was recommended that two permanent plague observation points be maintained further inland—in the west at Hailar and in the east at Mulin—with a capacity of fifteen hundred people each. The central functions of this monitoring system were to put all Chinese migrant workers under observation at a safe distance from the state border and to control and channel their movement.[164]

While the Chinese authorities had simply ignored the disease in Manzhouli in late 1910, they soon made progress in burnishing hygiene standards to modern specifications. They began to combat epidemics with the development of medical and sanitary infrastructures. In 1911 the Chinese government set up the North Manchurian Plague Prevention Service, which, in addition to adopting Western methods of public disease control, appointed foreign-trained physicians. A Chinese hospital with a laboratory and room for forty plague patients, twenty suspected plague harborers, and eighty persons in quarantine opened in Manzhouli the same year.[165]

The Manchurian pneumonic plague of 1910–1911 was the last devastating plague epidemic in East Asia, although it would not be the last epidemic in the region. In the following years isolated bubonic and pneumonic cases were reported to have killed some people on the Sino-Russian frontier, striking in Abagaitui, Dauriia, and other settlements. After the disastrous experience of 1910, Russian and Chinese authorities now cooperated in addressing these outbreaks. When in September 1911 plague struck about sixty kilometers west of Manzhouli in Transbaikalia, Russian officials inspected all passengers on the Harbin-bound trains.[166] In Manzhouli Russian mounted outposts patrolled all roads that led to villages, and two observation stations were established for persons traveling on foot or in carts. Beyond the railroad zone Chinese guards monitored the roads. The Chinese transferred all travelers to the Russian horse patrols, who, in turn, conducted them to the examination stations.[167]

Despite such achievements the plague epidemic had altered life on the frontier, even down to relationships between people. Policies of segregation along racial lines during the epidemic had produced estrangement among locals. The Russian press, calling for stricter controls, had done its part to further this process of alienation by depicting migrant workers from China as carriers of the disease. Interestingly, the Russian attitude toward the Mongols, Buriats, and other well-established men and women was not negatively affected by the epidemic. In that sense, to many local Russians being Russian often meant no more than condemning the Chinese. Thus, in terms of health and hygiene as much as culture and ethic or national allegiance, the border began to emerge as a bulwark against potential transmitters.

———

Despite the obvious porosity and vagueness of the Russia-China boundary, borders were established in minds and on the ground. At the beginning of the twentieth century the Manchu court had opted to implement New Policies in the imperial periphery for the sake of national defense, in other words adopting Western notions of territory with fixed boundaries, new mechanisms of control, and the encouragement of Han Chinese colonization. The Mongolian bannerlands, the last frontier area still under the old system and an intermediate zone between the Chinese and the Russian empires for centuries, were to be transformed into typical Chinese provinces.

The struggle against the plague and the quarrel over contested river islets intensified an emerging consciousness of the national border. Both events epitomized the process of nation formation as more complicated and far-reaching than the imposition of institutions or politics. They can be understood as formulations of local interests in national terms. Both incidents changed perceptions of the "other" and by so doing called customary relations among indigenous, Chinese, and Russian frontiersmen into question.

Though both states agreed on the need to delimit their respective dominions, the territorial benefits and losses on the Argun were nominal. More importantly the Cossacks' cause for grazing their cattle on the lush meadows of small Argun islands turned into a symbol of national security, thereby generating a consciousness of border issues within the remote Asiatic periphery. The plague produced additional ways to promote separation along ethnic and national lines. On the Sino-Russian frontier discourses evolving from the epidemic reaffirmed the metaphorical separation between "Europeans" and "Asians" and helped create physical boundaries. Thus, the adoption of national identities was grounded, to some extent, in a local sense of place.

These new national affinities did not necessarily replace local ones completely, however, not least because local economies often ran counter to national interests. For generations locals had been accustomed to purchasing everyday necessities across the river without constraint and therefore viewed their trade activities as perfectly legal. To counter such a conviction the metropoles established customs agencies, military disbursements, legal codes, economic policies, and other "tools of empire" to increase their control over the far-flung frontier. It was in fact in Manzhouli where, owing to closer connections to the heartlands of both empires by virtue of modern infrastructure, the frontier traits of the Argun basin began to fade. This new kind of border did not, however, universally translate into solidifying local acceptance of the international boundary. In fact the state's administrative presence in the lands along the Argun remained sparse, and the new restrictions served to intensify a thriving cross-border trade in which nearly the entire local population participated.

3

Revolutions without Borders

WHEN, IN LATE OCTOBER 1921, Zhang Guotao, both protagonist and narrator of the following story, boarded a Soviet train at Matsievskaia, other delegates from China and Japan were already waiting in the fairly horrid third-class car. They were bound for the Congress of the Toilers of the Far East in Irkutsk. Zhang, who recalls this episode in his memoir, was a founding member, an important leader of the Chinese Communist Party, and a key contact with the Comintern:

I registered at a Russian hotel, and then, following the directions Nicolaevsky had given me, I went to a certain barbershop for a haircut. I wrapped up in newspaper a shirt that needed laundering, and in its pocket I put the mysterious card. After having a haircut, I deliberately left the parcel behind. When I returned later to claim it, the proprietor ushered me into a back room, where he returned the shirt but kept the card. I told him the name of my hotel and my room number. He asked me to wait for him at the hotel after eight o'clock that evening.

It was nearly nine o'clock when the man arrived. Without a word he put the luggage into a sleigh waiting in front of the hotel. The sleigh was drawn by two horses. The three of us—the barbershop proprietor, the driver, and myself—climbed aboard; the proprietor wrapped a very thick blanket round the lower half of my body; and the sleigh shot ahead toward the border.

We passed through desolate country. There was no buildings at all. Nor did I see any sentries or the barricades that usually mark borders. White Russian guerillas and smugglers, it was said, were very active in the area; and so my two Russian companions held pistols under their coverlets, ready for any possible attack. The sleigh, shaking violently, careened forward over the meandering, rutted, snow-covered road.

About midnight we reached a railroad station eighteen miles from Manzhouli. It was on Soviet territory. In the cold night, with the temperature thirty degrees below zero, a thick mist gushed from the two Russians' mouths. "Feel cold?" one of them asked me. "We've arrived." I thanked them. Then, taking my luggage, they escorted me to the coach of a train standing beside the station.

The passport for Zhang's secret journey to Soviet Russia was the ordinary business card of some commercial house, a document given to him by Niko-laevskii, a Russian national living in Shanghai and assistant to the Dutch Co-mintern emissary Hendricus Sneevliet (alias Maring).[1]

Having dealt with the smugglers, medical scapegoats, and pastoral life of the sedentary Cossacks, we now turn to the notions of nationalism and na-tional belonging held by the nomadic frontiersmen and the multiethnic urban population of Manzhouli in times of revolution. Political upheaval and vio-lence accompanied the transition from imperial rule in China, after the Xinhai Revolution of 1911, and in Russia, after the October Revolution of 1917. Tradi-tional frontier policies were jeopardized, while new political developments such as the establishment of buffer zones, official and shady local govern-ments, warlord rule, and foreign intervention further destabilized frontier societies on the Argun. In Manzhouli during times of revolution nothing was ordinary: the border town was a hub for secret political agents and contraband trade, a meeting place for nomads, house dwellers, Cossacks, trappers, whores. Its location enabled extraordinary flows of people and ideas as well as a thriv-ing commodity trade.

China's 1911 revolution opened an interregnum decade. When the Qing dynasty was overthrown, autochthonous people, ever dissatisfied with Chi-nese and Russian incursions into their native lands, claimed independence from Beijing. Their aspirations to sovereignty did not last long, however. Fol-lowing the death of Yuan Shikai, China's first autocratic president, in 1916, the fragile republic descended into political chaos dominated by feuding warlords. In the process the illiterate soldier-bandit Zhang Zuolin established himself as the unchallenged ruler of Manchuria. In 1918 the nominal Chinese govern-ment in Beijing accepted Zhang's fait accompli by officially appointing him governor-general of the Three Eastern Provinces, or Manchuria. The author-ity of Zhang's warlord regime was certainly stronger than the indigenous uprising but, given its gamble on Japanese support, weaker than a proper nation-state.[2]

The Russian Revolution and the Civil War of course triggered changes in the structure of authority on the Russian side as well. At first, however, these produced a vacuum of power. As a result anarchy prevailed on the China-Russia frontier. The Transbaikal Cossack Grigorii M. Semenov, as a former captain (*esaul*) faithful to the old regime, exploited the disorder to establish a warlord-like reign in the railroad settlements east of Chita and west of the Great Xingan Mountains, using armored trains and horses. Further, and with the support of Japanese forces, Semenov and his subordinate Baron Roman von Ungern-Sternberg created political uncertainty in the minds of locals, a state of affairs that lasted until 1920. Their regime of terror collapsed after Japanese expeditionary forces retreated and the Bolsheviks established the nominally independent buffer state of the Far Eastern Republic (1920–1922) in the Russian territories east of Lake Baikal.[3]

Nascent Buriat Nationalism: Conflicting Sentiments toward Russia's Imperial Destiny

Nomadic people living on the imperial frontiers used to have a life both inside and beyond formal state boundaries, via cross-border migration or cross-border husbandry or simply operating under a notion of borders different from that of an emerging territorial state. In fact, up to the early twentieth century people in Hulunbeir and other nomadic areas were forbidden to cross between banners without permission, and often the internal (i.e., inter-banner) borders were more strictly enforced than the international one. Despite kinship links between different banners, "nomadic freedom" did not exist.

Life on the Sino-Russian frontier underwent profound changes in the tumultuous years during the collapse of the Qing and Romanov empires. Two key factors were responsible. The first was the migration of dominant ethnic groups to the imperial peripheries. Han Chinese and ethnic Russian immigration into Transbaikalia and Hulunbeir increased with the construction of the railroad but was also affected over time by the New Policies adopted in late Qing China, reforms in late imperial Russia, and collectivization in the Soviet Union. The second element was a concentration of power in the national centers. Russia and China strengthened their direct control over the frontier by adopting them as regular administrative units. Relations between metropole and periphery took on an increasingly hierarchical nature, based more and more on a subordinate relationship to the centers. The interimperial frontier turned, bit by bit, from a nomad's land into one of farmers and bureaucrats.

On the Russian side of the Sino-Russian frontier Buriat nationalism was born out of a strong reaction against increasing central control over previously independent ways of life. Representatives of the small russified Buriat elite not only condemned the Russian government for instigating land seizure but demanded the preservation of their clan and tribal organizations, self-government, judicial system, education, and religion.[4] The Khori Buriats also remained faithful to their Tibetan Buddhist beliefs.[5] By the turn of the century Aleksei M. Pozdneev, one of Russia's foremost authorities on Mongolian Studies, noted the "extraordinary success of Lamaism" in Transbaikalia. Instead of the allotted 285 lamas, 9,185 lamas served the Buriats in the province, and several new Buddhist monasteries were being built. Religious activities came under close surveillance by the state authorities, who feared, because of transnational spiritual ties, a religiously motivated Buriat separatism. The importation of theological writings and sculptures and the movement of lamas were controlled and often restricted.[6] The Buriats had not, however, been opposed in principle to all things Russian. Many had adopted a Russianized form of their names (such as Batuev from Batu). Under their own initiative they spread Russian education and contributed to the establishment of a high school for Buriat boys in Chita. Proper education, however, remained something for lamas, monks, and assimilated urban Buriat elites. In the entire Aga Steppe there was a single Russian elementary school. It is hardly surprising that by 1908 only about one in a hundred Buriats in the Aga Steppe could read and write in Russian, whereas over 5 percent were more or less literate in Mongolian or Tibetan.[7]

Arguably the most contentious issue was the repeal in 1904 of the Statute on Administration of Non-Slavic Populations in Siberia (1822), which had granted the indigenous peoples rights of autonomy and liberated them from the oppressive guardianship of the state.[8] In 1906, delegates of the eleven Khori Buriat clans traveled to Saint Petersburg to present a petition to the tsar. The petitioners demanded the abolition of the temporary regulations and the resignation of the recently appointed peasant heads. In their eyes, life before the reform had been quiet and economically secure. The first request concerned legal matters and administration. By 1901 the government had transferred the functions of the court and the prosecution to an interim regime. Since then local government or *zemstvo* courts claimed jurisdiction over even the smallest matters, and zemstvo police officers, according to the petitioners, abused their powers frequently.[9]

A second Buriat demand concerned their common land holdings. The land reform provoked clashes over the conflicting notions of place held by Russian imperial bureaucrats, on the one side, and Buriat nomads, on the other. In contrast to the Russian administrative unit volost', the Buriat tribal community (*buluk*), comprising up to several hundred yurts, did not necessarily constitute a fixed territorial unit, thereby illustrating the different notions of borders.[10]

By the time the Khori Buriats petitioned in the Russian capital some of their best pastures had already been conceded to peasants, and by 1908 about one-tenth of the Khori Buriat families in the Aga Steppe lived on estates belonging to peasants or Cossacks. Opposition to the reform, especially in the

Aga Steppe, was widespread, and territorial disputes between Cossacks, farmers, and Buriats lingered on. The Aga Steppe Buriats were dependent on fixed estates because they lived neither a purely nomadic life nor a purely settled one. They needed to stockpile hay during summer harvests to feed their stock in winter, when springs ran dry and rivers and lakes dried up. Yet the barren steppe was not suitable for haymaking. The allocation of land among the Russian farmers and Cossacks thus resulted in the decline of grazing areas, especially as the crucial hay growing areas tended to be better watered and therefore more suitable for cultivation.[11]

Adding to the change in land allocation and use, a 10 percent decline in livestock in the decade after 1897—due in part to animal diseases, changes in agriculture, and economic conditions—distressed the Buriats even further. These detrimental changes were mainly a result of the construction of the railroad, which was now transgressing many of their pastures. By 1908 the nomads in the Aga Steppe still had nearly 715,000 domestic animals, or about one-seventh of the total livestock in the province. But between 1897 and 1908 the total number of livestock per household had in fact plummeted from an average of about ninety-three animals to seventy-four.[12]

Despite the growing material difficulties of life, the nomads of Transbaikalia remained uncontained by international boundaries. Since the second half of the nineteenth century the Khori Buriats of the Aga Steppe had occasionally crossed borders into the Chinese Empire to graze their animals for several months a year. With the construction of the railroad, cross-border migrations intensified because of increased Russian settlement and expropriation of their lands. The Aga Steppe Buriats concluded informal agreements with the local Mongol officials over pasture rights. Official records show that by World War I migration had become a widespread phenomenon: about four thousand Buriats of the Aga Steppe periodically crossed into Mongolia, while roughly five hundred had settled there permanently. This new pattern had its implications, however. The Buriats' increased grazing of livestock, wood felling, and hay making in Mongolia sparked resentment among the local Mongols.

In the 1910s the Outer Mongolian independent government appealed to the Russian authorities to stop the uncontrolled movement of people and livestock across the border. Russian officials generally shared this view and sought good relations with the newly independent neighbor since the development of a local livestock industry on the still-open frontier was in Russia's interest. Searching for solutions, a Mongol-Russian commission convened in the village of Aksha near the Mongolian border in February 1917. The commission agreed to identify certain areas where the Aga Steppe Buriats would be free to migrate, pending joint approval by the Russian state, the Mongolian authorities of Hulunbeir, and the Tsetsenkhan district in Outer Mongolia.[13]

The retreat of the Khori Buriats thus long anteceded the arrival of the Bolsheviks on the steppes of Transbaikalia. Yet despite the roiling discontent generated by the economic, political, and cultural threats made to the Buriats during the late Romanov years, their nationalism was still nascent and much weaker than that of their peers in Khalkha and Hulunbeir: it did not demand separation from the deeply illiberal and imperial autocracy of the tsarist state. It was only after the Russian Revolution of 1917 and during the Russian Civil War that support for separation from Russia and the formation of a pan-Mongol state began to grow precipitously.

An Imperial Puppet on Standby: The Career of the Insurgent Tokhtogo

In Hulunbeir just as in Transbaikalia the absorption of nomads' territories into the former Qing and Romanov empires did not follow a linear path from a fuzzy multiethnic empire to a territorial state. Spurred by the Chinese Revolution in 1911, Russia supported the Mongolian independence movement to create a state between empires, which succeeded in the sense that China eventually lost influence over Outer Mongolia and temporarily over Hulunbeir. After the Revolution of 1911 borders between political entities were reconfigured and several states emerged, some of which collapsed over time. Mongolia exemplified this pattern with the transnational character of its history and its potential function as a buffer state. Overlapping the shared Sino-Russian frontier, Mongolia first emerged as the Bogd Khaanate (1911–1924) and then became the Mongolian People's Republic (1924–1992) under the strong influence of the Soviet Union.[14] The history of Hulunbeir, and therefore the history of the Argun basin, was closely related to that of Mongolia. Hulunbeir also became a semi-independent entity (1911–1915) and an autonomous region (1915–1920) before it was merged with Heilongjiang province and China again.[15]

Insurrections by nomads and informal Russian penetration into Mongol lands were not a new phenomenon but had occurred constantly since the mid-nineteenth century. However, with the implementation of the New Policies and the official opening of Inner Mongolian pasture lands for cultivation in 1902, the scale changed. Now massive revolts against aggressive Chinese colonization took place in most of the Inner Mongolian leagues.[16] The obstruction of land surveys, for instance, or the plunder of Chinese local governments, the murder of officials, and other forms of violent opposition fielded by the Mongolian rebels generally provoked military campaigns in response.[17]

With this new wave of active opposition to Beijing's reforms, the still easily penetrable Sino-Russian border began to play a crucial role. Those who challenged the reforms openly could seek assistance from across the border or take refuge in the neighboring country. Some Mongolian partisan biographies manage to convey a broad picture of the advantage of de facto uncontrolled state borders, the anger against Han colonization and the New Policies reforms, and Russia's collaboration in the struggle for self-determination. Self-testimonies of nomads, however, hardly ever appear in imperial archives, as few of the partisans were able to write and their scant written testimonies were hardly ever recorded in the archival files. Zorigt Baatar E. Tokhtogo,[18] interrogated in the summer of 1910 by the governor of Transbaikalia, was one of the resisters against Han rule. He spoke Chinese and Mongolian but was illiterate. Tokhtogo's Russian translator, however, wrote down his life story as a unique account.

Tokhtogo was born in 1862 as the hereditary son of the prince (*taiji*) of the south wing of Gorlos banner, far away from Hulunbeir and the border with Russia. That banner formed part of Jirim league (also referred to as Jirem, today's Tongliao Municipality) in Jilin province, one of the regions transgressed by the newly built Chinese Eastern Railroad. Han immigration in this banner had begun before the official opening and taxation of bannerland in 1902.[19] Tokhtogo was appalled by the Chinese colonization of the Jirim league, the ubiquity of unscrupulous behavior toward the Mongols on the part of the Chinese, the lack of protection against random robbery, and the absence of initiative among the Mongol nobility to resolve these problems.

Tokhtogo resorted to open resistance when Han Chinese troops advanced northward into Jirim in 1900. Under the camouflage provided by the Boxer Rebellion, the Han invaders grabbed land, seized Mongol livestock, and abducted women and girls. In response, Tokhtogo took up weapons. With support from a group of ten native elders whose families had all suffered from the invasion and massacre, he met the invaders in battle. None of the aggressors returned alive.

Tokhtogo's career as a rebel during the following decade reads almost like the fairy tale of an uncivilized hero from the steppe. Leading groups of ten to sixty armed men, never larger, he resisted imperial advance. He fought Chinese soldiers and farmers, captured Chinese colonization officials, and destroyed their bureaus. To survive, his militia robbed Chinese traders and distributed some of the loot to the poor. In 1907, with the prince's approval, Tokhtogo murdered a group of five Japanese topographers. They had been surveying territories in his native Southern Gorlos banner to ready them for colonization by the Chinese government. Afterward the Japanese government joined Chinese authorities in chasing the Mongol rebel. To avoid being

FIGURE 3.1. Zorigt Baatar E. Tokhtogo (1863–1922), a Mongol nobleman and zealous opponent of Chinese colonization.

captured, he went underground. Three of his sons and some of his partisan fellows joined him. The murder of the Japanese officials earned Tokhtogo fame and wide support among the autochthonous people. On occasion he would suddenly surface at different places in Khalkha, Hulunbeir, and the Nen River valley east of the Great Xingan range, as if the banner lands were still empty space. The Chinese genuinely feared the insurgent and his rebel force, who were said to have claimed more than twelve hundred killed or wounded between 1907 and 1910—most of them Chinese soldiers.[20]

Naturally, the Russian government followed the developments across the border, and the minister of war and other key political leaders sensed Tokhtogo's potential role in the interimperial struggle for control. In the spring of 1909 the head of the Transamur Border Guards, an important manifestation of Russia's military presence along the Manchurian railroad since 1897, surmised that Tokhtogo might be useful for Russian espionage, nomadic partisan organization, and subversive political action in Hulunbeir against the Chinese government: "Tokhtogo's popularity among the Mongols and Solons . . . determines the political significance of having him at our disposal. In case of any complications in the Far East Tokhtogo can be of special value to us and may be used as a means . . . to extend our influence in the region north and south of the railroad from Manzhouli up to Zhalantun station."[21] As early as 1908 Russian authorities in Harbin, the administrative center of Russian Manchuria, had proposed granting asylum in Transbaikalia to Tokhtogo and his supporters. After lengthy debates among the Ministries of War and Foreign Affairs, and almost two years of secret negotiations with Tokhtogo, the partisan agreed, accepting the precondition that Russia would grant him asylum only if he crossed the border without any open help. In the spring of 1910 Russian officials meticulously prepared the flight. His middleman received explicit instructions and documents from the Russian general consul in Harbin, as Russian officials knew that China would try to hamper the escape. They identified a suitable place in Khalkha where the Mongol group could pass the border without notice. To deceive Tokhtogo's Chinese persecutors, the Russian border commissioner of Kiakhta spread rumors among local Mongols that Tokhtogo was in hiding in a remote area of Mongolia, far from the Russian border.[22]

In spite of these efforts, the conspiracy failed. In April 1910 about eighty Chinese soldiers from an Urga battalion attacked Tokhtogo and his comrades in the Tsetsenkhan district of Khalkha the night before they crossed the border. Tokhtogo's men killed thirty-one Chinese during the fight and took six hostages, executing them after interrogation. According to his own perhaps too buoyant narration, Tokhtogo lost just two men in action, one of them his son. In the end Tokhtogo entered Russian territory with forty-seven male

Mongolian comrades, weapons, and more than two hundred horses. Yet the plan to hide the secret refuge of the Mongolian rebel had failed.[23]

A heated correspondence between Chinese and Russian diplomats and provincial authorities followed the coup. The Chinese imperial resident of Hulunbeir demanded that the Russians detain and deport the Mongolian insurrectionist. But the Russian military governor of Transbaikalia refused to hold diplomatic negotiations with the Chinese imperial resident of Hulunbeir. Instead, he reiterated the position of the Russian Ministry of Foreign Affairs, which classified the Mongol not as an ordinary criminal fugitive (who would have to be extradited) but rather as a political refugee.[24] In early June 1910 rumors circulated that in pursuing Tokhtogo about one thousand Chinese soldiers had passed Lake Hulun and approached Khalkha. In addition, about eight hundred banner troops from the Tsetsenkhan district were said to have been mobilized, supported by a hundred Chinese soldiers from Urga for protection in the event of Tokhtogo's return.[25] At the same time the Chinese were said to have sent spies to Transbaikalia to neutralize him on Russian territory. The Russian border commissioner of Kiakhta claimed to know the whereabouts of at least two Chinese spies who were in search of Tokhtogo. He described these "tourists" to the military governor of Transbaikalia as people "dressed in ragged Mongol garments; that is the usual Chinese way of espionage, disguise in poverty, feigning an idiot."[26]

But in Russia, Tokhtogo and his men were relatively safe at last. After the flight, the everyday lives of the rebels underwent significant change. One of Tokhtogo's companions told a journalist writing for the Chita newspaper *Zabaikal'skaia Nov'* (Transbaikal Virgin Soil) in 1910,

> For several years, we have attacked the Chinese in revenge for what they had done to us by plundering us and abducting our wives and children. We have never touched a single Mongol. The Chinese authorities have more than once attempted to detain us, and several times we were even surrounded by them, but we were able to escape and harm them. . . . We are accustomed to the harsh life. Our main chieftain Tokhtogo . . . speaks to us every day and suggests behaving modestly and living at peace with the population, not offending or insulting anyone. In other words, he makes us forget our previous military life. We endorse his teachings and wholly subscribe to them.[27]

Thus, even before Khalkha and Hulunbeir had declared independence the Russian press celebrated the noble savage.

Despite the value of Tokhtogo and his fellow refugees to the Russian government, the slow mills of Russian bureaucracy delayed in providing them aid. For more than a year the men camped in yurts on a temporarily assigned spot

FIGURE 3.2. Route of Tokhtogo's travels between 1900 and 1922.

in Western Transbaikalia, far away from Hulunbeir. Economic circumstances forced them to sell a quarter of their horses, undermining Tokhtogo's authority among his subordinates. Only in July 1911 were Tokhtogo and his followers naturalized as Russians and given an allowance of 13,500 rubles. They were further assigned about 1,635 hectares of land in the Aga Steppe, some 150 kilometers northwest of the Argun and about 900 kilometers away from his native Jirim league, where they were eventually assimilated into the indigenous Buriat Cossacks of this territory.[28] In the Aga Steppe the pacified rebel became, almost, an ordinary herder again, a fighter only in waiting.

The rebel for an independent Mongol state had been courted and supported by the Russian authorities early on. In retrospect his attempt to fight against Han Chinese colonization and the Qing New Policies provided significant impetus for the indigenous population of Hulunbeir and its neighboring territories to do the same. Therefore, Tokhtogo's story is emblematic of two themes: it showcases the resistance of the peripheral autochthonous population to Chinese imperial policies. At the same time it reveals how the Russian Empire attempted to spur on this insurgency to gain indirect control over Chinese frontier areas such as Hulunbeir. In sum, Saint Petersburg granted asylum to a negligible rebel, not out of altruism but from clear self-interest. As far as the indigenous insurgent was concerned, however, with respect to conflicting notions of territory and border his allegiance was still to the ethnic community rather than the Russian Empire. Tokhtogo thus embodies the type of "detachable men" that were caught between two competing empires both regarding him as their subject. Detachable people could fall victim to conflicting allegiances, which in Tokhtogo's case was his dependence on Russia as an external power as well as the link to his own group of followers.[29]

When the Subaltern Speaks Up: The 1911 Revolution and the Revolt in Hulunbeir

The introduction of Chinese administration and the attempt to populate the area with Chinese farmers induced protests on the part of Tokhtogo, the Barguts in Hulunbeir, and other Mongols on the Inner Asian margins and, further, their determination to separate from China. The effect of the New Policies on their lands and culture provoked the indigenous people of the interimperial frontier to assert independence even before the fall of the Qing dynasty. Russian policymakers were not caught unawares by these developments, as the asylum for Tokhtogo and his men has shown. By April 1911 rumors were circulating among regional Russian authorities concerning the Mongol elite and in particular Jebtsundamba Khutukhtu, the third-ranking lama in the Tibeto-Mongolian hierarchy also known as the "Living Buddha." The rumors suggested he was willing to seek refuge and adopt Russian citizenship in case of defeat and that the Chinese were building up their forces at Urga.[30] A diverse group of leaders from Inner and Outer Mongolia convened with the religious leader of the Mongols. They also sought help abroad. In July 1911 a delegation ventured to Saint Petersburg to appeal for Russian aid. Rather than petition for Russian intervention, the Mongols sought Russian aid in the form of diplomatic pressure, to stop Han migration to Mongolia and to force the Qing government to discontinue its reforms.[31]

Russia thus exploited growing discontent among the native people of Khalkha and Hulunbeir, pursuing a policy of quiet diplomacy to challenge these frontier areas as belonging to China's sphere of interest. Mongols were well aware that Russia's policy was by no means altruistic but driven by vested imperial interests. Yet they had no choice but to lean to one side. Russian expansion into Mongolia was also made possible by diplomatic agreements with Great Britain, which delineated spheres of interest for Great Britain, Japan, and Russia. Under those terms Outer Mongolia and Hulunbeir were designated parts of the Russian sphere.[32]

In the latter half of 1911, more than a year after Tokhtogo and his men had escaped to Russia, the state of affairs in China proper gave the Mongols a new opportunity to revolt. The Xinhai Revolution broke out under the banner of a rising Han nationalism. It meant, indeed, the end of Manchu rule, but viewed from China's ethnic periphery it was also a unique opportunity for secession from the Heavenly Kingdom altogether.[33] On the heels of the collapse of the Qing dynasty, Outer Mongolia declared independence on 1 December 1911. The leading nobles declared Jebtsundamba Khutukhtu to be Holy Khan (Bogd Khan) of Mongolia. Bearing in mind the example of Inner Mongolia, indigenous leaders in Outer Mongolia knew exactly what Chinese colonial policy entailed: they had seen the Chinese Republic fall prey to the New Policies and rally behind the Han colonization sponsored by the late Qing government. By separating from China proper, they hoped to avoid their kinsmen's fate in Inner Mongolia.[34]

Following the example of Outer Mongolia, the indigenous elites of Hulunbeir declared the region independent in January 1912 and called for unification with the newly created Khalkha empire.[35] Tokhtogo, however, who in the meantime had left his Russian refuge and hastened to Urga to take charge of the Holy Khan Jebtsundamba Khutukhtu's bodyguards, was not allowed to participate.[36] In addition, in some banners in Inner Mongolia where Chinese oppression had become intolerable, people rebelled and sought to join up with Outer Mongolia. Leaders in Khalkha supported their cause and launched a general military campaign. The Inner Mongolian bannerlands, however, were already too closely interwoven with the Chinese provinces to furnish the secular or ecclesiastical leaders who would be able to unify the indigenous people for a common political cause. In the end, Chinese Republican forces succeeded in suppressing the secessionist tendencies in those territories.[37]

Through an extensive network of informants, the Russian authorities stayed well informed about major developments in this rebellion. The first general assembly of influential Hulunbeir tribal leaders was held in September 1911—weeks before the Wuchang Uprising that marked the beginning of the Chinese Revolution erupted on 10 October. The banner leaders protested against their disempowerment and requested the Chinese authorities to remove Chinese officials, reintroduce autonomous regional administration, pull out all Chinese troops, and stop Han colonization. During a second congress in November 1911 it was decided, following orders from Urga, to proceed with the formation of troops for fomenting open rebellion. The first day of the revolt was scheduled for 15 December 1911.[38]

The Chinese authorities refused to accommodate the September demands of the Hulunbeir Mongols. The Mongols, in turn, distrusted Sun Yatsen and other Chinese revolutionaries and instead focused their hopes on Russia. Rumors circulated among the Mongols, indicting Chinese revolutionaries for slaughtering Mongols and suggesting that protection could be expected only from foreigners. Some Mongols in Hulunbeir even tried to adopt Russian citizenship. Corrupt Chinese authorities further fueled anxieties among the local Mongol population. In Hailar it was reported that the head of Chinese administration had jailed many Mongols who were innocent of any crime and that at night Chinese soldiers searched for Mongols to rob and beat. According to a secret Russian report, "arrests and prosecutions were carried out for the personal gain of the chief of prefecture, as he is willing to release arrested Hulunbeir Mongols for money." More diplomatically, the Chinese daotai of Hulunbeir tried to win the sympathies of the Mongol senior officials with a banquet. He anticipated that they could, in turn, influence the population.[39]

The hopes of the Chinese administrator were in vain, however. The rebels had removed the Chinese sentry posts on the border with Russia, one by one, without significant opposition from the Chinese guards. More and more armed banner men gathered in the vicinity of Hailar. By the Russian New Year their numbers had swelled to more than five hundred. On 15 January 1912 they encircled the Chinese administration and the barracks of the Chinese troops. The insurgents demanded the departure of all Chinese administrative officials and soldiers from the territory of Hulunbeir. On the night before the attack the Chinese daotai and his staff had taken refuge in the Russian-controlled railroad concession. Chinese soldiers made their way to the Russian concession within the city and agreed to a proposal by the Russian consulate to surrender their weapons. Thus, in the morning, without a single shot being fired, Hailar came under control of the Mongols. Public order remained perfectly intact: there were no reports filed about looting or violence against the remaining Chinese. Chinese traders opened their shops as they did every day. The nonviolent takeover did not last for long, however. One week after assuming control the new regime presided over a number of searches in residences throughout the city. The new masters discovered uniforms, weapons, ammunition, and 196 young Chinese men in civilian dress hiding in private houses. The men were arrested, handed over to the Russian authorities, and deported the same day on trains toward Harbin. Thus did the Russians support the Mongols in their quest to cleanse the region of Chinese forces.[40]

Negotiations were still ongoing between Chinese officials sent from Qiqihar and the rebels on the matter of Hulunbeir's future status when several hundred Mongolian soldiers began marching westward, approaching the Russian-controlled railroad town of Manzhouli on the international border. Since it was almost entirely inhabited by Russians and Chinese and was located inside the Russian-controlled alienated strip, the Mongols cared little about who ruled over it. Their prime concern was with the Chinese military detachment stationed at the nearby garrison of Lubin, about two kilometers south of Manzhouli. Officially only about 150 Chinese soldiers were deployed at Lubin, but in the wake of the rebellion the garrison had been fortified. Its head commander Zhang averred that he expected to engage in battle with the Mongols. Though confident he would win, he was also a realist, willing to withdraw his soldiers in case of defeat. He expected the rebellion to be brief and the regular Chinese military to reach the region soon.[41]

But these security measures proved ineffective and Zhang's assurance misguided. On 2 February 1912 Mongols captured and looted the Chinese garrison. They dismantled the buildings, sold the plunder, and set parts of the dusty military settlement on fire. According to Russian intelligence, Erwin Baron von Seckendorff, a German reserve officer in charge of the Chinese Customs House at Manzhouli, agitated among the Chinese in a successful bid to persuade them to resist the Mongols rather than surrender Lubin.[42] American sources confirm that the German baron had directed the fire of Chinese troops against the Mongol attack. After their defeat the Chinese soldiers and authority officials were made to march to the railroad station and then transported to Qiqihar. The customs commissioner Baron von Seckendorff, in turn, remained in charge of the Customs House at Manzhouli.[43]

Weeks before the Chinese defeat at Lubin, the Russian government was well aware of the looming insurrection. It reacted swiftly. In late 1911 Saint Petersburg increased its troop presence east of Lake Baikal. Two divisions were deployed at various railroad stations in Transbaikalia to protect Russian interests in North Manchuria and to regain full control over the Chinese Eastern Railroad line. About three thousand railroad carriages were being held in reserve at Manzhouli, fitted to accommodate forty soldiers each, so as to transport up to 120,000 men at very short notice.[44]

Whereas the occupation of Hailar had been carried out without direct Russian military assistance, Chinese, Russian, and foreign observers held different views about the extent of Russian support to the Mongols against the Lubin garrison two weeks later. Several possible motives drove Russian action near Manzhouli: the wish to maintain a buffer between thinly populated territories in Siberia and the increasing Han-populated areas, to forestall a strong Chinese military presence in Outer Mongolia and Hulunbeir, and to preserve an indigenous region free of significant foreign elements in Mongolia, enabling Russia to reap the benefits of economic development without competition. According to instructions from Saint Petersburg, Russia would remain strictly neutral in the event of hostilities between the Chinese and Hulunbeir banner people.[45] Yet there are good reasons to believe that some Russian military leaders did, in fact, openly intervene on the side of the Hulunbeir Mongols.

While the various accounts of the strike against the Lubin garrison near Manzhouli, of Chinese, Russian, American, and German provenance, vary in detail, they do agree that Russian assistance seems to have played a decisive role in the secession of Hulunbeir from China.[46] This interference was certainly in line with Russian interest at the time: the ousting of Chinese troops from its state border and its Manchurian railroad concession enabled Russia to secure the imperial periphery and exploit the economic benefits to be extracted from northeast China at lower risk and cost.

Weeks of uncertainty followed the expulsion of the Chinese civil and military corps. Suspicious of the peace, the Mongols remained on guard and stationed 250 soldiers in the Lubin garrison. Above Manzhouli's Chinese Maritime Customs office waved the flag of the Republic of China. On the roof of the residence of the Chinese delegate, however, the Imperial Dragon still flapped.[47] After the hostilities in Hailar and Manzhouli, the Mongols delivered their claims in a letter to the Chinese administrator of Hulunbeir: "We are determined not to recognize the Republic and not to submit to the oppression of the Chinese officials. We respectfully advise both of you gentlemen to promptly prepare and depart with your subordinate officials for your homes, and enjoy peace. All other people engaged in trade and other occupations will be left absolutely unmolested; on the contrary, they will be extended special protection. . . . If you oppose us by opening fire, we will be obliged to fight. Our righteous army of Hulunbeir respects the principles of humanity, and will not murder the Chinese."[48]

However, despite such promises, anti-Chinese violence erupted in Hulunbeir shortly after the capture of Hailar. Conditions became alarming, and Chinese officials warned the population that, if they supported the Mongols, their property would be confiscated as soon as the city was retaken by Republican forces. False rumors of Chinese reinforcements marching toward Hailar fueled the already-tense atmosphere.[49] On 21 April 1912 Mongolian soldiers, mostly Solons, looted Chinese shops and eateries in Old Hailar and arrested hundreds of Chinese. "According to recent rumors," the *Dumy Zabaikal'ia* (Transbaikal Thoughts) correspondent informed his readers, "The Mongols expelled all the Chinese out of the old city, driving them off to the alienated corridor, leaving only the merchants untouched."[50] Lester Maynard, the U.S. consul in Harbin, reported that "the principal buildings being entirely destroyed by fire, and the Chinese population, being subjected to great suffering and sustaining heavy losses . . . were in a panic, and tried to escape from the town, yet 600 Chinese were captured by the Mongols who apparently intended to hold them for ransom. The authorities were helpless, and looting continued. The only things being saved were articles that the owners managed to take to the Russian part of the town." Observers debated whether the total anarchy had been prompted by political or patriotic reasons, or whether a mutiny sparked by Mongolian soldiers who had not been paid set off the riots. In any case, the morning after the riots Russian authorities pressured the Mongolian administration to restore order.[51]

Thus, while Russia had been reluctant to get involved too closely in Inner Mongolia for fear of Japanese reaction, the tsarist empire was willing to become involved in Hulunbeir. Backed by the Russian military, the Mongols had succeeded in taking control of the steppe between the Argun and the Great Xingan Mountains and in restoring independence. For the nomads still living in the region, however, the future was less certain than ever.

Dependent Independence: Hulunbeir from 1912 to 1915

After the Mongols declared independence and expelled Chinese officials and the military, the status of Hulunbeir became a hotly debated issue among Russian politicians and commentators. In a speech to the Duma on 26 April 1912, three months after Hulunbeir became independent, Sergei D. Sazonov, Russian foreign minister, declared himself opposed to land annexation on Russia's periphery because the area did not pose significant military risk to the empire: "I cannot perceive any reasons why the annexation of Northern Mongolia [Khalkha and Hulunbeir] should be useful to us. Our interests require only that, as Mongolia lies on our frontier, no strong military power should be established there. Owing to the proximity of the Mongols, our Siberian frontier is better guarded than if we were to construct fortresses with large garrisons." Sazonov pointed to the differences between Inner and Outer Mongolia and cautioned that attempts to unite them were hardly likely to be a political success. He was even skeptical about an independent national existence for Outer Mongolia. The minister saw Russia's role as that of an intermediary between China and Mongolia, stressing that Russia must strive to have a seat at any negotiation table brokering an agreement between the two. He named three principal conditions to guide future relations between China and Outer Mongolia. First, he asserted, no Chinese administration was to be introduced. Second, no Chinese troops were to be deployed in the region. And third, Chinese colonists must be denied access to the region.[52]

The Russian foreign minister agreed that the restoration of Chinese sovereignty in Hulunbeir would be acceptable as long as the territory remained self-administered by locals and Russian economic interests were respected.[53]

The two treaty ports of Manzhouli and Hailar were subjected to scrupulous surveillance by the international community, foreclosing the possibility of a complete annexation of the area. At the same time the guarded Russian railroad concession in the area secured Russian claims sufficiently, and when in the future China was to assert its "interest in the railway, this would have confirmed Chinese connections with Outer Mongolia just when Russia was anxious to emphasize the lack of any such connections."[54] Though Russia had supported Tokhtogo prior to the end of Qing dynasty and the declaration of independence in Urga and Hailar, he was now no longer needed to support the Russian position in Hulunbeir. For the time being China's position was too weak to pose a threat to Russia's security and influence in the region.

Since Saint Petersburg obviously did not support the idea of a pan-Mongolian empire, it treated Hulunbeir's indigenous leaders lukewarmly and advised them to compromise with the Chinese authorities. These negotiations came to nothing, however, since Urga warmly received the pledge of the Hulunbeir leaders to be made a protectorate of independent Khalkha. In May 1912 Shengfu, chief of the small Ölöt banner and a member of the Daur gentry who had been a leading figure in the Hulunbeir rebellion, was installed at Hailar as the Urga Khutukhtu's viceroy and imperial resident. Shengfu's appointment followed a long tradition by which Daurs generally were more educated than members of other banners, and thus tended to dominate the tribal affairs in Hulunbeir by monopolizing official appointments.[55] By acknowledging China's command over Outer Mongolia while negotiating with the Mongols, Russia played a double game. With Hulunbeir becoming a Mongol protectorate, this strategy suddenly raised delicate questions. On the one hand, the Russian government was an advocate of national self-determination by the local elites. On the other, it accepted that the Chinese customs house remained open in Manzhouli.[56]

In China the retention of Mongolia and other frontiers as dependencies was disputed during the early years of the Republic.[57] At no point was Hulunbeir's independence stable and secure. By May 1912 the Heilongjiang provincial assembly was discussing two burning questions: namely, how to prevent foreign interference in Hulunbeir and how to convince the autochthonous tribes of the district to submit to rule by the Republic of China. That same month the Heilongjiang provincial government circulated leaflets in Hulunbeir aiming to win the hearts of the Mongols. The handbill, printed in Mongolian, promised equality among all ethnic groups in the Republic of China as well as respect for their rights to autonomy. It warned the people not to await support from Russia, as this would mean a violation of international law and was therefore unlikely to happen. In the next paragraph, however, the friendly tone turned frosty: "You cannot rely on your armed forces, for its strength does not exceed 1,000 men and thus is not able to resist the [Heilongjiang] government forces. Your soldiers are untrained and only a small minority of them is more or less able to handle guns. Such a quantity and quality of your soldiers is not enough to mess with Qiqihar military forces, of which 3 percent would be enough to definitely defeat you." The leaflet concluded with a call for a peaceful resolution to the various gambits for independence and the promise that the handover in January 1912 would have no repercussions.[58]

Nevertheless a punitive expedition carried out by a Chinese regiment against Tokhtogo's native Jirim league in Inner Mongolia in the autumn of 1912 raised concerns among the Mongols in Hulunbeir. Local Mongol officials in Hailar feared that the expedition augured an attempt by Chinese troops to cross the Great Xingan Mountains and retake Hulunbeir. However, Song Xiaolian, the new governor of Heilongjiang province and former Chinese administrator of Hulunbeir and as such an extreme advocate of sinicization, decided against the military option for the time being. Song seconded his delegates' request to negotiate with Mongols in Hailar and to work toward reunification with China.[59]

But a Russo-Chinese agreement signed on 5 November 1913 represented a defeat for the Chinese government. Russia recognized Chinese control over the entirety of Inner Mongolia, while China acknowledged the fait accompli of Outer Mongolian independence. Sovereign Mongolia was thus reduced to Outer Mongolia. Hulunbeir was not mentioned at all in the agreement.[60]

High politics between Beijing and Saint Petersburg on the matter of Mongolian independence proved to be a burden for the indigenous people, causing particular anxiety in Hailar. The disappointment following Russian rejection of support for Hulunbeir self-determination and the subsequent pact in November worried representatives of Hulunbeir's autochthonous elite and divided its people into two camps, along banner lines. The "Old Bargut" (Solons, Chipchin, and Daurs) banners swallowed the Russo-Chinese agreement while the "New Bargut" (Buriat) banners still agitated for unification with Outer Mongolia. Some even threatened to immigrate to Khalkha, on the chance that Hulunbeir would be incorporated back into China. In late February 1914 the imperial resident Shengfu had reached a preliminary agreement with diplomatic representatives from Heilongjiang province. First, the people of Hulunbeir were to become Chinese subjects again. Second, Hulunbeir was to be declared a special autonomous district outside the Chinese provincial administration but under the direct control of the Chinese central government. Third, military requirements were to be met with a local militia body so that the region might be free of any Chinese troops.

During a congress in spring 1914 the schism between the fractions of the Old Bargut banners on the one side and New Bargut banners on the other broke wide open. Officials from all seventeen banners gathered for eleven days in Hailar under the presidency of imperial resident Shengfu. The New Bargut openly accused the Daurs of accepting bribes and gifts from the Chinese. Daurs, for their part, tried to delay the close of the conference. They still waited for the approval of the preliminary agreement by the Chinese central government in Beijing and the Heilongjiang provincial government in Qiqihar. At one point a Daur regimental commander raised his voice to address the assembly. He took a gloomy tone, speaking for many in expressing his deep frustration with Russian perfidy and proposing instead a Chinese solution: "When we struggled for autonomy with weapons in our hands, we were convinced to unite with independent Khalkha, and the Russian government pledged to fully support us. Now it has become evident that the Russian government has broken its promises, putting us in a difficult position. If we do not take our fate in our hands now, our enemies will wipe us out. . . . Wouldn't it be better to accept Chinese authority right away instead of resisting and shedding our blood in vain?" With a military force of fewer than three thousand poorly trained and inadequately equipped soldiers, no one was really in the mood for fighting. Nonetheless the gathering ended without a satisfactory resolution.[61]

The Call for Independence Slowly Fades:
The Status of Hulunbeir after 1915

Russia's policy toward Mongolia following independence had been realistic and prudent, reflecting the different lights in which imperial officials saw Outer Mongolia and Hulunbeir. For Outer Mongolia policymakers in Saint Petersburg sought to preserve some degree of sovereignty, to prevent Chinese military deployment and colonization, and to obtain special economic interests and rights for Russia. According to this policy Outer Mongolia was granted a quasi-independent status in which it remained under both Chinese control and Russian protection, a decision born of international pressures at a tripartite conference of Russia, China, and Mongolia in Kiakhta on 7 June 1915.[62] To Russian observers the politically immature princes at Urga were mere puppets in a "Great Game" between Japan, Russia, and China. Russia's main concern had been the creation of a buffer state to prevent China from building up military forces at the border with Russia. A unified Mongol empire was not needed for this purpose and would, moreover, have provoked a conflict with Japan over interest spheres. "Mongolian nationalism," *Vestnik Azii* (Herald of Asia) concluded, "had unfortunately clashed with stronger forces."[63]

Indeed, when the "Hulunbeir question" was settled several months later, Russian and Chinese negotiators paid little attention to the needs and requests of Hulunbeir's indigenous representatives. The final arrangement dictated that the region's autonomy from China would be weaker than the quasi-independent status of Outer Mongolia. The agreement settling Hulunbeir, ratified by the Republic of China and the Russian Empire on 6 November 1915 in Beijing, adopted nearly all of the original Russian proposals, the ones Sazonov had initially doubted the Chinese would accept. Hulunbeir was declared a special district, directly subject to the central government in Beijing. The prereform administrative structure was restored: the Mongol banner deputy lieutenant general of the Hulunbeir garrison (fudutong) would enjoy the rank of provincial governor and was to be appointed via presidential decree. Collective ownership of land was granted to bannermen. In times of peace military presence would be limited to a standing local militia, although in cases of insurgency the Chinese government would maintain the right to dispatch its own troops after giving notice to the Russian government. Since Russia controlled the main passage to Hulunbeir—the Chinese Eastern Railroad—hidden military advance seemed unlikely. All taxes and duties, except customs, would continue to flow into the coffers of the local government.

With this agreement Russia assumed the role of mediator between Hulunbeir and China in return for additional privileges, as the declaration salvaged Russian economic interests in Hulunbeir. It was a grave defeat for Chinese diplomacy. Between 1915 and 1920 the region remained de facto under the joint control of Russia and China.[64] The agreement also marked a serious setback for the indigenous struggle for self-rule. Just as the Russian authorities had forgotten about Tokhtogo as soon as he had lost his possible strategic value for them, the voices of Hulunbeir's autochthonous inhabitants had been heard only insofar as they served Russia's strategic needs.

Thus it is hardly surprising that, despite the settlement excluding Hulunbeir from independent Outer Mongolia, the fight for self-determination from Chinese rule continued there after 1915. Probably the most prominent figure in that struggle was Babuzhab.[65] Born in 1875, he had been paramount in the revolt of the Kharachins, a sub-ethnic group in eastern Inner Mongolia. Babuzhab's freedom struggles gained more attention from contemporaries and historians than had those led by Tokhtogo, who had lived in Outer Mongolia since 1911, where he took to opium and, after his arrest by the Bolsheviks, died in 1922.[66] Certainly, Babuzhab became the more prominent figure because he did not give peace to Hulunbeir or to its contiguous neighbors, Inner Mongolia and Khalkha, after the annulment of independence.[67] In 1917 remnants of Babuzhab's troops surfaced again. But in this last campaign his reputation would be reduced to that of an ordinary robber. In May 1917, after the Kharachin bandits had chased Shengfu and other loathed Daurs out of their homesteads around Hailar, where they had largely stuck to two villages, they entered the native section of the city. There they looted all Chinese stores, the administrative offices and private properties of the Mongol fudutong, and the premises of the Daur oligarchy. Until soldiers from the Russian garrison checked the Kharachins in September 1917, the natives of Hulunbeir once again self-administered the region, this time under a regime of terror. In January 1918 the Chinese president Yuan Shikai assured monetary compensation to the victims. After months of violence the Daurs returned to Hailar.[68]

Not until the Russian Civil War did Russia's imperial position weaken along the Chinese border.[69] On 28 June 1920, when Russia no longer could guarantee indigenous self-rule, the 1915 treaty spelling out terms of governance over Hulunbeir was revoked and a Chinese presidential mandate finally rescinded the region's independence for good. It again reverted to the supervisory control of the administration of Heilongjiang province. The provincial government of Heilongjiang acted wisely, authorizing the office of the Mongol fudutong to continue administering the local affairs of the banner population in Hulunbeir. The Mongols thus retained a distinctive structure of local government within the Chinese Republic for the time being.[70]

Descent into Demimonde: The Dark Side of Manzhouli

In the volatile atmosphere of the late Qing and Romanov monarchies, toppled by revolutions in 1911 and 1917, respectively, and of the Civil War years, various powers competed not only for influence among the nomadic people on the faraway Argun frontier but also for influence among the cosmopolitan population of Manzhouli. Border towns are often breeding places for crime. During the tumultuous years of revolution Manzhouli was no exception. The Russo-Japanese War of 1904–1905 had washed all kinds of suspicious elements from other peripheries of the Russian Empire and China to the Manchurian border. Released exiles from Nerchinsk and from Sakhalin mingled with folk recruited from a pool composed of discharged servants, laid-off railroad workers, and ruined merchants. According to a governmental report they likely "were either on their way from Russia proper to Manchuria or in the opposite direction, were stranded temporarily, or took up permanent residence in the border settlement due to lack of funding or missing passports."[71]

The general public, stirred up by local media, soon found the chief culprits to be *kavkaztsy*—migrants from the Caucasus. Petty crimes like mugging and burglary were common, and even murder was not rare. Police often remained inactive, and ordinary residents became victims. One was shot and strangled by a group of Ossetians. Another named Suroveckii, a salesman of sewing machines, was killed in his house on a September night in 1905. The murderers left with money and other valuables. Locals demanded stronger police presence, but the local police staff was said to lack proper discipline.[72]

Most of the Russian and Chinese dwellers of Manzhouli lived in quarters isolated by nationality, rarely emerging to socialize with the "other" in daily life. Still, it is striking that despite the tensions caused by the imperial competition between Saint Petersburg and Beijing the Chinese rarely became the bogey in public Russian discourse around Manzhouli's history of crime. In contrast to other semicolonial urban spaces within China's Northeast, the Chinese seem to have avoided scapegoating. As Russians understood it the thievery of the Chinese was to target the construction materials of abandoned houses or public property like coal from the railroad storehouses, implying the kind of self-service culture not unpopular among Russian subjects, too. If Russians and Chinese competed at Manzhouli, it was usually at the bottom of society, fighting for stolen coal, timber, or the service charge for luggage transport at the railroad station. And if they fought, in most cases it was the Chinese that were the vulnerable party.[73]

The settlement-sized crime scene that was Manzhouli became an issue of national importance in Russia after a post and telegraph office were raided in 1908 and more than 210,000 rubles were seized by the bandits. After the raid the military governor in Chita described Manzhouli as a "reservoir" of criminals, triggering crime in the whole Transbaikal area. In his letter mailed to the Police Department of the Ministry of the Interior in Saint Petersburg, he drew a gloomy conclusion:

> A chronicle of crimes committed at Manzhouli would best show what kinds of elements find refuge there and how vigorous local police prosecute them. . . . The number of burglaries and murders in Manzhouli is enormous. I have no exact data on that. According to personal surveys I can just name several: For instance, 1) armed robbery of the postal train between Manzhouli-Harbin in the vicinity of the station, 2) larceny of Podliasok's pharmacy, 3) of Pakhatinskii's and 4) Partin's houses, 5) several cruel murders with theft. And finally 6) policeman Merzhinskii's assassination. Whole gangs of robbers committed all crimes except for the last. In none of the cases were the delinquents found.[74]

Police officers recruited from the Transamur Border Guards, who protected the Chinese Eastern Railroad, remained insufficient to meet this tidal wave of criminality. Their posts were located exclusively in the administrative village, far from the settlement's private districts, which remained guarded by infrequent and defenseless patrols.

Other traits of the city were typical of settlements with high numbers of visitors who were mostly men: a vibrant nightlife, prostitution, gambling, and spaces given over to the consumption of alcohol. Manzhouli counted about two hundred grocery and liquor stores selling beer on tap, eight wine taverns, about ten restaurants with "private rooms," and up to thirty canteens, most of them clustered around the bazaar, selling cheap booze and girls who entertained clients in various ways. Many of these institutions were open around the clock, generally packed with customers, and regularly attracted crime.[75]

The crime rate began to fall, however, when in 1910 the newly inaugurated public administration rented special observation posts overlooking the private village. Agents at these posts were able to ask for help from special patrols, who were immediately summoned at the first signs of any danger. Railroad police and a special Chinese police, designated in charge of Chinese subjects, supported the regular forces.[76] After a particularly gruesome fight between pations of a bazaar-canteen during Easter week in 1911, the municipal council also pondered how to fix the problem of Manzhouli's sex industry. Two patrons had attacked each other, one brandishing an axe, the other throwing glass bottles, one of which by mistake almost killed children playing on the street. In a lively discussion council members decided without a single vote of opposition to prohibit the services of prostitutes to men under the age of forty years. The employment of prostitutes by canteens and restaurants was banned too. The municipal council, in collaboration with the police and medical committee, began to search for a suitable place in the village to run the sex business.[77]

With the coming of World War I, Manzhouli was struck again by organized groups of criminals who raided people's homes, shops, and storehouses, forcing citizens to stay indoors, shopkeepers to close their shops, and the public administration to provide its servants with guns after nightfall.[78] The varieties of lawlessness characterizing the town and the origins of the marauding criminals recalled those of the town's earlier years. Manzhouli's history of crime thus demonstrates that offenses occurred by and large within the community of Russian subjects, rather than across the borders separating national groups.

Votes Bought, Taxes Evaded: Defining and Contesting Borders in the Town

Soon after the Russo-Japanese War had ended the tsarist government pursued its large-scale ambitions in the extraterritorial strip of Manchuria with renewed vigor. One key element of this effort was the establishment of municipal administrations in three settlements within the railroad concession:

Harbin, Hailar, and Manzhouli. The new municipal governments replaced and took up the obligations of the Chinese Eastern Railroad's civil department. They had the power to levy property, sales, and other taxes and controlled commerce, health care, city planning, realty, education, and other spheres of public life.[79] While this change generally helped improve living conditions, such municipal administrations did not constitute institutions of self-government for the residents. Their enactment signaled instead the desire of the Russians to shift the balance of power in hybrid railroad settlements to their favor.

In May 1908 the municipal government of Manzhouli took office. Until February 1921 it remained under the supervision and control of the Chinese Eastern Railroad board of directors. Russian was the official language and the mayor was to be a Russian national.[80] Manzhouli's municipal administration included two legislative bodies. One was the general assembly, convening at least twice a year. This body was limited by census suffrage. Only affluent taxpayers were eligible for membership. Members together decided on general matters and taxation in particular. The other body comprised the municipal council and the mayor (council chairman), three representatives of the general assembly, and one member appointed by the Chinese Eastern Railroad. The representatives of the general assembly were elected every three years.[81]

The electoral system had its more egalitarian elements. There was the fact that residents of all nationalities were allowed to serve on the general assembly, so that in 1912, for instance, the national composition of suffrage was distributed as follows: one hundred seventy-five Russians, thirty-six Chinese, eight Turks, and one German, Greek, Italian, Japanese, and American each, thereby mirroring the membership of the general assembly. And at least in theory Chinese and foreigners could also become members of municipal council.

Despite its façade of openness to equal representation by all nationalities, municipal governance in Manzhouli guaranteed the superiority of the Russians. Not surprisingly Lieutenant General Mikhail E. Afansev, Chinese Eastern Railroad deputy manager for civil matters, praised the electoral system as excellent because "the Chinese party will not matter to the outcome of the election, if only the Russian population keeps a certain solidarity and pays careful attention to the election."[82]

Yet the system played into the hands of the Russian government only as long as every Russian council member loyally adhered to the agenda of the Chinese Eastern Railroad. This was not the case in Manzhouli. Its administration attracted egocentric braggarts, often with a criminal history, who enriched themselves at the expense of the community. Aleksei N. Nikitin, who followed the rather even-tempered Sergei P. Golikov as mayor and chairman of the municipal council in 1910, was one of the loudest and most corrupt. During his reign it was not rare for insults and brawls to erupt during council sessions. Residents of Manzhouli demanded repeatedly to reform the general assembly, to end clientelism, nepotism, and populist brawlers.[83]

This spirit of reform received support from an unexpected quarter: the Chinese electorate. Despite the Mongol takeover of Hulunbeir and siege of the Chinese garrison in nearby Lubin in early 1912, Chinese representatives, some now without queues and suited and booted in the Western style, appeared on Manzhouli's political stage. Despite the political turmoil in China they were determined to assert political influence within the extraterritorial settlement. Yet their manner of political representation and participation was only dubiously fair. Vasilii I. Ablov, a Russian assembly member, criticized how the Chinese selected their representatives to the general assembly in July 1912. One such criticism was that clerks employed by local companies appeared in the assembly on behalf of the owners of those companies, thereby representing not themselves but an otherwise absent assembly member.[84]

The votes of those delegates turned out to be decisive for the election of the next municipal council. With the aid of loyal Chinese members in the council Nikitin remained chairman of the municipal council in July 1912.[85] The Russian press was enraged that "the Russian population has long ceased to be the master of the village. In fact it is controlled by the Chinese, led by Nikitin, the chairman of the municipal council, who, uniting all the Chinese, once for all fraudulently obtained their voices. . . . Of course, the Chinese, being a practical people, gave their votes to Mr. Nikitin not for nothing. They paid only half the taxes, and ended up becoming actual owners of the village."[86] After fierce protests from opponents of Nikitin the elections were restaged on 9 October 1912. Nikitin once again captured the vote and was confirmed as council chairman.[87]

During the next regular council elections in January 1916, in the midst of World War I and just one year before the abdication of Tsar Nicholas II, none of the Chinese electors who had supported Nikitin attended the meeting. The council chairman jockeyed again for reelection, but his days were numbered. Some of the two hundred attending members began to shout "Down with Nikitin." Angry, Manzhouli residents telegraphed the railroad administration in Harbin to demand the removal of Nikitin.[88] They were successful, and in February 1919, after the last elections to this executive body under Chinese Eastern Railroad control, the overwhelming majority of those elected were, again, Russian. There remained yet a long road from decorative to genuine democracy.[89]

On the face of it Russians seemed uniquely privileged in Manzhouli, since they were thought to dominate the municipal legislative body and all municipal institutions. Yet after Russia's defeat against Japan in 1905, foreign residents enjoyed privileges of extraterritoriality just as they did in other Chinese treaty ports. To satisfy Japanese demands, China had opened Manzhouli and other Manchurian towns to foreign trade after the war. Thus the presence of foreigners, whom Russia previously had tried to exclude from its sphere of influence, was now permitted, right up to Russia's very borders.[90]

When Manzhouli's municipal administration began to demand taxes from all businesses, including foreign ones, the tensions generated by the opening of trade escalated. For the Russians Manzhouli became a testing ground for Harbin and other railroad settlements in the alienated zone. Because it was small and located near Russian territory, a dry run in this settlement was more feasible than elsewhere. The additional tax revenue would have been small. Yet the Russian authorities were determined to charge foreign businesses, as they were concerned about an increasing reluctance to pay taxes among the Russians and the Chinese. Another and less obvious reason was the desire to reduce heavy drinking among the Russian soldiers due to the abundance of liquor on the Argun frontier. Explicit sanctions against liquor stores owned by French and German citizens were justified on the same pretext. To the U.S. consul in Harbin Roger Greene, this was absurd. No one, he reasoned, could believe licitly operating stores to be the real culprits. "Manzhouli is the known center for a large contraband trade in spirits, and . . . soldiers would have no difficulty in securing all the liquor they could pay for from other sources."[91]

Beginning in 1910 the municipal council at Manzhouli used all possible means to enforce the tax regime against non-Russian residents and businesses. They were ordered to pay their just proportion of duties, as were Russian and Chinese subjects. Russian officials argued that the taxes served the improvement of the settlement, providing infrastructure, sanitation, police, free education, and so forth to all citizens regardless of origin.[92]

Non-Russian and non-Chinese merchants refused to pay their share, however, and so Russian authorities resorted to extreme measures. On 17 June 1911 the newly hired guards were posted in front of all the foreign-owned businesses. Police had instructions to deny all customers access unless they could produce foreign passports. Those who attempted to enter the shops without complying were "roughly pushed back and threatened with arrest." The measures affected twelve Turkish-Armenian, three Greek, and one Austrian merchant, most dealers in liquor, grocers, or bakers. Later, notifications were circulated calling for a boycott of all foreign shops.[93] Russian advocates of the ban hid behind the pseudo-democratic camouflage of the local administration, informing the public via the press that it had been "not the Russians who prohibited the trade, but the municipal government, elected by Russians, Chinese, Japanese, Americans, etc." Deputy chairman of the municipal council Iakov F. Shardakov himself took matters in hand, demolishing the signboard of a Turkish grocer who rented shop premises in his house and then locking him out.[94]

Eager to defend extraterritorial trade privileges, German and French diplomats emphatically protested against the obstruction of businesses run by their citizens and other foreign merchants under their protection, and interfered in an effort to settle the dispute. The Chinese, however, took a passive stance in the conflict. The situation eased only after Dr. Franz Kuhn, the German vice-consul at Harbin, traveled to Manzhouli himself to mediate between the municipal council, the railroad administration, and foreign merchants.[95] On 4 August 1911, after seven weeks of government-imposed boycott, the police guards posted in front of delinquent foreign-owned shops were finally removed. The Russians then made a few concessions to the foreign businesses and the shop owners began to pay taxes to match the Russians.[96]

Until the Russian Revolution Manzhouli was a peculiar place on the border between Russia and China. Located on Chinese territory but within the extraterritorial zone of the railroad, the town came under de facto Russian control. Russian authority, however, was limited and often actively undermined. As it was a treaty port, foreigners enjoyed privileges of extraterritoriality, which they were eager to defend. Until 1912 China's ubiquitous influence was felt through the nearby military garrison at Lubin and the house of the Chinese Maritime Customs. In terms of its population, too, Manzhouli was a truly international place between empires. Borders were not always drawn cleanly between different ethnic groups in town. Some Russians formed coalitions with Chinese in the municipal council, while Russian nationals terrorized their countrymen.

Troubled Times: Manzhouli during Revolution and Civil War

In the wake of the February and October Revolutions of 1917 various groups competed for power in Siberia, the Russian Far East, the Russian concessions in Manchuria as well as on the steppes and in the villages of the Argun frontier. The attempt by the Bolsheviks to seize power was soon thwarted by the Transbaikal Cossack Grigorii M. Semenov. His newly formed Mongol-Buriat regiment cleared the settlements along the railroad east of Chita and west of the Great Xingan Mountains of communist forces. On 1 January 1918 his forces disarmed the Russian garrison in Manzhouli. After taking control over the border town, Semenov proceeded to crush a municipal government that to him "bore an obvious socialist coloration." His henchmen stormed into the railroad club, where several hundred delegates of the general assembly and observers had gathered. There Semenov personally disgraced and humiliated the communist assembly members in public, calling them "fools and donkeys who joined the Bolsheviks out of stupidity and inability to understand the essence of Bolshevism."[97]

Despite Semenov's rather arrogant cameo on the Sino-Russian border, the Special Manchurian Brigade, as his troops were called by then, sustained a defeat against the Bolsheviks in the spring of 1918 and then retreated eastward. In August 1918, however, Semenov succeeded in reclaiming his former sphere of influence in Transbaikalia. There, supported by the Japanese Expeditionary Army, the ataman of the Transbaikal Cossacks entrenched himself on the periphery of the Russian Empire and presided over a reign of terror that lasted for two years.[98] Semenov's brigade stands emblematic for the complex loyalties of the Cossacks who sometimes acted independently from the central Russian government. In following Semenov they were loyal to the tsarist regime, and they could not switch allegiance to the Bolsheviks without rebelling against their military code. The fact that Semenov's forces included Buriats, Mongols, and even a Jewish company is another example of the ethnic mixing that was characteristic for the Argun frontier.

Yet another name is connected to Manzhouli and the Argun basin during the Civil War years. In 1918 Semenov had entrusted Baron Roman von Ungern-Sternberg with the command at Dauriia railroad station. The offspring of a noble Baltic German family ultimately revoked his loyalty to Semenov and led the volunteer Asiatic Mounted Division, a ragtag group of Tatar, Buriat, Russian, Chinese, Mongolian, and other mercenaries. Until Ungern's 1920 retreat from Red Army units and Transbaikal partisans to Outer Mongolia, where he exploited anti-Chinese resentments among the Khalkha Mongols to revive the Great Mongol Empire, his troops often plundered trains passing through Dauriia to source their supplies. In the summer of 1921 rumors that Ungern's troops would move from Mongolia toward the railroad zone again created panic, particularly among Jewish and Chinese merchants in Manzhouli. Fortunately for them, in mid-August, Ungern was captured near the Russian-Mongolian border and executed.[99]

The Russian Revolution of 1917 and the Civil War of 1918 to 1921 undermined all efforts toward effective border control. Unstable power relations, a dearth of legislation, and the cacophonous existence of multiple currencies and barter trade networks meant that commodities and people crossed the Sino-Russian border literally uncontrolled. The reputation of the customs assessors had been sullied even before World War I.[100] And in many border villages Cossacks openly opposed Russian customs officers and tax inspectors. "Once there is no tsar, there can be no duty" became the motto of the day. Residents demanded that the customs officers leave their posts. If they resisted the mob insulted the officers and sometimes chased them away. Occasionally smugglers even fired at the officers.[101]

As soon as news broke of the February Revolution in 1917, even at major crossings such as Manzhouli, customs authority had become undermined. By October 1917 soldiers refused to have their luggage inspected, and local Cossacks disguised themselves as soldiers to cross the border unnoticed.[102] Then during the Civil War years Ungern and Semenov took advantage of the power vacuum between Chita and the Chinese border and so foreclosed any possibility of a tariff revision. At that point the railroad station of Manzhouli harbored so many speculators that regular passengers found it hard to obtain tickets.[103] When soldiers, Cossacks, and fortune hunters allied themselves against customs authorities, and when train services subsequently dissolved into chaos, it became obvious that the empire—and with it the still fragmentary border control—was on the verge of crumbling.

During the Russian Revolution and Civil War, Manzhouli also became a transit point for tens of thousands of refugees and exiles from the Russian Empire. In fact only because of the railroad was such mass emigration to China possible. For the majority of émigrés Manzhouli was only a stopover on their way to Harbin, Shanghai, and other destinations.[104] But leaving revolutionary Russia behind did not necessarily mean reaching a safe haven, as Semenov's men remained active on both sides of the border, hunting political enemies and searching for sources of income.

Fearing an arrest by henchmen of Admiral Aleksandr V. Kolchak's government at Omsk, Russian socialist and ethnographer Moisei A. Krol' reached the border in November 1918. In a hopelessly crammed third-class coach Krol' experienced half an hour of terror at Manzhouli: "Quite unexpectedly for the passengers, a Semenov officer began to go from car to car to check the passports of the travelers. As he came to our car he looked through the documents, taking some of them with him, including my own. Then burning anxiety seared in me and overwhelmed me. 'Are they not looking for me on a telegraph request from Irkutsk?' I wondered. . . . When the officer returned he handed me my documents very politely. I felt a deep sigh of relief and I scolded myself for being too nervous out of groundless fear."[105] In the summer of 1920, however, the situation at the border was to change. The hunters would become the hunted. At Manzhouli the Cossack Vasilii G. Kazakov testified to the Whites' hasty flight at the border: "Manzhouli was packed with convoys of military and refugee trains. Train cars had been turned into miserable housing for many thousands of people left to their own. A whole town of houses on wheels, from which day and night carry the melodies of songs, sounds of harmonicas, the cries of children and women, the shouts of the drunk, the moaning of the sick."[106] When in the fall of that very year Lialia A. Sharov crossed the border,

FIGURE 3.3. American Red Cross party giving provisions to refugees at Manzhouli, 1 September 1918. For tens of thousands of refugees from the Russian Empire Manzhouli became the main point of entry to China during the years following the Russian Revolution.

the Transbaikal side had already come under the control of the Bolsheviks. They had designated an international zone on the open steppe, on then-Russian territory, but fear was still ubiquitous among Whites in flight:

> The train stopped but there was no station. The doors of the railroad cars were locked. The soldiers exclaimed that the passengers were let out one by one and only from one car at a time. When my turn came I stepped down. The Russian inspector looked at my pass exclaiming: "What kind of fool gave you this pass? You will be arrested in Manchuria. . . ." He said it was not sufficient and suggested I should leave the train before reaching Manzhouli to avoid legal entry. I said I would follow his advice. I had no intention of jumping from the train. At Manzhouli I would be on my own railroad. It did not occur to me that the railroad was not ours any longer.[107]

Sharov was in luck. At Manzhouli the emigrant officer who checked her documents on behalf of the Chinese knew that her cousin was employed by the Chinese Eastern Railroad. She was allowed to continue her journey.

For many, however, the disorder meant hardship. Soldiers of all uniforms as well as civilian thieves stole anything of value. "Especially the women suffered. Before they arrived in Manzhouli on horseback, in the car or simply on foot, the Chinese soldiers took care of them."[108] The memoirs and recollections of the Civil War refugees illustrate primarily one thing: in times of war a border control regime as such does not exist.

An exodus of refugees from Soviet Russia continued to flow throughout the early 1920s, affecting everyday life in Manzhouli. Although most émigrés continued on their journey without lingering, some remained in town for some time. The population peaked at 24,990 in 1921.[109] The town on the border adapted to the new challenges only slowly, even as it became a primary entry port for thousands of émigrés. Until at least the fall of 1921 refugees lived in primitive tent camps on the outskirts of town or in shacks in the village north of Kuladzhi creek. In December 1921 the municipal council finally opened a free lodging house and a soup kitchen for the refugees and offered their children education on favorable financial terms, with support from local philanthropists.[110]

Despite such offerings, throughout the early 1920s life in Manzhouli remained difficult for refugees and residents alike. With little agriculture in the area people depended on food supplies from elsewhere; but cargo traffic on the railroad was interrupted repeatedly for weeks and even months.[111] Occasionally even access to information was restricted. The Chinese Post in Manzhouli held back letters from Soviet Russia, and thus thousands of émigrés waited in vain for news from home.[112]

A frontier spirit attracted people from various corners of the Chinese and Russian empires and from other parts of the world. An urban arena, Manzhouli generated new zones of contact between native frontiersmen, migrant workers, customs officials, traders, and fortune seekers, stemming mostly from economic but sometimes from political incentives, and often ignoring state-imposed borders. Despite a multicultural façade, these various ethnic communities remained separate in many respects. Segregated by the railroad tracks, the Chinese and Transbaikal neighborhoods kept their distinct characters for a long time. Encounters between subjects from Russia and China were often limited to the train station and the bazaar, to restaurants, gambling houses, and other public urban spaces.

Politically, Manzhouli was dominated by Russia in its early years. Despite putting into place a pseudo-democratic masquerade, the Russian state wielded political power indirectly over Manzhouli until the Russian Civil War. A municipal council was the key legislative body. Yet the council did not always act purely as an instrument of the Russian state. Its members often pursued their own interests, which by no means mirrored those of the government in Saint Petersburg. In fact the residents were commonly blessed or burdened with hybrid loyalties, and political identity often served as a strategic mask for essentially local or personal concerns. The issue of politics became more complex after the fateful year of 1917. For thousands of Russian émigrés Manzhouli was the first refuge on their flight from the advancing Bolsheviks. Soon Russian communists and defenders of the old regime fought over leadership in town and the latter began to align themselves with the new masters, the Chinese, to whom sovereign power had been transferred.

Long-established people in the pastoral surroundings of Manzhouli harbored conceptions of borders that contravened those held by states. Traditional cross-boundary economic and social networks were still wholly intact, and grazing areas were freely accessible and available for common use. But sedentary concepts of land use, based on exclusive property rights, began to gain ground, and these proved incommensurable with traditional nomadic frameworks. The most visible clashes in this regard were provoked by Chinese and Russian land reforms, which pitted notions of place held by imperial bureaucrats against those of the autochthonous borderlanders. Nomadic and seminomadic people refused to be assimilated into the new political geography, preferring to maintain their traditional lifestyles for as long as they could.

Transbaikal Buriats had been exposed to Slavic influences for some time. Yet land reform and the repeal of autonomy rights for the Buriats forced many members of the frontier minorities to flee to the neighboring Chinese steppe lands, fomenting border instabilities. The upheaval of the Russian Civil War further upset the rural population on the border. Yet although Cossacks and Buriats fought in the ranks of Semenov and Ungern, even those profound changes did not lead to a united secessionist front. The most common response of the autochthonous frontiersmen against economic, political, and religious restrictions in Transbaikalia was thus not rebellion but emigration.

In the Chinese frontier areas the interregnum period was perhaps even more complex politically, as an amalgam of Chinese claims, Russian ambitions, and Mongol hopes. Motivations for Mongol secession were multilayered, ranging from socioeconomic relief to political liberation, and from personal interests to the restoration of historical glory. The tsarist empire, in contrast to the Chinese, perceived the local populace in Hulunbeir as potential allies in its attempt to expand its informal spheres of interest beyond the state border. Russians and Mongols often disagreed over policy but were united in their opposition to the Chinese state. Rebellions in Hulunbeir flared up periodically during the late 1920s and early 1930s. Yet the insurgents achieved moderate success only through outside support, which is perhaps the most obvious sign that native women and men were on the retreat.

4

The Soviet State at the Border

AFTER 1917 the new leadership in Moscow professed commitment to anti-imperialism, declaring equality with China. Nonetheless Moscow tricked the Chinese by stating its intention to return the Chinese Eastern Railroad to China without need for compensation. As early as 1920 it became obvious that this pledge was not worth the paper it was written on. When the Soviet regime started consolidating its power along its borders with China, disregarding earlier promises to renounce tsarist privileges in that nation, it continued down the avenue that the tsarist government had pursued decades earlier.[1]

For its part, ignoring Bolshevik diplomatic maneuvers, the Chinese sought to exploit the roiling disorder of revolutionary Russia. In 1921, for instance, the Republic of China pressured the Far Eastern Republic to recognize Railroad Siding 86, the first station on Russian territory, as a neutral zone between both countries in the so-called Riabikov agreement, named after its Russian signatory. This Chinese military presence on Russian territory had been granted in exchange for continued operation of Soviet institutions in Manzhouli.[2]

But as soon as the Bolsheviks had gained control over the Russian Far East, they strove to recover colonial privileges in Manchuria and to revoke the Riabikov agreement. In the spring and summer of 1922, as Moscow began to clamor for this reversals, the Russian émigré press spread rumors about the imminent arrival of Soviet troops in the railroad zone, instilling fear among the Russians in Manzhouli.[3] Unbeknownst to them Soviet leadership was realistic about the utility of doing just that. Facing the army of Zhang Zuolin, scattered White troops, and Japanese garrisons, "our army is still too weak to occupy the railroad zone," wrote Georgii V. Chicherin, people's commissar for foreign affairs. Only on select occasions was the Red Army granted permission to cross the Chinese border to hunt down White units in the border areas.[4]

Between 1921 and 1923 conflicts occurred repeatedly in Manzhouli or on the border nearby, as both sides tested their limits. The Soviets impeded the free movement of Chinese soldiers on Railroad Siding 86, while Chinese authorities insistently demanded the transfer of the Soviet customs at Manzhouli to Soviet territory.[5] Taking matters into their own hands in June 1923, Chinese and émigré Russian police officers seized the Soviet customs post and arrested one Soviet guard.[6] The conflict further escalated, when a clash near Manzhouli between Soviet border guards and Russian émigrés working for the Chinese Maritime Customs resulted in a diplomatic crisis between Moscow and Mukden, the seat of the Manchurian Warlord government, in the fall of 1923.[7] Moscow steadily intensified its pressure on Zhang Zuolin, although the Soviets did not go so far as to deploy ten thousand soldiers to each of the two railroad terminuses, Manzhouli and Suifenhe, as was proposed in October 1923 by the ambassador plenipotentiary to China, Lev M. Karakhan. However, later on, after Chinese and Russian émigrés in uniform had attacked the crew of a Soviet train in Manzhouli, Moscow dispatched an armored train to Railroad Siding 86.[8]

The tense situation also had serious consequences for the civilian population. On several occasions Chinese police in Manzhouli maltreated Russians.[9] Remnants of local Transbaikal Cossacks, former *Semenovtsy*, repeatedly attacked their native Soviet Argun villages, further destabilizing the already frail situation on the border. In October 1922, for instance, about one hundred troops of the White movement attacked Abagaitui.[10] In the end the Chinese failed to alter the balance of border power in their favor. Following the incorporation of the Far Eastern Republic into Soviet Russia in 1922, they had to withdraw their soldiers from the Soviet Railroad Siding 86, while Soviet customs remained in Manzhouli. After long and hard-fought negotiations, the Beijing and Mukden governments agreed in 1924 to recognize the Chinese Eastern Railroad as a purely commercial enterprise, jointly administered by the Soviet Union and China.[11] The Chinese thus had failed to expunge old tsarist and new Bolshevik privileges from their territory. On 5 October 1924 the Soviet flag was hoisted above the consulate in Manzhouli.[12] The response offered by warlord Zhang Zuolin to this renewed Soviet imperialism comprised an extension of Chinese control into the railroad zone during the 1920s. Not surprisingly, joint administration of the railroad was undertaken by two very different parties in an atmosphere of unequivocal hostility.[13]

A Hornets' Nest: Reds and Whites in Town

In Manzhouli and other parts of the former railroad concession, the balance of power had in fact swung in favor of the Chinese, if only temporarily, after the Russian Revolution. In 1920, for instance, Russian extraterritoriality was revoked. When the municipal council came under supervision of the Chinese-controlled Special District of the Three Eastern Provinces in February 1921, sovereign power was transferred to the Chinese.[14] Chinese soldiers were stationed in town, and no longer Russian but Chinese police officers patrolled the streets. The Chinese dollar replaced the Russian ruble as legal tender. The warlord government of Marshall Zhang Zuolin tried to levy taxes directly on merchants and residents, calling local self-administration into question. Only after fierce protests from the municipal council, backed by strong support from Chinese Eastern Railroad general manager Boris V. Ostroumov, were most of the planned taxes repealed.[15]

But Russia's loss of political power over Manzhouli did not mean that old Russian and new Soviet elites were incapable of limiting the influence of the new Chinese political overlords. In fact the settlement's proximity to the Soviet Union enabled the Bolsheviks to wield power even more decisively than in Harbin. It thus became a site of Bolshevik and Russian émigré faction struggles for control. Former tsarist officials retained their municipal positions in Manzhouli, even as the Bolsheviks established their own formal and informal structures early on. In February 1921 the government commissioner of the Far Eastern Republic took office in the border town and Communist Party structures were implemented under his watch. Yet such political work among the Russian residents was difficult. The Chinese police, in part galvanized by the directives of Zhang Zuolin, was determined to eliminate Bolshevik structures, partly due to increased provocations by emigrants. This, in turn, forced the Bolsheviks to operate clandestinely. Secret members had only sporadic connections with their superior organizations in Harbin and Chita. Moreover, the informal structures of the Soviets competed with the formal ones. Consequently, gains made by Bolshevik agitators among the local population remained far from substantial until the mid-1920s.[16]

A key element of political work in town was the push for an advantage in influence over the public sphere, in this context defined by the political polarities between Reds and Whites. With several hundred railroad men working in town, the Soviets began to dominate public spaces early on. On the fifth anniversary of the October Revolution in 1922, public life in Manzhouli stood still. Most Russian shops and public institutions remained closed. Trade unions had given workers and employees a vacation day. People celebrated the holiday with a demonstration at noon and a play in the railroad school in the evening. Even the anticommunist council chairman Veniamin V. Sapelkin sent a congratulatory message to Boris A. Pokhvalinskii, Manzhouli's new government commissioner of the Far Eastern Republic.[17]

Soon, however, when emigrants began to suppress Bolshevik activities, public holidays, political rallies, secret meetings, and other events became arenas of conflict between Reds and Whites. One such incident occurred when the Soviet government commissioner organized a proper farewell celebration

for a group of Red Army soldiers in the railroad club on 2 February 1923. Announced for the evening's entertainment were a Russian orchestra and two
popular comedy acts by the emigrant playwright and satirist Arkadii T. Averchenko. Just as the first skit had finished, railroad police entered the scene and
blocked all exits. The infamous assistant commandant of the Chinese police,
whom the Russians in town called Vassilli Ivanovich, requested that the play
end immediately. After some discussion, as the policemen stood by idly with
bamboo poles drawn, it was agreed that the dances and tea drinking might be
permitted to go on. The guests, however, were no longer in a frame of mind to
celebrate. No more music was played, and soon everybody went home. Emigrants had succeeded in calling off the communist soirée. Although he was a
Chinese national, Vassilli Ivanovich was alleged to have acted on the order of
Lieutenant General Veniamin V. Rychkov, a former confidant of the White
leader Kolchak and head of the railroad police in Harbin.[18]

Communist holidays were a particular source of conflict. Chinese authorities simply refused to allow October Revolution celebrations in Manzhouli in
1923. In response, organizers moved the gathering to Soviet territory. Upon
returning home to Manzhouli they were met by a Chinese police squad. Russian émigré policemen in Chinese uniforms checked their documents and
arrested several people.[19] On May Day of 1924, Soviet railroad workers assembled inside Manzhouli's railroad depot. Even though this time the Chinese
authorities had approved the meeting, Chinese and émigré Russian police
demanded an immediate cancellation of the rally. They arrested several railroad men and confiscated banners and Lenin portraits. That evening the police
dispersed union members and their families who had gathered for a few plays
in the Modern cinema in the evening.[20] Still, after the Soviet takeover of the
Chinese Eastern Railroad in 1924, Russian émigrés could no longer expect
Chinese aid to underwrite the sabotage of Soviet rallies in Manzhouli. In
July 1924 Chinese authorities approved a Soviet summer outing to nearby
Matsieevskaia. Union members, girls and boys of the Soviet political youth
organization Komsomol, and Chinese pupils played soccer and did gymnas-
tics in the lush green steppe lands.[21]

In the second half of the 1920s, when Bolsheviks had consolidated their
power in the Manchurian railroad zone, they could expect their celebrations
to proceed without any interference.[22] Indeed, its strategic position as border
station led the Comintern to see Manzhouli as the principal secret channel
between China, Mongolia, and the Soviet Union. In the eyes of some émigré
authors, Manzhouli had turned into a repository for communists with "plenty
of Soviet spies, Chekists, Red Army soldiers and communists." Diplomats,
railroad and customs employees, and barbershop owners kidnapped White
émigrés and deported from the railroad zone Soviet workers believed to have

turned their backs on communist beliefs. They also facilitated the infiltration of Bolshevik agents on missions to China, and supported Chinese communists on their way to Moscow.[23] Recalling the personal impressions of Zhang Guotao's illegal border crossing in fall 1921, we know that the founding member of the Chinese Communist Party was just one of many who were assisted across the border in subsequent years.[24]

Despite the increasingly confident presence of the Soviets, the Chinese takeover of the railroad zone changed Manzhouli's character. Though it still resembled a Russian provincial town in appearance with Russian-type single-story buildings, a small public park, a church, and Russian-horse cab drivers, it also had transformed into a Chinese administrative town, home to the assistant commissioner for international affairs of Hulunbeir, the Lubin district administration, and the District Court as well as various other branch offices of the Special District of the Three Eastern Provinces.[25]

The Soviets, following in the footsteps of the tsarist regime, checked the influence of the Chinese in town, but these efforts hardly amounted to expulsion. By 1929, 2,937 Soviet citizens resided in Manzhouli, including hundreds of railroad employees, Soviet consular and customs staff, and employees of Soviet trading companies.[26] Due to the increase in freight and passenger traffic it gained further importance as the major transit hub at the border between China and the Soviet Union.[27] The town was home to consulates representing the Soviet Union and Japan, as well as Soviet and Chinese customs. It was an important export center within Northeast China and accommodated several offices of Soviet trading institutions as well as Chinese and foreign trading companies. Manzhouli, despite political and ethnic frictions, retained its status as a quite international railroad town on the border between the Soviet Union and China.[28]

Under Soviet Rule: The Gradual Halt of Local Border Traffic

In terms of economic border control, the first Soviet decade marked both continuity and change. Liquor trafficking and drinking remained ineradicable throughout most of the 1920s. By then the sad fate of the drunken Cossacks on the Argun had become a cliché that was grounded in reality, structuring, for example, the plot for popular plays such as a three-act piece that was staged in Harbin's People's House (Narodnyi Dom) in the spring of 1922. Its simple story line criticized both racketeering in the region and the inhumane punishments meted out by the Bolsheviks.[29] Constituting more than one-third of all contraband, liquor remained the major smuggled commodity. Its proportional share declined only as the illicit trade of other items grew. Liquor trafficking remained a key concern of the state since its consumption not only endangered public health and safety, but its purchase was often made with gold. Thus the government looked to end a two-sided financial loss.[30] But only during the second half of the 1920s, when the Soviet state switched to a hard-line approach, did Chinese petty traders on the right bank of Argun gradually disappear. As economic structures of the frontier continued to be extricated from one other, contact zones between locals gradually diminished. Soviet residents of the Argun villages no longer enjoyed the option to go for a drink across the river without the fear of arrest.

With the consolidation of Soviet rule on the Argun, the share of Chinese subjects in the Soviet gold fields, on Soviet markets, and in other economic sectors began to fall and then declined considerably during the 1930s, when the vast majority of the Chinese were expelled from the Soviet Union.[31] At that point border controls were tightened and crossing became increasingly difficult. Especially since bottles were too heavy to be easily carried by smugglers, profits from everyday commodities such as liquor were too small to be worth the risks and uncertainties. This was different with gold, which continued to be trafficked across the border.

Even if gold trafficking prevailed it was no longer the ordinary gold miner, Cossack, or train passenger who was up to the task. Different smuggler networks emerged, along with new strategies of trade. Smuggling rings henceforth involved specific borderlanders who used their multilingual and multicultural competences strategically. A key group, therefore, was the Chinese who had established roots in the Russian East. Many had spent years shoulder to shoulder with Russians many had even converted to Orthodoxy and married Russian women. Long-standing social and economic bonds to Russian inhabitants, discussed in detail later in this chapter, enabled them to create complex contraband networks that were well suited to the remaining loopholes of border supervision.

Many issues between Soviet and Chinese customs officials resembled the well-known problems of the period before World War I.[32] On the Chinese side the Maritime Customs limited its supervision by and large to the import, export, and transit of goods as well as passenger controls at the two major ports of entry on the Chinese Eastern Railroad (Manzhouli and Suifenhe) and at the mouth of the Songhua River, but they did not surveil the entire border.[33] To the Bolsheviks, however, the porous borders of the Russian Empire were unsatisfactory. A socialist economy required control of all goods and people and could not tolerate unregulated trade or capital flight. This principal change in policy fundamentally altered social relations and economic networks across the border.

Despite the Bolsheviks' gradual reintroduction of customs controls, the 1920s became the heyday of contrabanding. A report of the Dal'revkom, the Far Eastern Revolutionary Committee, estimated the value of contraband assets in 1924 at the borders of the Soviet Union's Far East at about one-third those of its European borders. The population in the European territories, however, was ninety times the population of the Soviet Far East. In 1923 the still-lax surveillance body of the state detained 1 percent of the population on the grounds of illicit border trade. It is therefore hardly surprising that in October of the same year the Far Eastern Customs District Commission noticed a "colossal increase of smuggling in the Far East that threatens in scale the foreign economic policy of Soviet Russia." Liquor, tobacco, tea, sugar, household goods, and clothing—the products with the highest tariff and tax rates—accounted for the majority of the illegally obtained foreign commodities.[34] To condemn the Russian, Chinese, and autochthonous people as smugglers would nevertheless be wrong by the jurisdictional standards of tsarist times. "Very few cases were reported in which the rural population of the border zone participated in the resale of trafficked goods on the black markets in the cities. Professional smugglers conducted the entire smuggling for the urban consumer, who, omitting the Chinese shopkeepers on the Argun, purchased large quantities of merchandise in the Chinese commercial centers."[35]

Three key reasons may be identified for the surge of illicit barter across the state border during the early Soviet years: First, the Bolshevik notion of contrabanding was fundamentally different from the cognate concepts during tsarist times. As early as 1918 the Bolsheviks had adopted a state monopoly on foreign trade. Its main objective was to gain full control over imports and exports. Prior to 1917 independent merchants in Russia, particularly in its Far Eastern realms, had largely run a trade deficit with China.[36] Some historians claim that by the mid-1920s the trade balance had transformed into a surplus due to the state clampdown on personal and informal trade at the border.[37] From that point onward trade with China was carried out only by state-licensed bodies—a situation ironically somewhat similar to the state-authorized Sino-Russian caravan trade during first half of the eighteenth century.

The second reason was the deficiency of the socialist planning economy. Continual shortages in the state-regulated consumer market, a poor sales network in the countryside, high prices on Soviet goods, and exorbitant tariffs on Chinese commodities worsened the supply situation of the local Soviet population on the international border. Unlike their countrymen in the interior, however, border residents still had a chance to overcome those shortcomings. For decades they had been accustomed to shopping on the Chinese bank. No one seemed willing to change this custom. Even Soviet men in uniform held on to this practice, which is why the civilian population soon returned to understanding local border trade as a "legal thing."[38] The new legislation and the deficiencies of the state-controlled consumer structure turned all local residents into smugglers in practice.

A third factor fueling the surge of smuggling was the restructuring of the border surveillance after the Soviet secret police agency had taken charge of border control in 1922.[39] This policy change also reflects the amplification of surveillance tasks. Border monitoring was no longer confined to the fiscal control and repression of illicit trade but henceforth emphasized passport control and the regulation of movement. With this reform the importance of the customs service declined. In 1924 many customs lookouts were liquidated in the Soviet Far East, eleven in the Chita customs district alone. At the remaining posts staff numbers were reduced.[40] Simultaneously the state injected more manpower into military surveillance. Five border brigades were formed in Transbaikalia. Among them was the ninth cavalry border brigade with headquarters in Dauriia. Surveilling of about six hundred kilometers of border, this brigade included four border commando offices, ten guard posts, and one border checkpoint at Matsievskaia.[41] Yet the strength of the Soviet border troops in the Far East, at about 2,282 men, remained extremely low. Each of the commando offices (with twenty-five to thirty men) and guard posts (ten men) along the entire Soviet Far East land border monitored a section stretching seventy-three kilometers on average. Low morale, a scarcity of horses, poor equipment, dependency on local peasants for their lodging, and a lack of discipline further decimated efficiency. Some Russians peered anxiously across the border: "Not only does the Chinese army outnumber our troops many times . . . , but British-controlled Chinese Maritime Customs shows no interest in cracking down on smuggling."[42]

Under such adverse conditions effective control was impossible. The porous border still allowed for widespread contrabanding sheltered from the eyes of the agents of the state. Members of the Anti-Smuggling Commission of the Far Eastern region, aware of these problems, tried to convince the government in Moscow to take pragmatic measures. In 1923 they proposed, among other things, a relaxation of state licenses on foreign trade, a higher allocation of everyday commodities to the border, the legalization of local border trade, and a drastic reduction of taxes on alcohol. Their demands, however, were largely ignored.[43]

Smuggling began to decline appreciably only during the second half of the 1920s, and in particular after the Soviet Union abandoned the New Economic Policy in 1928, which had tolerated commercial activity by private individuals to some degree.[44] Smugglers no longer had access to shops, fairs, or other easy places to sell their goods. Several other factors also contributed to this downtrend. In general during those years the Soviet policy toward trafficking gradually switched from a soft to a hard-line approach. In April 1926, to cleanse the border strip of contrabandists, the Central Executive Committee allowed the internal political-security apparatus to enact extrajudicial measures in the Soviet Far East. The state authorities sentenced the offenders to executions, camp imprisonment, and exile. In September 1927 Moscow decided to expel repeat contraband offenders from a fifty-kilometer section of the border zone. And due to the massive scale of smuggling the secret police in turn empowered provincial and district committees to enforce the deportations.

Cleansing campaigns and the severe punishments of members of professional contrabandist networks resulted in more than just the decline of smuggling. According to the plenipotentiary of the secret police in the Soviet Far East, by 1928 these extreme measures had also changed the nature and patterns of trafficking: "Whereas in the past individuals or small groups smuggled predominantly consumer goods, we currently observe exactly the opposite. Well-organized gangs now carry out the smuggling. . . . The transfer of contraband across the border is now being done largely by . . . Chinese, because they are . . . less vulnerable to our punishments and, often, when they are detected and detained they simply lose the goods they carry."[45] Members of such gangs were recruited among poorer migrant workers. Often employed by merchants as couriers, they earned much of their livelihood from smuggling.

From the late 1920s onward collectivization of nomadic herders and settled peasants, crackdowns on so-called anti-Soviet elements in the border regions, and the introduction of a border zone regime entailing large-scale extradictions further reduced the possibilities for contrabanding. In fact those deportations proved to be one of the most ruthless and formidable legal tools in the Soviet border control arsenal. Under Joseph Stalin trafficking became a severely sanctioned political crime. Smugglers were denounced as enemies of the social and moral order, and the word "contrabandist" could be mentioned in the same breath as the word "traitor." In many of those cases, however, accusations of smuggling were only convenient excuses for arrest. We will see in the next chapter that many of those detained and accused of smuggling had in fact never crossed the border, much less engaged in illicit trade.

Yet perhaps the most significant cause for the dramatic drop in the smuggling activity was the consequences of military confrontations on the border with Manchuria.[46] The Sino-Soviet conflict over the control of the Chinese Eastern Railroad in 1929 and the Japanese occupation of Manchuria from 1931 onward, discussed in the next chapter, triggered a hysterical war scare in the Soviet Union's eastern borderlands and led to a military buildup along the border of the Japanese puppet state of Manchukuo in China's Northeast. International machinations, not just state policies directed against contrabandists, resulted in the successful suppression of smuggling.[47]

It took more than three decades to establish such an effective customs supervision on the state border and thus to disentangle the informal Sino-Russian economies in the Argun basin. Implementing their own methods, the Bolsheviks continued what the tsarist government had begun. Some new cross-border networks did emerge after 1917, especially those geared toward illicit border trade, since the unregulated passage of commodities peaked during the early Soviet period. In the 1930s, however, due to internal reforms and military confrontations with external enemies, Moscow finally succeeded in breaking traditional and recently emerged economic cross-border ties.

The Strange Careers of Smugglers: Arkadii A. Ianechek and Xin Fanbin

The previous pages have focused on customs control mechanisms, patterns of transborder traffic, and the illicit passage of commodities. But the historical study of contraband trade is of interest not only in what it tells us about the loss of official revenues, gains to informal economies, and means of state surveillance. Smuggling networks and the biographies of traffickers also allow us to explore interethnic contact and the informed cultural choices of certain individuals in border regions. Smuggling thus provides a rare glimpse into the contexts and careers of smugglers and their enemies. They illustrate how the zones of contact bringing together borderlanders of different ethnic and national background evolved and disappeared again. The following pages, then, explore contrabanding across the Sino-Russian border on an intimate scale.

A diachronic comparison of different smuggler cases reflects the gradual shrinking of possibilities of encounter between autochthonous, Russian, and Chinese people on the Argun. Initially, in fact, trafficking was hardly anything out of the ordinary. Until well into the 1920s just about every border resident—be he a farmer, a vagrant, or a tax collector—could be a secret dealer. To many people buying goods across the border was still daily routine because import prohibitions had long applied only to certain commodities and the border could still be passed freely. For those goods that had been deemed illegal early on, however, it was common even before World War I for professional smuggling parties to supply the population further inland.[48]

By 1930, with zones of contact between Soviet and Chinese borderlanders contracting, no longer might the ordinary train passenger, Buriat herder, Russian Cossack, or Chinese gold mine worker, engage in the bootlegging of gold, liquor, or currency. In the enterprise of border transgression new strategies of contraband trade had evolved, and only more sophisticated smuggling networks prevailed. The transfer of commodities now mostly relied upon an equal share of Chinese as well as Russian and Buriat borderlanders who commanded multiple identities and often the ability to speak more than one language.[49] This moment lasted several years, until increasingly muscular military and political controls of the border and the border regions destroyed what was left of contact zones between native, Russian, and Chinese locals. Even the advanced networks of skilled contrabandists had by that time been dissolved. Secret transfer was then carried out only by people with special privileges granted by the state, as will be explained later.

To understand trafficking patterns around 1930, the case of a certain Soviet-Chinese smuggling ring is illuminating and should be taken not as an isolated instance in the archive but rather the norm. Its central figure was the forty-six-year-old Arkadii A. Ianechek from Borzia, less than two hours by train from the border on the Transbaikal branch railroad line. Secret police investigators raided Ianechek's house on 17 June 1931. Neither Ianechek nor his wife or their children were at home. Instead the officers encountered four Chinese men at the kitchen table.

During their search of the house inspectors found various silver and gold articles, dresses, suits, several meters of white silk, woolen pullovers, towels, and plenty of tea. According to Ianechek all of these treasures had been purchased legally and the clothes and fabric had all been used before. The inspectors accused Ianechek of illicitly importing foreign fabrics and tea from Manzhouli, destined for Russian consumers. It was also alleged that he would purchase gold and silver items in the Soviet Union to sell illegally abroad.[50]

Two Borzia citizens, the Chinese worker Wan Lichen and the cleaning lady Marfa E. Burtsova, acted as prosecution witnesses. Ms. Burtsova had recently observed how "some Chinese" took clothes stored at Ianechek's house in Borzia to transport them farther north to the Belukha mine, where they exchanged the fabrics for gold and silver. According to Burtsova the business went on for a year. Wan, married to a Russian, supported Burtsova in his statement. He added further allegations, claiming that Ianechek himself frequently sold contraband manufacture to people in the Borzia region. He was said to receive the imported fabrics from Chinese traffickers, who on their return smuggled the gold and silver they received from Ianechek.[51]

Arkadii A. Ianechek had many Chinese friends because he was no ordinary Soviet citizen. Born in 1885 in the Volynsk governorate (today's northwestern Ukraine), he had worked from 1907 to 1928 with the Russian and Soviet customs at different places and in various positions. His longest post was at the customs office in Manzhouli, where he had served for nine years as executive secretary. This was plenty of time to make friends with Chinese residents in town, as Ianechek admitted: "Of the Manzhouli merchants who were at my house I only know Xin Fanbin. The others I had not seen before nor do I have any contacts with them. I met [Mr. Xin] first when I lived in Manzhouli, as I always did business with him." Once interrogated, Xin, a native of Shandong province, also confessed to having close ties with Ianechek and recalled that they had done business since 1922.

After Ianechek left Manzhouli for Borzia in July 1928, his ties to Xin Fanbin did not languish. Between then and 1930 Xin Fanbin traveled to Moscow, Ekaterinoslavl, Kamenets-Podol'sk, and other cities in the Soviet Union, where he sold various articles on the streets. When asked by the Soviet officers what he and the three other Chinese men did in Ianechek's house in Borzia, Mr. Xin replied, in fluent Russian, that they were on their way to western China to seek work. They intended to reach Xinjiang via the Soviet Union. Since the men were traveling on a shoestring budget, they decided to buy tickets only to Borzia first, and to stop there for a flying visit to Arkadii A. Ianechek.[52]

The file reveals close contacts between the Chinese and Russians, where cultural barriers and national feelings recede. One could almost forget that in 1929 China and the Soviet Union were at war—with Manzhouli as the main battlefield. The social fabric of the sleepy railroad town of Borzia, about 110 kilometers off the border with China, reveals that around 1930 the border had by no means been hermetically sealed. Numerous Chinese nationals like Wan Lichen and the Chinese gold diggers in the nearby Belukha mine still lived and worked in the Soviet border region.

As other indigenous, Chinese, and Russian people of the frontier, Xin Fanbin and Arkadii A. Ianechek had both moved outside of prescribed cultural space. Ianechek had worked for almost a decade as a customs officer in Manzhouli. His job as a duties inspector exposed him to Chinese people every day, bestowing upon him a strategic competence that he could summon for the benefit of his illicit business. Xin Fanbin's ties with Russian culture were similarly close: for several years he had traveled the Soviet Union to trade on black markets. He spoke Russian well and was acquainted with Russian culture, embodying the widespread integration of Chinese migrants into Russian and later Soviet society.

What differentiates these smugglers, however, is the fact that Arkadii A. Ianechek, even after nine years in a multicultural city on Chinese soil, most likely had not learned to speak Chinese beyond a basic pidgin vocabulary. Already Owen Lattimore, in his time a leading scholar of Inner Asia, had pointed out this remarkable difference between Russians and Chinese. Successful Russians usually would not learn to speak Chinese nor intermarry with or live like the Chinese, while successful Chinese locals were more likely to learn Russian, marry a Russian, or "go Russian" altogether.[53] Like Ianechek, not all of the people participating in these networks had a migrant past. Still, because of continuing contact with the Chinese, he seems to have acquired a certain understanding of the Chinese mentality and got along well with Chinese people. Both had overlapping ways of life and—despite Ianechek's language gap—both had a profound knowledge of the "other" culture that enabled them, when needed, to make informed choices between cultural options, even as their frontier culture was increasingly undercut by state discipline and territoriality.

Throughout the 1930s contact zones between Russians, indigenous, and Chinese people grew smaller, and with them shrank opportunities for forbidden trade on the Soviet-Manchukuo border. Even for locals with cosmopolitan biographies, the covert transfer of commodities became increasingly difficult. Illicit activities were now mainly reserved for privileged elites. Certain professional credentials, such as those held by diplomats, became a precondition for bootlegging.

In the 1930s, the Russian exile press in Harbin occasionally leveled light-hearted accusations that Soviet diplomats were in the habit of trafficking Manchurian gramophone records and flower seeds at the Soviet-Manchukuo border.[54] In fact, émigré newspapers were entirely correct in pointing to a final set of border loopholes and their beneficiaries. It was during the Manchukuo years, when people like Xin Fanbin and Arkadii A. Ianechek could no longer keep in touch, that Manzhouli Soviet consular officials began to benefit from the growing trade links between Germany and Manchukuo.[55]

By 1941, Lidiia V. Zimina, wife of the Soviet Consul in Manzhouli, had become the key figure in those illicit transfers. At the consulate she worked in the passport office. There, according to the investigation files, by falsifying receipts and embezzling transit revenues from German companies, which had to pay transit fees on imports of peanuts and other goods from Manchukuo to the Soviet consulate, she enriched herself by more than nine thousand rubles, in addition to raking the agents of those companies. Her husband Mikhail veiled her activities. When internal inspectors began to check the bills more closely, he simply dissolved the inspection commission.

Outside of the consulate the diplomat couple had lived in the lap of luxury. Both had purchased all kinds of goods from local dealers in Manzhouli on credit. Only when the newspaper *Kharbinskoe Vremia* (Harbin Times) reported that a new Soviet consul was posted to Manzhouli did it dawn on these shopkeepers that the Zimins had departed for good, without paying their debts. The boldness of the Zimin family may have been exceptional. However, as Soviet consular officials in Manzhouli they enjoyed diplomatic immunity, shared contact with the locals, and could pass through the now-otherwise sealed boundary. The illicit activities of the Zimins thus had nothing in common with the ordinary smugglers of earlier times or with networks of skilled smugglers composed by the likes of Arkadii A. Ianechek and Xin Fan-bin. The Zimins were simply diplomats and their contraband was neither gold nor liquor.[56]

Even that brand of illicit activity was nearly quashed after the German attack against the Soviet Union in the summer of 1941, when the border became almost impassable even for diplomats. After the victory over Japan in 1945, however, the secret trade returned to the trains between China and the Soviet Union. But compared to its earlier scale, contrabandism of the postwar period is barely worth mentioning.

Taibog Nimaev's Eternal Flight: The Emigration of the Aga Steppe Buriats

While Chinese subjects had been deeply involved in smuggling on the Soviet-Chinese border for decades, the edge of Chinese peasant colonization was, as late as the end of the 1920s, hundreds of kilometers away from Hulunbeir. Although by 1927 Han Chinese accounted for almost a quarter of the region's population (17,177 of 72,021), they came as traders, contrabandists, or marmot trappers to the steppes and settled predominantly in the railroad towns of Manzhouli (8,735) and Hailar (4,810). Farther north only a slowly growing number of Chinese gold seekers—no more than a few hundred—worked at infrequent intervals beside the Argun River and its tributaries.[57] The agricultural development of Hulunbeir was confined almost exclusively to the arable land along the railroad and to small parts of Trekhreche, where Russian Cossacks tilled the fields. Hulunbeir, beyond the railroad concession, was still the domain of nomadic herdsmen.[58] In contrast to other former Mongol bannerlands in China's Northeast, where "the Russians, by driving the Chinese Eastern Railroad across North Manchuria in 1898, had been responsible for subjecting a rich belt of Mongol territory to Chinese colonization," railroads had not yet given Han colonization a similarly aggressive character in Hulunbeir.[59]

During the 1920s many people in Hulunbeir and other Mongol lands still belonging to Republican China retained aspirations for greater independence. Leaders echoed the rallying cries emanating from that region in the newly created Mongolian People's Republic. Though the Bolsheviks maintained the fiction that Outer Mongolia, after its foundation in 1924, was an independent state, it had in fact become the first communist satellite of the Soviet Union. Accordingly, the Mongols' ultimate goal, soon abandoned, of regaining Inner Mongolia and Hulunbeir, and thereby uniting a pan-Mongolian state, must be interpreted within this new political framework.[60]

In contrast to independence efforts during the late Qing years, when indigenous leaders sought aid from Saint Petersburg, the movement for self-determination in Hulunbeir of the 1920s was thus strongly influenced by ideological ties to Moscow. The Hulunbeir Mongols planned their revolt fully expecting to receive Moscow's secret assistance. Precisely because of its presumption of ideological contiguousness, the anti-Chinese rebellion of August and September 1928 was doomed to fail when Moscow ultimately refused to support its Daur leaders Gobol Merse (Guo Daofu) and Buyangerel (Fu Mingtai).[61] It would be the last flickering of an autochthonous resistance in Hulunbeir to gain even a modicum of support from the Soviet Union, to be understood by the latter as a blow against Chinese rule. In the assessment of Owen Lattimore by the late 1920s the "more or less unreal and romantic nationalism" of Inner Mongolia was in decline: "The question is no longer one of degrees of autonomy or nominal independence within rival Russian, Japanese and Chinese spheres of influence. On the economic side there is only the question of the presence or absence of colonial exploitation; on the political side, the degree of social revolution or counterrevolution."[62] Developments in Inner and Outer Mongolia over the ensuing decades support Lattimore's view. Following the Japanese occupation of the eastern and central parts of Inner Mongolia in the early and mid-1930s, the majority of the Mongol population fell under Japanese rule. That moment saw a movement for self-determination and unification blossom again for a few years under the leadership of Prince Demchugdongrub (De Wang) whose first moves were independent of the Japanese but soon supported by Tokyo, as the Japanese reckoned that Mongol nationalism could act as a counterweight to any possible Han Chinese domination. Japan also created a Mongol Xingan province within its satellite state of Manchukuo, which would become an enclave granted considerable autonomy. As the next chapter will illustrate, self-rule came at the cost, however, of the absorption of Mongol ambitions into the objectives of the Japanese empire.[63]

While the Mongolian territories of Republican China still retained a significant degree of independence due to China's weakness during the 1920s, Moscow had begun to control its Transbaikal periphery more assertively. Soviet nationalities policy was still based on concepts of order that had been developed in late imperial Russia, which held the ultimate goal of transforming the imperial autocracy into a national empire. In their effort to bring clarity to an unsettled environment, however, the Bolsheviks sought more radical answers than had their predecessors. Bolshevism, in this sense, was a new, more assertive form of imperialism. The national self-determination of ethnic minorities via the policy of *korenizatsiia* as well as the "sovereignty" of the Union's republics and autonomous regions were tactically useful fictions deployed by the state during the 1920s, but actual policy soon forbade any such movements. Stalin neutralized ethnic minorities by the forced transfer of entire populations or by liquidation. These violent policies deeply altered the social fabric of the lands on the Argun, eliminating the last pockets of resistance and laying the groundwork for a homogenous Soviet borderland. In such an alienated place there was no longer room for traditional economic and kinship networks that did not stop at state borders or strayed outside of formally demarcated sites.[64]

The Russian Civil War had brought matters to a boiling point, forcing many nomads of the Aga Steppe to flee the Russian frontier areas. As early as 1917 a Buriat banner had been founded in the Shenekhen area of Hulunbeir by a verbal agreement with the local government. The Khori Buriats, however, made use of this privilege only when the war reached the frontier, and thus when the Soviet agents began to see the Transbaikal borders as permanent sites for the defense of the Revolution. Between 1920 and 1923 more than seven hundred families fled with their yurts and livestock from the Aga Steppe to Shenekhen, a region of roughly three hundred square kilometers a day's ride southeast of the city of Hailar. The consequences of the flight were deeply felt in Hulunbeir's pastoral sector. The Buriats drove about forty-five thousand sheep and goats, fifteen thousand horned livestock, and twelve thousand horses across the border into Shenekhen.

Over the years they alienated themselves from their old homeland. Whereas during the early 1930s the majority of the adults still spoke Russian and could read and write Cyrillic letters, these skills were not passed on to the youth. And while good pasture land and a favorable climate created sustainable living conditions, heavy duties imposed by the Chinese local government marred the life of the Buriat diaspora. Chinese officials were said to have seized up to sixty-six hundred horses. As a result some families moved onward to Khalkha, founding their own banner in the Mongolian People's Republic. But their places were quickly taken by a new wave of Khori Buriat refugees from the Aga Steppe who arrived in Shenekhen during the turmoil of collectivization in the Soviet Union and the Sino-Soviet conflict of 1929.[65]

Indeed, in their quest for new land and secure grazing grounds many of the herders crossed the borders between the Soviet Union, China, and Mongolia several times before they reached their final grazing lands. In many cases the odyssey lasted for a decade, enjoining many trips across borders and then back. By that time, however, these transgressions had become dangerous. During the Russian Civil War soldiers and partisans lurking behind steppe hills represented the greatest risk, sometimes robbing and killing for personal gain. On one occasion in 1921 soldiers of the People's Revolutionary Army of the Far Eastern Republic held at gunpoint many Buriats returning from Mongolia

FIGURE 4.1. A Buriat family in Hulunbeir, early 1930s. The Russian Civil War and Soviet collectivization forced thousands of nomads to seek refuge in the Chinese frontier areas.

to the Aga Steppe. These unfortunates were robbed of their cattle, clothes, furs, money, and other belongings. Some were murdered. Many of those who survived fled to the nearby Tsugal'sk monastery. Indeed, the violence had taken on such proportions that the Ministry of Domestic Affairs of the Far Eastern Republic appointed a commission of inquiry in 1921.[66]

Danger lurked not only among the Bolsheviks. As late as October 1921 scattered Ungern-Sternberg troops, wending their way in from Manzhouli, advanced deep into Russian and Mongolian territories to steal cattle. The remnants of the White forces raided the Aga Steppe, stole more than nine hundred horses, and drove many Buriats across the border toward Manzhouli. Three days later, when the original owners arrived at the Chinese railroad town, many of their horses had already been loaded onto Harbin-bound trains. Meanwhile, Red partisans advancing from Outer Mongolia had looted the Aga Steppe in their absence. Horse theft, prevalent among Russians in general, was one of the most common violent and often lethal crimes within the region.[67]

Raids were also regular occurrences in the steppes of Dauriia following the defeat of the White armies and continued through the end of the 1920s. In September and October 1927 alone the authorities registered fifteen robberies in Borzia district, many carried out during daylight, totaling a loss of about five hundred horses in addition to other possessions. Often stolen animals were sold across the border. Buriats continued to be those most commonly victimized. Sometimes horses disappeared before the eyes of officials, as happened once at the residence of the secret police commandant's office in Kulusutai. The Soviet border guards and *militsia* were hopelessly undermanned, having only four officers stationed in the entire district at the time and thus in a weak position to respond.[68]

Keeping in mind that such perils confronted the postrevolutionary frontier helps us to understand the choices of Aga Steppe Buriats such as Aiuzh Zhamsaranov, Taibog Nimaev, and Munko Parshinov. For about ten years these herders roamed together, covering hundreds of kilometers as they circumvented the various risks posed by revolutionary times. When the Bolsheviks reached Transbaikalia in 1920, Nimaev, Zhamsaranov, Parshinov, and many other Khori Buriats retreated from the Aga Steppe to the land around the Khalka River in Outer Mongolia, where they remained until 1923. When late in that year the government in Ulaanbaatar (the former Urga) began to cooperate with Soviet authorities and so started collecting taxes from the Buriats, many returned to their native Aga Steppe, illegally crossing the border some fifty kilometers southwest of Borzia.[69] Dissatisfied with conditions in their now Soviet quarters however, and reluctant to give up their own local identities, some herders agitated for an ultimate migration to Hulunbeir. Nimaev and others negotiated a confidential agreement with the Chinese border guards to secure their secret passage across the border. On a December night in 1924 hundreds of Buriats crossed the border about fifteen kilometers south of the Dauriia station. As agreed they compensated the local Hulunbeir border officials with one sheep per yurt; some gave more. In 1925, however, when the authorities in Hulunbeir began to demand taxes from the herdsmen, they fled to the Soviet Union yet another time.

When forced consolidation of individual herder households into collective farms during collectivization and dekulakization began, many Buriats prepared for their final escape. By January 1929 Taibog Nimaev grazed his livestock some thirty kilometers from the international border on Soviet territory. Again a bargain with Chinese authorities and Russian emigrants had been made ahead of time. The great flight began on the night of 10 February 1929. The ice on the Argun trembled from the force of galloping horses, camels, sheep, and goats when three hundred families crossed the river near Abaigaitui with their entire livestock holdings, consisting of over a hundred thousand animals. Only when border guards' reinforcements arrived to help the still understaffed patrol were some herdsmen forced to stop at the river. At that point both sides suffered casualties. According to estimates by the Dauriia

border guards only about twenty thousand animals could be legally maintained in the country. Many of the herdsmen who had been stopped by the
Soviet guards, however, took advantage of the chaos and disappeared into the
night on the Soviet side. The border guards arrested only forty-three Buriats
and confiscated their livestock; among those arrested was Taibog Nimaev. The
families were convicted and given penalties of between 4,093 and 12,157 rubles,
depending on the number of animals they had attempted to shepherd. None
of the wealthy herdsmen, as they were now being labeled, were able to pay the
fines, however, and so in 1930 their herds were "sold" to the state.[70] The amount
of people and animals made this instance of collective flight exceptional but
not unique. Especially during collectivization the Khori Buriats of the Aga
Steppe made numerous other attempts, if on a smaller scale, to cross the Soviet
state border as a means of saving their cattle and thereby their livelihood.[71]

Khori Buriats were not the only locals who drove their cattle beyond the
limits of the Soviet state. Although a minority, the pastoral border crossers also
included Russian Cossacks and a few Chinese people.[72] Konstantin A. Ziablikov (born in 1876), from the village of Kulusutai in Borzia region, worried
about his cattle as well. In 1918 the former Cossack escaped alongside the
Whites to Mongolia. He returned in 1919 to Transbaikalia, only to be forced to
flee again, this time ahead of the advance of the Red Army in September 1920.
Upon his second return in 1921 he left his cattle in Outer Mongolia, where he
believed it would be safer from confiscation by the Red Army. Soon, however,
Mongolia was no longer a safe haven for nomads and Cossacks. In early 1929
Ziablikov hired the Mongolian herdsman Tsuku Kukunov to bring his livestock back to Kulusutai on Soviet territory. Ziablikov attempted to sell the
animals secretly, bit by bit. Soon, however, the local authorities learned about
his pursuit and his livestock was seized and later handed over to the local collective farm. Desperately, Ziablikov stole thirty horses and fourteen horned
cattle from the collective farm and tried to bolt to China. But on 7 February 1930 the old man was tracked down by a detachment of the Dauriia border
guard cavalry and arrested.[73]

By 1930 border guards and loyal executors of Moscow's directives for collectivization had come to represent a greater risk to the life of the herdsmen
than partisan looters. When escaping, Soviet soldiers sometimes chased Cossacks and Buriat herders across the border into Chinese territory firing
machine guns at them.[74] The emigration stirred by the Civil War and collectivization had caused Moscow to question the allegiance of the people on the
Argun. In a haze of paranoia the Bolsheviks created a new institutional and
legal framework for the Soviet border region, as we will see in the next chapter.
By then the steppe nomads had become quite conscious of where the state
boundaries ran and knew all too well the consequences they might face when

crossing them. What united them in taking the risk was a desperate desire to save their customary way of life.

Red Yurts on the Steppe: Collectivizing Rural Borderlanders

One key development giving the Soviets a higher degree of control over the borderlanders on the Soviet side was the process of collectivization itself. Between 1929 and 1933 it transformed traditional agriculture in the Soviet Union into large units known as collective farms (*kolkhoz*), thereby destroying the economic power of the supposedly wealthy farmer or mobile herdsman (*kulak*) and bringing about the mental and physical submission of the peasantry. In many parts of the country collectivization resulted in deportations, famines, and trauma, claiming millions of lives in the process.[75]

For the Soviet borderlands, collectivization was envisioned as a campaign that would reclaim contested and vulnerable areas from suspect people. Until 1930, most nomads and Cossacks in the Argun borderlands still lived largely isolated from national markets, within a subsistence economy of their own making. But within several years' time, Transbaikalia became the most successfully collectivized area east of Lake Baikal. Despite severe opposition from peasants and nomads along the border with China and elsewhere, by 1934 a total of 1,145 collective farms existed in the province.[76]

How rural frontiersmen became Soviet farmers or cross-border refugees can be divined by a look at the fate of nomads in the vicinity of Kulusutai, the very village from which Konstantin A. Ziablikov had fled. Founded in 1728 as a Cossack post some forty kilometers west of Borzia, close to the Mongolian border, Kulusutai became the residence of the *natsional'nyi somon* Novaia Zaria ("New Dawn").[77] It was established in 1925 after a large number of former Aga Steppe Buriats like Taibog Nimaev had returned from Outer Mongolia to Soviet land. Aside from twenty-seven Cossack villages, Novaia Zaria was the sole Buriat settlement in the entire Borzia district.[78] In February 1929 a total of 384 yurts and 1,503 people were listed in the registers of Novaia Zaria. The families were divided into 91 yurts belonging to rich peasants (*kulaki* and *zazhitochnye*), 49 yurts occupied by middling peasants (*sredniaki*), and 48 yurts held by poor peasants (*bedniaki*). The remaining 196 yurts were exempted from agricultural tax since the nomads were grazing their cattle within a range of three hundred kilometers from the somon's residence and therefore could not be included in the local government's peasant classification.

Since the mobile lifestyle of nomads was not compatible with the policy objectives at the time, a crucial step toward collectivization was the permanent settlement of the Buriats. Attempts to allocate land for the project were made as early as 1925 but did not come to fruition. Efforts to put in place a public school system were equally disastrous. An initial plan to open a school, in 1929, was canceled because few Buriats were willing to enroll their children in school. The lack of qualified indigenous teachers and the population's rejection of Russian teachers unfamiliar with Buriat-Mongolian script contributed to the apparent impossibility of the project. Additionally, permanent residence was a mandatory requirement for regular education, and naturally one strongly opposed by the Buriats.[79] The challenges encountered by the Bolsheviks thus resembled the problems that the Chinese officials had encountered two decades earlier, when they tried to force the Hulunbeir nomads to pitch their felt yurts at a defined location near a school and thereby fueled vitriolic opposition to their rule.

Although collectivization was in full swing in late summer 1929, the old social structures were still functional. The lamas and more affluent nomads had successfully agitated among the poorer nomads toward the end of latching onto old customs, despite the encroachment of the new state-imposed structures. Even the so-called poor and middling nomads asked with frustration how the transition to a Soviet society would work, if farmland, forest, bread, and other basic foodstuffs and agricultural machinery were not to be made available. Much more was at stake than a mobile lifestyle in the grasslands.[80] In Novaia Zaria, the kulak nomads and their families who did not flee early enough had been dispossessed of their livestock. The Buriat kulak Dair Batuev and his wife lost their sixteen horses, twenty-seven cattle, 335 sheep and goats, and eleven camels. In some cases Cossack farmers fared even worse than the nomads. The seven-member family of kulak Mikhail I. Kuznetsov of Abagaitui was threatened with eviction from their land when they owned as few as five horses, forty cattle, and 190 sheep and goats. Many Cossacks in the Argun villages saw no other way but to flog off their livestock at knock-down prices to the Chinese.[81] Animal husbandry and agriculture severely suffered from the consequences, and soon there was no privately owned livestock left in Abagaitui.[82]

Collectivization, as the examples of Novaia Zaria and Abaigaitui have shown, was another name for forced resettlement, expulsion, and denomadization of potentially disloyal people on the disappearing frontier. The population on the Soviet bank of the Argun declined dramatically during those years. Abagaitui, for instance, lost one-third of its residents between 1912 and 1935.[83] Moscow had succeeded in taming the nomads and Cossacks, to a degree. Those whom its officials considered suspect elements had escaped or been resettled by force, and the people of the steppes had ceased to cross the border in one or the other direction. Thus, incomplete as it was in the 1930s collectivization was a crucial element in establishing the center's control over the periphery and thus over the state borders.

Despite the pressure of sinicization the autochthonous people of Hulunbeir retained elements of almost all of their culture until the defeat of the Japanese in August 1945. In Hulunbeir collectivization commenced with the expropriation of the landowners and the establishment of people's communes in the early years of communist China as we will see in chapter 6. The borders to the Soviet Union and the Mongolian People's Republic, however, were firmly closed by then and played no role at all in these struggles. Emigration had ceased to be an option.

Pastoral Life in Emigration: The Russian Diaspora in Trekhreche

Similar to the nomadic Mongols and their cross-border livestock pastoralism the Cossacks on the Argun had a history of agriculture on both banks of the border river. Since the *fin de siècle* the fertile land in the valleys of Trekhreche had attracted members of the Transbaikal Cossack Host from the Russian bank of the Argun. Hulunbeir's accession to independence in 1912, discussed in the previous chapter, offered the Russians an opportunity to negotiate more favorable conditions for cross-border agriculture. At that point the weakness of the indigenous Hailar government controlling Hulunbeir between 1912 and 1915, its dependence on Russia, and its looser notion of land rights enabled Russian frontiersmen to hold certain rights for the first time. By 1914, the Mongolian-controlled Hulunbeir government had agreed to give Russian citizens the right to lease land for crop farming and horticulture, at the insistence of the Russian vice-consulate in Hailar. The agreement granted Russian subjects the right to rent plots for up to twelve years, a period the Russian authorities considered to be sufficient for capital investment without risk of immediate loss. Contrary to former agreements, Russians were now also permitted to erect permanent buildings on the leased estates. In addition, the region where Russians were allowed to lease land was larger than ever before and included some of the most suitable areas for cultivation in Hulunbeir. North of Starotsurukhaitui it stretched up to fifty kilometers from the Argun inland; it also included both banks of the Hailar River and finally the territories next to the Chinese Eastern Railroad.[84]

Hulunbeir's self-rule proved brief, but its conclusion did not dissolve Russian rural settlements on the Chinese bank. Cossack leasing of pastures and arable land on the Chinese bank continued even after the Chinese had regained full control over Hulunbeir in 1920. In the mid-1920s hundreds of Soviet

FIGURE 4.2. A party of farmers with horse wagons crossing the Argun by ferry
on 3 June 1929. In winter locals would use sledges to cross the frozen river. Due to the
Sino-Soviet conflict and the militarization of the border, such passages became increasingly
dangerous if not impossible just weeks after this picture was taken.

subjects still farmed on plots across the Argun River. The surrounding disputes were similar to those that had arisen prior to the Russian and Chinese revolutions. The Cossacks paid little or no rent. In response the Chinese authorities seized their cattle and grain and sometimes arrested the defaulting tenants. Agencies of the Soviet state, for their part, quarreled over what would be appropriate policies. District authorities were aware of the land shortage and advocated old practices of cross-border land use. But the security apparatus favored a nationally uniform policy of restrictive border controls, passage only at designated checkpoints, and increasingly stringent requirements for hunting, farming, and fishing permits on the Chinese bank, all toward the end of enforcing economic and political controls over the border. In fact, in the end it was not the Chinese state but an increasingly strict Soviet border control regime that restricted the practice of cross-boundary Cossack agriculture.[85]

Yet Moscow did not succeed in stopping the old practices. The Russian Revolution, the Civil War, and the collectivization of the Soviet countryside indirectly supplied the Chinese shore of the Argun with new frontiersmen from Transbaikalia. The new rural immigrants, many of whom had crossed only the Argun and settled within sight of their old homes, continued to live as farmers and hunters on land already known to them for generations. In contrast to the nomadic diasporas formed within the Sino-Soviet border region and the exodus of Russians to Harbin, then, the migrations of the Russian Cossacks remained local. Unlike before they did not return after the harvest to their native villages on the Russian bank. These people were now political refugees and could not go back to Soviet Russia on pain of death. The Cossacks in particular became enemies of the state since so many of them had supported the White Russian Ataman Semenov. The Argun no longer connected both shores but divided them, and the Trekhreche delta was transformed into a rural Cossack diaspora in China. And it is an irony of history that the Trekhreche district, where the Chinese had first burned down the Russian wooden cabins and primitive earth houses, proved the most attractive for the Cossack refugees.

Cossacks' emigration across the Argun can be divided into four phases. The first wave of refugees came during and immediately after World War I and were not immigrants in a conventional sense. Some were among those who had held pastures on the Chinese bank for generations, where they made their hay in winter but now no longer returned to their native Cossack villages on the Russian bank. A second wave of emigrants, mainly richer Cossacks from Eastern Transbaikalia, fled during the Civil War era. In hopes of being able to beat a quick retreat to their native country, many initially lived in transitory earth huts. The so-called "people of the 1930s" (*tridtsatniki*) represented the third and numerically largest emigrant wave. Those emigrants were Russian Cossacks and peasants who fled during the collectivization, fearing the decossackization practices of the Soviet regime. Around the same time a smaller number of unemployed former Chinese Eastern Railroad personnel from Harbin and other settlements in the railroad zone moved into the region. The rural Russian diaspora grew from 2,130 in 1927 to 5,519 in 1933 and to about 11,000—or more than 80 percent of the population of Trekhreche—in 1945.[86]

Due to its central location and connection with Hailar via dirt road, Dragotsenka became the principal village in the region. Its population grew sharply during the Manchukuo era, from four hundred fifty predominantly Russian inhabitants in 1933 to about three thousand people in 1944, half of them Russians, along with one thousand Chinese and five hundred Japanese residents. By the 1930s Churin & Co., Hayashi Kane, and other trading houses had opened branch offices. The village also boasted an electricity plant, a refinery for vegetable oils, a dairy plant, saddlers, tanneries, leather manufacturers, car workshops, a post and a telegraph office, and a bank.[87] Its amenities made Dragotsenka rather an exception among the twenty-one Cossack villages in the region. Tranquil and with larch wood blockhouses framing wide streets— almost identical to those of traditional settlements on the Transbaikal bank of Argun—the villages seemed to have fallen out of time. Similarities ran beyond architecture: the Trekhreche Russians also retained their prerevolutionary

FIGURE 4.3. A Russian teacher in the Trekhreche village Dubovoi in July 1932. The child's
father is Chinese. Mixed marriages, usually between Chinese migrant workers and local
Cossack women, were common in the Argun borderland.

faith and morals and wore traditional Transbaikal Cossack dress, and the Orthodox Church still played a pivotal role in people's lives.[88]

To visitors the village denizens gave a sense that they had been transplanted
to China and had thus managed to preserve their translocal identities and a
rural Russian lifestyle that had ceased to exist in the Soviet borderland after
collectivization. When a Soviet scientist visited the region in the late 1940s he
wrote of a feeling of having traveled backward through time: "Life here is not
very different from that in the remote Transbaikal villages of the Russian Empire. On Soviet visitors, the region registers the impression, almost, of a
museum."[89]

This impression was, however, largely a fabrication, a manufactured idyll
representing a bygone era on both shores of the Argun. Even as early as the
1920s, when China had regained complete control over Hulunbeir, Russian
settlers faced an expanding set of constraints. At that point, the Manchurian
warlord government appointed Han Chinese officials to administer the region.
For the first time Russian settlers had to register with Chinese authorities.
Russian subjects in Trekhreche were included within the Chinese passport
system to undermine any extraterritorial reach into Chinese territory. The

burden of taxation rose steadily as well. The horse tax, for instance, almost quadrupled from 1921 to 1929. The Russian émigrés were now subject to a partial Chinese judiciary—or, at least, this was how they perceived the Chinese courts, whenever a case between a Russian and a Chinese was heard. Religious freedom was increasingly restricted. The Chinese authorities prohibited, among other practices, observance of Orthodox holidays. Policy measures extended even to key representatives such as Harbin's Archbishop Mefodii, who was arrested during a visit to Trekhreche. Overall, Russians believed that rationale behind those policies was to drive them out of Trekhreche, back to the Soviet shore of the border river.[90]

Staying put in defiance of such policies, however, meant a life of isolation for the emigrants, with long periods apart from their families across the Argun. In addition, caught between the crossfire when the Soviet Union clashed with the Manchurian warlord regime and Manchukuo, the civilian borderlanders of Trekhreche, some of them having fought with Semenov, would soon find themselves stigmatized as bandits, spies, and enemies of the Soviet people.

––––––––

When the Bolsheviks had strengthened their hold over Transbaikalia by the late 1920s, the possibilities of contact between Russian and Chinese subjects on the Argun frontier began to shrink. The permeable border was much more unsatisfactory to the Soviet than to the tsarist government because a planned economy based on autarky could not tolerate informal trade. The control of economic and commercial affairs was, however, just one way of laying claim to the borderland. The Bolsheviks sought to create a different form of state that required a different form of border society. Their project demanded loyal people in a coherent nation-state, united on the march toward communism. Nomads and Cossacks engaging in husbandry in the borderlands were indifferent to Marxist theory and modern notions of borders and posed a potential threat to the Soviet ideology and economy. Although the process of taming indigenous borderlanders had been set in motion before 1917, the Soviet state imposed control over religious affairs and lifestyles more decisively and comprehensively than had the tsarist regime.

As a consequence, many of the Argun Cossacks and Transbaikal Buriats were forced into emigration. After the Russian Revolution many Cossacks took up permanent residence in an area long familiar to them on the Chinese bank. There they erected their new homes exactly in the same spot in which the Chinese state had previously banned them from harvesting fodder for winter. Now, however, it was the Bolshevik regime that prevented them from returning to their native villages in the Soviet borderland. Their small rural diaspora offered powerful evidence that the border had become an undeniable reality for local people as much as for state bureaucrats. The Argun Cossacks retained—as did nomadic borderlanders—local identities resistant to the top-down processes of nation building. They were adamant in preserving ethnic and cultural pride and thereby claimed quasi-national allegiances to the by-gone Russian Empire. Just like their nomadic peers the Cossacks thus faced a double bind: social stigmatization in their own countries and demonization as bandits or enemies from the neighboring state.

The militarist Zhang Zuolin remained in power until Japanese officers as-sassinated him in 1928.[91] Manchuria came under full Japanese control three years later. After two decades of relative prosperity, during which Northeast China had flourished economically, the region again served the purposes of an imperial military. This time it was the Japanese army that used the region as a staging ground upon which to prepare for the war in East Asia and the Pacific. As we will see in the next chapter, these developments had a profound influence on the political landscape of the Argun basin and the everyday lives of every single one of its inhabitants.

5

An Open Steppe under Lock and Key

ON 6 SEPTEMBER 1931 a special correspondent from *Zaria* (Dawn) visited Manzhouli. *Zaria*, then still an independent, moderately liberal, anti-Soviet emigrant paper in the cosmopolitan city of Harbin, devoted one page to his article. Less than two weeks before the Japanese would begin to occupy China's Northeast, he told his readers about the rather sudden change in the Soviet border regime:

> Some people from the city go through the fields toward the border. They walk calmly, since it is still about one and a half versta to the border and no one seems in sight. Suddenly . . . three-four Red Army soldiers on horseback appear and rush straight to the people. They have to hurry to get away, because the Soviet border guards have "a very poor knowledge" of where exactly the boundary is located and with particular fervor they are trying to catch anyone in this manner at the border. . . . Previously, until relatively recently, the border guards did not show much effort in tracking down people on the border. Though they knew exactly where the boundary was located, they often allowed people from both sides to cross the border freely. Now the guards begin to show eagerness, apparently because they have received new orders. . . . Therefore the people of Manzhouli advise others not to walk too close to the border anymore and generally recommend hiding from the Soviet patrols, if they come into view.

For the border population of Manzhouli the aggressive action of the Soviet guards, determined to keep people away from the border space itself, was a radical change. The opposite side of the border, with Railroad Siding 86 just minutes away by train, slowly began to disappear from the everyday lives of the borderlanders. It was the beginning of a long process of alienation of the people in the wide grassy steppe. "No villages, no farms are in the Soviet border strip and no one but Soviet border guards are allowed to be there," continued the *Zaria* correspondent. "There are only bare hills and empty fields. It is difficult to see in this area or even hear any birds. A sense of eeriness appears if one takes a long look at this deserted Soviet area."[1] The silence of the birds heralded a new era.

During the late 1920s and throughout the 1930s routine interactions across the Soviet-Manchurian border were practically nonexistent due to animosities between the regimes on both sides. Political disputes, warfare, nationalism, ideological friction, cultural dissimilarity, and ethnic rivalry fueled this alienation. Face-to-face contact and international trade became increasingly difficult and in many cases even forbidden. Continuous tension left the Argun borderland both economically underdeveloped and sparsely populated. The border gradually became a social fact. With contacts across the border cut off, old networks adopted the contours of the border and emerging networks simply assumed its total acceptance. As such, as this chapter will demonstrate, the border reemerged in the Soviet Union in the late 1920s with new ideological weight and new legitimacy as both sacred and inviolable.

With the Japanese occupation of Manchuria in 1931, a new player entered the scene. Strictly speaking, the fourteen subsequent years of Japanese rule might be regarded as an interlude in the borderlands' development since, in a political sense, the Soviet Union did not encounter China at its borders. This rupture notwithstanding, that decade and a half might also be regarded as extending or perhaps even accelerating the process of border formation and the alteration of the borderland because many of the changes inscribed by the Japanese remained after their defeat in 1945.

The history of the Japanese puppet state of Manchukuo (1932–1945) was not a repetition of seemingly similar developments of the imperial expansion of Russia or the West but something that Prasenjit Duara called "new imperialism."[2] During the period of High Stalinism that coincided with the Manchukuo years, the Soviet Union itself was a country under siege as it underwent immense changes, which redounded to the borderlands. After the tragic completion of collectivization Stalin intensified his regime of terror and violence, mapping out ethnic cleansing and other terrorizing policies in the Soviet borderlands.[3]

What the Soviet and the Japanese-Manchukuo governments had in common was their broad reach of rule. The two no longer relatively weak imperial metropoles encountered each other on the Argun. Both regimes were now able to increase their power at the periphery considerably, and each found new ways to impose its will on the borderlands. To understand why the region went through such a rapid and radical change one must consider the internal and external factors that triggered the change. On the one hand the key internal element driving this transformation was an intensification of the political control imposed by both regimes on their respective populations in the borderlands and beyond. The establishment of border zones, propaganda warfare, and ethnic as well as political cleansing campaigns were among the crucial internal factors that altered the character of the region. The critical external element that ultimately transformed the once open frontier into a tightly controlled borderland, however, was the threat of war between Japan and the Soviet Union, which led to troop reinforcements, military clashes, and intensified espionage work.

Understanding this military dimension is critical to comprehending the history of this particular borderland during the 1930s. Military history, in its crude material sense, is a subdiscipline that until recently had little to do with social or cultural history. However, although tanks and soldiers seem to have fallen out of academic fashion, they have to be kept in mind as factors within studies of the physical landscape. More than any newly passed regulation or propaganda slogan, the armored vehicle shattered informal cross-border networks. Therefore, this chapter shifts the perspective away from borderlanders' lives to policies imposed by the metropoles.

The Sino-Soviet Conflict: A War at the Border

Toward the end of the 1920s, tensions arose between the Soviet Union and Zhang Zuolin's warlord regime in Northeast China (as well as the nationalist government in Nanjing) over the control of the Chinese Eastern Railroad. Ostensibly a dispute about the railroad, the crisis was in fact the outcome of a complex mix of political, social, and economic disharmonies. On 27 May 1929 the Manchurian authorities raided the Soviet consulate general in Harbin and arrested eighty Soviet nationals, including the general manager of the Chinese Eastern Railroad, Aleksandr I. Emshanov. On 13 July, after China had taken full control of the railroad, Moscow sent an ultimatum to the Chinese nationalist government, demanding they return the railroad to Soviet control within three days. Both sides moved troops to the border. Only a few weeks later the Soviet Union formed the Special Far Eastern Army,[4] amassing about a hundred thousand men in the region, to face off against some sixty thousand Chinese soldiers. In the ensuing war for the control of the Chinese Eastern Railroad, Vasilii K. Bliukher, commander of the Special Far Eastern Army, defeated the Chinese warlord forces. The ratification of the Khabarovsk Protocol in December 1929 settled the conflict and restored the status quo ante.[5]

Throughout these maneuvers in the summer and fall of 1929 the atmosphere remained tense in Harbin and in the border towns. Local Chinese authorities in Manzhouli harassed Soviet diplomats, and Chinese soldiers intimidated local Soviet citizens. Once the Soviet ultimatum to return the control over the railroad had expired in mid-July 1929, Soviet companies and

FIGURE 5.1. Manzhouli passenger station building, early twentieth century, with bilingual Russian-Chinese signs and travelers from all over the world.

institutions began to close their branch offices in Manchuria. By 22 July more than three thousand Soviet nationals had left Northeast China via Manzhouli, followed by Transbaikal railroad workers who left the border town at the end of the month. Local Chinese authorities prepared lists of emigrants to fill vacant positions on the railroad. They were instructed to put all remaining Soviet citizens under house arrest and, at the first possible opportunity, to deport them to the hinterland.[6]

Because of its strategic railroad station Manzhouli was at the center of the Red Army campaign against the troops of the northeastern government of the "Young Marshal" Zhang Xueliang. Aside from some minor incidents the Red Army offensive proper began on 16 August 1929. Several thousand Soviet soldiers attacked fortified Chinese positions in the vicinity of the Zhalainuoer mining region southeast of Manzhouli. In a second strike Soviet troops shelled Manzhouli with artillery and dispatched infantry and armored trains. In October artillery again pummeled the city several times and aircraft dropped bombs.[7]

Comrade Bliukher explained why the Soviets did not occupy the border region right away but instead allowed the conflict to drag on for five months: "It was not war and not peace, but a 'conflict.' . . . If the outside world would have learned about our preparation for the operation, the howl of the imperialist powers and their intervention would have had obstructed our plans in many ways, and perhaps would have disrupted the Manchurian operation. . . . For none of our operations did we give the assurance that they would not at the last moment be canceled for foreign policy reasons."[8] A new attack wave followed on 17 November 1929. Two days later, after suffering heavy losses, the general of Manzhouli's Chinese garrison declared his willingness to surrender unconditionally. Without even waiting for a peace envoy Soviet troops occupied the border town.

In Manzhouli they discovered that the Chinese had looted all the shops and many private apartments and that many soldiers were trying to disguise themselves as civilians. Immediately after the occupation the Soviet military command disarmed about eight thousand Chinese soldiers and imposed a curfew. The Soviets then proceeded to carry out a political cleansing of the border town. With lists of names in hand, the political police of the Soviet Union GPU arrested numerous Russian and Chinese residents, though almost all citizens of either nationality were soon released.[9] However, some two hundred fifty more or less well-off Russian emigrants and former officers of the White Army were interrogated and isolated. Together with the Chinese prisoners of war, they were deported to camps in the Soviet Union and subjected to intense political agitation.[10] Soviet forces then took Hailar and chased the retreating Chinese troops eastward. In complete disarray, the Chinese soldiers finally withdrew to Qiqihar. Only forty-eight hours after the Soviets had launched the attack warlord Zhang Xueliang declared himself willing to negotiate.[11]

In terms of economic and material damage the war had a particularly devastating impact on the western terminus of the Chinese Eastern Railroad. As early as the 20 August 1929 the *New York Times* depicted Manzhouli as a "dead town": "The streets are deserted, most of the homes are empty and stand with windows and doors nailed tight. No saddle horses or farmers' teams are tied to the hitching posts along the main thoroughfares; the great shipping pens built for Manchurian and Mongolian horses and cattle are empty. Even the railroad yards are practically empty, for since Russo-Chinese relations were broken off three weeks ago the Transsiberian trains have not been run over this route."[12] Soon after the first attacks Manzhouli residents had crowded the Harbin bound trains. Many shopkeepers and merchants had closed their businesses and left the border town. The staff of the Chinese Maritime Customs had decamped as well. Consequently supplies fell to catastrophic levels. Manzhouli's population is said to have dropped from 12,954 in early 1929 to about 3,000 residents in the summer of 1931.[13]

The conflict on the international border fueled hostilities among civilian residents. Yet anti-Chinese attitudes were nothing new to the people of

Transbaikalia: Moscow had long attempted to manipulate their political views and emotions. As early as the mid-1920s, the Bolsheviks nourished Sinophobic sentiments among the Soviet borderlanders. After Zhang Zuolin ordered his army to arrest the Chinese Eastern Railroad general manager Aleksei N. Ivanov in January 1926, an anti-Chinese lecture series was staged in the Soviet Argun villages. Yet just about 10 percent of the war-weary population were said to be hostile toward China.[14]

The ferocious attacks of 1929, which had deeply affected the lives of the civilians, undoubtedly sharpened the dividing lines between "them" and "us," between "the Soviets" and "the Chinese." For people who had pointed guns at each other, smuggling could never again be simply normal business. In a grander political sense, too, the Sino-Soviet conflict had somewhat united the otherwise divided Soviet borderland community once again. At the beginning of collectivization in 1929, all three classes of the peasantry—kulak, sredniak, and bedniak—were said to have supported the Soviet position against China.[15] The poor peasants allegedly assisted in protecting the border by organizing self-defense units. Some even participated in the battles. Sometimes the border guards also supported the population. When floods struck the Argun between 1927 and 1929, the *pogranichniki* saved lives and property.[16] Even the Khori Buriats of Novaia Zaria somon and other nomads, more often than not indifferent to imperial rivalries, were said to have stood firm with the Soviet position in the conflict over the Chinese Eastern Railroad.[17]

Additionally, the self-perception of Red Army soldiers had changed. In 1929 they had proven themselves, protecting the borders and their civilian populations for the first time. The Sino-Soviet conflict thus boosted the pride of the Soviet men in uniform. "Showing them our strength, we made the Chinese generals talk to us" was the conviction held by the staff of the Border Guards and soldiers of the Red Army with regard to the operations near Manzhouli. To the Soviet men in uniform it had been a complete victory and as such strengthened their confidence in the power and capability of the Red Army.[18]

The "Trekhreche Tragedy": Soviet Punitive Expeditions in the Chinese Borderlands

Although Manzhouli was the center of military conflict, a glance at Trekhreche, a rural region on the Chinese bank of the upper Argun, shows the same conflict in a different light. Until the late 1920s widely dispersed White units occasionally attacked Soviet border guards and operated on Soviet territory to steal horses and stir up the peasants against the Bolsheviks.[19] The armed conflict over the railroad thus offered Moscow a pretext to finally eradicate these units and to carry out genocidal policies against the Cossacks who had moved to that region.[20] A severe flood in summer 1929 inundated numerous villages in Trekhreche and on the Argun riverbanks. Though high water claimed several lives and left many farmers homeless, the disaster was a blessing in disguise. It cut off the connections between Hailar and the Soviet border and averted a Soviet attack as well.[21] Only in early August, when small Red Army squads shelled and invaded the border villages on the Chinese shore of the Argun without warning, did people in Trekhreche learn about the conflict over the Chinese Eastern Railroad.[22]

Punitive raids on the river villages continued until fall. On 28 September 1929 about 150 Red Army soldiers crossed the Argun and cordoned off the village of Damasovo. According to eyewitnesses Soviet troopers went from house to house, throwing grenades everywhere they suspected people to be hiding. Soon the entire village was in flames. Only four houses remained unharmed, and twenty-three men out of one hundred fifty total inhabitants were killed. Nine Chinese border guards stationed nearby tried to protect the villagers but soon became victims of superior force themselves. Five of the guards were killed; the others were able to escape. The Soviet soldiers acted with extreme brutality against the civilian population. Efim Ia. Volotkin, an eyewitness, reported, "The Reds did not only beat men but also women and children. The latter were driven into the river and, if they wanted to come back, they were hit with rods and sticks, or even shot. Infants were seized by their hands and feet and thrown into the water." Death lists of Argunsk and other raided settlements reveal a similarly gruesome picture. The victims' bullet wounds suggest killings by execution.[23] Archpriest Vladimir I. Izvol'skii of Manzhouli district church of the Orthodox Diocese of Beijing was shocked when he examined the bodies of priest Modest V. Gorbunov and eight other Russians from Verkh-Kulei, all of whom had been killed by the Soviets.[24]

The Trekhreche Russians were de facto unprotected from Soviet assaults. A small force of Chinese soldiers, the majority stationed at a garrison in Labudalin, south of the Trekhreche delta, guarded the border and villages in that area. No later than August 1929 Russian émigré representatives tried to persuade the Chinese authorities to establish a self-defense structure not only for Trekhreche but for Manzhouli and Hailar as well. The Chinese military initially sanctioned the formation of paramilitary units, with the stipulation that weapons were to be handed out only in case of war. The proposal, however, ultimately failed. The Russian emigrants could not dispel the doubts of the Chinese about their loyalty.[25] Without approval from the Chinese authorities the emigrant farmers had set up a small informal force to defend themselves.[26]

As the tide receded the Soviet troops pushed deeper into the interior. Tynykha, a village far away from the border river, was the site of perhaps their most brutal punitive raid. If one believes eyewitness accounts published in the Harbin émigré press, its strategy was particularly horrific. On 30 September a Soviet detachment of about two hundred soldiers crossed the Argun into China. In the evening several soldiers went into the village Tsenkir-Bulak, where, dressed in civilian clothes, they pretended to be refugees and inquired about villages where emigrants from the Soviet Union had recently settled. One resident agreed to accompany them to Tynykha. As they reached the village in the early morning hours of 1 October, only farmers milking their cattle were awake. The Soviet soldiers killed their guide and entered the village, burning all the houses and the hay, which had been prepared as winter feed. The whole population was taken to a nearby hill where the Soviet soldiers separated the men and boys over twelve years of age. "From a distance of only five or six steps they fired machine guns. All 76 people fell in a heap. The Red executioners, not trusting the machine guns, began to turn over the bodies, stabbing them with bayonets and finishing them with their revolvers." On their retreat, the Soviet soldiers raided Tsenkir-Bulak and another village, killing twenty-seven more people.[27] Two days after withdrawing to the Soviet bank, the Soviet unit again emerged to assault two villages on the Argun, allegedly killing over a hundred twenty people.[28] Harbin's Russian émigré papers soon estimated the total body count to be a thousand people, although these numbers seem highly exaggerated.[29]

Harbin's Archbishop Mefodii announced 13 October to be a Day of Mourning.[30] Church services in memory of the victims continued over the next days in Harbin. On 15 October émigrés tried to gather in front of the German consulate in Harbin but were soon dispersed by police.[31] While the Soviet press was silent about skirmishes, the massacre at Tynykha sparked outrage and widespread condemnation among the émigré Russian, Chinese, and international communities of China's Northeast.[32] Through the global network of Russian emigrant communities, the "tragedy of Trekhreche Cossacks" gained international attention as well. In Shanghai, for example, the Russian Ladies Relief Committee, together with local Cossack organizations, scheduled a benefit concert for the victims. Shanghai's Russian community also sent U.S. president Herbert Hoover a telegram informing him of the "inhuman massacre of innocent people" and urging the president to pressure Moscow to end the "bloody nightmare of red executioners."[33] These were the international echoes of a soon-forgotten tragedy.

The brief return of Chinese rule over the Russian émigrés meant no return to normalcy for the Cossacks on the Gan, Khaul, and Derbul rivers. The settlement of the Sino-Soviet conflict, with the signing the Khabarovsk Protocol on 22 December 1929, not only restored the status quo ante on the Chinese Eastern Railroad but also bound the Chinese authorities to disarm the émigré Russian forces, expel their instigators, and suppress emigrant organizations. The warlord government in Mukden at least gave the impression that it pursued a crackdown on the White Russians in Harbin, Trekhreche, and other Russian settlements in Manchuria. Among the nine emigrant leaders who the Soviet Union had demanded surrender was Ivan A. Peshkov, the famous leader of a small White guerrilla force in Hulunbeir. Instead of arresting him and other leading figures, who, according to a German diplomat, "with an energetic will on the Chinese side" probably could have been captured by the authorities, the Chinese arrested pawns and nonentities, whom they labeled "partisans." A Chinese court in Hailar, for example, sentenced seven young peasant lads from Trekhreche, between sixteen and twenty-four years of age, to death.[34] By putting such people to death the government in Mukden attempted to assign blame for the conflict on defenseless scapegoats.

Throughout the confrontation floods, lootings, and an animal epidemic caused additional suffering among the local population. It deepened after the Chinese resumed their rule over Trekhreche in March 1930. Armed gangs continued to roam the area and terrorize the population.[35] In a letter from July 1930 locals complained to the American Committee for the Aid to the People of Trekhreche about violence committed by Chinese soldiers against "us the European people of the white race" in various villages and hamlets. Besides committing these assaults Chinese military authorities are said to have demanded food staples such as flour and other levies from the civilian populations. Moreover, despite a strict ban Chinese soldiers allegedly engaged in opium cultivation in areas populated by Russians. Cossack farm animals who stomped on these fields were beaten to death in sight of residents. Freedom of movement for the Russian émigrés was restricted too. The Cossacks were not only denied to leave Trekhreche but also not even allowed to move from one village to another.[36] The Slavic people who were once at the forefront of Russian colonization on the Argun now came under attack from all sides.

The year of 1929 thus marked a watershed in the lives of the borderlanders—not only for the people on the Argun.[37] Moscow's planners had anticipated in vain that these purges in the shadow of the Sino-Soviet conflict of 1929 could be waged silently, in hopes of avoiding international attention. The mass executions in Trekhreche permanently alienated the Russian emigrants from their old homeland. For decades, if not centuries, the Argun had connected the lives of traders and cross-border agriculturists. But now, living at the very edge of their native country, the Argun became a line of separation to the women and men of the Trekhreche region. For the people living far away from the border, the extensive, anxious press coverage in the Soviet Union, China, and across the globe made the border region appear dangerous.[38]

The media coverage and public commemoration of the Sino-Soviet conflict had a lasting impact on borderlanders in the Soviet Union and China alike. To commemorate the fallen Soviet soldiers, Dauriia was renamed the Soldiers' OKDVA on 6 August 1930—the first anniversary of the Special Far Eastern Army's founding. Both a monument to the fallen soldiers and a war cemetery were built at this major army garrison. To promote patriotism it was ordered that all passenger trains—including express trains—stop at that station.[39] Dauriia was not the only settlement that was renamed. Due to its highly symbolic and strategic position at the border, Railroad Siding 86 was named Otpor (repulse).[40] By the early 1930, popularized by a marching song commemorating the battles of 1929, the word was on everybody's lips. With lyrics by Bolshevik worker poet Aleksandr N. Pomorskii (Linovskii), its refrain ended with the line "Fight back!" (*Daesh' otpor!*)[41]

Even before the Japanese occupation of the Chinese Northeast, then, the borderland had undergone dramatic changes. The Sino-Soviet conflict of 1929 changed the region in three important ways. First, with the establishment of the Special Far Eastern Army in August 1929, it paved the way for the militarization of the borderlands. Second, it furnished a welcome pretext for Moscow to purge the White émigré communities that still mingled with borderlanders on the Soviet Argun bank. Third, the brutal fighting accelerated the breakup of formerly intense transcultural cross-boundary networks and battered the still-dynamic borderland economy. Manzhouli's deterioration from a vibrant border town into a gloomy backwater epitomized this decline. Within months the conflict had paved the way for a transformation that would gain momentum and unfold fully in the 1930s.

New Neighbors in the Steppe: The Japanese Occupation of Manchuria

Just days after the Manchurian Incident of 18 September 1931, when Japanese troops used the pretext of an explosion on the Japanese-controlled railroad near Mukden to occupy China's Northeast and start a fourteen-year war between China and Japan, Moscow began to reinforce its troops in the Soviet Far East. Cavalry and motorized units were moved from Dauriia to Abagaitui on the border to reinforce patrols and to protect the Chinese Eastern Railroad in the case of a Japanese attempt to seize control of it.[42]

Tumultuous months preceded the ultimate seizure of Manzhouli by the Japanese Army in December 1932. Railroad employees loyal to Moscow had left Manzhouli and other stations of the Chinese Eastern Railroad's western line and sought shelter in the Soviet Union already in early 1932.[43] Chinese soldiers mutinied in March 1932 in the border city. To protect Japanese civilians from their assaults, the Japanese community requested military assistance from the Japanese consul in Harbin. It took five days to restore civil order. Customs officers raised the flag of Manchukuo over the customs office at Manzhouli as Manchukuo border guards assumed their duties on 27 April 1932.[44]

During the conflict between the Chinese and Japanese troops Moscow acted cautiously, choosing a path of mediation and troop noncommitment to avoid a clash with the Japanese, whose armed forces were soon within striking distance of the Soviet borders. Moscow was placed in a difficult position when the Chinese army commander, Lieutenant General Su Bingwen, staged a mutiny, seizing hundreds of Japanese civilians and isolated military personnel as hostages. On 27 September 1932 the Chinese insurgents shelled the Japanese consulate in Manzhouli and assaulted Japanese residents in the border town. The customs office remained closed, and about two hundred fleeing Japanese nationals sought refuge in the Japanese consulate as they prepared for an evacuation by train through Soviet territory via Chita and Vladivostok.[45] From late September to early December 1932 about thirty thousand Japanese and Manchukuo soldiers and some forty-five hundred Mongol cavalrymen directed a fierce campaign at the Chinese troops. His back against the wall, Lieutenant General Su finally agreed to negotiate with the Japanese. Su discussed terms with the Japanese negotiators indirectly through Manzhouli's Soviet consul. The Chinese general took the Japanese community hostage, releasing them only gradually.[46]

These negotiations failed in late November.[47] Fleeing from the advancing Japanese and Mongol troops, more than four thousand men of Su's remaining forces and other Chinese elements entered Soviet territory on 4 and 5 December, some by foot and others on several captured trains. Once on Soviet soil they were disarmed and detained at Otpor and Dauriia.[48] The immediate danger of a military confrontation between Japanese and Soviet forces as a result of turmoil at the border had been averted.

In an emotional address to his followers delivered from an improvised stage in the internment camp, Lieutenant General Su called for discipline and cooperation with the Soviet authorities. He praised the good treatment extended by their hosts and then appealed to the patriotism of his followers: "In the Soviet Union a colossal program is under way to modernize the country. All those who want to work and learn in the Soviet Union shall remain here. . . . Those who stay here are, however, reminded that our main task is the future of the Chinese Republic and the salvation of the Chinese people."[49] For the Soviets, however, the Chinese soldiers were of little use, and Moscow deported them as soon as possible.[50] The drama at the border met its end even more expeditiously. On 6 December Japanese airplane pilots dropped handbills on Manzhouli. Troops entered the town and restored order. A few days later a newly formed police force and border guard began to patrol the city and the border. By mid-December 1932 the still Soviet-controlled Chinese Eastern Railroad had resumed its Manzhouli-Harbin train connection and international train services.[51]

In the short term Japan's seizure of the Chinese Northeast once again stirred flight, violence, and unrest at the border. In the long term, however, stable institutions replaced the weak blend of warlord, Republican, and semi-colonial infrastructure that had so often frustrated Moscow's attempts to install a rigid regime along the border during the 1920s. This new regime would, in turn, accelerate the evolution of a segregated borderland.

Two Very Different Stops at the Border: Manzhouli and Otpor

The Japanese occupation of China's northeastern territories forced the Soviets to move almost their entire border and passenger control facilities—still located within the right-of-way strip in Manzhouli—onto Soviet soil. In late 1931 Soviet authorities hastily ordered the relocation of the Soviet luggage and passport control temporarily to Matsieevskaia and later to Otpor. Essentially, they pulled out the railroad staff of nearly five hundred as well as all equipment belonging to the Transbaikal Railroad Administration. Though many Russians remained in town, Manzhouli slowly began to shed its distinctive administrative character—that of a dual city with (Soviet) "Transbaikal" and "Chinese" sides.[52] The abrupt Soviet withdrawal from Manzhouli anticipated the sale of the Chinese Eastern Railroad in 1935 to Japan.[53] Most of its thousands of Soviet employees and their families in Harbin, Manzhouli, and other settlements along the tracks were forced to return to the Soviet Union. Ambitious Soviet plans to relocate at least the freight handling infrastructure from Manzhouli to Otpor to ensure economic profits from transit traffic and the regional economy generated on Soviet territory did not materialize.[54] The sale thus meant, ultimately, that Manzhouli retained its position as transit hub on the Soviet-Manchukuo border and that Moscow had lost its economic benefits in this last major foothold in Manchukuo.

If one believes contemporary travelogues, however, the establishment of Japanese administrative control over Manzhouli did not instantaneously transform Manzhouli into something other than a multicultural border town. The border-crossing experience of Western train passengers passing the border

FIGURE 5.2. Street scene in Manzhouli, June 1935. Although electrification had existed since the early twentieth century, horse carts were still the most common means of transportation.

does not quite correspond to what might be our intuitive landscape, featuring strict and highly symbolic borders. Comingling of cultures and revisions to imperial power made necessary by local realities, visible if one looked past the thin surface of national symbols, were still quite evident to many travelers of the 1930s, like the British adventurer Peter Fleming, who arrived on Manchukuo soil in 1933:

> The flag of a brand new kingdom, the flag of Manchukuo, flew above the station buildings. It was yellow, with a pleasant agglomeration of stripes in one corner. But the flag was the only outward sign of change. True, there was a little Japanese official who took the German consul and myself off to a remote part of the village, and there, when we had filled up forms the size of sagas, issued us with the new Manchukuo visas. . . . But even this bureaucratic interlude had its typically Chinese side. We travelled to the passport office in a tiny decrepit droshky, pulled by a mouse-like pony. Crowded though it already was, we were saddled with a supercargo in the shape of an enormous coolie. He did nothing at all except slightly retard our progress, but his presence was clearly part of a recognized routine and when it was all over he demanded a tip. He described himself as a "visaporter."[55]

Like Fleming, the German China hand Ernst Cordes began his jaunt through Manchukuo in 1935 at Manzhouli. For him, as for Fleming, entering the "New State" Manchukuo at Manzhouli was anything but ceremonious. The border settlement did not yet appear as the symbolic stage of a new nation. To get his passport endorsed Cordes, like Fleming, had to get off the train. It was the multicultural atmosphere of Chinese, White Russian, Soviet, and Japanese residents that most fascinated the Beijing-born son of a German diplomat during his brief stopover in Manzhouli.[56] While waiting for his travel documents Cordes sat next to a group of Japanese officers in the station restaurant. The room was decorated with overgrown palms, cactuses, and giant ferns. A large oven radiated oppressive heat. European classical music sounded from a gramophone: a waltz by Strauss, followed by an oratorio by Bach. The uniformed Japanese ordered lemon tea, ham, and eggs. Though the waiter was Russian, their order was in Chinese. The colonizers had become colonized, Cordes realized. After lunch he obtained his travel documents in a henhouse, where the visa office was temporarily set up. The Manchukuo authorities evidently still put little emphasis on representation.[57]

In the late 1930s, however, things had changed. Manzhouli had become a heavily secured border town. Transit passengers were no longer allowed to leave the station, guards being posted at all exits to observe the foreign travelers.[58] Communication with the Soviet Union was now highly restricted. Zones of contact between Soviet and Manchukuo subjects nevertheless endured, as Soviet consular staff and railroad employees attending to passenger and freight transfers stayed behind.[59] Yet it was no longer fun to be there, as it may have had been for the German traveler Cordes. To an American journalist who crossed the international border in 1938, Manzhouli was a place where foreigners were not welcome any longer: "Perhaps it's the world's largest city without a bona fide hotel for the very simple reason that visitors are not allowed to stay in the city, unless they can provide a specific reason. . . . During the entire search [of the train], the passengers may neither enter the platform nor leave the Soviet sector of the station building. . . . With a world in times of peace this border town has nothing in common."[60]

Compared to Manzhouli, the Otpor border station, twenty minutes away by the slowly moving train, was tiny and literally at the end of the world. Mikhail I. Sladkovskii, the famous Soviet economist and scholar of Russian and Soviet economic relations with China who worked as head of the Soviet border guard's Special Purpose Service in Otpor from 1932 to 1933, shared with his wife the modest comfort of a four-seat coupe in a Pullman car that was parked on a siding and served as temporary accommodations for the border guards. Besides such railroad cars Otpor consisted only of a station house, one dozen residential and administrative buildings, barracks for the railroad workers, the garrison *bania*, a tall watchtower, and the border arch, where locomotives passing under sounded the horn.[61] According to the 1939 census just seventy-five residents lived in Otpor.[62] Throughout the Manchukuo period the customs post boasted fewer than ten employees because there was so little to control as cargo trade and passenger traffic had greatly declined.[63] The apparent insignificance of this very last *forpost* on Soviet soil does not, however, reveal its very real strategic importance, which it would take on in the years to come.

Barbed-Wire Fences: The Militarization of the Border

Though Otpor had been named for the Soviet resistance to China in 1929, its epithet fit especially well during the ensuing Soviet-Japanese confrontation. The old rivalry over supremacy in Northeast Asia had long caused trouble between Japan and Russia or the Soviet Union. For decades tension and enmity had simmered between these two powers. In particular the debacle of the Russo-Japanese War (1904–1905) and the Siberian Intervention during the Civil War (1918–1922) raised these specters in Moscow. As the Soviet Union confronted Japan for the first time along a 4,200-kilometer land and river border, such fears became even more justified.

Beyond a doubt, starting in the late 1930s at the latest, the Soviet government was aware of a possible attack from Germany and therefore prepared for war.[64] Nevertheless, Japan's occupation of Manchuria meant a threat on two borders, precipitating a decade of measures to increase Soviet military strength in both quality and quantity. Consequently, in some respects the border situation was similar to the western border of the Soviet Union. Bare numbers of troops deployed in the regions of East Siberia, the Soviet Far East, and Manchukuo suggest the scale of the arms race. From 1931 to 1941 the numerical strength rose from just over thirty thousand to eight hundred thousand soldiers in the Soviet Union east of Lake Baikal and from zero to seven hundred thousand troops in Manchukuo.[65]

On the Soviet side the reorganization and rationalization of the Far Eastern command structure got under way in 1935 with the consolidation of the Transbaikal Military District from the various western garrisons of the Special Far Eastern Red Banner Army. As a consequence of deteriorating Soviet-Japanese relations, especially after Tokyo had signed the Anti-Comintern Pact with Berlin on 25 November 1936, Soviet military presence there shot up in the late 1930s and reached its zenith in 1941. But a statistical indicator of troop strength can give only a one-dimensional picture of the changing military presence in the borderlands. Crucially the Soviet military also transformed during the 1930s from a horseback into a motorized and mechanized army equipped with planes and tanks.[66]

Even now it remains difficult to judge the range of military planning in the Soviet-Manchukuo borderlands. As early as 1934 foreign military experts predicted that in the event of a Soviet-Japanese war there would be two main fronts, a western one in the Transbaikal area and an eastern one in the Maritime region. Bruno Plaetschke, a German geographer, expected the principal battlefront to stretch "west of the Xingan Range in the highlands of Hulunbeir ... and west of the city of Hailar, which would become the main base of the Japanese forces. The very much exposed station of Manzhouli would probably soon fall into Russian hands."[67]

Practical schemes outlined by both sides support this opinion. Already in 1933 evacuation plans were drafted in the Soviet Union for the full administrative staff, livestock, and important property held by collective farms and food processing plants in the border region. People and assets were to be relocated by train from Borzia deep into the interior for the event of mobilization for war. By the late 1930s medical staff, railroad personnel, and the civilian population in Dauriia, Borzia, and other Soviet settlements near the border took part in regular aerial defense exercises.[68] As early as 1933 Soviet military planners designed simulations for an occupation of the Great Xingan Mountains by Transbaikal Army divisions, in case of a Japanese attack on the Soviet Far East.[69] In a similar fashion the Japanese had developed a variety of invasion plans for a strike against the Soviet Union, or, pending a Soviet invasion, how to contain Red Army breakthroughs.[70]

Soviet and Japanese military defense investments support these predictions as well. Both sides deployed huge resources in the fortification of the borderlands. As early as spring 1932 the Russian emigrant paper *Zaria* reported massive Soviet troop reinforcements across the border of Manzhouli and other pivotal areas.[71] Soviet border guards built barbed-wire entanglements and dug trenches along the less secure sections of the border. The Otpor border sector, which comprised roughly eighty kilometers of barren steppe from Abagaitui to the Mongolian boundary, was particularly vulnerable.[72] As they had in the vicinities of Blagoveshchensk, Birobidzhan, Grodekovo, and other strategically important border areas, the Soviets erected ferroconcrete pillboxes across Manzhouli. Called *tochkas* in Russian, they mimicked military barricades that had been built earlier along some parts of the Soviet border with Poland.

Those rather urgent measures, taken by Moscow after 1931, were followed by more durable border defense positions in the Soviet borderlands, later termed fortified regions (*ukreplennye raiony*). The purpose of the Borzia and Dauriia fortified regions was to defend the borderland, cover the strategic deployment of military forces, and shield important Borzia and Karymskoe railroad junctions along the Transbaikal trunk line. Those fortifications were equipped with a broad set of installations, such as antitank obstacles, artillery emplacements, communication trenches, gas-attack shelters, and stocks of war materiel. The barricades of the five main defense areas were not positioned right along the boundary line but rather placed in strategic positions. In the western sector of the border with Manchukuo, for example, military planners chose the right bank of the Borzia River, an area more than one hundred kilometers west of Manzhouli. In 1939–1940 a construction battalion erected a second defense line closer to the border. The new facilities near the garrison town of Dauriia were built in response to the border clashes at Lake Khasan (1938) and Khalkhyn-Gol (1939) that will be discussed later on in this chapter. About sixty-five kilometers long and up to five kilometers wide, this line of defense spread from Abagaitui to the steppe hills west of Dauriia.[73] At the same time hundreds of acres of collective farmland in the Argun borderlands were transferred to the administration of the Transbaikal Military District to provide space for new airfields and other military installations.[74]

Troop deployments transformed the borderlands beyond bolstering their capacity for force. With thousands of new soldiers stationed in close proximity of the border, the military became a major element in this sparsely settled and economically underdeveloped region. When the German journalist Wolfgang Sorge passed Dauriia, a major Soviet military base near the Chinese border, by train he reported seeing "a town with cobbled streets, about 50 massive stone barracks, several villas and many mud huts."[75] The sheer size of new military bases changed the economic, ethnic, social, and cultural nature of the borderlands.

Japan's position in Hulunbeir remained relatively weak. Its population numbered only about forty-three thousand people until the acquisition of the Soviet railroad concession in 1935.[76] The number of Japanese in Hailar is said to have increased over the two years following the occupation in December 1932, from three hundred to fifteen hundred.[77] Hailar was home to the headquarters of a single division stationed west of the Great Xingan Mountains. During the following years, however, the army further enhanced the garrison, and the city itself developed into a fortress that by 1939 hosted one of the eight Guandong Army border garrisons.[78] Manchukuo's fortified military zones resembled its Soviet equivalents to some extent. One stood at the Amur River between Heihe and Fuyuan, another in the eastern sector in the vicinity of Suifenhe. The third and most important of these fortified zones, however, lay in the Hailar-Manzhouli area.

Similar to Soviet bans on travel in fortified areas, Manchukuo regulations rigorously restricted access. According to a report by the U.S. consul in Harbin, it was forbidden to inspect the condition of the district and to photograph or sketch drawings in those zones as well. Furthermore, passengers who traveled by train between Manzhouli and Hailar were not permitted to look out of the windows of railroad cars. To prevent illicit gazing, the shades in the coaches were pulled down. Since the authorities in Changchun (Xinjing) and Tokyo feared sabotage, they restricted access to Japanese military installations in those zones to the Chinese. The borderland was thus made increasingly inaccessible through militarization. And it was secured not only on the ground: the Guandong Army declared almost the entire Hulunbeir region a no-fly zone.[79]

Numerous infrastructure projects in the borderlands were part and parcel of the efforts of the two powers to improve their strategic positions. Aside from the few railroads, proper transport infrastructure and signal communications simply did not exist before 1931. As early as May 1932 Turar R. Ryskulov, vice chairman of the Russian Council of People's Commissars, complained about the poor conditions at the Far Eastern borders: "There are no roads along the border and no bridges over the rivers. Border guards crossing rivers regularly result in fatal accidents. Border patrols are forced to make large detours, making border surveillance and communications between border posts difficult." A three-year plan listed the construction of bridges, purchase of barges and patrol boats, construction of roads, clearing of patrol trails, and cleansing of a four-meter border strip from forests and woodlands as central investment projects. These, however, were often jeopardized by lack of funding.[80]

In the Argun borderlands the Chinese Eastern Railroad and a parallel road were the only lines of communication worthy of that name, aside from often hardly visible trails in the steppe plain and forests. But by 1934 the Trans-Siberian Railroad had been double-tracked up to Karymskoe and work was under way to double-track the Amur Railroad as well. In the borderlands the most important enterprise was the construction of a branch railroad stretching from the southeast of the Transbaikal region to the east of the Mongol People's Republic. Built between 1936 and 1939, this line ran from Borzia via Choibalsan to Tamsag, flush with the border with Manchukuo, mainly for strategic purposes.[81] To secure passage of patrol flotillas through the border waters, both powers equipped their own sides of the lower Argun riverbanks with navigational lights in 1936 and 1937.[82] During the 1930s the Soviet-Japanese arms race put an end to sparsely controlled borders in this manner, transforming the borderland into a no-man's land strung with barbed-wire fences.

Limiting Access: The Establishment of Border Zones

To step up controls over the Argun borderland, territories along the state border were no longer just cut off from the outside world but also closed to the core country. Though restricted access zones were not unique to the Soviet

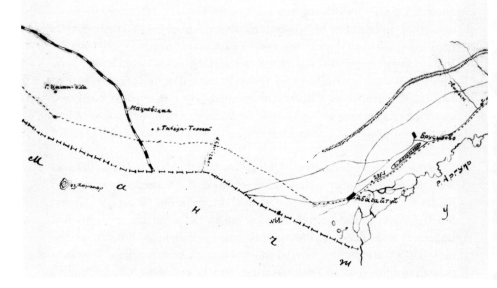

Схематический чертеж Государственных границ
Монголии и манчжурии, с указанием установленной
постановлением президиума Борзинского рика от 21-5-36г.
границ пограничной полосы; - указанной на данном чер-
теже пунктиром красной тушью.

Масштаб 10-вер. в дюйме

FIGURE 5.3. Detail of a sketch map of the Borzia region along the borders with Mongolia and Manchukuo in May 1936. The forbidden border zone, here marked by a thin dotted line, was 7.5 kilometers wide, but it was soon expanded to stretch across dozens of kilometers.

Union, Moscow's administrative and ideological conception of border zones went further than those of other modern states. The objective of those restricted access terrains expanded from the mere establishment of military security to achieving political and economic dominion as well as the control of local people.

A decree, ratified by the Central Executive Committee of the Soviet Union on 7 September 1923, identified a special continuous administrative territory along the entire Soviet border, what would be termed "border districts" (*pogranichnye raiony*) for the first time. Within this territory several different

strips—4 meters, 500 meters, 7.5 kilometers, and 22 kilometers in breadth—
were established. All came under the exclusive control of the Soviet border
guards, part of the secret police GPU and invested with far-reaching powers
that were already established by the fall of 1922. Zones were now controlled
ultimately from Moscow rather than the local administrations of the border
regions. The new regulations allowed entry into the innermost border strip
only with special permission. The border districts were soon expanded significantly. By 1929 they included not only all districts touching the international
boundary but also all adjacent districts. These primary border zones or "front"
(*frontovye*) districts and secondary border zones or "rear" (*tylovye*) districts
greatly enlarged the area of regulation.[83]

During the 1920s Moscow's overriding concern lay with the western borderland. The shift of power in East Asia reversed that trend during the early
1930s. Some of the new policies were first implemented in the east. In 1932
another border regime, the "forbidden border zone" (*zapretnaia pogranichnaia
zona*), was created, two years before the Politburo imposed this type of regime
on the western border regions. Security measures in the forbidden border
zones were even more severe than in the districts.[84] Originally the restricted
access zone was only 7.5 kilometers wide, but depending on the strategic position, topographic features, and other factors, it was expanded in some areas to
stretch across dozens of kilometers. In Chita region Moscow expanded the
closed security zone in 1938 to encompass the corridor of the Trans-Siberian
Railroad and the vast territories south of it.[85] The border itself was thus expanding farther into the heartland, putting greater parts of the country under
a tight security regime.

Restrictions on the movement and migration of people were not limited to
the Soviet borderlands. In December 1932 the Soviet government introduced
internal passports to enforce restrictions on all migration, particularly to cities.[86]
However, the rules applying to the border zones were the strictest. Access was
forbidden even to Soviet citizens, unless they were registered as permanent
residents or had special permission from the authorities to gain entry to the
closed security zone. For that access all visitors were required to register with
local authorities upon arrival. Restrictions were imposed not just on human
beings: all vessels needed to be catalogued. Furthermore, border guards had
an unlimited right of search and seizure at any time. During the mid-1930s
Moscow further toughened the regime, instituting ever more severe labor
camp sentences for violations of the forbidden border zone regime and illegal
border crossings.[87]

The rigorous rules within the forbidden zone reveal the Soviet state's intention to monitor the borderlanders and to limit the access of other Soviet citizens and foreigners to both the border regions as well as the neighboring

country. By that time, however, there had been only a negligible number of registered foreigners left in the Soviet border regions on the Argun. In 1931, for example, just 117 foreigners were enlisted in the Borzia region, 21 fewer than the previous year. Not a single foreign national lived in Novaia Zaria, and there were just two in Dauriia and seven in Abagaitui.[88]

Even the freedom of movement of diplomats was affected by the new regulations. By 1941 it was mandatory for staff of consulates and embassies to acquire travel permits in advance to travel through "forbidden places and areas." Categorized as "forbidden" were border zones as well as numerous republics, regions, and cities, including all regions bordering with Manchukuo. During World War II conveyance rules became even stricter. The Soviet Union and Manchukuo agreed that each side had the right to send diplomatic couriers across the border on fixed routes by train four times a month. Manchukuo diplomats were obligated to travel to their Chita and Blagoveshchensk consulates via Otpor only, just as Soviet representatives had to journey through a single channel to reach the consulates in Harbin and Dairen.[89]

Beginning 1 February 1937 Manchukuo adopted a quite similar border zone regime. Mirroring the measures implemented several years earlier on the Soviet side, some Manchukuo districts, and in some parts entire provinces, became subject to such boundary zoning if they were adjacent to the territory of the Soviet Union. The virtually identical wording of the Manchukuo laws and the earlier Soviet regulations indicates a certain level of transfer and imitation: all persons over the age of fourteen years residing within the border zone were required to register with the police and to obtain a special certificate of residence. Strangers who wanted to visit the zone were obligated to obtain a travel permit in advance. Offenders were punished with imprisonment or a fine. The law gave the authorities carte blanche to bring the border zone under their heel. The state granted itself the convenient tool of being able to prohibit residence or travel or repress whatever it deemed oppositional to Manchukuo rule.[90]

As demonstrated earlier in the fight against smuggling, regulations written in the metropoles were often hard to implement on the ground. The same holds true for movement-regulating border directives. Yet through an increase of border guard personnel and other security measures, the authorities nonetheless succeeded in enforcing these restrictions over the years. The establishment of border zones in the late 1920s and 1930s was, in the long run, probably one of the most profound changes of the early Soviet period. It had a long-term impact that would continue to affect the daily lives of ordinary people until the 1980s through a high degree of central authority over the borderlands.

The Spy Scare: Intelligence Warfare and Purges
at the Border

On a summer evening, while the Soviet border guard Mikhail I. Sladkovskii was chatting with his wife in their dacha not far from Otpor's wooden border arch, a sharp cry cut through the evening silence: "'Stop, hands up!' . . . 25 to 30 steps from us stood with his hands raised a red-bearded, shaggy-haired tramp, and behind him, 10 to 15 steps away, the border guard Nikitin aiming a rifle with a bayonet at the unknown." Sladkovskii was perplexed by the detainee's appearance. At first glance the man looked like a homeless vagrant, but his manicured hands, pink skin, and a smart look in his eyes exposed him as spy.[91]

Until the late 1920s border transgressors had been for the most part smugglers, and migrants crossing the Argun and the steppe border in such numbers that an airtight sealed boundary was no more than a political fantasy. But this situation changed after the Sino-Soviet conflict and Japan's occupation of Manchuria. Smuggling and flight became, increasingly, a mortal risk. This narrowing of zones of contact was reflected in the change of the kind of people engaged in cross-border activities. Through the 1920s essentially anyone local could commute or buy and sell across the border. By the end of the 1930s the searches and patrols by the border guards reached a point of such intense rigidity that only privileged people like diplomats, such as the wife of the Soviet Consul in Manzhouli, were allowed to slip through and to smuggle commodities. Underlying this decline of smuggling, informal networks and uncontrolled contacts across the state border were improvements in border control, joined by cleansing campaigns and the severe punishment of nomads and members of professional contrabandist networks. Additional key factors were international hostilities that curtailed forbidden cross-border activities. All of this resulted in a decrease but not a full cessation of legal and illegal border traffic. Throughout the 1930s the border still remained permeable and one of its most typical trespassers was the spy.

Espionage was above all a way to counteract the sealing off of the border. Soviet authorities knew the borderlands better than the Japanese, although Tokyo had begun to gather anti-Soviet intelligence years before Manchukuo became a neighboring nation.[92] According to secret Soviet reports the Japanese commenced the comprehensive exploration of their Manchukuo borderlands in late summer of 1933, which included information on topography, land routes, waterways, climate, and soil. The Japanese placed great emphasis on intelligence regarding Soviet army positions. They studied the geography of the Trekhreche region, the vicinity of Manzhouli, and other areas between one hundred and two hundred kilometers from the boundary inland. In the summer and fall of 1933 Japanese airplanes took aerial photographs of the border, encompassing three to five kilometers of Soviet territory and the first fortification zones.[93]

Mapping the border required manpower, but intelligence operations were a far more complex operation. Both sides obtained information through agents who entered enemy territory, analysis of radio broadcasts and publications, wireless interceptions, and the interrogation of army deserters and defectors. They did not limit their efforts to the narrow meaning of intelligence work. Rather they embraced a broader understanding of intelligence that included propaganda handbills, posters, radio broadcasts, and the like, along with cross-border espionage and counterespionage, sabotage and countersabotage.[94]

From the early 1930s on and throughout the Pacific War, the mission of Manchukuo's Soviet Territory Observation Teams was to keep the Soviet borderlands under close surveillance around the clock to detect any preparations for an attack by the enemy forces.[95] The Soviets installed similar observation positions along the border at strategically important sections, such as Otpor, Abagaitui, and the border outposts further northward along the Argun River, usually spaced about ten kilometers apart. Those units recorded, in detail, any movements of even so much as a single Manchukuo vehicle or soldier and submitted detailed daily reports to headquarters.[96] More importantly, however, the records disclose how each side had deployed sufficient military staff to keep its opponent under close observation along the border, day and night. Compared to prerevolutionary times, when one might have calculated less than one soldier per kilometer of boundary line, the protection and surveillance of the border had indeed changed.

Espionage was an additional component of intelligence gathering. Both Japan and the Soviet Union worked hard to penetrate the other. Long before Japan occupied China's Northeast the Soviet Union operated a tightly knit underground network of intelligence agents, who used the border stations at Manzhouli and Otpor as junctions for information exchange.[97] Secret services infiltrated the borderland and spies scrutinized the territory there, studying distinct strategic points on both sides of the river. As early as September 1932 Manchukuo authorities identified the first Soviet spies on Harbin-bound trains in Manzhouli.[98] The central body of the Japanese espionage was the Japanese Military Mission, whose branches settled first in Harbin, Mukden, Manzhouli, and Suifenhe and soon expanded into various other cities in Manchukuo.[99]

Following bloody clashes on the border that will be discussed momentarily, Japan and the Soviet Union intensified their intelligence activities during the late 1930s. Between January and September 1939 the Soviet secret police tracked down 108 illegal border crossers in the Chita border district, allowing only two into Manchukuo. The remaining 106 persons were trying to cross the border into the Soviet Union. Of those, one-third were classified as spies. Compared with figures from the early 1930s, these seem incredibly low. For Soviet counterintelligence, however, this was a major cause for concern, explained by "intensified activity to establish a bridgehead in northern Manchuria for a future attack on the Transbaikal area . . . and to increase the intelligence work in the region."[100]

In the eyes of the Japanese, perhaps the most valuable agents were the White Russians of Manchuria due to their ideological convictions and ethnic background. The emigrants were familiar with the language, culture, and territory of the Soviet borderland.[101] Potential spies were usually sought out by the Japanese Military Missions in Hailar, Manzhouli, and Dragotsenka as well as the branch offices of the Bureau of the Affairs of Russian Émigrés (BREM) in these places.[102] After the emigrants had received training, they were sent to the Soviet Union. Those who succeeded in infiltrating Soviet territory were, despite their cultural background, confronted with multiple obstacles involving identification documents, dress, and new Soviet vocabulary in the Russian language. Although they were supposed to return after collecting information, only a few did so. Some, after being arrested, succumbed to threats or bribery and became counterspies. It was not uncommon for the detected agents to linger a while in the border zones and submit false reports upon return, claiming that they successfully completed their mission.[103] Both sides, in fact, feared that their spies were double agents. The Soviet authorities successfully operated counterintelligence divisions and bogus anti-Soviet groups that collaborated with Japanese intelligence.[104]

Not every trespasser was sent across the border by state directive. But as was not the case during collectivization, these were neither the shepherd with his livestock nor groups of hundreds of refugees but desperate individuals by themselves or in small groups, escaping political oppression and poor living conditions. Many, fearing arrest, fled during the Great Terror. Some of them were prominent, like Genrikh S. Liushkov, commissar of the Far Eastern Regional directorate of the People's Commissariat for Internal Affairs (NKVD), who had been in charge of massive deportations of ethnic Koreans and Chinese from the Soviet Far East during the mid-1930s. When he received the news that in the next few days he would be called to go on a *komandirovka* to Moscow in June 1938, he defected to Japan since such "calls from Moscow do usually end with arrests." After a Manchukuo patrol detained Liushkov on the border he was sent to Tokyo, where he worked for the Japanese Army's intelligence and propaganda apparatus until 1945 and provided the adversary with valuable intelligence on troops in the Soviet Far East. Japan spun the story of his escape into widely disseminated propaganda purporting to give an insider's view of the war preparations within the Soviet Union and the causes of the Great Purge.[105] Others who fled the Soviet Union in the mid- or late 1930s, whether Buriats or Russians, whether hidden on a railroad coal car or carried over a frozen river by foot, described the Soviet Union in Manchukuo's press as hell on earth, populated by sullen, intimidated, and starving people deprived of their civil rights.[106]

People like Liushkov feared the mass arrests of the Soviet elite as well as hysterical campaigns directed against ordinary civilians in the climate of spy mania. Foreign factors also formed a crucial element during the years of political repression, which were motivated by Stalin's struggle to consolidate his power and the stability of the regime he had created. Deep-rooted fears of internal enemies merged with xenophobic traditions and a fragile political and economic system, and this dangerous combination generated an image of ethnically defined internal foes called "enemy nations."[107] Until 1938 the Kremlin had expelled almost all Chinese migrant workers and Korean farmers from the Amur and Maritime provinces but allowed the Khori Buriats to stay in the Transbaikal region. Those cleansing campaigns against so-called undesirable labor and plans for an infusion of new permanent settlers from other parts of the Soviet Union thus deeply affected the ethnic composition of the borderlands on the Amur and Ussuri, and to a much lesser extent the ethnic structure of the Soviet population on the Argun.[108]

Russians and other Slavic peoples of the Soviet Union were not spared during the years of terror. The search for spies in the country's peripheries was particularly pervasive. Moscow accused tens of thousands of individuals of conducting intelligence work for Germany or Japan or having ties to anti-Soviet spy rings. People who had lived or traveled abroad or had contact with foreigners were significantly more likely to be accused of espionage.[109] During 1937 and 1938, the height of Stalin's terror, arrests for espionage soared from 10 percent in 1937 to 26.8 percent of all arrests in 1938. In those same two years 18,341 and 34,565 people respectively were accused of spying for Japan— roughly one-fifth of all arrests for espionage during this period.[110]

Espionage trials had already begun by the mid-1930s in the Soviet Far East. But only with the approval of the Soviet secret police agency operative order 00447 by the Politburo in July 1937 did killing by quota begin and Japanese spies were "uncovered" everywhere. Soviet railroad men working at Manzhouli were not spared from the purges. Out of thirty-nine Soviet employees sixteen were considered politically disloyal or suspected of being Japanese spies, some because they had read émigré papers, others because they were said to be active in local fascist circles. Among them was Andrei S. Sizinov, Manzhouli's Soviet stationmaster. Twenty-one Russians who had been hired on the spot and were working mainly as janitors or caretakers were excluded from this classification. Thirteen foreigners (all Chinese) employed for menial work were, for their part, allegedly Japanese spies.[111]

Hiroaki Kuromiya has attempted to give some of those murdered in 1937 to 1938 a voice by reading the personal files of the executed, that were compiled by the Soviet secret police. These documents are often the only available sources to historians but are essentially fiction. As fictional as the interrogation records are, they still offer a glimpse into how cross-border espionage networks might have worked.[112]

One of these cases is that of Petr P. Purin. When he was interrogated on 21 February 1938, Purin was accused of spying for the Japanese. Before his arrest the battalion commissar had served as the head of the technical department of the intelligence division in the Transbaikal Military District. The life of this ethnic Latvian, born in 1897 at the western edge of the Russian Empire, ended in tragedy in the eastern borderlands. Purin's only "crime" was that he came under suspicion of political disloyalty. Written by his interrogators, his "confession" contains just enough detail to be credible to the naïve reader. Whether he had actually collaborated with the Japanese, however, remains unknown.

In early 1929, Purin, then secretary of the Soviet consulate in Hailar, rented a room in a house shared with a Japanese company agent called Terada. Because Terada was fluent in Russian, these two men soon became closely acquainted. Purin allegedly sensed an opportunity to recruit a Japanese national into the service of the Soviet Union. To build trust in this friendship, avers the trial dossier, Purin presented Terada with Soviet consular files on Hulunbeir and the railroad. Once in possession of the materials Terada said that he would return them only if Purin would accept to work for Japan. Having no choice, Purin agreed. After the Hailar consulate was evacuated in July 1929, during the turmoil of the Sino-Soviet conflict, Purin was dispatched to Otpor. Later posted to Starotsurukhaitui on the Argun, he supposedly remained in contact with the Japanese Secret Service, albeit through local contacts rather than Terada. According to his dossier Purin provided the Japanese with information on the Red Army troop strength, deployment location, and data on mining and industry, the last especially relating to the armaments industry in the Soviet border province. Without any material evidence to support this claim, Purin was sentenced to death and shot.[113]

The secret police file listed, accurately and truthfully, the names of the villages and towns where Purin had lived and worked. His dossier shows striking similarities with other testimonies in structure and content and even in the use of essentially interchangeable narratives.[114] Foreign connections were the greatest risk factor for arrest and execution. Contrabandists, refugees, former diplomats, and ordinary railroad men alike were labeled as spies or traitors. According to the Stalinist xenophobic ideal people who lived at the international border should have had no experience with the culture of the bordering nation.

Where the Subaltern Rules: The Japanese and the Mongols of Hulunbeir

As much as Japanese strategies to infiltrate the neighboring state resembled those in the Soviet Union, their approaches to administering the borderlands differed. Even relative to late tsarist Russian efforts to control the Hulunbeir Mongols and absorb their territory into a buffer state, Japanese rule, at least on the surface, was far less aggressive. The nomads of Hulunbeir, then still almost half the population of the region,[115] were uncompromisingly anti-Chinese and had maintained a degree of autonomy that had allowed them to resist Chinese inroads more successfully than had Mongols in other parts of China's Northeast. The struggle of the Mongolian partisan Tokhtogo at the beginning of the twentieth century exemplified the Mongol attitude toward the Chinese. This disdain for settled peasantry was deepened by resentment of the Chinese agriculturalist colonization policies adopted by the imperial court, which were further entrenched under the government of the Chinese Republic. Though the Mongols of Hulunbeir did not hail the Japanese as saviors, as some had the Russians, Japan's promise to protect their grazing lands from further Chinese colonization, its creation of semiautonomy in Manchukuo, and its respect for politically influential Mongol princes and lamas led some of the indigenous borderlanders to regard their new sovereigns initially as liberators.[116]

The new Japanese regime added a distinct Mongol Xingan province to Manchukuo that was on at least equal footing with the other provinces. In spite of Chinese colonization and their disproportionately low population, the Mongol territory was still the largest unit within Manchukuo. Unlike any other Manchukuo province, through a decree in March 1932, Xingan was internally reorganized into four subprovinces: the Northern (Hulunbeir) with Hailar as seat of the subprovince, the Eastern (Nen River valley), the Southern (Tokhtogo's native Jirim league), and the Western (Jo-oda league). Similar to the organization of Chinese provincial governments, each of the four Xingan districts was allotted a Mongol subprovincial governor who was "aided" by a Japanese advisor. At the same time all four subprovinces were garrison districts, presided over by a Mongol garrison officer and his Japanese aide. In this manner the Japanese had complete control over the administration of Xingan, just as they had over the other Manchukuo provinces.[117]

FIGURE 5.4. Hailar, 1942. "Directing goats is beneath the dignity of the Hailar traffic cop,"
reads the caption to this photograph in *National Geographic*. On a banner slung across the
street Chinese and Western companies advertise "Wholesale and retail, prices low."
The door at right offers a "Japanese-style haircut." The rider is Mongolian,
the Manchukuo policeman Chinese.

In Xingan the Mongols were granted significant autonomy, at least on
paper. This can be attributed to the fact that they were seen as potential liaisons
in maintaining the strategically cardinal position held by the Japanese in the
parts of Inner Mongolia controlled by Republican China. Japanese willingness
to concede Mongol autonomy, therefore, can be understood only in conjunc-
tion with the Soviet goal of forcing the nomads to abandon their migrant
economy. It can also be seen only in light of the situation in Outer Mongolia,
where purges of the old elite and the installation of a government organized
along Soviet lines stirred anti-Soviet sentiments among the Mongols of
Manchuria.

There were several novel aspects of this administrative autonomy. The new
administrative unit was no longer part of Heilongjiang province. Instead, this
autonomous Mongol region, headed by the Xingan Province Board, answered
directly to the State Council of the Manchukuo government in Xinjing. It was

the only province in which a native population dominated over Japanese residents. Indeed the special characteristics of the Xingan Province led it to resemble a kind of national reservation. According to official statements the area was to be administered as a virtually autonomous domain, with Mongol princes and other hereditary chiefs retaining their posts. They were also given the promise that all the Mongol-inherited faiths, customs, and institutions would be retained, as long as they were compatible with the new age. In theory this partial self-rule allowed the Mongols to regulate their own lives to a considerable extent.[118]

The province even fielded its own troops. In January 1933 newspapers in Manchukuo discussed government plans to set up an indigenous conscripted army for patrols along the western state borders with the Soviet Union and the Mongolian People's Republic in Northern Xingan province (Hulunbeir). By June 1933 headquarters for the Mongolian army units were set up in Hailar under the auspices of a Japanese advisor. Some fifty Mongolians underwent officer training, and twelve were even sent to Japan for instructions. The conscription call was said to be for Mongol males between twenty and thirty years of age, to create a body of a standing army of ten to fifteen thousand soldiers.[119] By November 1934 two Mongol cavalry regiments, totaling a thousand men, were in the service of the Manchukuo army in Northern Xingan province. To the British travel writer Peter Fleming, who paid a visit to a Mongol regiment near Hailar, the introduction of soldierly discipline along Prussian-Japanese patterns seemed to be causing problems among the autochthonous populations. The result, he found, was a hybrid army of native Mongol soldiers with modern equipment. The conscripts found it difficult to live in barracks after the yurts:

> The barracks were cold inside. All the men stood ready to attention when we came in except one, who went on eating out of a bowl with the air of one has right on his side although the next man kicked him on the bottom. . . . Some bring their own horses. All bring their own saddles, and these, a gay, outlandish assortment, were laid out on trestles in the yard. . . . There was an officer with an aquiline nose, sloping shoulders, a curious drifting gait, and the air of a demon. He said some of them understood machine-guns. The rifles are new and I think the same as the Manchukuo rifles. The kit was quite neatly kept and the place clean. Most of the men are literate.[120]

To breed a loyal indigenous elite from all the Xingan provinces, a Xingan Officers Training Academy was opened on 1 July 1934 in the village of Wangyemiao (Ulanhot) in the South Xingan province. Its fundamental purpose was to inculcate the lower ranks of the future army into the new regime and to impress upon them the destiny of the Mongol nation within its realms as well as to advocate rapprochement with and dependence on Japan. Aside from morning and evening worship, the daily life of the cadets closely mirrored the life of cadets in the Japanese Imperial Army. Indeed, one important task of these young soldiers was to spread a positive image of Japan and Manchukuo among their peers. One can easily concur with a contemporary American diplomat who judged the work of the academy to be an index of the nature of Japanese attitudes toward the Mongols: "There is reason to believe that the [training] methods [adopted in the academy], in which a strong Mongol state under Mongol leadership is promised, will eventually result in lessening the Mongols' disinclination to accept Japanese rule. The school will no doubt increase the combat efficiency of the Mongol cavalry units in Xingan and will place these units under direct control of the Japanese staff."[121] The establishment of Mongol army units therefore reveals Tokyo's attempt to integrate autochthonous peoples into Manchukuo, which with any luck would prove useful for border protection and other self-serving purposes.[122]

Though the Mongols certainly enjoyed some degree of autonomy, this relative freedom was not simply benevolence on the part of the Manchukuo government. By the mid-1930s, once the Japanese had firmly established their position as the new power, they began to restrict the Mongols' political and economic privileges. The banner system lost its exclusively Mongol character. Local Mongol authority was abrogated and increasingly steered by the Manchukuo central government as well as by the development of a largely Manchukuo local bureaucracy in each banner. On the local level, just as the power of the banner chief diminished, self-government councils that had been set up in 1932 with local legislative, fiscal, and advisory functions also gradually lost their influence. By the close of the decade the banner chief needed the approval of the provincial governor to make an increasing number of decisions and was flanked by a Japanese councilor to "assist" him. Even the term banner resident was watered down. According to a 1932 ordinance only males who had resided in the banner territories for at least three years were defined as banner residents. Under a decree passed in 1937, however, any person who resided in a banner was to be considered as a banner resident. Therefore, "Manchurians" (a euphemism for Han Chinese citizens of Manchukuo), Russians, and Japanese could also become banner residents.[123]

Increasingly, Mongols were also marginalized economically. The Great Depression and the Sino-Soviet conflict of 1929, the Japanese occupation of Manchuria in 1931, and ever-stricter border enforcements temporarily brought the famous trade fair next to the Ganchzhur Monastery, a two-day horseback ride southwest of Hailar, to a near standstill. Demand from merchants in Harbin, among the last customers of horned cattle and sheep traded in Ganchzhur, had fallen sharply. What mattered most, however, was the change in the nomadic lifestyle that accelerated the decline of this fair. Compared to figures from 1912, 95 percent fewer horned cattle and 94 percent fewer sheep were sold in 1934. Figures for horses were slightly better, reaching a quarter of 1912 levels, because the animals enjoyed a good reputation and were exported as far as Shanghai and Hong Kong.[124] A Manchukuo travel guide, printed in 1941, still mentioned Ganchzhur as a "typical Mongolian affair" in a list of Hulunbeir attractions but admitted that it "has now lost much of its former importance."[125]

The Manchukuo government initially limited its efforts to freeing the nomadic economy from volatile pricing. But in 1938 the Mongols "voluntarily" contributed open lands in the Xingan province and other areas to the state, which transferred these areas to Japanese farmers who would also serve as colonizing agents. In addition to the nationalization of tribal lands, indigenous representatives agreed to relinquish the Mongolian land tax, and other taxes hitherto collected by local authorities, to the Manchukuo central government. Despite their loss of power, the Mongols were permitted to keep their positions, in name only. The archaic social strata of the Mongols was thus preserved. As they had in other occupied territories, the Japanese froze the existing social order on paper, thereby maintaining the appearance of autonomy.[126]

It would be wrong, however, to give these new stricter regulations the sole responsibility for the decrease of Mongolian autonomy. With the construction of new railroads and telephone lines as well as the ongoing integration of the nomad economy into international trade, some commentators saw religion as the only hope in saving Mongolian cultural identity. Though such observations certainly smacked of salvation ethnography, even religious practice had been on the decline. In the Ganchzhur Monastery the number of lamas had drastically dropped from fifteen hundred to just about two hundred in 1934.[127]

Freedom was even more limited in Outer Mongolia, the Soviet satellite state. Moscow established the greatest possible control in this former Qing frontier. It converted the Mongolian People's Republic into the first line of defense for its vast and vulnerable Siberian territories. Separation from China was wrought in exchange for the violent transformation of Mongolian society from feudal to socialist.[128] From the mid-1930s until the dissolution of the Soviet Union in 1991, Moscow's utter control over the Mongolian People's Republic secured one of the longest and most vulnerable stretches of the Soviet Union's eastern border.[129] After a long period of transition Mongolia was finally divided into spheres of national interest and thus integrated into its neighboring empires. The nomads to whom those steppe borderlands had once belonged had been neutralized by the metropoles. From that point onward they no longer played a key role in the formation of this border.

Old Russia in a Nutshell: The Cossack Émigrés under Manchukuo Rule

The presence of a large Russian emigrant community in Manchukuo offered Japan the chance to leverage the loyalty of this group against its hostile neighbor across the Argun, much like they had sought to pit the Mongols of Manchukuo against the Han Chinese. Maintaining good relations with the Russian émigrés was therefore crucial since it offered the potential to irritate the Soviet Union not only with bandit attacks, but with various iterations of soft power, as we have discussed earlier in this chapter. The other side of the coin, however, bore the chance that this prospective ally might easily turn into an unpredictable confederate if relations soured. Administering this emigrant community was therefore a delicate task.

The Russian emigrants had, much like the Mongols, mixed feelings about their new masters.[130] In the beginning they rather welcomed Japanese seizure of control since the Chinese had so repressively dealt with them. Further, there were lingering wounds from the fierce fighting with the Red Army during the Sino-Soviet conflict of 1929. In general, the roughly five thousand Trekhreche Cossack farmers found comfort in their new, strong guardian.[131] On 23 December 1932 a delegation of Trekhreche Russians handed the Japanese authorities in Hailar a declaration that embraced the new "era of order and justice" and affirmed a will to cooperate.[132] Many were ready to collaborate, in the spirit of their anti-Soviet convictions.

In the beginning the Japanese too were sympathetic to their new European subjects. With regard to culture and the economy the Japanese authorities largely preserved the old traditions and living patterns of the Russian agriculturists in the Manchukuo borderlands. Paradoxically, they were even obsessed with it. Japanese ethnographers compiled in-depth studies of Russian village architecture and agriculture and the rural way of life in general. During its decade of its existence, Manei—the Manchurian Film Association—produced a number of silent films reflecting the realities of Cossack life at the Argun. Preserved clippings of one documentary depict the life of the Trekhreche Cossacks. One can see farm workers do the afternoon's threshing, with horses drawing a plow slowly through a field. In another scene a blond girl makes cheese. The film thus illustrated a traditional life that had in fact ceased to exist in Soviet Russia.[133] Similarly, Russian-language journals and newspapers published in Manchukuo emphasized the preservation of "community and family in the old patriarchal way."[134]

But this euphoria vanished as the Japanese began to control the Russian emigrants more closely. The central colonial tool was the Bureau of the Affairs of Russian Émigrés (BREM). This organization, created in 1934, presided over the Russian population of Manchuria. Headquartered in Harbin, it maintained branch offices in various Manchukuo cities and villages. Its goal was to stamp out underground Soviet activities and to unify the politically divided Russian population by encouraging them to forget their misunderstandings and to unite them in a struggle against Bolshevism. Its staff sought to oversee all aspects of Russian life, carrying out policies favoring the Japanese, confirming the loyalty of the Russians to Manchukuo and Japan, and ensuring their material well-being.[135]

The Xingan Regional Office, located in Hailar, was in charge of the Russian emigrant communities in Hulunbeir. As of December 1944, about 237 employees worked in fifty bureaus, branch offices, and representative offices, which were maintained in literally every Hulunbeir village listing Russian residents. This bureau was nominally under Russian control. In Trekhreche, for instance, the Cossack ataman headed the office, a nod to the prerevolutionary organization of the Russian Empire.[136]

All adult Russian nationals were required to register with BREM. Those émigrés who refused to do so were disfavored. They were denied employment and education for their children and were apt to come to the attention of the Japanese Military Missions and the police. Though not everybody enlisted and statistics remained inaccurate, the numbers give some sense of population. The bureau's records listed a total of 68,887 Russian emigrants in Manchukuo by 1944. With 21,202 persons registered with the Xingan Regional Office, Hulunbeir was second only to Harbin (39,421) in population size.[137] According to official statistics, more than 90 percent of Manzhouli's Russian population (or 1,499 Russian emigrants) were registered with the bureau as quickly as by 1 September 1936.[138]

What function, then, did BREM serve for the border regime? One important task was to select loyal emigrants to populate the villages of Trekhreche and other sections of the Manchukuo-Soviet border. The results of the colonization policy were, however, mixed. Although the Japanese encouraged Russian migration to Trekhreche, the flow of people to this part of the border zone was highly regulated and filtered through a strict registration procedure. Likewise, some Trekhreche Cossacks were deported from the border region, often because of political concerns. For example, the Cossack Grigorii I. Kudin asked the Japanese authorities three times to return to Trekhreche, his old place of residence. They rejected his request and allowed him to return only briefly to fetch his family and belongings.[139]

But even before BREM was founded in 1934, the Japanese had begun to administer the Russian border population. The Japanese Military Missions, with their far-reaching policy influence, had ulterior reasons for taking an interest in helping organize White Russian communities in Manchukuo. Secret

FIGURE 5.5. Ranch life on a Russian farm near Manzhouli, 1935. Unlike the Russian Cossacks in Trekhreche, most of the smallholders had few animals and lived in poor conditions.

Soviet intelligence reports about conditions across the border suggest that the Japanese soon revived existing White paramilitary units to their own ends. As early as the winter of 1932–1933 the activity of the White Russian bands in Hulunbeir had significantly increased. The Peshkov brigade, concentrated in the Trekhreche area, is said to have amassed about a hundred men in those months. Under the direction of Colonel Hashimoto, Gun commander of the Japanese Military Mission in Hailar, the Japanese began to form Cossack self-defense forces and distributed one to two rifles per household.[140]

Corruption and hunger were phenomena that were known not only to the Soviet population on the Argun, suffering under the collectivization. Great sorrow befell the people, including Russian emigrant communities, on the other side of the river too. The establishment of Soviet rule and the war of 1929 had already caused great damage to the Russian emigrants in Hulunbeir. The Manchukuo years, however, brought even further decline. By and large the position of the Russians deteriorated rapidly under the new regime, and many emigrants became strongly anti-Japanese. Manzhouli devolved from a frontier town with a lively trade into an isolated steppe village. Many residents could no longer make a living from trading or from railroad work but were instead forced to keep goats and other animals to survive. Yet even their lean stores of harvested steppe hay were not enough to feed this livestock because authorities allowed the people to retain only two-thirds of the harvest. The remaining third went to BREM and eventually to the Manchukuo army.

Injustice, poverty, and miserable living conditions divided the local Russian emigrant community of the local BREM elite. In July 1936 angry residents submitted a letter to the bureau's headquarters in Harbin calling for an investigation into corruption within the local structures. To be sure the case received attention, a copy also went to the head of the Japanese Military Mission in Manzhouli. The authors accused Manzhouli employees of not pursuing the goals of the BREM and instead working for their own material and personal interests. Some staff allegedly diverted a portion of the hay duty to themselves and failed to ensure an even distribution of land. While the pastures of the privileged were located in the vicinity of the settlement, those of the ordinary people were, in many cases, more than twenty kilometers away.[141]

Agitation was one crucial task to counter anti-Japanese feelings and to foster anti-Soviet sentiments among the Russian population. In December 1936, *Binjiang Shibao* (Harbin Times) reported about a joint anticommunist mass rally of Japanese, Manchukuo (Han Chinese), and Russian émigré Manzhouli citizens, almost one-third of the population.[142] In 1938 the authorities instituted an anti-Comintern day. The Japanese further played their hand with the establishment of the Hailar-based Xingan Anti-Communist Committee to coincide with the twenty-fifth anniversary of the October Revolution in November 1942, whose task was to coordinate and promote agitprop work among the emigrants.[143] Russian youth especially were regularly called to BREM for interrogations, discussions, and training. Patterns of administering the emigrant youth were quite similar to the younger generations' organizations in the Soviet Union. The Circle of the Cossack Youth organized regular gatherings in Dragotsenka's Cossack House. Similar circles of Russian youth, operated by the local bureau youth departments in Hailar and Manzhouli, arranged various Russian cultural spectacles and oversaw political indoctrination.[144] In Manzhouli the BREM-founded House of the Russian Emigrants was the official center of emigrant life. Opening in 1942, it boasted a large stage and auditorium, a conference room, a restaurant, several club rooms, and a library, housed various cultural and sport groups, and organized traditional amateur plays, ballet, and sport performances. The local BREM branch regularly scheduled anticommunist educational propaganda evenings in the House of the Russian Emigrants, which were said to have attracted many people.[145]

Yet the propaganda failed to generate enthusiasm for a war that further increased demands made on the emigrants. Just two days after the attack on Pearl Harbor, Cossack General Aleksei P. Baksheev, head of the BREM Xingan Regional Office, chair of the Xingan Anti-Communist Committee, and head of the Union of Cossacks of East Asia, ordered "each Cossack and Russian émigré to be prepared at any time for the common defense and thus to assist the Nippon and Manchurian Imperial Armies, which firmly protect the borders of the Manchurian Empire."[146]

News of Japan's falling star soon reached the Manchukuo borderlands. General Lev F. Vlas'evskii, who directed BREM from 1943 to 1945, warned the Russian residents of Manzhouli not to believe "false rumors . . . which are of great harm to the emigrants and the state" on 4 October 1944, while on an inspection tour.[147] The emigrants were forced to do their bit to serve the Japanese. Manzhouli residents donated metal for the arms industry to the fascistic Kyōwakai mass organization.[148] The Russian civilians were channeled into manual labor, such as constructing roads or harvesting. They also underwent air raid protection exercises during the war years to practice first aid and window blinding.[149]

Russian squads within the ranks of the Manchukuo army, which in the 1930s had operated secretly, became regular units after the outbreak of the Pacific War. The army supplemented open recruitment calls with food support as well as other economic incentives for conscripts' families. On 11 December 1941 Lieutenant Colonel Taki of the Japanese Military Mission ordered the formation of the Hailar Consolidated Regiment, to consist of two divisions that in theory would include all of the area's male Russian emigrants between the ages of seventeen and fifty-five. Similar to the Mongols, the men were compelled to undergo regular reserve duty training. The eventual inclusion of emigrant women and girls in military preparations, as well as the organization of a Reservists Union by the Japanese Military Mission, amounted almost to a confession of failure—a desperate papering over or deflection of the fact that the end was near.[150] While securing the loyalty of the Russian and Mongol borderlanders in Manchukuo had been a major concern for Japan until the very last days of the war, it was the violent border incidents and their medialization that shaped this borderland most profoundly during those years, subjects to which we now turn.

Khalkhyn-Gol and Beyond: Negotiating the Bloody Border

On the morning of 31 January 1939, some five kilometers southwest of Kailastui, a village approximately halfway between Manzhouli and the Trekhreche delta, Soviet troopers suddenly came under fire on an Argun island as they were checking a border control strip. Both the Soviet Union and Manchukuo claimed the river island to be part of their territory. As a consequence eighteen Manchukuo soldiers posted on an island at the mouth of the Gan River opened fire on the *pogranichniki*. Soviet reinforcements arrived quickly, cordoned off the area, and forced the Manchukuo soldiers to retreat. According to Soviet accounts, the fighting resulted in seven dead or seriously wounded among the

Manchukuo troopers and one injured Soviet commander. This incident is illustrative of many skirmishes that occurred along the border between the Soviet Union and Manchukuo during the 1930s. Illegal acts took various forms, from airspace violations by reconnaissance aircraft to illegal incursions into enemy territory or attacks on border guards. In most cases, however, they ended nonviolently.[151] Though these incidents were less prominent than the border clash at the Khalkha River at the Mongolia-Manchukuo border, their purpose was generally the same: to negotiate power along the border by deliberately provoking the opponent and, above all, to create a strained atmosphere among the people in the region.

The illegal acts became the subject of numerous diplomatic talks. A fundamental disagreement, of course, concerned the placement of the boundary itself. The Soviets maintained that it did not need to be redefined since it was already perfectly clear. To the Japanese, on the other hand, river islands and many parts of the land border lacked clear definition. Indeed, boundary landmarks were few and poor. In some sections of the western border area only low piles of stones indicated the course of the boundary, as before, and these were easy to scatter, shift, or remove.[152]

In the treaty between Moscow and the Manchurian warlord regime as well as the final stipulations between the Republic of China and the Soviet Union, both signed in 1924, Moscow had agreed to redemarcate the boundary through a commission—a term that had been only vaguely delineated in prior treaties between the Russian and Chinese empires. This redemarcation, however, never took place. In the conflict with Tokyo during the 1930s, Moscow insisted that the boundary had been clearly defined by binding agreements and that no skirmishes over territory had occurred before the Japanese invasion.[153] In other words, despite the massive technical resources at hand, no clear boundary had ever been established because the Soviet Union feared that it would lose territory with a redemarcation. In return Japan made use of this imprecision to provoke Moscow with border violations. This policy of constant confrontation aimed to force the Soviet Union to the negotiating table.

Until spring 1935 Soviet objections took the form of discreet diplomatic notes routed through its consulate general in Harbin. However, this muted form of protest did not yield results. Finally, in April 1935 Moscow addressed a letter of protest directly to the Japanese foreign minister, Hirota Kōki. This diplomatic note meticulously listed the border violations by Japanese and Manchukuo soldiers occurring between 18 March and 17 April. By the summer of 1935 the Soviets had accepted a Japanese proposal to set up mixed border commissions to handle the dispute. The negotiations soon failed, however.[154]

At the same time Manchukuo approached representatives of Outer Mongolia with concerns about the vague course of the boundary in southern

Hulunbeir and beyond. To Moscow the Outer Mongolian border with Man-chukuo was almost as important as its own border with the Japanese puppet state since Mongolia occupied a strategic buffer position between the Soviet Union and Manchukuo.

With two internationally unrecognized states at the negotiating table, this conference became a true diplomatic curiosity. Even deciding upon its loca-tion was something of a litmus test. Manchukuo proposed convening in Ulaanbataar, Xinjing, or Hailar, but Moscow pressured the Mongols to meet in Manzhouli on Manchukuo territory. By doing so Russian diplomats sought to limit access for Japanese delegates to Mongolia and to be able to exert influ-ence on the Mongolian delegation through its experienced Soviet consul, Vladimir V. Smirnov, at the same time. Outwardly, however, the Soviet Union preserved a façade of noninterference: not a single Soviet delegate was among the Mongolian delegation. The Manchukuo government was less hypocritical and sent Japanese, Chinese, and Mongol delegates.[155] Negotiations began in June 1935. Yet by the end of the same year they had broken down, in part because new border clashes had already occurred. Unsettled boundaries there-fore continued to provide a pretext for further border conflicts.[156]

The situation along the borders between Soviet Union and Japan and their client states remained tense during the second half of the 1930s. Border patrols now fired without warning, even if the violator crossed only a few dozen me-ters of territory. Moscow's inner leadership circle closely monitored every incident, no matter how trivial, and handled the border issues with great care in hopes of preventing escalation.[157]

It became evident that such hopes were in vain when the border skirmishes culminated in two large-scale clashes in the late 1930s. From 29 July to 11 Au-gust 1938 the first heavy armed conflict broke out in the region around Lake Khasan at the eastern border sector between Manchukuo and the Soviet Union. This clash was prompted in particular by Soviet troop reinforcements at Lake Khasan and by the defection of NKVD commissar Liushkov who had provided Tokyo with essential intelligence on the Soviet forces in the Far East.[158] The following summer, from mid-May to mid-September 1939, both sides concentrated troops along the Manchukuo-Mongolian border in what was to be the second and more serious conflict of Khalkhyn-Gol (Nomon-han), some 180 kilometers south of Hailar. The conflict started when a small Mongolian cavalry unit had entered the disputed area on the Khalka River and was expelled by Japanese forces. It quickly escalated with Soviet and Japanese forces drawn into the conflict. The newly opened strategic railroad between Borzia and Tamsag in the easternmost corner of Outer Mongolia had given Soviet forces a clear strategic advantage during the battles. Japanese troops were further overwhelmed by Red Army tank attacks led by Georgii K.

Zhukov, which nearly annihilated an entire Japanese division and left thousands dead.[159] Reflecting close military cooperation, this time Mongol troops fought and died side by side with the Soviet and Japanese forces—yet another example of how local people became caught up in the struggles of the major powers.[160]

Those two clashes were the heaviest but not the last giving weight to perceptions of the border as a perilous site of confrontation without end. Yet despite these, and even while surveys along the Soviet-Manchukuo and Mongolian-Manchukuo borders were never completed, both sides settled upon spheres of interest after Khalkhyn-Gol. Moscow recognized Japan's client state Manchukuo in exchange for Tokyo's recognition of Outer Mongolia. The danger of Japanese aggression against the Soviet Union finally lapsed with the Soviet-Japanese Neutrality Pact of April 1941 and then further receded with the Japanese surprise attack on the U.S. Pacific Fleet at Pearl Harbor.[161] The defeat of the Japanese forces at the Khalkha River confirmed a political and military alliance between Ulaanbaatar and Moscow and thus held strategic value for the Soviet Union's national security in the Far East. At the same time it mirrored a new balance of power between Japan and Manchukuo on the one side, and the Soviet Union and People's Republic of Mongolia on the other.

"The Border Is Under Lock and Key": Ritualistic Reaffirmations of the Border

"The border is under lock and key" was deployed as a national slogan from the mid-1920s onward, long before the border clashes at Lake Khasan and on the Khalkha River. The Sino-Soviet conflict of 1929 had brought the Far Eastern border into the center of nationwide discourse and triggered an obsession with secure borders.[162] During this conflict the state border emerged as sacred and the border guard appeared as a positive figure in a wider official discourse, replacing the heroic image of the Cossacks of prerevolutionary times. Soon an entire repertoire of songs and poems about border guards came into being. During the period of High Stalinism in the mid-1930s this notion developed into a national preoccupation simply with borders. The state created various ritualistic reaffirmations of the sacred borders in the West and in the East as protecting the socialist *rodina* against imagined enemies from within, as well as danger from the outside. What lay beyond these borders was the unknown home of the enemy. On a conceptual level borders thus were represented as an equilibrium of safety and fear.[163]

Through the prolific production of pamphlets about Soviet border guards as heroes of the nation, the international border on the Argun, Amur, and Ussuri rivers was given the attention of a national audience and was put on the

ГРАНИЦА НА ЗАМКЕ

МОЛОДАЯ ГВАРДИЯ 1930

FIGURE 5.6. Detail of Nikolai K. Kostarev's booklet cover *Granitsa na zamke* (The Border Is Under Lock and Key). Published in 1930, this semifictional collection of "facts" about the Sino-Soviet conflict of 1929 found a wide readership in the Soviet Union.

mental map of the ordinary Soviet citizen, part of a broader strategy to create new Soviet heroes.[164] One key example is Nikolai K. Kostarev's booklet *Granitsa na zamke* (The Border Is Under Lock and Key). Finished in April 1930, it is a hastily written "book of facts" about the conflict at the Far Eastern border in 1929, taking Otpor—the last train stop on Soviet soil—as its setting. Upon his arrival from Leningrad an officer takes Kostarev to a Soviet border patrol. Looking through binoculars at a surveillance post, silhouettes become people. "There, behind the barricade, a handful of Chinese soldiers. One can even see their gray cotton coats as huge and clumsy as they are. They gaze at our armored train. Yesterday they shot at it."[165]

Kostarev's text is a semifictional medley of different "good" and "bad" border stereotypes, which together produce a distorted mirror image of the actual conflict. For instance, the reader learns about Sibiriakov, a supposedly heroic Red Army soldier and loyal party member, who is exposed as a traitor and sentenced to death. A few pages later Kostarev chats with comrade Boris N. Mel'nikov, Soviet consul general in Harbin, who almost fell victim to an assassination by a White guard in Chinese police uniform. The writer and journalist describes the pitiful Chinese refugees from the Zhalainuoer coal mines, irregulars from a small Mokhova gang, and many more protagonists. Kostarev pens every possible border character, from friend to foe, in his small booklet that soon became a bestseller.[166]

Kostarev's border figureheads were not the only characters in the emerging Soviet propaganda offensive. Moscow also began to stigmatize the Russian Cossacks in Trekhreche as antiheroes. Similar to Russian émigrés in Manzhouli, they were labeled Semenovtsy in reminiscence of Ataman Semenov's insurgents and deemed aggressive and backward, people with a deep aversion to the Soviet Union. This phantom of "Cossack resistance" likewise played a crucial role in establishing a Soviet identity in the Far Eastern borderlands. The specter of the mythical evil Cossack had several functions, which remained valid in the Soviet border propaganda of later periods: it connected people emotionally with the Bolshevik struggle in the Civil War, stirred vigilance against a new enemy, presented the borderland as an area of confrontation, and consolidated the outlying areas of the Soviet Union as one against eternal enemies from behind the Argun River.[167]

Soon after the Japanese occupation of Manchuria the propaganda battle flared up again, echoing the incessant border skirmishes.[168] This time it was aimed at a broad audience at home, across the border, and also abroad.[169] International press correspondents led their readers at home to believe that the outrages they described could, at any moment, turn into a major conflagration.[170] Various Soviet and Japanese printings dramatized the Khalkyn-Gol battle in particular. Those booklets clearly identified both aggressor and victim, provided detailed descriptions of causes, developments, and results of the war campaign, and cast their respective sides in a rosy light. In the second issue of *Nomonhan Incident*, a pamphlet published by the Dairen-based *Manchuria Daily News* in summer 1939, Japanese publicists were presumptuous enough to write that borders of Manchukuo would remain unchanged, since "the irresistible determination of the combined Japanese-Manchukuo forces has completely annihilated the mechanized might of the Soviet-Outer Mongol forces in a modern warfare." Despite the florid language, this was far from the truth.[171] Still, the Japanese propaganda itself appeared particularly modern. It published some materials in English, illustrated the articles with high-resolution photographs, and spiced up reports with seemingly objective eye-witness perspectives solicited from American and German journalists.[172]

Both regimes were eager to capitalize on the Khalkhyn-Gol battle and on similar incidents. Each side accused the opponent of being responsible for the violence along the border and assured their public that its own officials were able to remain patient in the face of provocation. Manchukuo counted well over five hundred Soviet offenses between 1932 and 1938. If one believes these reports the western border area was the least troublesome, with just thirty-four incidents during those years.[173] Throughout the 1930s the same accusations were widespread and captured headlines in the Manchukuo-aligned Russian and Chinese presses.[174]

In spreading such accusations of alleged Soviet provocations at the border, the Japanese sought to manipulate or bend the Russian immigrant community of Manchukuo to their advantage. The media, it was hoped, would incite war-like spirits to "keep the Whites in the desired state of inflammation, and to direct their hatred of the Soviets in the interests of the Japanese."[175] After the ratification of the Soviet-Japanese Neutrality Pact in 1941, Manchukuo's anti-Soviet propaganda took on a milder tone. Sharp attacks on Moscow receded from the papers to lectures and meetings. The propaganda in the press depicted the puppet state as an outpost to defend the so-called Greater East Asia Co-Prosperity Sphere from dangers in the north.[176]

With tighter border surveillance, the covert distribution of propaganda items in enemy border territories became increasingly difficult. Radios were common in Moscow, Tokyo, and Harbin but not yet in the borderlands.[177] Therefore in the late 1930s Manchukuo leaflet airdrops gained particular importance as a way of instilling uncertainty and anxiety among the Soviet borderland population. In summer 1937 the rain of Manchukuo propaganda pamphlets was so incessant that additional Soviet fighters were deployed in military districts on the border with Manchukuo.[178] But even those channels seem to have lost significance over time. Despite their proximity to the Soviet Union, the Japanese did not observe any oral or printed enemy propaganda among the Russian émigrés of Manzhouli in the last years of war. But they took no chances: to prevent close ties between the subjects of both states the Japanese authorities in 1943 prohibited the Russian emigrants of Manzhouli from any information exchange with Soviet nationals.[179]

Compared to the Manchukuo propaganda, the language used by Soviet agitators at home and abroad was rather meek. Soviet newspapers tried to unmask Japan's militaristic ambitions and propagandistic designs, mainly by translating compromising book essays and newspaper articles from the

„Мы крепко на .замок запираем наши границы. Наши границы опоясаны железобетоном и достаточно прочны, чтобы выдержать даже самые крепкие зубы. Об эти укрепления разобьется любая империалистическая голова, охваченная военным угаром". (БЛЮХЕР).

FIGURE 5.7. Anti-Japanese caricature published in 1934 in *Otpor*, the official newspaper of the Political Department of Transbaikal Railroad, with a quote from the commander of the Special Far Eastern Army Vasilii K. Bliukher: "We firmly close our borders with this lock. They are girded with ferroconcrete, are strong enough to withstand even the most powerful teeth. These fortifications break any imperialistic head obsessed with militarism."

Japanese.[180] Soviet radio transmissions to the still-limited number of listeners in Siberia and the Soviet Far East and news from abroad received minimal broadcast time.[181]

The radio-owning Russian community in Manchukuo, however, was a main target of Russian-language programs over the airwaves. In a November 1937 interview with *Zaria*, the director of a local radio station informed émigré radio listeners about various restrictions: in particular, the possession of radios with strong receivers and the ability to receive airwaves other than medium-wave frequencies were forbidden. All radio stations broadcasting from Man-chukuo, Japan, and Korea lay within this range. Devices with receivers beyond this range had to be converted. People caught listening to "illegal stations" or in possession of "illegal receivers" were at risk of prosecution and up to one year of imprisonment.[182]

Despite countless violent incidents at the border it was not a tank, a soldier, or a fence but agitation via radio, newspaper, and evening lecture that most pervasively confronted the common people in their daily routines. Propaganda warfare created growing aversion to the neighboring country and bred alienation between Soviet and Manchukuo borderlanders, ingraining the border as a line of separation cleaving unambiguous concepts of "us" and "them." And to people living far from the boundaries, the media coverage and the reports on distant and yet so close places made war a part of everyday life. In the end the myth of the Soviet border guard heroes enjoyed a much longer after-life than their Japanese peers.[183] This hero of the people would reappear in the Sino-Soviet split of the 1960s and 1970s, as we will see in chapter 7.

———

The Sino-Soviet conflict over the control of the Chinese Eastern Railroad and the Japanese occupation of China's Northeast substantially altered the Argun borderland from the late 1920s until the mid-1940s. Only at a few junctures in the history of this region did extraordinary measures emanating from the metropolitan elites transform the periphery as rapidly. The steppe land on the Argun was built up into highly militarized zones, effectively putting an end to uncontrolled cross-border contact.

The arms race meant troubled times for the borderland. The nightmarish prospect of a two-front war caused the Soviet leaders to think twice before choosing to provoke Japan. Principal leaders in Tokyo knew this and played their trump as long as they could. By military clashes and staged incidents Japan pushed for a constant pinprick war. Both sides disagreed over the de-limitation of the border, but at the same time neither was willing to draw precise physical boundaries. Unreliable and ambiguous boundary demarcation continued to provoke various conflicts. The tense atmosphere at the border, in turn, enabled both parties to pursue their own strategic internal objectives, both within the borderlands and beyond.

Two of these features were the propaganda warfare and intelligence work along the boundary and in the hinterland. Japan's sophisticated disinformation machinery had the potential to undermine newly established Soviet authority.

The response of Moscow was rather clumsy, but it was successful in creating a foe and a border in the minds of the ordinary people—especially among those who lived far away from the state's perimeter. The border gradually emerged in a metaphorical sphere, as it was displayed as a bulwark against the hostile neighbor in the propaganda of both regimes. The mental maps of the long-established borderlanders, however, had yet to vanish. While physical separation could be achieved instantly by force, instilling psychological alienation was a protracted process.

Another important measure intended to strengthen the rule of center over periphery was the establishment of border zones, which laid the foundations for the border regime that would endure until the demise of the Soviet Union. The aim of Moscow, as well as Tokyo, was to control all movements of people, to allow only loyal subjects to reside there, and to restrict the access of foreigners and unreliable "elements." Tied to the inscription of these new policies were various cleansings of the borderlands. During the Great Purge "enemy nationalities" and unfaithful subjects in the Soviet Union's borderlands faced deportation. New settlers, often from distant parts of the Soviet Union, replaced them. Their unfamiliarity with the local culture facilitated the growing isolation of the borderland from undesired influences of the world outside and inside. The Japanese principals of Manchuria, too, experimented with their border residents and redefined the roles of different ethnicities. Imperial Japan was able to redistribute the power among the various ethnic groups for its own benefit. To weaken the nominally dominant Han Chinese, Tokyo granted Mongols some illusory autonomy and limited privileges. To some extent the same was true for the Cossacks in Trekhreche and the Russian railroad employees in Manzhouli. Quite soon, however, all the minority Manchukuo borderlanders were to realize that the Japanese interest in them was not an aimless philanthropic endeavor and had its price.

6

Staging Friendship at the Barbed-Wire Fence

IN AUGUST and September 1945 the Soviet Army crushed the Japanese forces in Manchuria in a lightning campaign and then occupied Manchukuo.[1] The Japanese positioned in Manzhouli were caught by surprise when the attack began on 9 August. Though they offered robust resistance, the Japanese units were driven out of the border town with little time to destroy infrastructure. The Japanese civilian population also fled in panic. Within a few days' time tracks and bridges had been repaired and the first Soviet trains were running from Manzhouli toward Harbin to supply the Soviet Army. Chita based newspapers crowed that normal life had returned to the border town, red flags were hanging in front of houses, and restoration work was under way, with local Chinese residents offering their helping hands to Red Army soldiers.[2]

On 18 August 1945 as the victory of the Red Army was only a matter of days away, Mikhail A. Matkovskii, the temporary acting chief executive of the Bureau of the Affairs of Russian Émigrés, wrote a letter to the Soviet consul general in Harbin. Hypocrisy and fear hovered between the lines, as servile in language as the declaration that Trekhreche Russians had handed the Japanese authorities upon ceding control of Hailar in 1932. Bold enough to speak on behalf of all remaining Russian emigrants of Manchukuo, Matkovskii confirmed that they, although living outside the Soviet Union, had "never separated themselves and their thoughts from their own people. They considered their primary and sacred duty to prepare themselves and their children to fulfill their duty to the homeland." Furthermore, promised the letter, "those who had been involved in any activities that harmed the native country will remain on site and will own up to their responsibility."[3] Perhaps Matkovskii did not yet fully know how right he was. Under the surface of Sino-Soviet friendship propaganda the military advance brought fear to the borderlands: weeks of looting and rape by Soviet soldiers in August 1945 and thereafter made that year particularly devastating for the population.[4] About six months later the Red Army withdrew from China's Northeast. Chinese Communist forces quickly "liberated" many parts of the region, and Manzhouli came under control of the Chinese Communist Party on 17 May 1946. Thus, more than three years before the founding of the People's Republic of China on 1 October 1949, the Chinese Communists became masters of Hulunbeir, with direct links to the Soviet Union.[5]

This chapter deals with the late 1940s and the 1950s, a period that is generally perceived as a honeymoon between the People's Republic of China and the Soviet Union, albeit one marred by the seeds of future conflict. Though the social and economic fallout of World War II was certainly felt in the borderlands,[6] many things had changed for the better compared to the years leading up to 1945. There was no longer the threat of war to tyrannize the local population and transform the borderland areas into highly militarized zones. On the Soviet bank of the Argun the siege mentality against enemies from within, the dull hatred of anything and anyone foreign, cultivated in the Soviet Far East and in other regions of the Soviet Union since in the 1930s, gradually withered. Under Nikita Khrushchev, who succeeded Stalin in power, people in the Soviet borderland no longer feared deportation, imprisonment, and other repressions dealt out by their own government as much.[7]

It was in this generally more relaxed atmosphere that the Sino-Soviet friendship evolved. While a spectrum of transborder contacts had already resumed by the second half of the 1940s, officially the alliance began only with the Treaty of Friendship, Alliance and Mutual Assistance, signed by Stalin and Mao Zedong on 14 February 1950 in Moscow. Though the title suggests otherwise, the agreement itself was not negotiated in harmony, and both Communist parties entertained some degree of bad faith, due to historical frictions. While the treaty may have improved relations on paper, it was only in 1953, with Stalin's death and the armistice of the Korean War, that the relationship entered its "golden years." The war had created some sense of brotherhood between the two alienated regimes, and Stalin's overbearing attitude no longer burdened bilateral ties. Economic cooperation, technical assistance, and cultural exchange reached new heights. Over eight thousand Chinese students enrolled in universities across the Soviet Union, while more than twenty thousand Soviet experts were sent to China.[8] Unsurprisingly, border problems receded. Beijing showed a tolerant attitude toward the historically disputed regions as promised in the 1950 treaty guaranteeing mutual respect for territorial integrity. The few border incidents that did occur were solved peacefully, by processes suffused with proclamations of mutual goodwill.[9] However, as this chapter will demonstrate, despite an ubiquitous rhetoric of friendship and increasing bilateral cooperation in economic, educational, cultural, and other spheres, Beijing and Moscow continued to retain their own state border controls and limit cross-border interactions among the local population in their shared periphery.[10] In other words relations between the metropoles warmed, whereas contacts in the borderlands chilled.

A Twin City on the Border: The Making of Zabaikalsk

Stalin's diplomatic triumph at Yalta in February 1945 had resulted in a temporary reestablishment of the terms that had been dissolved in Manchuria as a consequence of the Russo-Japanese War of 1904–1905. The agreement between the Allied leaders had an enormous impact on the fate of Manzhouli. It determined that the two trunk lines of the former Chinese Eastern Railroad and the South Manchurian Railroad would be operated under joint Soviet-Chinese management. From August 1945 onward these two lines were together known as the Chinese Changchun Railroad and were managed by the Soviet Union and Republican China together, until the influence of the Chinese Nationalists in the region weakened. On 1 May 1950, seven months after the People's Republic of China was established, the Chinese Changchun Railroad was formally reestablished, again under joint Sino-Soviet management. On 31 December 1952 the Soviet government transferred its railroad rights, including tracks, land, rolling stock, real estate, and adjacent workshops, to the government of China without payment, as agreed by Mao and Stalin in the 1950 Treaty of Friendship, Alliance and Mutual Assistance.[11] Thus, after a seven-year interregnum China regained full sovereignty over the railroad and Manzhouli. In the post-1949 period, Otpor and Manzhouli again each became a key economic hub for bilateral commerce and the first stop for delegations from the neighboring country. The twin communities became the connecting hinges of the two communist countries and their ally states.[12]

These new circumstances and the intensification of economic and technical ties between the two communist regimes triggered the growth of both border settlements. Within ten years' time Manzhouli's population nearly quadrupled, from 9,180 inhabitants in 1949 to 35,131 in 1959—almost exclusively Han Chinese.[13] Despite the sharp increase in population in Manzhouli in particular and across the Chinese borderland in general, a phenomenon we will discuss momentarily, the situation in Hulunbeir was difficult. Manzhouli, Hailar, and other settlements were affected by the political turmoil marring the first decade of Communist China. Living standards were extremely poor, and residents suffered from severe supply shortfalls.[14]

While all transfer of passengers and cargo prior to 1949 had been handled exclusively in Manzhouli, the full return of the Manchurian railroad to China in late 1952 required the quick revival of Soviet railroad infrastructure at

Otpor, which is why we will now focus on developments in the Soviet borderland.

The Soviet border regions suffered, as did the Chinese borderlands, from several major structural problems that slowed the progress of border settlement on Soviet soil. Even though the state encouraged immigration through material incentives and ideological appeals, the nonetheless sparse and scattered population meant a constant shortage of manpower, limiting further development. In the ten districts of the Chita region that bordered on the People's Republic of China and Mongolian People's Republic, the population density in 1950 was only 1.5 persons per square kilometer. Rural populations in some border areas had even declined since the collectivization. Another problem was their remoteness from urban and industrial centers. Chita, the provincial capital, was 6,208 kilometers from Moscow by train, and many consumer goods, machinery, and even food and fuel had to be imported into the border region by railroad.

In the postwar years the region had a low berth in national hierarchies for the allocation of capital, and its economic output lagged far behind the countrywide norms. The situation for agriculture was similar. Tractors were few and dated back to the early 1930s. Only 9 out of 241 collective farms in the ten border districts of the Chita region had electricity in 1949, and three-quarters of housing in the rural areas either needed repair or was past all hope. Public health care was poor, and the school system was underdeveloped. Yet due to a lack of material incentives the severe shortage of physicians and teachers could not be remedied.[15]

Despite these obstacles, and despite its previous insignificance as a Soviet outpost on the border with Manchukuo, the population in the settlement exploded from about 2,300 in March 1952 to 7,767 by early 1954 due to high demand for railroad personnel to clear the cargo trains. As a consequence Otpor was elevated from a station to an urban-type village (*rabochii poselok*) on 3 July 1954.[16] During the early 1950s, however, living conditions in Otpor remained poor and the railroad lacked manpower across the board, despite the population increase. Instead of the desired number of almost 1,200 railroad workers, only 980 worked at the station in Otpor in 1952. Railroad administration could provide only half of its Otpor staff with more or less normal housing. Rather, whole families usually shared one small room. A total of 185 people lived in simple wooden houses or dugouts, and 298 in dorms or rooms for train conductors. Moreover, nearly 500 railroad employees lived in the "red village," a train car park, which in 1952 consisted of eight passenger and fifty-six heated goods cars known as *teplushka* in Russian.[17] Until at least 1951 the people of Otpor shared one public bathhouse. The food supply was bad. A single railroad car grocery store commuted irregularly between Borzia and Otpor, and canteens were as poorly stocked as one might expect.[18] Only by the mid-1950s did the housing situation improve. In the summer of 1956 all families on the railroad cars could finally move into newly built houses and the "red village" was closed down.[19]

The pioneer stories Otpor veterans tell today often sound similar. In 1955, right after her graduation from Chita Railroad College, Vera P. Zolotareva arrived in Otpor to work at the station. Like most of the new residents she was still an unmarried teenager. Zolotareva was lucky to share a room with five colleagues in one of the six railroad dormitories. In 1953, at the age of sixteen, Iurii I. Kozlov began a lifelong career on the Soviet railroads in Otpor, which was to be interrupted only by one year of military service in the Far East. In the beginning he worked as a locksmith and was later retrained to become first a stoker and, yet later, an engine driver. Kozlov spent his first year on a teplushka. His future wife Valentina, who came in 1957, was shocked once she got off the train: "What a savage landscape, I thought, when I first arrived from Briansk, neither trees nor shrubs, few buildings." When the Kozlovs married in 1958 they were assigned to a flat in a newly erected two-story building.[20]

It was the growth of not just a railroad settlement but also a politics of toponymy that was necessary to establish an operational channel for the transfer of people and commodities between China and the Soviet Union and to create the new state-promoted border of friendship. Otpor, like many other border settlements, embodied a well-remembered political history, as we have seen in chapter 5. During the Sino-Soviet conflict of 1929 the settlement, then still known as Railroad Siding 86, was at the center of conflict. After Soviet troops had defeated Chinese and White Russian forces in Manzhouli, the railroad siding, with its highly symbolic and strategic position at the border, was dubbed Otpor (repulse). In 1953, however, provincial authorities tried to persuade Moscow to rename the border dwelling Zabaikal'e (Transbaikalia), arguing that its current name "at present no longer conforms to the friendly relations" between the two states.[21] The Soviet Ministries of Foreign Affairs and Railroads fully supported the proposal as the current name would "certainly cause confusion among many Chinese comrades passing through the station on their way to the Soviet Union."[22] Other possible names circulated as well. As late as 1958 it was rumored among Otpor's inhabitants that their hometown would soon be renamed Druzhba (friendship).[23] Maybe bureaucrats in Moscow were attentive as bilateral relations began to cool after Khrushchev's "secret speech" at the twentieth congress of the Communist Party of the Soviet Union in 1956. Perhaps nervous that another renaming might be required in the near future, the principal decision makers opted for the neutral geographical choice. Thus Otpor was finally rechristened Zabaikalsk in 1958.[24]

Though in some respects the Soviet border settlement reflected Manzhouli's frontier spirit of half a century earlier, differences prevailed. While Manzhouli was partly built by private capital, construction in Otpor/Zabaikalsk was underwritten entirely with state-allocated funds. The motives of people who put down roots in Manzhouli in the 1900s and Otpor in the 1950s differed as well. Whereas the former came individually, attracted mainly by business opportunities, the latter were sent in groups, assigned by the state to take up work in public enterprises.

The mobility of such people, from nation proper to borderland, marked another striking difference between the Manzhouli pioneers of the late tsarist years and the Otpor pioneers of the 1950s. Valentina V. Kozlova and Vera P. Zolotareva had spent their childhood and teenage years in the Soviet heartland provinces, far away from the Chinese border. Only Iurii I. Kozlov, born in 1937 in a small village in the Borzia district, was a "native" borderlander. Nevertheless, because of the tight border regulations in place during the Manchukuo years, even Iurii had never set foot in China, and after 1945 the border remained essentially closed for locals, as did the border zone for ordinary Soviet citizens.[25] Ever since the 1930s people in the Soviet borderlands had been required to obtain a special pass called *propusk* to enter the border zone. This passport stamp distinguished borderlanders from ordinary Soviet citizens. The authorities maintained a strict border regime despite their proclaimed friendship and a persistent rhetoric that "the old notions of boundaries, as such, will gradually disappear" within the communist hemisphere.[26] Zabaikalsk remained a "closed settlement" inside a zone whose limits were enforced by border guard patrols.

Railroad Traffic Back on Track: The Establishment of a New Transport Hub

Though the Soviet Union had transferred its railroad rights over to the Chinese government by late 1952, it took another two and a half years for the Transbaikal Railroad to hand over Manzhouli's broad gauge tracks and adjacent railroad equipment, houses, car park, and rolling stock to China. On 1 July 1955 Chinese Railroads began its independent operations at the border station, and Manzhouli's more than three hundred Soviet railroad personnel, who had lived permanently in a dormitory attached to the Soviet consulate, returned home. Other Soviet institutions and enterprises subsequently left. The Soviet consulate was closed in December 1956, and the Soviet Far Eastern Freight Traffic Company, which employed up to sixty Soviet laborers in Manzhouli during the 1950s, closed its doors in late 1962. Most of the Soviet workers who left the Chinese border city settled in Zabaikalsk. The number of Soviet nationals (Russian émigrés included) in Manzhouli fell from about 4,000 in 1945 to 2,944 in 1951, then to 138 in 1955 and to just 66 in 1960.[27] The full restoration of Chinese sovereignty over Manzhouli and the repatriation of Russian émigrés, to be discussed later in this chapter, thus resulted in the further disentanglement of the Chinese and Soviet border regions. While during the early 1950s Soviet nationals still belonged to the townscape and Chinese shopkeepers still greeted Soviet customers in reasonably fluent Russian, a European face in the streets of Manzhouli had become a rarity a decade later.[28]

Such processes of ethnic and national homogenization notwithstanding, railroad traffic increased steadily in the postwar period, suggesting closer ties between the metropoles. Transbaikal Railroads inaugurated express trains, running from Otpor to Moscow twice per week, in May 1950, and the Chita-Otpor-Chita train began to operate daily. Chinese Railroads also increased their inland passenger traffic throughout the 1950s, by adding five new train connections to and from Manzhouli. The railroads also reintroduced direct international passenger service between Moscow and Beijing. The first express trains departed from Moscow's Iaroslavskii station and Beijing's main station on 31 January 1954.[29] The people at Otpor station greeted the Moscow-bound train with great fanfare after it had crossed the border on 2 February.[30]

Cargo traffic surged as well due to the intensification of economic cooperation between the Soviet Union and China.[31] The outbreak of the Korean War in June 1950 was another important factor in the sharp increase of international cargo on the railroad line. Since the second half of 1950 the border settlements became the major hub for military equipment shipments en route from the Soviet Union and its allies to the Korean Peninsula.[32] Several civilian agreements facilitated cargo traffic on the railroad. On 14 March 1951 Soviet and Chinese Railroads concluded the Sino-Soviet Treaty of Coordinated Railroad Transport, in 1954 Chinese Railroads joined the International Railroad Cooperation Organization, and in 1956 cooperation with eleven socialist countries resulted in the further expansion of railroad cargo capacity. Within five years international transit cargo increased by more than six times, from 719,000 tons in 1951 to its peak of 4,864,000 tons in 1955, which would then steadily decrease from the late 1950s onward to settle, at the height of the Sino-Soviet split in 1970, at the nadir of 119,000 tons.[33]

Though the figures might suggest otherwise, the cargo terminals at Manzhouli and Otpor never met the government's planning objectives throughout the 1950s. Inadequate discipline and security, incomplete railroad equipment, and technical deficiencies were common problems at Otpor station.[34] A limited deployment of Soviet customs officers resulted in insufficient controls,

TABLE 6.1. Annual international cargo shipments through Manzhouli (in thousands of tons)

Year	Import	Export	Total
1951	515	204	719
1952	1,149	1,146	2,295
1954	1,952	1,664	3,616
1956	1,608	1,991	3,599
1958	1,998	1,426	3,424
1960	1,902	913	2,815
1962	1,817	412	2,229
1964	879	280	1,159
1966	1,159	203	1,362
1968	291	38	329
1970	73	46	119
1972	210	124	334
1974	271	131	402
1976	157	108	265
1978	208	99	307
1980	153	97	250
1982	351	84	435
1984	1,273	422	1,695
1986	1,981	988	2,969
1988	1,509	1,104	2,613
1990	1,814	761	2,575

Note: Manzhouli zhan zhi, 133.

and the lack of railroad employees led to delays in cargo shipments.[35] Transit goods often waited weeks, not days or hours, for clearance.[36]

The increasing transit figures disguise the fact that, in contrast to imperial times and the tumultuous late perestroika years, Sino-Soviet border trade amounted to less than 1 percent of overall bilateral trade volume in the late 1950s. Whereas long-distance trade by train continued to rise throughout this period, the benefits of this increase at the border were insignificant.[37] Consequently, the figures suggest closer connections between Moscow and Beijing than between the Soviet and Chinese borderlands. This tendency also points to the stronger centralization and integration of the Chinese and Soviet borderland economies with their respective metropoles. Over the years central state planning had marginalized the regional economy.

In addition to the international cargo traffic and the insignificant formal border trade, informal forms of commodity exchange unquestionably prevailed during the alliance period, if on a smaller scale. After the Soviet victory over Japan in 1945 illegal trade had returned to the trains between China and the Soviet Union.[38] Compared to the scope and pattern of early twentieth century contraband, however, the illicit trade of the postwar period is barely worth mentioning. It cannot be compared to the bold trafficking of liquor on horse carts or sophisticated contraband networks choreographed by well-established borderlanders, such as the smuggling ring of Xin Fanbin and Arkadii A. Ianechek, with their secret deals hammered out at Ianechek's kitchen table.

Rather, smuggling in the postwar years was largely the province of people working or traveling on international trains. Probably most important in this regard was the outflow of illegal currency, such as the exodus of Soviet rubles to Port Arthur and other destinations in China's Northeast where they enjoyed a high purchasing power, and schemes for the profitable exchange to Chinese yuan during the dispersal of Soviet soldiers, advisors, and railroad personnel to Manchuria from the late 1940s to the early 1950s.[39] Soviet railroad employees in Otpor and Manzhouli were also involved in small-scale illegal barter. The conductor Vasilii V. Aleshin, for instance, purchased two bottles of vodka and several pairs of shoes for his colleague Anna P. Sedova in Manzhouli in August 1947 and received twenty packs of cigarettes in return.[40] Yet despite the increase in goods and passenger traffic in the mid-1950s, smuggling on the freight and passenger trains actually declined.[41] The scale of smuggling was nothing compared to earlier days, not least because customs examinations in times of so-called amity were carried out meticulously, as the Polish traveler Ryszard Kapuściński discovered in 1958:

> A search of the compartments begins, a rooting about on the shelves, under the seats, in nooks and crannies, in ashtrays. Then sounding of the walls, the ceiling, the floor begins. The examining, looking, touching, smelling. Now the passengers take everything they have—suitcases, bags, packages, bundles—and carry them to the station building, in which stand long metal tables. Everywhere, red banners joyfully welcome us to the Soviet Union. Beneath the banners, in a row, customs inspectors, men and women, without exception fierce-looking, serve, almost as though they were bearing some sort of grudge, yes, very clearly a grudge.[42]

Even if the officers did not find any suspicious items, such screenings imprinted upon the minds of the travelers the layers of instructions, prohibitions, limitations, and secrecies that sedimented to form the Soviet state. Only with the border opening in the late 1980s, when more people were allowed to travel again and surveillance structures were no longer as strict, would the mass trafficking of illicit goods recur.

Distant Brothers: Engineering Friendship
in the Borderland

Besides the thousands of cargo carriages that rumbled across the border, and despite the stern expressions of Soviet customs inspectors, the most visible element in cross-border exchanges of the 1950s was arguably the cultural representation of friendship at the shared border. While Soviet-Chinese Friendship Societies in the Soviet Union were established only from 1957 onward, Soviet authorities organized these badges of amity between the two peoples in important cities on the Chinese side even before the founding of the People's Republic.[43] In Dalian (the former Dairen) on the Bohai Sea, for instance, a branch was formed in late 1945 and in Manzhouli no later than 1946. Their task was to foster positive local Sino-Soviet relations, as the Soviet Union urgently needed to polish its image in China. Memories of Soviet abuses of the civilian population during the 1945 military campaign had to be dispelled, so the image of the Russians as colonial oppressors and the Soviets as ill-mannered liberators of China's Northeast would be erased.[44]

During the initial stages of the project, however, propagating friendship was rather difficult. In Manzhouli, publications intended for distribution among the locals were scarce and available only in Russian. Newspapers and journals were passed from hand to hand until they dissolved but did not reach most of the local Mongols and Chinese. Russian émigrés proved to be ignorant of the new rulers' culture and way of life.[45] The association held regular member gatherings and organized rallies on commemorative days like Pushkin's one hundred fiftieth birthday as well as on Soviet and Chinese communist holidays. By 1949 the Manzhouli municipal authorities had fully adopted the Soviet repertoire of public performance. For the Anniversary of the October Revolution, about two thousand Chinese and two hundred Soviet citizens gathered in the park around the Soviet War Memorial for a minute of silence, followed by several speeches on the Sino-Soviet friendship. An orchestra played and the streets were decorated with flags, slogans, and portraits depicting Marx, Engels, Lenin, Stalin, Mao, and Sun Yatsen. Membership tripled within two years' time, rising from almost 500 members in October 1947 to 1,641 members in September 1949—roughly 18 percent of the city's overall population.[46] In 1952 the Chinese-Soviet Peoples' Friendship Palace was opened, to become the heart of Manzhouli's various friendship activities.[47]

From early on the Sino-Soviet Friendship Society tried to reach a broad audience in Manzhouli. It ran a number of cultural circles, a theater group, a choir, and sports teams and it set up photo exhibitions. It organized a campaign against illiteracy and a Russian language-training program—each with fifty to one hundred participants in 1949. The association was in charge of a small library, which soon enjoyed popularity among the Mongol, Chinese, and Soviet communities of Manzhouli. The city housed two cinemas, one Russian-language movie house run by the Association of Russian Émigrés in Manzhouli and one privately owned Chinese theater that screened only Soviet movies and Chinese productions from the Harbin Studios. Both movie houses were very popular among the citizens. Ivan M. Golkin, head of the Society of Soviet Citizens in Manzhouli, was a member of the Sino-Soviet Friendship Society's managing committee. Some of the committee members, like Zhang Yanqin, who had joined the Chinese Communist Party in Yan'an in 1933, prided themselves on their revolutionary past. The society's first secretary was Manzhouli's mayor Liu Fuzu.[48]

Though these biographies might suggest otherwise, it was difficult to recruit suitable cadres for the group. Since at least 1947 Liu's leadership was understood to be temporary, continuing only because other candidates were rejected and some even imprisoned due to their economic background or political past as members of the Guomindang, the Chinese Nationalist Party, or collaborators with the Manchukuo regime.[49] Yet despite these standards, admission to the friendship society did not require even the most basic grasp of the culture and language of the Soviet Union. Though the neighboring state was literally within sight, some of the leading committee members had never or only briefly visited the Soviet Union and lacked essential language skills and any familiarity with the culture of the neighboring region. The aim of the organization, however, was not really to bridge cultures. Though called Sino-Soviet Friendship Societies, their objective was to regulate and channel contacts rather than unify the two peoples.

Basketball Diplomacy: How Best Friends Crossed the Border

The public representation of the encounters between the two peoples in the borderlands nonetheless suggested a pure and abiding bond. From 1950 onward, Manzhouli's railroad station became the stage for countless reception ceremonies and lavish friendship performances portrayed endlessly across newspapers and booklets in both countries.[50] The story line contradicts Kapuściński's bad impressions of the border, but, dubiously, is almost interchangeable in Chinese and Soviet publications. Witness, for instance, this recollection of an Uzbek artistic group on tour in China, published in *Pravda* (Truth), the central organ of the Soviet Communist Party, in February 1953: "A bright, sunny day. We left the Soviet Union as our train passed the border. Manzhouli. Even before we got off our car we heard the voices of the people who greeted us. Then we got off the car. Enthusiastic welcomes from every direction, 'Stalin, *wansui*,' 'Stalin, *wansui*,' 'Long live friendship with the Soviet Union.'"[51] Though the true feelings and excitement of the travelers were certainly embellished, such statements at least prove that, in contrast to the Manchukuo period, foreign travelers were again allowed on the trains in great numbers. Chinese papers mimicked these exaggerated descriptions, such as the *Renmin Ribao* (People's Daily) article celebrating the arrival of a Soviet delegation at Manzhouli in late October 1951: "Silk banners of every color are flying at the station. The railroad platform is furnished with portraits of Chairman Mao, Soviet and Chinese flags flutter in the wind. A huge red cloth is emblazoned with a slogan proclaiming, 'Long live the everlasting deep friendship of the Sino-Soviet peoples' and 'The Sino-Soviet friendship is the powerful guarantee of peace in the Far East and the world.' Accompanied by music, the sound of drums and enthusiastic applause the train pulls into the station."[52] Otpor became, like Manzhouli, a stage for such artificial friendship performances. Every time a special train pulled into the station railroad workers got off to wave their handkerchiefs. When young Asian delegates passed the border to attend the Sixth World Festival of Youth and Students in Moscow in the summer of 1957, they were greeted warmly by the citizens. "Everybody went to the train station to welcome the delegations. . . . Foreigners were greeted with a brass band and dances in a friendly, you could say joyful, atmosphere," as Valentina V. Kozlova recalls this simulated friendship reception.[53]

It was not only in the national papers that the border stations became symbolic of the eternal friendship between both countries. Chinese travelogue authors who visited the Soviet Union, whether they were directorate members of friendship societies or participants in youth delegations, universally depicted the northern neighbor as heaven on earth and its people as enlightened and charming paragons of virtue. Chinese pilgrims of that time routinely opened their narratives with the familiar border-crossing scene in which they had to change trains and would then pass through the still dwarfish wooden state gate between Manzhouli and Otpor to begin their journey into the bright future.[54]

Confirming trade statistics, state-sanctioned writings describing the amity between the two peoples of that time suggest that after two decades of confrontation and mistrust the border had become fully permeable once again. Yet the number of locals who were actually allowed to cross the state line illustrates that that portrayal was inaccurate. In fact forms of cooperation and encounter in the Sino-Soviet borderland of this period were quite deliberately kept to a minimum.

Beyond the performance of friendship in the media and social organizations, cross-border cooperation was a theme of disaster relief and forest and steppe fire prevention, and it made its mark in medical assistance and scientific

КРЕПИМ ДРУЖБУ ВО ИМЯ МИРА И СЧАСТЬЯ!
讓我們為和平與幸福來鞏固友誼!

FIGURE 6.1. "We strengthen friendship in the name of peace and happiness!"—Soviet propaganda postcard by Viktor S. Ivanov hailing the alliance with Beijing with a print run of 100,000 copies, 1954.

research, among other realms.[55] In 1956 Moscow and Beijing agreed to organize bilateral scientific research commissions to explore the boundary rivers' potentials for water transportation and energy provision. In the second half of the 1950s scientists studied the topography, hydrology, and geology of the Argun and Amur basins for the benefit of joint future mining, hydroelectric, and other economic projects.[56] *Renmin Ribao*, mouthpiece of the Chinese Communist Party's Central Committee, assured readers in the fall of 1956 that China and the Soviet Union will "work hard together to explore and develop" the border rivers and depicted the collaborative explorations as a remarkable step to further "strengthening the friendship between the Chinese and the Soviet people."[57]

Hydro-geological research was just one among several fields in which the fleeting thaw in relations had created tangible cross-border ties. When ice floes on the Argun River threatened to cause the flooding of some eight hundred houses across several villages in the Trekhreche region in April 1958, Soviet military planes bombed the ice barrier, saving the Chinese villages.[58] As late as January 1960 both governments signed agreements stipulating measures for forest and steppe fire prevention. Volunteers from both sides extinguished fires near Zabaikalsk in the spring. That same year workers built a sixty-meter-wide protection belt along several sections of the border zone to prevent fires from crossing the border, and several Soviet planes and helicopters took up regular fire-surveillance flights along both banks of the Argun. To further bolster fire protection bilateral commissions negotiated plans to erect watchtowers and to clear undergrowth from the area over the following years.[59]

Yet even at the zenith of the alliance regional cross-border exchange beyond disaster relief was highly limited with few real day-to-day contacts between ordinary people. Contact was rare even among railroad men at the border stations. Besides the three daily shifts of workers, each consisting of eight to twenty Chinese men who lived in a dormitory at Otpor station from 1952 onward, there were literally no Chinese citizens who stayed on the Soviet side. The tally of Soviet railroad men who worked shifts in Manzhouli was even lower after 1955. They did not stay overnight but commuted from the Soviet border settlement every day by car.[60]

Yet these few routine encounters were often depicted glowingly by the Chinese and Soviet press. For instance, on 1 October 1959 a report appeared in the local paper *Leninskii Put'* (Lenin's Way) on the railroad workers of the border stations of Zabaikalsk and Manzhouli, purporting to illustrate the peculiar friendship between the two peoples. Raisa A. Kuznetsova is the protagonist in this report, which bore the telling title "Russian and Chinese—Brothers Forever," tasked with recounting the everyday working life of Soviet duty officers at the border railroad trading post. Kuznetsova worked together with a Chinese colleague in her office for eight years. In the beginning she could communicate with him only through an interpreter, but "now they converse in simple sentences, and when the words run out, they make use of gestures and sketches." The text comes to an emotive close: "In many divisions of Zabaikalsk, Russians and Chinese work shoulder to shoulder. All are united by the strong friendship and one goal—to move more rapidly into the bright future. The workers of this border station often visit their friends on the other side of the border. They discuss and agree on forthcoming work, exchange their experiences, learn all that is useful from one another. This good friendship, hard as steel, unites the railroad workers of both border stations."[61] At best such enthusiastic accounts of everyday encounters between Chinese and Soviet professionals were only partially true. Such articles veiled the fact that the Transbaikal and the Qiqihar Railroad administrations as well as the Soviet and Chinese border guard structures seem to have been among the few institutions that collaborated and had even established a routine exchange of delegations. In addition to top-level talks, Manzhouli and Zabaikalsk railroad men held regular meetings on work experience, drawing several hundred participants annually.[62] Both railroad stations exercised a limited degree of cooperation—apart from train cargo matters—in other fields, such as road maintenance and medical assistance, as well. Zabaikalsk offered health care to the children of the Chinese railroad men, while a Chinese doctor shared his knowledge of acupuncture with his Soviet colleagues. Between September and October 1957 alone nine Chinese nationals are said to have been treated in nearby Soviet hospitals.[63]

Beyond expert exchange among the Soviet and Chinese railroad authorities and collaboration on medical assistance, other forms of regulated encounter occurred. After a Communist Party of the Soviet Union's Central Committee resolution (passed in January 1956) permitted international tourism for Soviet citizens, Chita region tourist groups started to vacation in China. But the program was insignificant, attracting fewer than a hundred tourists annually. The first Chinese tour groups visited the Soviet borderlands in 1959. Membership in tourist delegations, however, was reserved for select cadres. Those hoping to become part of a tour group needed to obtain travel permissions and were asked to write a resume.[64]

Besides nomenklatura tourism of political elites, authorities also organized regular small delegation exchanges during national holidays. Soviet railroad men from the border station visited their Manzhouli colleagues during Spring Festival, on the occasion of China's national holiday on 1 October, or for the Anniversary of the People's Liberation Army. Other groups participated in this form of public friendship performance too. Annually, on national holidays, several delegations commuted between the Chita region and the Inner Mongolian Autonomous Region to which Hulunbeir belonged. Between 1956 and 1958 about twenty Chinese groups visited the Chita region, but the numbers declined afterward and tourism was halted in full after 1961.[65] Even during the alliance regime, being included within a delegation or serving as an employee of the railroad was the only chance for many people to see those across the border, as private visits had long become a thing of the past.[66] Being a railroad worker or delegation member did not necessarily mean being in touch with people from across the border. Compared to the early twentieth century, crossing the border had become something extraordinary.

At the same time metropolitan diktats were not the only force keeping apart the people of the borderland. Many of the locals, as Iurii I. Kozlov puts it, "simply had no desire" to see the world on the other side of the fence. Most of the people who had migrated to the border in the 1950s, in fact, would not cross it until the late 1980s.[67] With no clue about the workings of the neighboring state or about indigenous life in the borderland, they had moved to Otpor from the Urals or the Volga region and to Manzhouli from south of the Great Wall. Their lack of language skills or familiarity with the region and the clash of different cultures generated indifference toward the distant neighbor. In addition, a low standard of living on both sides impeded economic incentives for informal cross-border exchange.

Yet the occasional organized trip across the Argun River disrupted the general detachment to bring people from both river banks closer together, if only for brief moments. In fall 1958, on the occasion of the ninth anniversary of the People's Republic of China, a large youth delegation from the Chita region visited the Chinese borderlands on a five-day trip. The group included volleyball and basketball teams, the Transbaikal Military District dancing ensemble, and a choir of twenty singers from the Chita Music Academy, plus several translators. After an arrival ceremony at Manzhouli station and two volleyball and basketball matches in the afternoon, the day ended with a mass meeting in support of eternal friendship attended by some fifteen hundred young participants.

The next morning the Soviet delegation left for nearby Hailar. An evening banquet in a clubhouse, a highlight of the trip, "demonstrated the vivid friendship and union of the two Great peoples." The Soviet delegates sang "Katiusha" and "Moskva-Pekin," and the evening concluded with traditional dances performed by representatives of both countries. On the morning of 1 October some twenty thousand people joined the anniversary parade. The full program in Hailar went on for two more days, with yet more concerts, volleyball and basketball matches, visits to a school and several factories, and the ceremonial laying of a wreath for the fallen Soviet soldiers of August 1945. On the fourth day, after three days of constant gifts, exchanging of communist devotionals and cordial words and phrases, and tables groaning with food and cigarettes, the program diverged from the frenetic performance of bonhomie to visit an autochthonous cooperative some forty kilometers outside Hailar.

To many of the Soviet delegates the nomadic way of life on display there must have seemed rather exotic since nomadism had been in retreat in the Soviet borderlands for quite some time. Nomads on the Chinese side of the border had, however, deftly adapted to the new political regime. First, they showed off traditional horse riding skills, then the Soviets were assigned to small groups to be offered tea in yurts furnished with Mao portraits. The head of the cooperative lectured on the nomads' past, "the destitute prerevolutionary life of the Mongols, feudal oppressors, and Japanese imperialists."[68] After tea the Soviet visitors inspected newly erected backyard blast furnaces in the grassy steppe. Very much in the zeitgeist of the Great Leap Forward, a catastrophic attempt by Mao to hasten industrialization and crop production, the visitors reassured their Mongol hosts that China would overtake Great Britain in steel production in a short time. With such rapid progress "you very soon will drive the U.S. imperialists out of your territory," *Neimenggu Ribao* (Inner Mongolia Daily) quoted one of the Soviet delegates.[69]

The last stop on the way back home was brief and particularly delicate. The Soviet delegates met two dozen Russian emigrants, most of them between eighteen and twenty-five years old, in a Hailar school—allegedly at the émigrés' request. In a reserved atmosphere and with an attitude of superiority, the Soviet youth delegates enlightened "these inadequately informed Russians" about the Chita region's achievements during the last four decades and about the freedoms enjoyed in the Soviet Union. On the fifth day of its trip the delegation returned home after one last basketball game in Manzhouli in which the Soviets defeated the Chinese again, this time by a score of 97 to 72.[70]

The tour across the border, though still orchestrated, even stilted, seems to be one of the few encounters in which delegates were actually permitted to meet locals living across the Argun River. They might have had a chat with a Chinese sportsman after a volleyball match or with a Mongol in a yurt. The journey to the East certainly did not change people's mind-sets in a fundamental way, and its effects hardly reached a mass audience. Yet it was at least some kind of cross-border encounter. But what was a carefully prepared visit between a young selected Soviet delegate with a likewise selected herdsman in a yurt decorated with a portrait of the Great Helmsman of the 1950s, compared to an accidental and informal meeting between a lonesome Chinese trapper and a young Cossack woman of the 1900s, possibly the beginning of a romance or a lifelong relationship? In short, compared to earlier times, state authorities now regulated cross-border flows of people, areas of contact between borderlanders from both Argun banks had shrunk, and forms of encounter had taken on a much more formal shape.

When No One Dares to Speak Russian Any Longer: The Sinicization of Hulunbeir

The meetings of the Soviet delegates with the Russian émigrés at Hailar, and with nomads in a cooperative, point to the fact that both the towns as well as the countryside of Hulunbeir became more integrated into the Chinese heartland during the first decades of the People's Republic. As a corollary to this development, both groups with whom the young Soviet delegates had mingled on their trip across the border, the Russian émigrés and the nomads, were dying species in the borderland by that point.

Russian life in Hulunbeir was in decline, as was reflected in the decreasing number of Soviet nationals residing in Manzhouli. Circumstances in the Trekhreche delta were similar. After "liberation" in 1945 the Cossack community had faced strong repression from the Soviet authorities and had fallen victim to Sovietization policies. Officers of the Soviet secret police agency NKVD followed in the shadow of the army. They arrested about a quarter of the male Cossack population, mainly those who had left the Soviet Union during collectivization or had collaborated with the Japanese, and deported them to the camps of the Gulag. The other residents were given Soviet passports after the Presidium of the Supreme Soviet of the Soviet Union had in November 1945 issued a decree announcing the "restoration" of Soviet citizenship to Russians residing in China. In autumn 1949, after an exceptionally good harvest, the remaining Russian farmers in the Trekhreche area suffered an expropriation campaign. Though there are no reports about human executions, dekulakization went hand-in-hand with the mass extinction of livestock. Until the mid-1950s agitators sent by the Soviet consulate in Manzhouli and approved by the Chinese state urged Cossacks to return "home." Those who followed such calls were resettled in large numbers in Kazakhstan and the Urals. Some, like Vasilii M. Iakimov, who left the Trekhreche region voluntarily in 1959, were allowed to settle just across the river unless their names were on a list of the secret police. Iakimov moved with his family to Abagaitui. But since the collectivization the formerly prosperous Cossack village on the Argun had been impoverished, its "entire state farm possessed less than one Russian farmer in Trekhreche," Iakimov recalls with resignation. Once Beijing allowed those Cossacks who had dared to remain on Chinese soil to apply for third country citizenship in 1962, the majority opted for relocation to Australia or Latin America. With most of the former population now gone, Chinese settlers took over deserted Russian farms.[71]

As Sino-Soviet relations continued to deteriorate in the 1960s, the Chinese authorities further restricted the activities of the remaining ethnic Russians in Hulunbeir. A case in point was the shutdown of the Association of Soviet Émigrés, as the organization was euphemistically termed, in September 1962.[72] Those who had continued to live in their wooden houses in the Trekhreche villages and hamlets were mostly poor, did not have relatives in the Soviet Union, and were commonly the offspring of mixed Chinese-Russian couples. A few years on, during the Cultural Revolution (1966–1976), the political upheaval in China that was intended to bring about a return to revolutionary Maoist beliefs, Russian people were blamed for spying for the Soviet Union. Adherents of the Russian Orthodox faith were accused of belief in superstition. Soviet passports protected some émigrés during the peak of the turmoil. Those of mixed origin, who generally lacked Soviet documents, however, were brutally assaulted: some were tortured and killed and "their bodies thrown down the wells."[73] Yang Yulan, alias Tamara V. Erekhina, daughter of a Chinese father and a Russian mother, remembers those days with horror: "Back then we were not even allowed to speak Russian at home, though we were born here and there had been Russians living here for about one century."[74] As a second-generation borderlander and descendant of a mixed couple, Yang was fluent in both languages.

FIGURE 6.2. Abagaitui with Manzhouli across the Argun in the far background in 2009.
Founded as a Cossack village on the Russian river bank in the eighteenth century, it became a
typical Soviet village with an animal husbandry state farm.

During the Cultural Revolution and the Soviet-Chinese rift, Moscow organized one last repatriation campaign. As part of that effort members of the
Russian diaspora in Trekhreche were resettled just across the river on the
Soviet bank of the Argun. For most repatriates it was not a return but rather a
new beginning in an alien country that they had never before visited. Ivan M.
Sokolov, for example, emigrated with his wife and his eight children in 1970.
Sokolov was born in 1927 in the Trekhreche village Verkh-Urga, where his
parents had fled during the Russian Civil War. On the Chinese side they had
owned a cattle farm. But after the Sokolovs had found a new home in Soviet
Abagaitui, the former Cossack village further upstream near Zabaikalsk,
Ivan M. Sokolov was assigned to work in the local state farm (*sovkhoz*) to feed
state-owned animals. His family had been among the last on the Argun, familiar with both cultures, fluent in both languages, and accustomed to traditional
forms of agriculture.[75]

It was not just the prerevolutionary way of life of the rural Russian diaspora
that came under pressure from the long arm of Beijing's Communist autocracy. At first, after the August 1945 Soviet military campaign against Japan, the
borders once again became permeable for some time. Many nomads in Inner
and Outer Mongolia had high hopes for a reunification of the two divided
territories into one country. In the years to follow, as had been the case in the

FIGURE 6.3. Russian Trekhreche Cossack Ivan M. Sokolov at his kitchen table in Abagaitui, 2009. He was born to Russian Cossack emigrants in Trekhreche in 1927, and his entire family was repatriated in 1970 to the Soviet Union—a country he had never set foot in before.

1910s and 1920s, when due to land grabs the Russian and Soviet governments supported indigenous secessionist activities, Moscow once again regarded Hulunbeir as an area of special interest. A new Moscow-supported autonomous province was proclaimed on 1 October 1945, with a government largely modeled on the old Manchukuo administration of the Northern Xingan province. Khorloogiin Choibalsan, leader of the Mongolian People's Republic, expressed his hope to fuse Hulunbeir, the northeastern end of Inner Mongolia, and other Mongol territories in China with the Mongolian People's Republic. In January 1946 the Eastern Mongolian Autonomous Government was established under a united procommunist leadership. During the following years many Hulunbeir Mongols sought refuge in the Mongolian People's Republic. In the end, however, the Soviet approach to the indigenous borderlands proved once more too opportunistic. By May 1946, once the Chinese Communist Party had gained a foothold in Manchuria, Stalin discontinued his support to the indigenous separatists in Hulunbeir and other Chinese borderlands and the territories were transferred to the Chinese Communists during the so-called second partition of Mongolia.[76]

As in other parts of the Inner Mongolian Autonomous Region, the autochthonous society in Hulunbeir was subject to violent reorganization by the Chinese Communist regime after 1949.[77] Interethnic relations, especially those between Han and indigenous nomadic peoples, were anything but harmonious. Ethnic minorities were integrated into the new Chinese state with massive sinicization efforts and with a view toward raising a barrier between the formerly connected transborder peoples on either side of the Argun.[78]

The new masters restricted religious freedom and removed all special privileges granted to nobles and lamas. During a campaign against "counterrevolutionaries" in 1951, half of the twenty-two temples in Hulunbeir were subject to violent attacks, though Buddhism was not entirely eradicated and some monasteries remained undamaged. At the Ganchzhur Monastery, where a huge trade fair was held annually until the mid-twentieth century, for example, monks were grouped into brigades in an attempt to secularize them. Yet they continued to live near the temple, to read sacred books, and to pray. Eventually, however, during the Cultural Revolution, this sanctuary was destroyed and the monks suffered terribly. By that time too the popular practice of Lamaism was nearly wiped out.[79]

In addition to the aforesaid disruptions, the post-1949 period may also be described as revolutionary in its rearrangement of land ownership and forms of agriculture. Under a land reform campaign promulgated during the first years of Communist rule, a comprehensive redistribution of property from herdsmen with large livestock to the "poor" was carried out. To improve agricultural production the Maoist leadership expanded the "rationalization" of Hulunbeir's pastoral production with the introduction of people's communes during the Great Leap Forward in 1958–1960. Although in the words of the Chinese state media Hulunbeir's autochthonous population was "skipping several stages of social development," rapid progress came at a high price. As a result of deficient planning the number of livestock dropped rapidly. At the same time the area of farmland more than doubled during the campaign, only to fall sharply again after 1961. With collectivized ownership, distribution, and consumption patterns, most of the stock farming economy was now in the hands of the state, and little remained of the pre-1949 traditional pastoral economy.[80]

———

In the postwar era, the world's longest land border was briefly a background to friendship but returned to serve more durably as a great divide. If we limit our glances to its first decade, as this chapter did for the most part, the alliance period appears to be one of growing cross-border contact, especially in the area of international passenger and cargo trade. As vehicle for transit, however, the railroad functioned as a narrow corridor that hardly affected its surroundings. The passengers on the trains usually traveled long distances between Shanghai and Warsaw or Pyongyang and Leningrad, making only a brief stopover at the border when the bogies were changed. Consequently, the rail line facilitated the expansion of an international flow of people and commodities, whereas local and informal forms of border trade did not rejuvenate under the two communist states.

Official friendship rituals at both border railroad stations, if celebrated with hollow phrases in the press, also did not bring the people on the Argun closer to one another. When locals from across the border came to pay a visit their trips had been approved and even neatly choreographed by government bodies well ahead of time. Thus contacts between men and women of the borderlands were no longer spontaneous but ritualized. Ultimately, then, such official displays of harmony reaffirmed rather than mediated the differences between nations.

Such formalized transborder connections were also caused in part by new demographics, which had changed significantly on both shores of the Argun. Whereas the Soviet territory near the international border had been ethnically homogenized during the 1930s, the Chinese borderland caught up over the following two decades. Moscow assisted in this process as both governments collaborated in the "repatriation" of the Russian emigrants. Simultaneously with the expulsion of the Russians from Trekhreche villages and Manzhouli the Chinese government also began to curb the traditional living sphere of the nomadic herdsmen in Hulunbeir—the genuine borderlanders. Thus, by way of forced denomadization, restriction of religious practices, and the prohibition of Russian as the language among the people of the Russian diaspora, Beijing attacked the last symbols of borderland unity and suppressed still-existing border cultures.

With the influx of new women and men from the heartland provinces of both states a new kind of borderlander gradually replaced the indigenous and quasi-indigenous denizens. Han Chinese were relocated to the eastern shores of the Argun by the means of political campaigns reminiscent of Stalinist practices. Immigration strategies in the Soviet borderland were less brutal in the postwar decades. The Soviet authorities attempted to attract new settlers mainly by economic incentives and were, judging by the numbers, far less successful than the Chinese. The majority of these colonists were indifferent toward the traditional borderland milieu, as they had no previous border-crossing experiences and were unfamiliar with the culture and language of their new surroundings. These new settlers were less likely to challenge the state-imposed regimes but implicitly accepted and followed the contours of the political border.

7

Invisible Enemies across the
Frozen River

DURING THE 1950s all along the Sino-Soviet border, a rhetoric of friendship had carried the day. Soon, however, the border would again become an arena of conflict, this time between the two leviathans of communism. The rapid deterioration of their partnership, which culminated in violent border clashes on the Ussuri in March 1969, altered not just the rhetoric but also the reality of everyday life in the borderlands. Even more so than in the tense Manchukuo years, people on the Argun were separated and isolated. Only from the mid-1980s onward did subtle signs of reconciliation bring new hope.

Whether it fell under the banner of friendship or enmity the border of the post-1949 period remained a grim place, an ugly symbol of imposed statehood, staffed with hostile soldiers and customs inspectors. When Ryszard Kapuściński, a globe-trotting journalist from Poland, arrived at the Soviet border station Zabaikalsk in 1958, it was difficult for him to glean any sign of friendship. His writing describes, rather, the continuation of a strict border regime despite an officially proclaimed amity:

> Barbed wire. Barbed-wire barriers are what you see first. They protrude out from the snow, hover over it—lines, trestles, fences of barbed wire. . . . On the face of it, this thorny, rapacious barrier stretching along the border seems like an absurd and surreal idea, for who would force his way through here? As far as the eye can see there is only a desert of snow, no roads, no people, and the snow is two meters high; taking a single step is impossible. And yet these walls of barbed wire have something to say to you, have something to communicate. They are saying: be careful, you are crossing the border into a different world. You will not escape from here; you will not get away. It is a world of deadly seriousness, orders, and obedience. Learn to listen, learn humility, learn to occupy the least amount of space

possible. Best mind your own business. Best be silent. Best not to ask questions.[1]

At first sight the Polish journalist and travel writer's impression seems an anomalous observation by a peculiar passenger, far from representative of everyday life for most in the borderlands. Yet Poles, Vietnamese, Swedes, and all manner of nationals soon were to become the major border passers in much more significant numbers than people from the Soviet Union or China or even locals from the Argun borderland. And whether Kapuściński's reflections were as overstated, even fictitious, as they might seem at first blush is one key question to bear in mind.

Before we discuss how the nature of the Argun borderland changed during the time of the Sino-Soviet split, we must briefly outline developments in high politics, as by this point the metropoles very much determined the local transborder relations on the ground. Khrushchev's criticism of Stalin at the twentieth congress of the Communist Party of the Soviet Union in February 1956 is often perceived as a watershed moment in the history of the Soviet-Chinese alliance, initiating a second phase of enmity. Mao perceived Khrushchev's denunciation of Stalin as threatening because the Chinese Stalinist leadership was drawing the ideological justification for their regime from Stalin's role in Soviet history. In the years that followed deep-rooted disagreements over ideology, economy, military affairs, border territories, foreign policy, and leadership in the communist hemisphere led to intense diplomatic quarrels and public attacks.[2] In 1960 bilateral trade went into free-fall, and Moscow withdrew Soviet experts from China.[3] In the spring and summer of 1962 a border incident in the Xinjiang Uigur Autonomous Region—over the course of which about sixty thousand residents illegally crossed the border from China into the Soviet Union—laid bare the unsettled border issues between the two regimes.[4] Another issue was reparations demanded by the Soviets from China for previous assistance. The Chinese government had to make large repayments, which in popular nationalist myth caused the famines that hit rural China.[5] In addition the fact that Moscow submitted to the United States during the Cuban Missile Crisis of October 1962 while Beijing was victorious in the Sino-Indian border conflict at almost the same time gave Mao Zedong new self-confidence in his rhetorical war against the Soviet leadership. The detonation of China's first atomic bomb in 1964, Mao's decision to end party relations in 1966, and the intervention of Warsaw Pact military forces in Czechoslovakia in 1968 added fuel to the fire in what was becoming a rapidly deteriorating relationship.[6]

The conflict culminated in violent border clashes on the then unheard-of island of Damanskii (Zhenbao), in the Ussuri River, in March 1969. The factors that may have prompted China to launch the attack are myriad, ranging from local conflagrations and domestic politics to international pressures.[7] The clashes on the frozen border river signified two issues. First, there was a revival of disagreements over lines of demarcation, which Beijing now employed for its political agenda.[8] Second, the fighting marked a major realignment in the Cold War. As the Sino-Soviet border skirmishes on the Ussuri were relatively minor in terms of bloodshed, they can be seen as Beijing's signal to Washington that the Sino-Soviet alliance was over and a new alliance could begin.[9]

Throughout the 1970s there was no substantial rapprochement between Moscow and Beijing, although the two countries exchanged ambassadors once again, resumed border talks, and reinstated bilateral trade on a small scale. The situation again threatened to get out of control, however, when Moscow's ally Vietnam attacked Beijing's vassal state Cambodia in November 1978. In retaliation the Chinese leadership launched a punitive campaign against Vietnam in early 1979. With these conflicts in Southeast Asia and the Soviet Union's intervention in Afghanistan in 1979, relations between the two communist countries again went downhill.[10]

This chapter argues that the rift between Beijing and Moscow had a lasting influence on the situation along the border, with direct and indirect consequences for those living in the area. The two communist regimes, armed to the teeth, confronted one another on the border with even more weaponry and soldiers than had been assembled during the Japanese-Soviet arms race in the 1930s. Propaganda campaigns resuscitated old motifs of infiltration, sabotage, espionage, and disinformation, imbuing the border with new legitimacy as a space of enmity. The conflict was, of course, not just about winning or losing the hearts and minds of the people. Though no major war broke out, the war scare affected the security, economy, and demography in the border regions of Hulunbeir and Transbaikalia, and its concomitant outpouring of nationalism altered how the local populace in the divided Argun borderland perceived the border and its adjoining states.

Control Tracking Strips in the Barren Steppe: New Techniques of Border Surveillance

Even during the golden period of the alliance Moscow had never entirely dissolved its border regime of the 1930s. In fact, via several resolutions from the early 1950s onward, the Council of Ministers of the Soviet Union expanded legislation from the 1930s regulating the internal border zones.[11] Local newspapers informed the population of the new rules with full-page announcements about those border laws.[12]

From the 1960s onward some new features were added to the existing monitoring mechanisms of sentries, observation posts, patrols, passport control posts, mines, and barriers on the border with China. The most notable installation was the extension of the "control tracking strip" (*kontrol'no-sledovaia polosa*) directly behind the boundary line and running along at least ninety kilometers of the Sino-Soviet border near Zabaikalsk. The strip consisted in part of two lengths of barbed wire enclosing a primitive raked corridor. The highly granular soil in this corridor served as a crude sensor showing footprints or tire tracks, virtually preventing any surface crossing from going unnoticed. The second row of barbed wire triggered an alarm if touched. Floodlighting, 260 kilometers of electric signaling systems, and other monitoring devices complemented this security system.[13]

Adjacent to the "control tracking strip" was "Zone A," a generally uninhabited area, and fences separated much of this zone from the interior country. Settlements and state farms, which had existed before the zone had been set up, were the only exceptions. Only in such places could ordinary citizens live immediately at the border or cultivate land within sight of the neighboring country. The Kozlov family in Zabaikalsk, for example, farmed on "a tiny plot of land inside the zone . . . directly behind the border, just 400 meters away." Thus, the Kozlovs were within earshot of the Chinese border guards when harvesting cucumbers and, by and large, unafraid of being shot.[14]

The second (populated) zone had been established during the 1930s and was called a "forbidden border zone." It stretched at least thirty kilometers in front of the boundary and "Zone A" itself but often extended even further inland because it encompassed the entirety of every district bordering on China. Warning signs, highway checkpoints, border guard squads on the trains, and patrols making rounds in the open steppe separated this area from the interior. As they had in the past, Soviet citizens had to obtain a special passport from the Ministry of Internal Affairs to enter the zone.[15]

Borderland surveillance was practiced behind the barbed-wire fence on the Chinese side as well throughout the 1950s. There, overall monitoring structures were less strict than on the Soviet side. Yet under the slogan "monitoring the entire border, blocking the sensitive areas" Shiwei, Manzhouli, and seven other settlements and strategic sites in Hulunbeir's vicinity to the state borders had been made restricted zones and cordoned off as early as 1953. This border zone was further extended in 1963, when a total of 84,977 square kilometers were added to the "border restricted area"—about one-third of Hulunbeir's overall territory. The rules for residents living in or passing through the restricted area resembled those of the Soviet Union in their rigidity. Only local residents could obtain the special permits that allowed entry.[16]

When relations between Beijing and Moscow began to cool, both sides implemented stricter border controls. Beginning in September 1962 observation posts were set up at Hulunbeir's international borders with Mongolia and the Soviet Union. The border-control division of the police in Hulunbeir was complemented with additional military police as well as 156 groups of the people's militia recruited from the local population. Within a year structural improvements and an increase of staff shortened the surveillance section assigned to each border guard post, from an average of 343 to just 60 kilometers (73 kilometers at the Mongolian border).[17]

Already by 1964 the Soviet Union had begun to upgrade its existing border protection facilities as well as their vehicles and radio communication technology, which sometimes dated from the Manchukuo period. Border guard posts at the Dauriia division were equipped with additional shelters and holding devices for machine guns. Two large Antonov An-2 biplanes were brought into service for reconnaissance flights. Between 1967 and 1969 six additional border outposts were erected along the roughly 1,050-kilometer-long border with China to guard a zone of about 20 kilometers in length and up to 5 kilometers wide. Motorized observation units further sharpened this scrutiny.[18]

Throughout the escalation of Sino-Soviet tensions the Kremlin pursued a dual strategy of negotiation and quiet military buildup. In January 1966 Leonid Brezhnev signed a new defense agreement with Mongolia, giving Moscow the right to station troops and maintain bases there, just a few hundred kilometers from Beijing. China too began stationing large military garrisons next to the border of the Mongolian People's Republic and the Soviet Union. By 1968 six Soviet divisions in Mongolia and another sixteen in the Soviet Far East were amassed near the border with China, ready for combat. They faced forty-seven lightly armed Chinese divisions. Between 1968 and 1973 the number of People's Liberation Army divisions doubled and Soviet troop strength tripled.[19] In subsequent years, and in particular after Vietnam attacked Cambodia in 1978, testing Sino-Soviet relations once more, Moscow and Beijing continued to consolidate and modernize their border installations and defense structures. In the Soviet Argun borderland, for instance, minefields and fortified regions were reactivated, like the one near Dauriia, or were newly built, like the one between Zabaikalsk and Abagaitui.[20]

During roughly two decades of conflict the Transbaikal Military District was a major base for Soviet Army troops on the Soviet side. Although there was never actually heavy fighting along the upper Argun, the Damanskii bloodlettings of March 1969 were echoed in Zabaikalsk and other places in the borderland. "Our fighter planes were flying along the border and armored personnel carriers were positioned at the border. . . . The entire village went on state of red alert, which lasted for several weeks," Vera P. Zolotareva recalls of the spring of 1969 in Zabaikalsk.[21] To Zolotareva and other borderlanders, the noise of airplanes and tanks heralded a new era.

Hunters, Lovers, Deserters: Trespassing the Locked Border

Amplified border surveillance probably reduced the number of border trespassers but never fully prevented people from crossing the boundary. In the years 1960 to 1965 Chinese records registered fifty-four escape attempts from the Chinese borderland region Hulunbeir to the Soviet Union. Between 1970 and 1979 only fifteen Chinese nationals escaped from Hulunbeir to the Soviet Union. During the same time period sixty-eight people, mainly nomads, were reported to have fled from Hulunbeir to the Mongolian People's Republic.[22]

Chinese and Soviet sources on border violations vary significantly. Both are unreliable as they are impossible to verify, and it is difficult even to reconstruct how categories were defined and how data were generated. According to Soviet sources illegal crossings from China to the Soviet Union on the Transbaikal-Hulunbeir border in fact increased in the years following the 1969 battles. Soviet authorities arrested hundreds of violators. In 1973 alone 315 violations were recorded within the operational area of the Dauriia division, almost half committed by Chinese citizens, though numbers are much higher than those in Chinese statistics. New control mechanisms certainly facilitated surveillance and the detection of border violators. On 13 June 1972, for instance, Soviet guards detained Pan Xuebo in the no-man's-land near Zabaikalsk. His arrest was preceded by a large-scale search after a signaling system had triggered an alert and footprints had been sighted on the control strip.[23]

Such disobedience in the face of border regimes was punished on both sides. Border transgressors were subjected to "educational measures" or more severe criminal penalties.[24] Not every trespasser faced severe legal consequences, however. Chinese authorities deported drunken or mentally ill border trespassers who had illegally entered Chinese territory by mistake mostly on the same day and at the latest within two weeks. When Chinese border guards, for instance, spotted the mentally handicapped Vladimir I. Sorokin near the railroad tracks between Manzhouli and Zabaikalsk on 20 June 1966, he did not face a long prison sentence. He was sent back to the Soviet Union eleven days later. However, those suspected of intentionally crossing the boundary, to seek asylum in China, were detained for months or years. A group of five Mongolian soldiers faced a particularly harsh fate when their private hunting party ended on 29 December 1972 within Chinese territory in an unfenced section of the Chinese-Mongolian border. The sources do not reveal whether or not their crossing was unintentional. Only after six and a half years in prison were they allowed to return home.[25]

Individual border transgressors were not the only sensitive issue to inflame the labile situation on the border. State-provoked incidents, grounded in territorial disputes, further destabilized the border truce. Soviet and Chinese accusations read like an endless game of tug-of-war, echoed by propaganda, and call to mind similar allegations in the Manchukuo period. Chinese sources speak of no fewer than 198 incidents along the Hulunbeir section of the international border with the Soviet Union between 1959 and 1965. These alleged Soviet provocations included unnecessary detentions, use of firearms, theft, violations of airspace, illegal patrols on Chinese territory, and the relocation of boundary stones. In 1960 the Soviets are said to have erected five kilometers of metal fencing on a hillside, thereby expropriating three square kilometers of territory that the Chinese claimed to be theirs. As a result the old differences over territoriality flared up again. The Soviet Union was also alleged to have agitated Hulunbeir's ethnic minorities to rise up against the Han Chinese via loudspeaker exhortation and secret agents.[26] Soviet accusations followed a similar pattern.[27]

Each side had its very own view on those incidents. For the head of the political section of the Transbaikal border district Ivan A. Skotnikov, the question of guilt was cut and dried. Chinese provocations were part of the "anti-Soviet strategy of the Maoists, with 'hysterical spectacles' and riots according to a prearranged plan . . . to provoke reactions on our side, which could then be represented as an armed attack on the peaceful Chinese population." False allegations against the Soviet Union thus belonged to the repertoire of Chinese "psychological warfare," he averred:

> At first sight, such obvious old wives' tales do not seem worth our attention. Say, for instance, a car drives not far from the boundary line and the headlights' beam drops somewhere on Chinese territory. We would be immediately criticized on grounds of espionage for deliberately illuminating Chinese territory, disturbing the great Chinese people and keeping them from working. Or to give another example, just some days ago, two hunters fired two shots somewhere about one kilometer from the Chinese border. The next day the Chinese raised charges of a supposed shelling of Chinese territory by Soviet soldiers. We are literally receiving piles of such allegations every day. The Maoists accumulate such materials for the indoctrination of the Chinese population and for their propaganda abroad.[28]

Though separating brothers in arms, the Soviet-Mongol border was also thrust into the spotlight during the Sino-Soviet split. The surveillance of the almost eight-hundred-kilometer stretch in Transbaikalia was reinforced, as it poten-tially allowed various backdoor routes to border transgression.[29] Since at least 1964 Moscow and Ulaanbaatar exchanged information and assistance in sur-veilling their mutual border.[30] At the regional level Soviet executive powers were requested to remind the Mongolian guests of the need for strict compli-ance with the border regulations and to bear in mind "the consideration of tact and sensitivity in dealing with the Mongolian friends."[31]

Surveillance of the border restricted areas was another important strategy in tracking down foreign transgressors as well as saboteurs, denunciators, and other "enemies" of the Soviet population. All Soviet districts bordering with China were deemed operational areas subject to surveillance. After the 1969 events observations were carried around even beyond those boundaries, es-pecially along lines of communication that might be of use to the transgressors and near possible hideouts, such as deer stands and shepherd's cabins. Though surveillance of the interior generally followed well-trodden protocols and its practices had involved civilians in assistance brigades as early as the 1930s, it had become a collective task involving every element of borderland society more so than ever before. Party and Komsomol organizations, regional and local administrations, trade unions, in short, the entire population was called upon.[32]

By performing patrols, inspections, and identity checks, the volunteer people's militia (Dobrovol'nye Narodnye Druzhiny, DND) formed the core of the effort. In particular, these volunteers were charged with tracking down any unauthorized accommodation or transport provided to foreigners and Soviet citizens. The DND also had paramilitary groups who would assist the military in wartime.[33] In 1977 about 4 percent of the local population in the Chita region border districts belonged to this civil surveillance body.[34] Among its members there was a high proportion of women. Liudmila I. Mashukova, stationmaster at Matsievskaia, about ten kilometers northwest of Zabaikalsk, was one of them in those years. Apart from managing the small railroad sta-tion, she would observe the tracks and station surroundings and immediately report any suspicious person to the border troops. For Mashukova being a member of the people's militia was an honor: "I worked for the DND because I was a true patriot," she later recalled.[35]

Even outside of formal surveillance channels, many citizens like Mashu-kova voluntarily reported suspicious individuals in the border zone to the authorities.[36] In the small communities adjacent to the state border virtually everyone knew everybody else. The common fate of living in the last *forpost* of the Soviet Union certainly nurtured a distinctive identification of residents with their environment and led to increased skepticism about everything alien. Most of the suspicious persons tracked down by volunteer patrols in the border zones were Soviet nationals, not Chinese. Their motives for violating the border regime ranged from secret visits to a girlfriend in the border zone or other harmless offenses to defection and other serious infringements of border regulations.[37]

Despite such all-out controls on external and internal borders, loopholes might still be found. Though members of the people's militia paced on permanent patrol at the railroad station in Zabaikalsk, railroad employees repeatedly violated the border regime by hiding unknown persons or not properly registering them with the authorities, and guests could check in without properly identifying themselves at the station hotel.[38] Yet, it was said, due to the involvement of the civilian population in protecting the border zone, illicit crossings into China and other infringements of the border regime dropped significantly after 1969 in many parts of Transbaikal region.[39]

Patronage relationships between units of the Soviet border guards (who had remained under control of the internal political-security apparatus) and the DND, the Komsomol, and other bodies were structured so as to further blur bonds between civilians and the soldiery. Border guards, agit-brigades, and veterans were sent out to the population to promote political vigilance in the border regions through lectures and concerts. Military games of the Volunteer Society for Assistance to the Army, Aviation and Fleet (Dobrovol'noe Obshchestvo Sodeistviia Armii, Aviatsii i Flotu, DOSAAF) prepared youth for their future paramilitary duties. To the Soviet public the people's militia volunteers were presented as heroes.[40] When the entire family became involved in the task of border protection, the border became part of normal life.

What had changed since the Manchukuo years, then, aside from a few technical innovations was the degree to which border protection had become a collective task. "The border is guarded by all Soviet people"—a dictum that had been proclaimed over the media and that was displayed at Zabaikalsk's railroad station entrance and on the clubhouse façade—met residents' eyes at almost every turn.[41] Or in contemporary Soviet military prose, "If the warning signal will sound, not just the border guard is ready to serve. Young and old will leave their domestic hearths, to seal off all roads and trails. All the people on the border keep watch. Whether soldier, tractorist, teacher, agronomist, Communist or Komsomol member, they form the second line of border defense."[42] Certainly even a border with a sensor-equipped control strip and the watchful eyes of the civilians could still be overcome. Yet in the perceptions of many ordinary locals the border was strong, as they themselves were a crucial element in its protection.

"Coffin Allowances": Demographics on the Argun

In May 1969, two months after Chinese and Soviet troops had clashed on the Ussuri, Vasilii S. Rudometkin, director of the fishing and sheep-breeding state farm Abagaitui, relocated his family and their belongings away from the border without approval from state and party authorities. Within sight of the border to China, the state farm Abagaitui no longer seemed a safe place for the Rudometkins. Even prior to the skirmishes Rudometkin was anything but a dedicated Soviet borderlander. He did not cooperate with Soviet border troops, did not participate in the people's militia, and stayed at home whenever the village was put on alert. "Rudometkin was scared by the tense situation on the border and simply decided to run away," the district committee's plenary session report tersely read.[43]

The decision of the Rudometkins illustrates the far-reaching economic and demographic impacts of the Sino-Soviet split on the economically underdeveloped borderlands. Depopulation and a shortage of skilled labor were the most pressing problems. With a total of only 90,050 people (or 7.4 percent of the total population of the Chita region) the districts bordering China were sparsely inhabited to the extreme.[44]

The Chinese were also alleged to be in the practice of obstructing the economic activities of the area's Soviet civilian population, such as fishing or hunting.[45] Yet China was not the main reason why many Soviet borderlanders considered the Argun lands to be uninhabitable. The issuing of internal passports to the peasantry from the early 1960s on, legally necessary for any domestic travel, facilitated the massive outflow of people from the 1960s onward. Yet to Mikhail M. Matafonov, first secretary of Chita's regional party committee, the internal economic failings were the major cause for the exodus: "Poor energy supply, underdeveloped construction and transportation sectors, skills shortages, . . . and inadequate housing, services and cultural facilities are essential factors in the population exodus from the border districts. . . . The massive outflow of people from the borderlands between 1966 and 1976 resulted in the complete liquidation of 10 settlements."[46]

For quite some time the Soviet authorities had been aware of the difficulties of living in Siberia and the Soviet Far East in general and on the border with China in particular. Since the postwar years Moscow had designed policies offering economic incentives that might lure citizens to the regions bordering with China. Yet such programs were only partially effective.[47] Even after tensions with Beijing had somewhat diffused in the early 1970s, the Kremlin was reluctant to reopen any significant bilateral trade with the People's Republic. Regional officials in the Soviet border regions, by contrast, urged a resumption of border trade to ameliorate the stagnant economy. Yet the

Soviet border regions remained cut off from their Chinese neighbors until border trade resumed in the 1980s.[48]

The Kremlin tried to overcome this self-created problem with internal development programs. In 1976 the Council of Ministers of the Soviet Union adopted a long-term plan to accelerate economic development in the districts bordering China. Its main objective was to attract new residents from the central regions of the Soviet Union. Incentives for settlers in the border districts included one-off payments, rental deductions, tax rebates, and increased holiday entitlements. Salary bonuses, or, in the vernacular, "coffin allowances" (*grobovye nadbavki*)—since people living next to the border would probably lose their lives in the event of a Chinese attack—were to be significantly higher than in other districts of the Chita region.[49]

Additionally, remote areas adjacent to the state border were to be made more attractive to potential immigrants thanks to infrastructure investments. Members of Chita's regional state planning committee drafted a comprehensive scheme for the border districts that solicited investment in agriculture, forestry, mining, and infrastructure. Housing and service issues, however, were at the top of the priority list. Hoping that more municipalities near the border would benefit from such largesse, the regional party committee's first secretary Matafonov lobbied in Moscow to expand the forbidden border zone in the Chita region significantly. In fact many party secretaries of towns and villages requested inclusion in the proposed zone.[50]

With slightly more than ten thousand residents, the population of Zabaikalsk remained stable throughout the Sino-Soviet split. Zabaikalsk's position on the international border with China was recognized in an administrative-territorial reform in 1967, when it became an urban-type village and the seat of a newly formed district. It then benefited further from a small number of construction projects.[51] The standard of living was certainly higher than in many other Soviet settlements of comparable size. Yet who would move to a sleepy urban-type village in the steppe, offering no prospect of a better life?

The situation in the border villages was much worse. Hoping to attract new settlers from other regions, the Zabaikalsk district administration published annual advertisements with headlines such as "Come to live and work" in the local paper.[52] Yet seeking better payment and some modest cultural entertainment, the youth moved to the cities, leaving behind an aging population.[53]

The depopulation of the countryside remained whitewashed by local media. In 1982 Valentin P. Rumiantsev, who had succeeded the runaway Rudometkin as director of Abagaitui's state farm, gushed about his new home on the Chinese border. After his family had moved from the Perm region in 1978 they were given a three-bedroom house, a barn, a vegetable garden, and a cow.[54] Yet such government support and the expansion of state-operated agricultural estates, existing and new, could not reverse the trend.[55] Instead of the expected population increase in structurally underdeveloped border areas, the number of residents continued to decline.[56]

Revisiting the massive inflow of Han Chinese, denomadization, and assimilation of the autochthonous nomads in Hulunbeir discussed in chapter 6, it becomes obvious that the situation in the Chinese border areas was different. Beijing did not foster population increases by devising incentives, economic or otherwise. Chinese borderland policies resembled, rather, the managed destruction reigning in the Soviet borderlands during the Stalinist period.

The last traces of the traditional Mongol way of life disappeared when groups of Red Guards terrorized Hulunbeir's pastoral regions during the Cultural Revolution of the late 1960s. These teenage soldiers attacked families who had been classified as the herdlords, in addition to Mongols with "bad" political backgrounds. Mao's regime of violence thus targeted anything associated with the traditional indigenous borderland society. Because it was largely Mongols who fell victim to those campaigns and Han Chinese who were blamed for organizing them, the Cultural Revolution reaffirmed the already extant distrust of the Chinese among the autochthonous borderland population. The chaos and confusion of Mao's last decade in power certainly marked the violent high point of assimilationist state policies.[57]

Rounding out collectivization and the restriction of religious freedom, heightened migration was perhaps the most durable symptom of the transformation of the Chinese Argun borderland in the post-1949 period. Even though Han Chinese by far outnumbered the Mongol population in Hulunbeir when the People's Republic of China was founded in 1949, the communist state succeeded in doing what Song Xiaolian, the Chinese circuit intendant of Hulunbeir, had failed to achieve in the last years of Qing rule. Already by 1950 the share of autochthonous inhabitants had fallen to about 10 percent. During the Great Leap Forward the population of Han ethnicity in Hulunbeir jumped steeply, as many unofficial migrants fled there from further inland to elude famine. When ethnic conflicts over land became too serious the central government in Beijing made efforts to stop spontaneous migration to Hulunbeir and other peripheral regions. As a result of those restrictions, and the famine from which the people in Hulunbeir had also suffered, Han immigration into Hulunbeir was temporarily reversed. Yet it soon began to increase again, particularly during the Down to the Countryside Movement in the late 1960s and early 1970s, when urban youth were recruited to live and work in the countryside. By 1970, despite a population increase among the autochthonous inhabitants, only 4 percent of Hulunbeir's population were of Mongol origin.[58]

As an integral part of postwar transformation in Manzhouli's urban milieu, Cossack villages in Trekhreche, and the pastoral Hulunbeir grass steppe, the

TABLE 7.1. Population development estimates in Hulunbeir

Year	Mongols	Han Chinese	Total
1927	32,000	17,000	49,0000
1950	25,000	240,000	265,000
1952	26,000	270,000	296,000
1954	28,000	360,000	388,000
1956	30,000	450,000	480,000
1958	36,000	670,000	706,000
1960	40,000	1,090,000	1,130,000
1962	39,000	840,000	879,000
1964	38,000	940,000	978,000
1966	39,000	990,000	1,029,000
1968	43,000	1,110,000	1,153,000
1970	48,000	1,190,000	1,238,000

Note: The numbers between 1950 and 1970 are rough estimates taken from figures 3.4 and 3.5, in Sneath, *Mongolia*, 97 and 99. Figures for 1927 are approximated and taken from Kormazov, *Barga*, 44. Soviet nationals, Russian émigrés, Japanese, and other nationals are not included in the figures shown.

previously heterogeneous ethnic composition of the Chinese borderland became gradually homogenized by design and thereby integrated into the Chinese heartland. Ultimately this process realized state objectives formerly pursued by different means. Both metropoles now exerted firm control over their respective, separated borderlands. In the case of the Russian diaspora both governments cooperated for some time and opened their otherwise locked border to bring the Russians "home." As a consequence zones of contact between Russian émigrés and Chinese borderland peoples had almost completely vanished by the 1960s.

In the contrasting case of the Buriat, Oroqen, Daur, and other nomadic people of Hulunbeir, the gradual process of sinicization and denomadization was directed from the Chinese central government and allowed the Soviet Union and the indigenous borderlanders no say in the matter. The vigor of Beijing's campaigns—some similar to earlier Soviet campaigns, others not—created an inflow of Han Chinese to the right bank of the Argun. Consequently Chinese farmers and Chinese forms of sedentary agriculture triumphed over autochthonous nomadic life. With the Sino-Soviet border firmly sealed the mobile borderlanders were unable to take refuge across the border, as their ancestors had.

However, these shifts did not yet mark the end of pastoral nomadism and the legacies of a borderless world. This becomes apparent in the short history of Cuogang (Tsagan), located about forty kilometers southeast of Manzhouli on the railroad to Hailar. Though Cuogang had already existed prior to 1949 as a small station with a few houses, most residents arrived in the communist era.

In 1956 Cuogang became an agricultural producers' cooperative. Conducting anthropological fieldwork in the late 1980s, Burton Pasternak and Janet W. Salaff observed the still-lingering legacies of transborder social and cultural entanglements in Cuogang:

> Where people live together, traditions combine. Town-dwelling Mongols live in homes like those of the Han, and grow vegetables in their compound gardens. Most Mongol adults can speak Mandarin, and most dress like the Han. Mongol youngsters, too, carry their milk cans to collection stations on bicycles. But here the Han favor beef and mutton, not pork. Like the Mongols they drink milk-tea, and share the regional penchant for hard liquor. . . . And when they cut hay or herd on the open grassland, they, too, live in yurts. . . . There are also traces of the earlier Russian presence. A white haired, blue-eyed, Russian-born woman married to a Han Chinese, the matriarch of a three-generation household, still lives in Cuogang. Some Chinese occupy the wooden houses with gingerbread façades built by Russian railroaders near the train station and along the track.[59]

Yet by the late 1980s little else evoked the bygone open interimperial borderland.

As a result of the continuous tensions between Beijing and Moscow the Argun borderland remained economically underdeveloped and, particularly on the Soviet side, sparsely populated. Though both metropoles recognized balanced demographic conditions as important preconditions for stability there, Moscow failed to attract significant numbers of volunteer immigrants to the region. On the Soviet side, conversely, many people moved away from the borderland despite the incentives. Others were to replace them, but those few newly arriving settlers were attracted by economic privileges offered by the government. This differentiated them from the earlier generations of borderlanders, who had come in search of gold, marmots, or profits skimmed from alcohol contraband. On the Chinese side those who came were often forced to do so by the state. Many would not return to their homelands once the campaign was over but choose to stay.

In Transit: Zabaikalsk Station as Showcase of the Soviet Union

Most local borderlanders like Rudometkin never crossed the Argun, though they often lived within sight of it. Yet in spite of conflict between Moscow and Beijing plenty of people moved back and forth. The majority of border crossers, however, were passengers on the international express trains who came from afar.

Train service operated normally for the most part, with infrequent delays, despite the saber rattling emanating from Beijing and Moscow and provocations during the Cultural Revolution, such as the destruction of Manzhouli's Chinese-Soviet Peoples' Friendship Palace by an angry mob in August 1968.[60] The small number of incidents demonstrates how smoothly the railroads worked on the technical level, despite the doctrinal divergence and geopolitical contest between Moscow and Beijing and despite the breakdown of political, economic, and cultural relations that culminated in a seven-month undeclared military conflict between China and the Soviet Union on their shared border in 1969. But a closer look into the compartments of international express 17/18, running between the two capital cities, as well as into the *wagons-lits* of the special passenger trains forces another interpretation of the conflict's impact on the border. Passenger statistics can sometimes be more revealing than secret intelligence dossiers, for this purpose.

Just a few crossing points, through which commodities and people could pass with official blessing, remained open after the border had been sealed during the Manchukuo years via militarization, the creation of control mechanisms, and various propaganda campaigns. These efforts had resulted in a tight physical surveillance of people moving across and living near the state border as well as in the creation of a metaphorical bulwark in the hearts and minds of the people that defended the nation against the hostile and alien neighbor. When bilateral relations between Moscow and Beijing deteriorated, the number of passage points declined further. Zabaikalsk was for a long time the only railroad crossing open to travel between China and the Soviet Union. During the split, with only a few hundred passengers crossing the border every week, the overall number of travelers had been very low, even at this very last point of passage.

The most striking finding to be gleaned from passenger statistics is the decline in Chinese and Soviet nationals on the trains. In 1966 Chinese travelers still constituted the majority (54 percent). In 1969, however, only two Chinese passengers crossed the border by train out of nearly seven thousand passengers in total. Though the data on Soviet travelers are incomplete, it can be assumed that the number of Soviet passengers was subject to a similar trend over the years. The number of Soviet and Chinese commuters thus became a mirror of the Sino-Soviet rift, which meant that Manzhouli-Zabaikalsk in that era was most consistently a point of transfer for people from other countries.

During the 1970s the overwhelming majority of passengers originated from the socialist sister states North Vietnam and North Korea. Being close allies of Moscow, both countries sent students and business delegations to the Soviet Union as long as Beijing allowed their transit through Chinese territory.[61] Beginning in the late 1970s the number of travelers from third countries (all countries except the Soviet Union, China, Vietnam, and North Korea) swelled. On the international train covering the Beijing-Moscow-Beijing route, the share of this group grew from less than 1 percent (1974) to one-third (1981). Most were from Eastern Bloc and Western European countries. There were very few U.S. citizens (just two persons between 1966 and 1976) but hundreds of Finns, who may have benefited from the nonalignment status of their country.[62]

The traffic statistics thus reflected political relations in East Asia and beyond. They give an account of a highly regulated border that could not be crossed easily by ordinary tourists, world travelers, or businessmen. For each statistical anomaly there is a plausible political explanation. With 19,280 people crossing by train at Zabaikalsk in 1973, the international passenger traffic, for example, rose by two-thirds compared to the previous year because delegations of several thousand young citizens from Vietnam and North Korea crossed the Sino-Soviet border in special trains to attend the Tenth World Festival of Youth and Students in East Berlin.[63] What is perhaps the most significant detail in the data, however, is the aforementioned ratio of Chinese and Soviet passengers. With just a dozen or so Soviet and Chinese travelers annually aboard the international trains, they can be seen as a gauge for the political atmosphere between Moscow and Beijing. At the time of the Sino-Soviet split there were virtually no passengers from either country seated on the Moscow- and Beijing-bound trains because both governments restricted the travel of students, experts, and tourists in times of diplomatic vagaries and military confrontation. The lingua franca of the Beijing-Moscow-Beijing coaches was, therefore, primarily Vietnamese and Korean. All other languages, including Russian and Chinese, attracted attention. It was not until the mid-1980s that the proportion of Soviet and Chinese passengers rose again, as relations between the two countries began to improve.

Precisely because border passage was limited to a smattering of crossing points and to a small circle of people, the Soviet authorities paid special attention to the experience at these portals. As at Brest in the Belorussian Soviet Socialist Republic on the border with Poland, trains in Zabaikalsk were directed into the bogie-changing shed, where carriages were jacked up and the Chinese standard-gauge bogies were changed to the Soviet broad gauge. The two-hour stopover at the Soviet border station offered Moscow the opportunity to present a good impression of the Communist party-state to the international traveler, an impression that, at least in theory, would contradict Kapuściński's memories of grim faces and rude customs inspectors in 1958.

When the new representative passenger terminal officially opened in fall 1953, in a joint Sino-Soviet ceremony at Otpor it became a flagship station and a source of pride in the Soviet Union, designed to impress incoming travelers

FIGURE 7.1. Zabaikalsk passenger station building, 2009. Opened in fall 1953, it became a
showcase of the Soviet Union on the border with China.

with the superiority of the communist system.[64] Manzhouli's new passenger
station building, built around the same time by the same group of Novosibirsk
architects, replaced the prerevolutionary art nouveau terminal of the Chinese
Eastern Railroad. With neo-Greek, Renaissance, rococo, and Byzantine styles,
it was basically a clone of the Soviet terminal just across the international
border.[65]

Yet in spite of all the station's pomp and eclecticism, construction and deco-
ration work remained unfinished at least on the Soviet side, the platforms were
dirty, and the station building, restaurant, restrooms, and hotel train car were
frankly unsanitary. The waiting lounge and the customs declaration room remained cold in winter due to a perennially broken heating system. Virtually
nothing was on display in the station's buffet except for pyramids of canned
Kamchatka crabs and alcohol. Many locals mingled with regular customers in
the restaurant and often, after a few drinks too many, raised a ruckus.[66] Station
staff treated international passengers disrespectfully.[67] Many of these shortcomings tarnished the effect of a structure intended by the state to convey the
sensibilities of a civilized and advanced nation.

During the years of conflict with China, however, Soviet efforts to burnish
service, to refurbish the station building, and to leave a generally pleasant

impression on the transit passengers intensified. In its ideological battle with China and the West the Kremlin sought to impress and win the hearts and minds of the East Asian travelers on the international trains. During the mid-1960s the station facilities were modernized. The platforms were extended, the exterior premises were better maintained, and thereafter flowerbeds were tended each year, their several thousand blooms a striking sight in the harsh desert climate. A new archway at the border welcomed travelers from East Asia. Inside the station building the railroad administration set up a new souvenir stand, installed automated luggage lockers, and fitted all waiting rooms—Soviet and international travelers waited in separate rooms—with new Hungarian upholstery. Starting in November 1965 the customs inspection hall was equipped with a cinema system and from 1970 on boasted a large screen.[68]

Thus, in theory, transit passengers from East and West alike were to hear, see, and smell the land of milk and honey. During the stopover a loudspeaker system transmitted propaganda programs for travelers in all public station rooms and on both platforms, in Russian, Chinese, English, Korean, and Vietnamese. Broadcasts included features about Soviet cosmonauts and Soviet art, Siberia, and Soviet revolutionaries and programs like those on the "Exhibition of Economic Achievements—Our Country as a Miniature," which proclaimed the imminent victory of socialism.[69]

Starting in the mid-1960s, in addition to the acoustic exposure, three propagandists—two young high school graduates, one with language skills in Chinese and English, and a loyal Chinese colleague, who worked as an interpreter—took care of passengers in the flesh. Over the following years these propagandists were supported by a growing number of Chinese language translators. Every employee who interacted with foreigners underwent special training, and some had a basic command of English or Chinese.[70]

A central task of the propagandists and interpreters was carrying out ideological and political work among the foreign travelers, such as offering them free books or inviting them to structured discussions. In such meetings while passengers awaited their trains in the terminal the propagandists tried to call attention to international and national politics as well as business and culture in the Soviet Union. In 1969 alone sixty-seven such gatherings were organized. Agitation among travelers, however, was hampered by a communication problem. During the staff selection procedures the railroad administration had expected primarily Chinese nationals. The target audience, however, turned out to be mainly Vietnamese and Korean travelers, who spoke only poor Russian and Chinese if at all.

Film screening was probably the most crucial propaganda tool in reaching a wide audience. In 1974, for instance, 125 screenings with a total of 8,350 viewers, or roughly half of all international passengers, were organized. The border station received feature films from Moscow in Russian, English, French, German, Korean, and Vietnamese. The repertoire varied little over the years, and many of the films were out of date by the time they were shown. Another drawback was a simultaneous audio broadcast of programs over the speaker system on the platforms and in the waiting rooms. International travelers thus suffered from a polyphonic overload of outdated propaganda.

A wide range of newspapers and magazines, such as *Moskovskie Novosti* (Moscow News), *Sovetskii Soiuz* (Soviet Union), and *Sovetskaia Zhenshchina* (The Soviet Woman), were available in English, French, Vietnamese, Korean, and other languages. Brochures, booklets, and postcards were offered by the thousands every year to passengers as *compagnons de voyage*, stacked beneath a sign reading "For free—in memory of your stay in the Soviet Union" in the station building and on the trains. Even Lenin badges and other souvenirs were provided.[71]

Despite the ideological immersion on offer at Zabaikalsk, it is perhaps not surprising that the conflict with China did not weigh heavily on interaction with international travelers at first.[72] In 1971, out of a selection of more than one hundred different books and pamphlets available for international travelers, only the English edition of Boris M. Leibzon's *Anarchism, Trotskyism, Maoism*, available in forty copies, contained anti-Chinese content. It turned out to be a shelf warmer: fewer than half of the copies were taken.[73] Three years later, however, the selection of anti-Chinese propaganda was wider: one in ten books contained direct or indirect anti-Chinese propaganda—most of them in Chinese. Booklets such as Aleksei N. Zhelokhovtsev's *Pochemu maoisty kleveshchut na SSSR* (Why the Maoists Slander the USSR), in runs of several hundred copies, were out of stock.[74] Technical problems with printing can only explain the delay during the first months following the Ussuri clashes. Rather, it seems that propaganda officials in the government bureaucracy wanted to avoid any direct provocation at the border, at least in the early years of the conflict with China. Overall, anti-Chinese proselytizing was limited at the border station. Emphasis had been placed, rather, on showcasing Soviet "achievements."

Despite all efforts, however, Zabaikalsk was everything but a showcase of Soviet socialism. In 1972 an inspector from Chita identified many shortcomings that defied recent remodeling to recall those of the 1950s: the waiting room for foreign travelers lacked a Lenin portrait, for instance, as well as posters of the five-year plan. He also admonished the education and appearance of the employees. The cashier, the projectionist, the employees of the baggage department, and even the station manager were not dressed in the required uniforms. Lacking toothpaste, sewing kit, socks, and other travel items, the station shop and newsstand "Union Press" were meagerly stocked. In the restaurant passengers were served by a single waitress and could choose from only a small selection on the Russian language menu. The local press complained too that diners there were regularly cheated.[75]

When the Soviet-Chinese border was no longer the border between sister states, Moscow strove to present the Soviet Union as a progressive country at the border station of Zabaikalsk, the first stop in the heartland of communism, making use of loudspeaker announcements, film screenings, and directed conversation "among friends." And indeed, despite all the shortcomings and the rituals attached to the organized friendship meetings and propaganda, the station may have actually been bathed in a rosy light in the memories of at least some travelers from North Vietnam or North Korea because they saw things for the first time that did not exist in Hanoi or Pyongyang and usually were unavailable in the Soviet Union outside Moscow or Leningrad. Many Finnish and West German passengers, in turn, might have been amused by the crude propaganda or the odd photo displays with pictures of calves and the like. But no matter whether impressions of the propaganda show were good or bad, after the two hours of passport controls, customs inspections, movie screenings, and shopping, everybody knew that they had crossed a border.

Diplomacy of Shunters: Borderlanders as Agents of Diplomatic Exchange

Even as bilateral relations cooled markedly in the early 1960s, Soviet railroad employees with professional cross-border ties maintained amicable contacts with Chinese colleagues and the local population.[76] Though zones of contact between Soviet and Chinese borderlanders had shrunken, at the railroad stations of Zabaikalsk and Manzhouli the presence of professionals from across the border was nothing particular. Only when the Cultural Revolution was at its height did transnational exchange between the railroad employees turn frosty.[77]

The number of border-crossing shunters and engine drivers had declined steadily. This was primarily due to the decline in exchange of goods. In 1970 just 119,000 tons of international cargo transshipment (a substantial part of which was Soviet military equipment for North Vietnam) were handled at Manzhouli and Zabaikalsk—just 3 percent of the cargo volume of the mid-1950s. With fewer freight cars to clear, fewer workers were required to couple and uncouple wagons.[78] Around 1970, as a result, the majority of the about fifteen hundred railroad workers in Zabaikalsk knew China only from distant glances across the steppe hills.[79]

In contrast to the majority of her coworkers the shunter Vera P. Zolotareva belonged to a limited circle of borderlanders allowed to travel to Manzhouli on duty, even during such politically fraught moments. Zolotareva was acquainted with the distant neighbor state through contact with Chinese colleagues. Born in 1938 Zolotareva had moved in 1955 to the Soviet border station settlement, where she worked in the railroad freight depot to clear commodity trains to China for many years. Several dozen other railroad men, staff of the Soviet export companies, postal officials, and employees of several other companies also traveled to Manzhouli on duty, even in moments of fractiousness with China. Their special role put people like Zolotareva at the mercy of the great powers, for better or worse. Zolotareva confirms that the schism between the two communist powers affected the way she was seen by her professional contacts and occasionally imperiled her. Recalling one such situation in January 1967, she testified,

> Of course there still were a few contacts. I was friends with one Chinese colleague, but for him it was dangerous to express such amiability because they mutually spied on each other during the Cultural Revolution. Overall, it was very difficult to work.
>
> I had a shift on the day after their students marched to the Red Square in Moscow to demonstrate. Instantly there was a response in Manzhouli. It was as if the entire city had gathered . . . opposite the train station. . . . I do not know how many people came together, certainly more than one thousand. . . . And then the entire crowd invaded the train station. Their railroad staff hid somewhere, and that day there were only three Soviet railroad employees in the shift. We really did not know what we should do. We were completely baffled. We tried to call the stationmaster in Zabaikalsk but the connection failed. . . . Yet somehow our stationmaster arrived later in Manzhouli, but they did not let him into the station building. Some time later the new Soviet shift finally arrived. I don't know what held them up, but the Chinese demonstrators did not enter our room. Yet on the walls, they wrote: "Down with Brezhnev! Down with Kosygin! Down with the Soviet government!"[80]

Another confrontation occurred in the late 1960s while the Beijing-Moscow train was handed over to the Soviet railroad staff. "The Chinese had daubed it completely with paint and our train manager did not allow the express to depart from Manzhouli station. Back then the Chinese had only weak shunting locomotives. Nevertheless they still tried to move the train toward Zabaikalsk, but the Soviet train manager pulled the emergency brake. The train stood at least a whole day, probably even longer, until our government gave permission to allow the train to be moved on to Zabaikalsk. In Zabaikalsk they put the passengers on a local train and cleaned the international express."[81] During the Cultural Revolution people like Zolotareva sometimes experienced risky confrontations in Manzhouli. The stories they secretly shared with their neighbors and friends might have been even more alarming than Moscow's anti-Chinese propaganda, to which we shall turn momentarily. Yet even before the propaganda war intensified in 1969 the ordinary citizens of Zabaikalsk could feel that a major confrontation was under way. Since at least 1963 rehearsals of evacuation scenarios and civil defense drills had impressed upon the residents that times had changed for the worse.[82]

Thus, the engine drivers and shunters of the two border railroad stations did far more than clear goods and passenger trains. Sometimes they assumed delicate and critical tasks made necessary by relations between Moscow and Beijing. Chita's regional party committee received instructions from and regularly reported to the Central Committee in Moscow on meetings between Soviet and Chinese railroad men. On 1 May 1972 twelve Manzhouli railroad men visited Zabaikalsk. The program included a reception at the station's hotel Intourist, the screening of a movie on the Great Patriotic War, and lunch in the railroad club. The Chinese delegates proposed toasts for May Day, for solidarity, for the friendship between the Chinese and Soviet peoples, and for the railroad men of Manzhouli and Zabaikalsk. Together they sang the "Internationale." Then the Soviet participants continued with the Russian wartime song "Katiusha" and presented souvenirs to the Chinese guests. During their brief visit "not a single time did the Chinese guests bring up 'ideas of Maoism and the Mao Zedong thought.'" To the Central Committee in Moscow this was probably the most important passage in the report. Following a similar format Soviet delegates paid a return visit to Manzhouli the next day to find a "welcoming and friendly reception." With the permission of the Chinese authorities the guests also got the chance to visit Manzhouli's Soviet war memorial.[83] Though more sporadic and smaller in scale, these resembled the exchanges of delegations that had taken place under the alliance regime in form and content. In times of conflict, however, those meetings fulfilled the governments' desire to exercise goodwill diplomacy at the lowest level.

Moreover, depending on the changing state of diplomatic relations, both sides occasionally rejected proposals for visits. In 1975 the party leadership in Manzhouli declined a request by Zabaikalsk's district party committee for a ceremonial laying of a wreath for the fallen Soviet soldiers at Manzhouli's war memorial to mark the thirtieth anniversary of the liberation of Manchuria from the Japanese. The decision was made in consultation with the central government in Beijing. Zabaikalsk's stationmaster Evgenii I. Dorogoi was then informed by his Manzhouli colleague that the Chinese people did in fact

honor Soviet men who had given their lives, with annual wreath-laying ceremonies at memorials and cemeteries.[84] Yet with deployments of large Soviet
military forces at the Sino-Soviet border and in Mongolia and with a looming
Soviet-Chinese proxy war in Indochina between the pro-Soviet governments
in Vietnam and Laos and the pro-Chinese government in Cambodia, Chinese
officials insisted that joint commemorations would be inappropriate. In the
end Dorogoi secured a face-saving deal on behalf of the Soviet government.
On 3 September 1975 Soviet employees on duty in Manzhouli carried memorial wreaths. They were granted permission by Manzhouli's railroad department to lay down the wreaths on behalf of the railroad men of Zabaikalsk. A
spontaneous crowd of more than one hundred local Chinese spectators surrounded the Soviet railroad employees at the memorial.[85]

Some railroad workers in Manzhouli and Zabaikalsk composed almost the
sum total of legal border crossers in the period of conflict. Sometimes they
were exposed to the risks of political turmoil. Sometimes too they assumed
the roles of weather balloons. As these metaphorical balloons rose through the
atmosphere, they gathered important data on behalf of the political leadership
in Beijing and Moscow. Their visits were quite accurate ways of measuring
conditions on the ground, given the bilious relationship between the two communist giants. In most cases, however, shunters and engine drivers simply did
their jobs. And in allowing them to do so both governments acknowledged,
obliquely, that the border would never be hermetically sealed.

The Propaganda War in the Borderland: A Revival
of an Almost Bygone Hero

Alongside the military confrontation between the two communist countries
and the legal restrictions placed on travel across the almost locked border,
ideological warfare played a key role in the conflict between Beijing and Moscow. Visual and acoustic bombardment was seen as crucial for winning or
losing hearts and minds in the borderlands and beyond. Beyond up-to-the-
minute media coverage in newspapers, on radio, and on television, it also extended into the spheres of pseudo-scientific literature, textbooks, and novels.
With rising literacy rates among the borderland people as compared to the
Manchukuo period, propaganda was more successful.[86]

Already throughout the 1960s an anti-Soviet line was disseminated over
Chinese radio programs and newspapers.[87] When the most serious of all border clashes occurred in the vicinity of Damanskii Island on the Ussuri River
on 2 March 1969, leading to an undeclared military conflict between the Soviet
Union and China that lasted for seven months, this shrill propaganda war

FIGURE 7.2. "All reactionaries are paper tigers"—Chinese border guards laughing about a
captured Soviet helmet. Illustration in the anti-Soviet propaganda booklet
Doloi novykh tsarei! (Down with the new tsars!), published in several
languages and distributed widely by Beijing's
Foreign Language Press in 1969.

intensified to unprecedented levels. Within no more than twenty-four hours
of the incident strategists in Beijing had coined the catchy slogan "Down with
the new tsars!" which they would subsequently use to agitate against Soviet
leadership at home and abroad.[88]

The Kremlin, by contrast, failed to produce any popular slogans, but the
centrally controlled Soviet propaganda machine likewise quickly gained momentum and began to use the events on the Ussuri to appeal to the Soviet
people's patriotism. On 14 March the Central Committee of the Communist
Party of the Soviet Union adopted, for immediate release, a propaganda plan

for the press and for radio and television broadcasting with the aim of "exposing the treacherous actions and hazardous course of the Maoist group." This directive set out the topics to be reported in the print media.[89]

In Soviet domestic propaganda, especially in the border regions, film also proved a fruitful medium. Perhaps one of the best-known anti-Maoist documentary films was *Noch' nad Kitaem* (Night over China, 1971). The message is apparent from the title. Director Aleksandr I. Medvedkin showed how the Red Guards drove an old, once respected cadre through the streets of Beijing like a performing bear, knocked out his teeth, put a fool's cap on his head, and, with all this humiliation as a mere prelude, forced him to do backbreaking work in the fields. In 1973 alone about 12 percent of the Chita region's population watched this movie.[90] In criticizing the detrimental course upon which the People's Republic had embarked the Soviet agitators were always keen to urge political vigilance on the part of the people at home. The message was clear: patriotism and readiness to defend the motherland at all times. Its impact on audiences is, however, hard to assess.[91]

Displaying the evil of China's Communist leadership was one facet of Soviet propaganda. Another key motif during the Sino-Soviet rift was the heroic myth of the border guard, a myth that had existed since the 1920s, long before the Chinese spilled Soviet blood on the frozen Ussuri. The pogranichnik reappeared not only in the shape of monuments honoring Committee of State Security (KGB) border guards as folk heroes or rituals such as the Border Guard Day celebrations every year on 28 May, entailing meetings, lectures, parades, and fireworks, but also in Soviet national media formats such as *Pravda*, *Izvestiia* (News), and TASS news agency reports.[92] At the regional level, district and local newspapers of the border regions devoted much space to the military clashes on the Ussuri in early and mid-March 1969, divided between readers' letters to the border guards, reportage on the same, and illustrations of border soldiers. In locally produced stories the roles were also clearly divided: "Chinese bandits" were confronted by Soviet "heroes of Damanskii Island," who demonstrated "bravery and heroism" in the defensive battle against the enemy.[93] Their deployment was staged as part of an ongoing historical mission to protect the border: "Those serving at the border posts are the sons of those men who defeated the Japanese samurai and defended the fronts in the Great Patriotic War. The echo of the shots fired on Damanskii can be heard all along the border. Redoubled vigilance is the only answer for our boys on guard."[94] Those men who had fallen in the March battles were acclaimed martyrs in the name of the security and happiness of the motherland. Anatolii M. Kovalev, just nineteen years old, was one of the soldiers who lost his life in the second battle in mid-March. The *Zabaikal'skii Rabochii* (Transbaikal Worker), an organ of the regional party administration with a circulation of 130,000 copies,[95] wrote, "His mother was on the way home when the sad news of Anatolii Kovalev's death reached the village of Bal'za. The whole village mourned the border guard, who had been a local boy. Everyone, young and old, gathered for the funeral service in the village club to remember those who 'loved their lives and their Motherland.' . . . Things will be peaceful along the border, for it is reliably guarded. The heroes of Damanskii have proved as much."[96] The same newspaper had published a similar article three days earlier, which, typically, took up at least one page: "'Addressee: Chita 2, Dachnaia 17, Gladyshev, Viktor Semenovich. Message: Your son Sergei has died the death of the brave while protecting the national border . . . ,' the telegrapher . . . read the telegram once again. What is to be done? How on earth I am to tell his mother this terrible news, when her heart is already so weak?"[97] The fate of eighteen-year-old Sergei V. Gladyshev and his posthumous cult were taken up by almost every newspaper in the region, including *Na Boevom Postu* (On Guard), mouthpiece of the Transbaikal Military District. The journalist had talked to those close to Sergei and reported that the deceased was considered an "active Komsomol member," someone who liked to read, travel, and play basketball, the son of "a normal working-class family."[98]

Chita grieved for Gladyshev. Ulan Ude grieved for Nikolai N. Petrov.[99] In short every town was assigned its own heroes, invariable from "next door," with "normal" Soviet biographies. Their martyrs' deaths, embellished by the media, lent emotion to the conflict and further alienated the borderlands. The myth of the Soviet hero of the Ussuri River had a long half-life. It cast a bright shaft of light that would begin to wane only many years later.

The Frosted Glass Border: The Disappearing of the Other Halves

The Sino-Soviet conflict remained an important topic in the regional and local Soviet media throughout 1969, but less so during the following years. For the most part the regional press reprinted reports from metropolitan newspapers on the clashes on Damanskii Island, usually with a one week delay. The front page of Zabaikalsk's newly launched local paper, *Zabaikal'ets* (The Transbaikalian),[100] included TASS news agency articles on the funeral of the fallen Soviet soldiers and the content of a press conference at the Soviet foreign ministry. On the same page, in a prominent position in the upper-left column, under the heading "With Full Voice," the paper reported on a rally of Zabaikalsk's residents, which the party leadership had convened on a Sunday morning, one week after the first exchange of fire on the Ussuri. Local employees had gathered in the station building and were informed about the new situation. Nasak I. Iudinov, first secretary of the district committee, opened the meeting.

Leading employees of the local rail operations then gave speeches, but there were also contributions by workers and railroad men exhorting the protection of the "sacred borders." If the event's printed excerpts are to be trusted, the railroad worker Mikhail M. Voitkov rose at one point to deliver a stirring speech: "Through the border violation, the Chinese provocateurs have shown their true colors. So it is our duty to protect the border like the pupil of our eye. The Chinese leadership has gone from provocations on the ideological front to armed struggle. We Soviets now bear the stigma of shame because of the Chinese provocateurs. We mourn with the mothers of the fallen border guards."[101] Over the following weeks and months the journalists of the district newspaper reported on similar organized assemblies. The most important gathering of this kind in Zabaikalsk was held on a July evening in the square behind the railroad men's club. *Zabaikal'ets* printed an in-depth piece on this "Meeting with the Heroes of Damanskii," as the title dubbed it. Pupils, workers, and senior citizens came together there to listen to the speeches of the border guards, some of whom had fought right on the front lines. They not only spoke of the Chinese provocations on Damanskii but also recalled earlier skirmishes and their heroic defense of the homeland, eliciting "thunderous applause" from listeners.[102]

In 1969, alongside these exclusive reports from the region, the district newspaper—among others—published statements by the Soviet government of several pages on China, interviews with the "Heroes of the Island of Damanskii," reports on the Soviet retaliation of 15 March, as well as TASS photo reports on the border guards on the Ussuri and on soldiers and border guards from the region of Chita who were involved in the clashes, some of them posthumously decorated.[103] Through an eyewitness report the newspaper roused memories the Sino-Soviet conflict of 1929, highlighting what it argued were the Red Army's heroic struggles in the conflict over the Chinese Eastern Railroad.[104]

But from 1970 on China was to appear in the local newspaper only sporadically, when Moscow anticipated new acts of aggression along the border emanating from Beijing, became aware of new anti-Soviet sentiments in China, or reported on China's domestic political difficulties and the suffering of its people.[105] Apart from reports on Chinese politics in the state media Soviet border dwellers learned surprisingly little about China during the period of conflict. Until the late 1950s, when official relations between Beijing and Moscow had been cordial, the case was quite different. In chapter 6 we analyzed an article from the 1959 run of the local paper *Leninskii Put'*, discussing railroad workers at the border stations of Zabaikalsk and Manzhouli and in the process illustrating the seemingly amicable joint working life of the Soviet and Chinese duty officers at the border railroad trading post.[106] The wording even then would have sounded stereotypical and crude. Yet the descriptions in the story were astonishingly specific and vivid. The people in it, like protagonist Raisa A. Kuznetsova, had names, as did places on both sides of the border.[107] The reader might know the places and perhaps even some of the people. But it was to be the last such local report to make explicit mention of dealings between Soviets and Chinese in the borderlands and, in fact, would be the final article to name Manzhouli for many years. Though Zabaikalsk and Manzhouli lay just ten kilometers apart and one could gaze at the other across the border from the peaks of the steppe hills, the Soviet regional press refrained from mentioning Manzhouli and other places in the Chinese border region for twenty-six years.

Only in the summer of 1986—when the ideological rivalry as the main driver of Sino-Soviet tensions had disappeared, new interests of Beijing and Moscow pushed the two regimes toward normalization of their bilateral relations, and local cross-border exchanges slowly resumed—did China once again bask in a positive light in the regional publications of the Soviet borderlands. It was first reintroduced in general reports on the recommencement of friendship societies and the exchange of delegations in July 1986,[108] and, one and a half months later, on the visit by a four-person delegation of the Manzhouli Sino-Soviet Friendship Society to the district of Zabaikalsk. The report was brief and the language matter-of-fact, but the editors gave a photo of the joint Soviet-Chinese delegation a prominent position.[109]

There was as yet no sign of a return to the typical effusive style of twenty-six years earlier in *Leninskii Put'*, which sang the praises of the friendship between the two peoples, but the trend was clear. It took another four years for the first multipart report on the neighboring town of Manzhouli to appear in August and September 1990 under the title "Seven Days in China." The reader was certainly meant to feel the journalist's enthusiasm. Evidently he could hardly believe his eyes.[110] These reports meant the end of the frosted glass border, behind which the neighboring country beyond the Argun River had been a blurred outline for a quarter of a century. These portrayals implied the rehabilitation of the concrete "other," the return of people and places.

War over the Airwaves: How Radio Programs Transgressed Borders

Though Beijing and Moscow also waged a propaganda war of greater territorial scope, the border region was the front line of propaganda in the war over the airwaves during the Sino-Soviet split.[111] Those within and beyond immediate sight and earshot of the border were the main target of agitation. More than five years after the military clashes on the Ussuri Island of Damanskii, Efim B. Malikov, the chair of the television and radio broadcasting committee of the Chita region, described the situation on the border: "On the Chinese side, attempts continue to be made to exert an ideological influence on the Soviet people and especially the border guards through special organs and special units. In the Chinese villages near our border radio broadcasts of an anti-Soviet character are constantly being transmitted from powerful loudspeakers, and slogans and banners with anti-Soviet themes are regularly put up across from Soviet settlements."[112] Yet it was not just the people near the border who became targets for Beijing's Russian-language broadcasts. Early on the Kremlin had recognized the weak spots in its own provision of radio in its eastern regions, even before Beijing went on the air in the Soviet Union. And as early as 1960 a secret report for the Central Committee of the Communist Party of the Soviet Union stated that provision of radio news in the morning and evening was unsatisfactory for those living in Transbaikala and other Siberian regions as it did not reach these people.[113]

By December 1962, shortly after Radio Beijing had begun to transmit radio broadcasts in Russian, Moscow followed its anti-Soviet content with concern. At the time Moscow still hesitated to establish expensive and often ineffective jamming stations and hoped to prompt Beijing to back down through effective counterpropaganda.[114] It quickly became apparent that such expectations were in vain. In 1969 listeners in the Soviet Union could receive propaganda broadcasts from China day and night, on no fewer than ten radio frequencies. Such programming was jammed as early as August to October 1963. Starting in mid-1964 Moscow broadcaster *Maiak* (The Lighthouse) tuned its Far Eastern and Central Asian transmitters to those frequencies used by Radio Beijing for its Russian broadcasts, in order to disrupt them. The same thing happened later with half a dozen medium-wave transmitters, but it was not until many years later that the Soviet Union would succeed in "soundproofing" large parts of the country.[115]

One key technological means of protecting broadcasting operations from deliberate interference by the enemy was the Soviet Union's rapid development of a cable radio network. The choice of programs was left in the hands of a local functionary since the hardware simply could not pick up on Chinese broadcasting any longer. All that was required of the listener was to adjust the volume. Though the border districts were supposed to be a priority for cable broadcasting, it did not by any means reach all citizens. In 1974 the district of Zabaikalsk, with its 26,169 inhabitants and 6,218 households, had a total of 2,078 cable radio connections in homes, of which merely 1,528 were operational. In Matsievskaia, Abagaitui, and a number of other settlements in the district there was no cable radio at all. Those who wished to listen had to turn on the traditional wireless.[116]

Beijing made skillful use of these deficiencies. News programs, press reviews, and reports on life and the "colossal" progress in China arrived over the Chinese airwaves in the Soviet borderlands.[117] According to Matafonov, the first secretary of the regional party committee, a significant number of people, particularly the steppe herdsmen, listened at least occasionally to Chinese radio broadcasts. While it was believed that the vast majority of the population put little faith in what they heard from Beijing, he reflected, it was also naïve to trust "that everyone is endowed with sufficient immunity to anti-Soviet propaganda." That Chinese propaganda resonated with some Soviet citizens was evident in "panic-fueled rumors . . . in the form of declarations of sympathy for Maoist policies and word-of-mouth propaganda based on radio broadcasts from Beijing."[118]

Radio was not the only problem. While television played practically no role for people living in the border regions of China,[119] the Soviet Union was catching up in its television services. By the end of the 1960s around twenty-five million Soviet households had television. In the early 1970s, when the "Orbita" radio antenna in Krasnokamensk, about ninety kilometers northeast of Zabaikalsk, was brought into service, most of the settlements in the upper Argun border region could receive television broadcasts. But even at the end of the decade households with a television in the border region were still a minority.[120] And the privileged sector of families with a television set already sitting in their living rooms did not necessarily receive the Moscow channels, but might secretly watch "eastern television."[121]

During the Sino-Soviet conflict both governments succeeded in controlling and curtailing flows of people and commodities, but they would never manage to seal the border completely. Yet, in retrospect, border transgressions by radio waves seem rather harmless. Perhaps it was not the technical incapability to crack down on enemy radio stations by jamming radio waves that was decisive in this airwaves battle. Much of the content was crude, manifestly false criticism of the enemy that bored its listeners to death.

Other Channels: Face-to-Face Propaganda Work among the Borderland Peoples

Alongside newspapers, radio, and television broadcasting, other methods facilitated indoctrination about the conflict with China. Museums, for instance, were important vehicles with which to disseminate the key messages of enmity. Aleksandr P. Tarasov experienced the events on the Ussuri as a pupil at a Chinese language school in Chita. As early as March 1969 his class was led through a hastily erected exhibition at the Museum of the Transbaikal Military District in Chita. "An entire room was dedicated to the March events, featuring outsize photographs of the bodies of Soviet border guards. Death on their faces and the bodies uncovered—so that we could see their injuries and the clotted blood more clearly."[122]

An equally important role was played by the Znanie (Knowledge) organization. After the escalation of the conflict, particularly in localities near the border, this body deployed propaganda groups and more than three hundred qualified lecturers in the region of Chita. These provided the masses with "information" on Maoism and the foreign policy approach of the Communist Party of the Soviet Union, through talks and discussion evenings.[123] Questions relating to China were also tackled in the events and exhibitions displayed on an agitation train—complete with museum, club, cinema, and library cars—which visited Zabaikalsk, Dauriia, Borzia, and other stations in the region in 1970 to commemorate the hundredth anniversary of Lenin's birth.[124]

Further, border guards and soldiers in the Transbaikal border district were not only meant to defend the border from enemy attacks but also tasked with carrying out propaganda work among civilian borderlanders. Groups of border guards visited villages and agricultural stations in the immediate vicinity of the border to give the residents talks on the "domestic policies of the Chinese government" and "the anti-communism and anti-Sovietism of the Chinese leadership." In the clubhouses of some villages information stalls on "Maoism, supporter of imperialism" and the like were erected with the assistance of border protection officers.[125]

Though soldiers and border guards were certainly tasked with disciplining the civilian population, agitprop activity among the men in uniform was likewise important because the armed forces were deployed right on the front lines and thus especially susceptible to the enemy's inculcation. The military headquarters, political divisions, and party sections paid special attention to two groups: first, soldiers deployed far from their bases because of their particular duties and, second, young recruits who were ideologically "impressionable" and, according to Aleksandr I. Biks, head of the political section of the Transbaikal Military District, did not understand "the essence of current events in China" and so sometimes exhibited pacifist attitudes. The proportion of presentations, lectures, and film screenings devoted to informing people about enemy ideologies increased to one-third of all the educational work.[126]

A last important means of transmitting the message of enmity with Mao's China was an emphasis on the friendship with the third country in the borderland region: the Mongolian People's Republic. While under the alliance

ГРАНИЦЫ РОДИНЫ СВЯЩЕННЫ И НЕПРИКОСНОВЕННЫ!

FIGURE 7.3. Reprint of a propaganda poster by graphic artist Georgii V. Gausman titled "The Borders of the Motherland Are Sacred and Inviolable!" appearing in the local paper *Zabaikal'ets* in July 1978, depicting two deliberate and vigilant members of the Soviet border and coast guard.

regime Mongolia had constituted a territorial link between Beijing and Moscow, joined by a common ideology, it once more transformed into a loyal Soviet buffer during the Sino-Soviet confrontation, supporting Moscow "unexceptionally, unqualifiedly, and unhesitatingly."[127] It was not only the deployment of Soviet troops at the strategic position of the Sino-Mongolian border that made the Kremlin's oldest satellite state an important ally. For propaganda purposes the friendship with Mongolia was much more vigorously emphasized in the Soviet Union when relations with China reached the freezing point. On his 1974 state visit to Ulaanbaatar, General Secretary Brezhnev said in the Mongolian capital, "Friendship with People's Mongolia, our oldest brother-in-arms in the struggle for socialism, is for us Soviet people a matter of honor and internationalist duty."[128]

Mongolian cities and provinces demonstratively developed alliances with neighboring Soviet cities and provinces. The Chita region established twinning agreements with the Dornod (Eastern) *aimag*, among others. By 1968 officially arranged exchanges of delegations, screenings of Mongolian films, friendship evenings, and guest performances by musical groups from nearby Mongolian towns had become key elements of external cultural policies in the Borzia district. They were echoed in the regional media to reaffirm the friendship between the Soviet and Mongolian peoples.[129] Patterns of staging friendship with Mongolia thus resembled the Sino-Soviet friendship performances of the alliance period, but now they targeted Beijing. With the Mongols lauded as friends of the Soviet people, the Chinese might be seen more starkly as enemies.

———

The period of enmity of the 1960s to the early 1980s accelerated processes of alienation between Chinese and Soviet locals in the Argun borderland. The Sino-Soviet split provoked an exceptional concentration of military force along the border—unparalleled even by the military deployments of the Manchukuo period. Despite this display of power, the hermetic seal on the external border remained fiction. Even an overstaffed and technically sophisticated surveillance grid—which extended deeply into the hinterland and, more than ever before, trained its gaze on the civilian borderland population—did not result in complete isolation.

Indeed, Zabaikalsk and Manzhouli were among the last open border checkpoints between China and the Soviet Union through which legal border crossings continued to be possible, at least on a small scale. Local transborder contact, however, was professional and not private, largely configured to maintain railroad and postal services between the two countries. Yet it was mainly passengers on the international express trains, who hailed in large part from third-party countries, rather than local borderlanders who passed through this last narrow slit in the barbed-wire gate between the People's Republic of China and the Soviet Union.

The militarization of the border regions also had dire consequences for their economic and demographic development. In the Soviet borderland, despite a sharp increase in population in the postwar years, depopulation became a major issue as the economy and infrastructure remained underdeveloped. Soviet youth were not so much afraid of China as reluctant to continue harsh and boring everyday life in sleepy Soviet border villages. Chita, the next chief economic and cultural city, was hundreds of kilometers away and separated by the internal boundary between the heartland of the Soviet Union and the restricted border area. Manzhouli was within sight of some Soviet border dwellers, but due to the locked international border and the cultural indifference toward China, the Chinese town seemed distant and alien. Thus the Soviet borderland was isolated twice over, cut off from the Soviet interior and from

China. This peculiar situation created a frontier ethos, a sense of life in a well-fortified "zone," among the local borderlanders. For ordinary Chinese nationals access to the Chinese borderland was likewise restricted and the situation in the border areas of Hulunbeir overall was certainly even more troublesome than on the Soviet side.

In addition to the economic and demographic fallout of the military confrontation along the shared periphery, the crisis of ideological legitimation provoked by China was the greatest threat emanating from Beijing. The staged peace border of the 1950s was unceremoniously replaced with an almost exclusively rhetorical front of enmity. Both countries fired from all propaganda barrels. The border thus not solely functioned as a practical means of controlling transborder flows but simultaneously operated as a symbol of state power. Ideological warfare took on an even greater importance than it had during the Soviet-Japanese confrontation of the 1930s, as it was now a confrontation between two communist regimes. Compared to the earlier period, the concept of the enemy produced in Beijing and Moscow, however, was now much more abstract, for the names of places and people in the neighboring country were eradicated from public discourse. This blurred outline of the adjacent borderland was made possible since the border was now under lock and key and the majority of locals on both Argun banks no longer had personal memories of the neighboring state.

8

Watermelons and Abandoned
Watchtowers

DURING A RARE VISIT in February 1981 two American journalists were allowed to inspect the Chinese border protection facilities near Manzhouli. This fact alone suggests a significant change in the surveillance and defense regime on the Chinese side. During their trip Michael Weisskopf and Howard Simons found a virtually undefended Chinese border, guarded only by 280 lightly armed soldiers scattered across the few border posts outside Manzhouli: "At the last outpost along this critical section of the Sino-Soviet border, seven young Chinese sentries and a German shepherd dog are all that would stand in the way of an invading army if the Soviets were to move into this vast frozen plain in Inner Mongolia. This tiny band of soldiers stands guard . . . , peering through binoculars at the busy, well-armed Soviets across the border." By the early 1980s, with little hope of blocking a Soviet land invasion supported by superior air power, the Chinese army had withdrawn dozens of kilometers inland to the Great Xingan Mountains to protect the region's heartland. This marked a sudden change of heart. Two years earlier, in February 1979, while Beijing was fighting a Moscow ally in the Sino-Vietnamese War, Chinese troops on the Argun were put on alert against a possible attack. For several days afterward Soviet troops at Zabaikalsk drove their T-54 tanks within a few hundred meters of the boundary, as the skies overhead were crisscrossed by MiG-23 fighter planes. By February 1981, with the Soviet military bogged down in Afghanistan and a declining economy at home, this display of Soviet military dominance and the degree of tension prompting it were things of the past.[1] Border incidents resulting in bloodshed also had become extremely rare.[2]

This final chapter examines the development of Sino-Soviet relations and their impact on the Argun borderland from the post-Mao and post-Brezhnev years to the early 1990s. It explores how the boundary between the two communist states gradually became permeable again through center-driven political and economic reconciliation between the two countries and how, with slackening control at the border and the simultaneous political and economic power breakdown of the Soviet Union, informal cross-border contacts grew as well. While the border was still heavily guarded, the borderland soon slipped out of the control of the metropole, at least on the Soviet side of the barbed-wire fence. Indeed, it will be argued here that local initiatives accelerated the process of rapprochement between the two sides. Officially approved contact channels were quickly replaced by zones created by the local border people.

The Last Chapter of Unfathomable Enmity: The Propaganda Movie That Was Never Aired

The echo of the Sino-Soviet rift slowly faded away, drowned out by signs of a cautious reconciliation. In Zabaikalsk anti-Maoist propaganda work among railroad personnel continued, despite increasingly regular contacts with their colleagues from across the rolling grassy prairie hills that sometimes went beyond the professional realm.[3] As late as December 1980 the Central Committee of the Communist Party of the Soviet Union contemplated the production of a televised film that would once again expose its neighbor's malevolent activities in the border region. The script was to revolve around statements by unmasked Chinese spies, recorded on video by the Soviet secret service, explaining how spies were recruited in the territory of the Soviet Union and the intricacies of their infiltration activities. The film could then, according to a KGB statement, "be broadcast at a politically suitable moment within the Union and in third countries with the aim . . . of achieving a favorable opinion of our country in the societies of the international community."[4] Only when Mikhail Gorbachev rose to power in the mid-1980s did the Soviet government begin to reconsider its approach to information control and to move toward glasnost and objectivity in reporting. The KGB propaganda movie never went on air, and in late September 1986 the Central Committee in Moscow resolved to stop jamming broadcasts from Radio Beijing, a task that had required an enormous expenditure of resources.[5]

Already when Deng Xiaoping reassumed Chinese leadership in 1978 Beijing's foreign policy toward Moscow underwent a cautious revision toward rapprochement. In 1982, at the twelfth Congress of the Chinese Communist Party, the Chinese regime declared that it would pursue an independent foreign policy and thus refrain from allying with either the United States or the Soviet Union. Yuri Andropov's cautious China initiatives during his brief interregnum from 1982 to 1984 were insufficient to achieve a fundamental break with inflexible Soviet foreign policy, but they nonetheless paved the way for a more pragmatic Soviet China policy under Gorbachev. Upon his taking office in March 1985 the Kremlin's new foreign policy agenda thus explicitly addressed the resolution of what Chinese officials called the "Three Obstacles" to normalization: first, Moscow's invasion of Afghanistan; second, its support for the Vietnamese occupation of Cambodia; and third, and certainly most important for the Argun borderland, the issue of Soviet military presence in Mongolia and along the Soviet border with China.

Further, during the perestroika years a consensus emerged among Soviet foreign policy elite around the need to devote resources to economic reform rather than costly international conflicts. Border talks, suspended since 1978, resumed in early 1987. The Kremlin was now much less concerned with a Chinese military threat. In their eyes Deng's China, like the capitalist world, was no longer inherently militaristic and aggressive, thereby making cooperation possible. Simultaneous reform efforts in the People's Republic of China helped solidify cooperation and trust. The Sino-Soviet summit in mid-May 1989 in Beijing became a symbolic breakthrough in their relations. Both sides agreed to the resumption of relations between the two communist parties and to base bilateral relations on peaceful coexistence.[6]

Rapprochement from Above: Reestablishing Contacts in the Borderlands

Even before Gorbachev's rise to power, Moscow and Beijing took steps to ease political tensions, if only on a cultural level. The friendship societies restored contact in 1983. The societies resumed some of their activities in the capitals: exhibitions and educational evenings were organized to pay homage to writers or historical dates of the neighboring country. The first top-level delegations commuted between Moscow and Beijing. Exchanges of students and tourist delegations began in 1984.[7]

When the affiliates of both friendship societies resumed their work in the border regions, about sixteen years had passed since Manzhouli's Chinese-Soviet Peoples' Friendship Palace had been demolished during the Cultural Revolution in August 1968.[8] On the Soviet side of the border with China the Soviet-Chinese Friendship Society added new local branches in Zabaikalsk, Blagoveshchensk, Pogranichnaia, and Nakhodka.[9] The presidium of the Soviet-Chinese Friendship Society urged regional staff to hold an inauguration meeting at Zabaikalsk in the first quarter of 1984. This was followed by a regional conference in Chita to elect the local branch president, vice-president, and secretary. The first official delegation of the local Manzhouli branch of the Sino-Soviet Friendship Society embarked upon a twenty-four-hour-visit

FIGURE 8.1. A Chinese delegation visiting Zabaikalsk, mid-1980s. These official exchanges
were a crucial part of reviving formal economic ties during the *perestroika* years.

to Zabaikalsk in November 1984 to commemorate the October Revolution's
anniversary. Five Chinese and five Soviet professionals assembled there, all
locals, most of whom worked for cargo companies. Their program included a
tour of the Zabaikalsk middle school, two movie screenings, and participation
in an October Revolution celebration demonstration. Zabaikalsk delegates
had already paid a visit to Manzhouli one month before, during the ceremonies marking the thirty-fifth anniversary of the People's Republic of China.[10]

As is evident, central and regional authorities in Moscow and Chita maintained the tradition of organizing and scripting "friendship." With the exception of provisions for cooperation in disaster relief, the Soviets moved cautiously toward resurrecting cross-border contacts. The regional party
committee advised its Zabaikalsk subordinates to commemorate crucial historical dates of the Chinese Communist Party and the Chinese Revolution.
Exchanges of delegations on 1 October and 7 November 1985 continued in a
"cordial atmosphere" according to the by-now well-trodden tradition. During
those meetings Chinese delegation members repeatedly expressed their willingness to expand social, cultural, and professional activities and to come together "not just during anniversaries." They proposed "gatherings between

veterans, women, youth, working experience exchanges of teachers, agronomists etc." The Soviet side had to slow the enthusiasm of its Chinese partners,
reminding them that "all activities are oriented according to relations between
the two central organizations." In fact, as in the 1950s it was the Moscow-based
party authorities who were empowered to sanction activities of the local
Soviet-Chinese Friendship Societies and regional government exchanges.[11]

By 1986 Moscow and Beijing allowed members of the two local friendship
societies to come together for substantial working meetings for the first time.
The three-day visits of the Chinese to Zabaikalsk in August 1986 and of Soviet
friendship delegates to Manzhouli in fall 1987 proved especially fruitful. The
cultural façade of the program was sustained. However, economic issues dominated the agenda. Chinese delegates visited the state farm Stepnoi and the firm
Agroprom. In a brief article the local Soviet newspaper *Zabaikal'ets* finally
broke the news of these meetings to its readers.[12]

In return, the Chinese hosts showed their Soviet guests around the prerevolutionary Russian-built Zhalainuoer coal mines, about thirty kilometers southeast of Manzhouli, joined them on a tour of a chemical plant in Manzhouli,
and then took them on a walk through the city. Manzhouli's party vice-
secretary Wu Yihan used each and every stop on the junket to express his hope
"that the visit will stimulate deeper contacts between the two border regions
in the economic and cultural spheres." What Wu had in mind was cooperation
between Manzhouli and Zabaikalsk in matters of culture, sports, labor activ-
ism, and organized tourism; but direct cross-border trade was head and shoul-
ders above the rest in importance.[13]

For the first time in their history both friendship societies became more
than just a stage for state-sanctioned amity. At least on the Chinese side they
were to become agencies of economic cooperation. Just one month after the
Soviet delegates had taken a stroll through Manzhouli, comrade Wu visited Zabaikalsk again. There he presented his ideas with unabashed clarity. He offered
to set up a Chinese canteen in Zabaikalsk, staffed and supplied from across the
border, and invited the Soviets to open a Russian lunchroom in Manzhouli.
As Wu inspected the new dormitory for Chinese railroad men constructed at
the train station of Zabaikalsk he further proposed sending more permanent
Chinese workers to meet the growing need for loading freight.[14]

Indeed the increase in railroad freight traffic over the border was one of the
first visible signs of growing economic ties between the two countries. Since
the early 1980s China's leadership had urged Moscow to expand contacts beyond cultural folklore. In October 1982 the two sides held negotiations on the
resumption of cross-border business in Khabarovsk. Two agreements were
signed in April 1983, restoring border trade between the Soviet Far East and
Heilongjiang province as well as between Eastern Siberia and Inner Mongolia.[15]
In Zabaikalsk and Manzhouli international freight rates between 1980 and 1985

FIGURE 8.2. Manzhouli's party secretary Zhang Zhi and the first secretary of Zabaikalsk's District Executive Committee Viktor I. Kolesnikov during the negotiations of the economic agreement in Manzhouli, April 1988.

had jumped more than tenfold and transport infrastructure soon proved to be inadequate, although the freight rates failed to reach the all-time high of the mid-1950s.[16] Since business started off from almost zero in 1980, however, these figures are more impressive than they seem at first glance. Even in 1990, Sino-Soviet trade represented only a small percentage of total foreign trade. Because almost all goods were transported by rail, moreover, the increase in bilateral business ran through the border settlements without directly affecting them beyond securing additional jobs in the cargo terminals and therefore had only a limited impact on people's lives in Zabaikalsk and Manzhouli.[17]

An economic agreement brokered in April 1988 brought about a break-through in regional transborder collaboration between the Zabaikalsk district and the city of Manzhouli. It listed several areas ripe for the development of professional cooperation: exchange of technical know-how, delivery of Chinese building materials, assistance in construction and the allocation of labor, and Soviet delivery of raw materials. Since both countries circulated nonconvertible currencies, barter transactions dominated the exchange of goods. Additionally, a mixed trade-economic working commission replaced the rather inflexible friendship societies, which had proved to be inappropriate for quick economic development due to a lack of relevant expertise.[18]

Both sides were to profit from the revival of economic exchange. In Zabaikalsk, where the population had fallen to seventy-five hundred in 1989,[19] most buildings dated back to the 1950s. Lethargic workers and a pervasive lack of materials as well as antiquated cranes and excavators slowed canalization and the construction of housing projects. Even small but prestigious installations such as the station's archway remained uncompleted.[20] The city's first Chinese construction projects, built by some two hundred fifty workers of the Harbin Railroad Administration, started in 1988, and included several apartment buildings, a canteen, a dairy, and a gymnasium with an indoor pool. Unlike in tsarist times Soviet regional papers no longer wrote xenophobic reports on "yellow laborers" but praised the effort of the "Chinese friends."[21]

Agriculture became another important domain of cooperation. Unlike in China, where rural reforms and privatization after 1978 had caused a big increase in agricultural output, Soviet agriculture was still mostly collectivized, centrally planned, and inefficient. Chinese peasants were waiting to cultivate potatoes and other crops in the vicinity of Zabaikalsk. "Our Soviet neighbors would like to learn to produce melons the way we do here," Manzhouli mayor Xu Shaoan told a *Time* journalist in 1988. Siberian farmers would learn Chinese techniques for planting, growing, and harvesting. To a Soviet trade official from Zabaikalsk such cooperation not just resulted in a booming local melon crop but brought about a range of mutual benefits. "Business is booming. We manufacture what they want, they grow what we want."[22]

In fact the taste of a Chinese-made watermelon could increase sympathy of the local Soviet border populace for the former enemy more efficiently than any friendship performance. The remote settlement soon became one of the symbols of a nationwide discourse of Soviet-Chinese friendship. "Zabaikalsk—border station" reads the headline in a front-page story in the high-circulation daily broadsheet newspaper *Izvestiia*, next to a photograph depicting two smiling cargo managers, one Soviet and one Chinese.[23]

Nevertheless the gaps in the barbed-wire fence were still narrow and contacts between the ordinary people remained limited to a few state-approved projects. Formal relations were restricted to contacts between a relatively small circle of railroad workers, customs officers, farmers, construction workers, and local cadres. In the fall of 1989 Manzhouli's mayor named the lack of a regular highway checkpoint as a major shortcoming. Local politicians of both sides of the border were eager to address this but had to wait for central approval before they could build. Authorities in Moscow remained hesitant, fearing a loss of control, as road traffic is primarily made up of individual movements, in contrast to trains operated by the state.[24]

Although friendship societies lost their status as discreet diplomatic channels, they continued to fulfill their original role as agents of cultural, social, and professional exchange, monitoring relations between the people of both sides, as contacts and exchange gradually intensified. The activities of the Zabaikalsk local branch were largely restricted to the field of transport. Those who did not work in that sphere rarely got in touch with Chinese people. Soviet-Chinese Friendship Society members, librarians, teachers, and doctors had virtually no contact with Chinese citizens. Recognizing this, officials aimed to improve the situation through measures such as placing a higher emphasis on teaching Chinese in middle school.[25] By 1989, however, professional exchanges in other disciplines, such as between doctors and between agronomists, had been established and binational sports events had been organized. But not until 1990 did the two local friendship society branches in Manzhouli and Zabaikalsk consent to meetings of less prominent members of their societies, allowing delegations of teachers, translators, health care workers, and veterans to meet.[26]

By that time, however, many borderlanders did not need such organizations as pretexts for visiting the neighboring country any more. Most members of the insignificant Chinese diaspora in the Chita region had spent time with relatives in their homeland or were visited by Moscow-based Chinese diplomats.[27] Further, for the first time after more than half a century the descendants of the Russian Cossacks in Trekhreche and the Khori Buriats in Shenekhen region—whose ancestors had fled to China in the turmoil of revolution, civil war, and collectivization in Russia and who had survived the repressions of the Cultural Revolution in China—were now able to see their Soviet family members across the Argun. Previously Soviet and Chinese authorities had prohibited any contact between families.[28] Yang Yulan, the daughter of a Russian mother and a Chinese father, having spent her entire life in the rural Cossack diaspora on the Chinese bank of the Argun, now made use of a bilingual background that once had been stigmatized. In 1991 and 1992 she worked as a translator for a Manzhouli company, accompanying Chinese business delegations to Chita and other places in Transbaikalia in the midst of a crumbling Soviet Union.[29]

Lifting Barriers: The Widening of Cross-Border Contact Channels

The reestablishment of cordial relations between Beijing and Moscow also benefited international travel. Tourism was no longer as exclusive as it was in the early 1970s, when just a handful of Westerners were permitted to cross the border every year.[30] Yet in the late 1980s international train travel still remained the preserve of the privileged. In 1988 the Swiss-owned Nostalgie Istanbul Orient Express Company train drew much attention from international and local audiences. A *New York Times* advertisement praised the nineteen-day journey from Paris to Hong Kong for re-creating travel "as it was experienced by the royalty of yesteryear."[31] A Japanese broadcaster produced a two-hour documentary about the journey to the East and *Zabaikal'ets* covered the four-hour sojourn at the Soviet terminus in great detail.[32]

When the luxury train passed the border it marked the quiet before the storm. Motor traffic between Zabaikalsk and Manzhouli expanded significantly. While a total of fifteen to twenty cars daily were cleared by customs in 1988, these figures multiplied within three years to up to three hundred vehicles per day. Every month about twelve thousand people used the highway checkpoint in 1991, double the number of railroad passengers. In 1992 it became the largest motorcar checkpoint along the Sino-Russian border but remained a makeshift site lacking appropriate customs facilities.[33]

The number of passengers on international trains rose at a slower pace, yet growth rates were nonetheless impressive: within five years they had seen a fivefold increase from 16,004 in 1988 to a postwar peak of 76,605 passengers in 1992.[34] The facilities of the train station of Zabaikalsk had not been built for such high numbers of travelers. At times two to three hundred passengers crowded the smelly station, finding "no place to rest or snack."[35] Immigration procedures remained much the same as in the 1950s. After traversing the 6,293 kilometers from Moscow to Zabaikalsk, the train was emptied and briefly removed so that the bogies on all carriages could be switched. Meanwhile passengers filed their visas and then decamped to the station building in Zabaikalsk, strolling by its Corinthian pillars, to exchange their leftover rubles for dollars. After two to three hours the railroad journey continued. At slow speeds trains passed a wall emblazoned with the slogan "USSR builds Communism," to reach Manzhouli after fifteen minutes.

The winds had changed on both sides of the border. Douglas Fetherling, a Canadian writer who traveled the Trans-Siberian in the spring of 1990, was surprised by some of these developments: "Foreigners were even allowed to take photographs of the platform, an activity forbidden at many other, less sensitive facilities of the Soviet railroads." In Manzhouli passengers exchanged

FIGURE 8.3. A Moscow-bound international train passing the Soviet state gate under the watchful eyes of armed guards patrolling the border in 1991. The coat of arms with hammer and sickle is welcoming the passengers to the Soviet Union.

freshly retrieved dollars for Chinese Foreign Exchange Certificates at the station, as foreigners were not allowed to pay with the local currency but had to buy these certificates. Fetherling experienced the Chinese immigration and customs officials who climbed aboard to be "courteous as well as efficient." He even had a chat with a young customs inspector, who asked him if he might sit down and join him in a conversation to practice his English.[36]

It was not only the Western adventurer or the Vietnamese student who took the train from Beijing to Moscow. The route became increasingly popular among the Chinese and Soviets. By 1991 it was almost impossible to obtain tickets for the Beijing-bound train in Chita. The train ran once a week and was often fully booked. People in the Chita region usually had to take the local train to Zabaikalsk and to cross the border from there to Manzhouli by bus, where they would eventually get on a Chinese train. Nevertheless, entering China was still not an easy task. "It takes forever for people to cross the border. Many camp at the train station. There are too few train tickets, and too few cars pass the highway checkpoint," as *Zabaikal'skii Rabochii* quoted a Soviet customs official. To meet the increasing demand Chinese and Soviet railroads scheduled the train to run twice a week and added an additional passenger car from Chita to Beijing. To ease local border traffic to some degree a regular shuttle bus between Zabaikalsk and Manzhouli started to commute in August 1991.[37]

With swelling cross-border traffic and subsequent proliferation of economic activity, one negative side effect of relaxed controls recurred. Illicit trafficking, undeniably, had never been entirely wiped out. Even at the height of political tensions smuggling had occurred on a small scale, but it now picked up again along the border. By 1990 the subject, banned as a topic of official public discourse for decades, reappeared in Soviet media. An article in *Zabaikal'ets* explained the etymology of *kontrabanda* and informed the readers of some popular means of deception on Beijing-Moscow trains: lipsticks in sealed cigarette packs, electronic watches wrapped in toilet paper, jewelry in thermos cups, and—perhaps most daring—ruble bills squirreled away in the window frame of the train car lavatory. The situation at the Manzhouli-Zabaikalsk highway border crossing was similar. The head of Soviet customs there admitted that smugglers were caught almost every day. People were as creative as they had ever been. One Chinese truck driver hid ruble bills in the air filter of his Dongfeng truck. But Russians accused the Chinese contract workers of being the most vigorous smugglers. "After finishing their jobs . . . Chinese citizens carry many export-restricted items home to their motherland."[38]

Soviet and Chinese nationals were not the only ones involved in smuggling circuits. In 1990 the "Polish pearl necklace scandal" became an incident widely discussed in local and regional papers. A group of Polish nationals, mainly university students, used their academic holidays to take an illicit shopping tour in China. That June at the train station in Zabaikalsk, Soviet customs nabbed at least fifteen such delinquents and sent them to the KGB prison in Chita. The Poles had acquired at Chinese bazaars bags filled with pearl necklaces that they intended to sell on black markets at stations along the Trans-Siberian Railroad, in their native Poland, and, probably, at the premiere European bazaar of that time: Berlin's long-deserted Potsdamer Platz. Due to variant pricing systems in China and the Soviet Union, the Soviet customs estimated their overall value at the absurd amount of nearly 2.5 million rubles.[39]

"Run on the Freight Wagons": The Collapse of the Border Control Regime

Such stringent customs procedures proved ephemeral, however. Economic disruption across the country and political power breakdown in Moscow fostered a dramatic increase in Sino-Soviet cross-border contacts and, in the end, led to conditions that were close to anarchy. Many of the shortages in consumer goods and food products in the Russian border regions were compensated by imports from Chinese border cities. In 1992, then, international trains were laden not only with human cargo. Sino-Russian shuttle trade had expanded rapidly. In 1993 the Russian border trade of Heilongjiang province accounted for one-third of the overall Sino-Russian trade balance. Beijing's policies accelerated this trend, as China granted the four border cities of Manzhouli, Heihe, Suifenhe, and Hunchun the right to establish economic cooperation zones. These zones aimed to stimulate foreign investment, technology exchange, and labor exports.[40]

Arguably the most important preconditions for this trend were slackening Soviet control at the border with China and the changed economic policy in China, which meant that small manufacturing blossomed. Following the end of communism in the Soviet Union and the disintegration of the state itself, the border zone regime was lifted. People no longer needed special permits to enter Zabaikalsk and other settlements adjacent to the state border.[41] Although passports were still checked at the border, local cross-border exchange soon challenged the control of the center at large. Zones of encounter between the Russians and the Chinese expanded beyond the train stations. And anyone could travel, not just the privileged who crossed the border for professional reasons. Zabaikalsk, once a sleepy and isolated border settlement, transformed into an El Dorado for the new post-Soviet caste of businessmen. They came from all corners of the former Soviet Union. The railroad administration revamped two passenger carriages on a siding to enlarge the station hotel's capacity in early 1992. Within several days all beds were fully booked.[42]

Accordingly, state-sanctioned commissions no longer directed trade between the two countries. Beginning in early 1992 people of both nations took barter trade into their own hands. By that time roughly fifteen hundred Chinese street traders had taken up permanent residence in Zabaikalsk. In the streets, on the tracks, in the passenger waiting hall, and soon everywhere Russians "bartered gold for . . . 'Adidas.'" Locals no longer dressed in Soviet gray or brown but in luridly colored Chinese attire. Tolerated by local authorities, the small square in front of the station building was converted into a bazaar, to emerge as the center of a grassroots economy, known as "Five-Kopecks" in the vernacular. In the end it was not the expert smuggler but the cross-border shopping tourist who most assertively challenged Russian border control. Newly established private travel agencies started to offer routine trips to China. For many Chita citizens a trip to Manzhouli became as common as going fishing or mushrooming.[43]

As the numbers of shopping tourists swelled central authorities pulled the emergency brake. Moscow ordered the highway crossing point to be closed in early August 1992. Only official delegations and goods were allowed to pass. An official statement declared that the checkpoint had never been sanctioned for private border crossing.[44] Prices for Chinese goods instantly skyrocketed. Crowds of Chinese day-trippers waited in Manzhouli. Countless people from all former Soviet Republics and Eastern Europe waited in Zabaikalsk to cross the border. In the turmoil accompanying the disintegration of the Soviet Union, orders from Moscow impressed only a few. Instead people at the border came up with new ways of acquiring a Chinese-manufactured Western lifestyle. "Everything started with people sick of their monotonous existence in front of deserted shop windows. They turned their eyes to the railroad tracks, with its cargo trains, and considered their freight to be 'humanitarian aid.' During that moment among parts of the population the 'Run on the freight wagons' war cry was born. Very soon it became evident that looting the cargo trains was not a difficult task."[45] A reform of the Soviet customs system that had terminated state monopoly on exports brought about a surge in the number of train cars eligible for customs clearance in the late 1980s. And not long afterward the first theft of railroad cargo was reported in Zabaikalsk.[46] Over the next few years the scale of such operations was to expand massively. In 1992 up to two thousand wagons with imports from China simultaneously waited to be cleared by Russian customs. Manzhouli was clogged with goods cars too. This left carriages with shoes, bikes, electronic devices, vodka, cigarettes, and other expensive consumer goods standing in the open almost unprotected for months. Sidings lacked ordinary fencing, there was just one guard per thousand wagons, and floodlights did not work. Russian railroad staff often abdicated their duty to safeguard shipments and instead assisted the raiders. The once isolated border settlement degenerated into the heart of the regional crime scene. According to Russian media the looting frenzy started in spring 1992 and lasted for ten months.[47] Media reported regularly on lootings, gunfights, and rampant moral decay, proffering images of people exchanging their consciences for sneakers. "Children abandoning school, adults their jobs, the disabled and the retired blank out their indispositions, railroad men ignoring their duties. All rush on the freight depots mercilessly plundering goods wagons. . . . They seize everything from condoms to leather jackets and fur coats. Entirely without shame, they get on the car, take off Soviet clothes to dress in Chinese garments." Families and entire school classes, with pupils as young as nine years, raided the cars together in organized groups. Local youth established their own black-market economy on the schoolyard. They dealt in everything that was fetched from the trains. The herdsman Apilov seized 107 leather jackets and sets of sportswear as well as forty-five bottles of vodka, with his wife and his daughter. Zabaikalsk soon bred its homegrown nouveaux riches. The biggest burglars settled around Victory Street, next to the tracks. Residents soon dubbed it "Millionaire's Street."[48] The disorder culminated in December 1992, by which time Zabaikalsk looked like a frontline village in war. Machine guns shelled the black-marketers' dwelling, and some were killed.

In early January 1993 provincial authorities in Chita reestablished the border zone control. Reinstating rules in application from the 1930s onward, only locals, visitors with proper documents, and passengers bound for China were allowed to enter the Zabaikalsk district.[49] An extremely frigid winter there brought life to a standstill and may have contributed further to the reduced influx of adventurers.[50] Only in the spring were authorities able to fully reestablish control. Freight depots were fenced in and observation towers and additional floodlight poles were erected. But some sources assessed economic losses up to that point in the billions of rubles.[51] Authorities estimated the number of casualties within the settlement from the skirmishes of the past year at seven people dead and eleven seriously injured.[52] Among them was a local resident who was shot for stealing six feather beds. Police searched his corpse and found 72,217 rubles and a tear gas cylinder. During winter the police and the military detained suspects numbering in the hundreds. In February 1993 alone more than three thousand were caught. Many of them were prosecuted for theft and taken into custody. Still most were likely never taken to trial. Many became "national heroes" among their peers.[53]

The final chapter of this book on the people of the Argun basin ends with this looting frenzy. Even though the plunderers were mainly newcomers to the region, their motives were manifold, ranging from revenge against the restrictive state to a pent-up desire for the goods of the ancient forbidden "other." Their motives also included a feeling of having been—as people on a remote border—unfairly left behind in poverty when the metropole was in presumed prosperity.

———

Diplomatic rapprochement accompanied the dissolution of barriers at the shared border, which had been sealed during the Sino-Soviet conflict of the 1960s and 1970s and during the Manchukuo years. Within a few years the agendas of official meetings had shifted from cultural to economic itineraries and zones of contact between the people of both countries widened again. Now not just the customs inspector or train conductor crossed the international border but also Chinese farmers and construction workers, whose social worlds were far less circumscribed there. Numbers of passengers on international trains swelled too, and twice a week the arriving trains gave the once tightly secured train stations a polyglot charm. Yet all those entanglements remained formal and under state command.

When political weakness and economic disorder reached the restricted border area of the Soviet Union, however, the shift from formal to informal came almost overnight. Perhaps for the first time since the 1920s the periphery clearly prevailed over the metropole, as bottom-up initiatives now dictated relations at the border, bypassing the formal channels between Moscow and Beijing. Soon after the Soviet flag was lowered above the Kremlin in Moscow and the Russian tricolor had been raised in its place the bunkers were abandoned and the minefields along the vast border between the Tianshan Mountains in the west and the Sea of Japan in the east were cleared. Various new economic, social, and cultural transborder networks that are part of a new chapter of post-Soviet Sino-Russian relations have since emerged.

Conclusion

MANY OF THE NEW entanglements of the post-Soviet era were made possible by a power shift that can probably be studied best in Manzhouli and Zabaikalsk. Michael Wines, a *New York Times* correspondent, observed the result of this fundamental change in 2001:

> For a lesson in 21st-century geopolitics, come to this border town, until just a few years ago an outpost for Russian infantry awaiting a Chinese invasion. Russian gun emplacements are crumbling now but the invasion is underway anyway: Chinese built the town's few new apartments, China Telecom connects the cellular phones, and Chinese traders hire busloads of jobless Russians to tote Chinese-made clothes and electronics through the Chinese-built border crossing. . . .
>
> For the Zabaikalsk residents, paradise begins 50 yards across the border, past abandoned Russian tanks and rusted barb-wire fences. There the Chinese have built a gleaming free-trade center, a small city of hotels, freight-forwarding offices, wholesale stores and pagodas. On the horizon, 10 minutes down a freshly paved highway in China, is the city of Manzhouli. Ten years ago a Chinese version of Zabaikalsk, it is today a staging area for Russian trade—a forest of skyscrapers and cafés.[1]

Nowadays, nearly three decades since the dissolution of the Soviet Union, Manzhouli is no longer just an obscure outpost on the China-Russia border, a cargo hub between Asia and Europe, or a shopping destination for Russians living nearby. With an exploding population, currently around three hundred thousand people after decades of stagnation, and an airport, with regular service to Beijing, Irkutsk, Ulaanbaatar, and Harbin, the city is modernizing at the speed of light.[2] While a few Russian-style log houses still line the streets, the city has turned into a pastel-painted Russian-inspired theme world annually attracting millions of Chinese tourists, who come to visit its new eclectic architecture. Halfway between Manzhouli and the international border is a bizarre park filled with a Gothic-style wedding palace, a Russian doll square

FIGURE 9.1. Manzhouli as seen from the railroad tracks in 2009. The obscure border outpost with only a few two-story buildings has transformed into a bustling city with a skyline of high-rise buildings within only a few decades.

dotted with matreshkas and Fabergé eggs, and a copy of Volgograd's *The Motherland Calls* statue. What visitors from Beijing, Xi'an, or Guangzhou see is a boomtown of hotels, restaurants, and shops now catering mainly to the Chinese market—a commercialized Chinese version of "Russia," without having to cross the actual state border. Their exploration usually ends at the bombastic Chinese state gate through which trains pass on their way to Moscow. Beyond the gate lies the sleepy backwater Zabaikalsk surrounded by low-rolling grassy hills. Nearly fifty meters high the Chinese gate absolutely dwarfs the Russian gate on the opposite side of the boundary, just as the glittering world of Manzhouli's skyscrapers overshadows the desolate cluster of gray concrete structures in Zabaikalsk.[3]

The pompous gate thus mirrors the new power relations between Russia and China and underscores the persistent symbolic force of this border despite its porousness. Though their fortunes are reversed dealings between Moscow and Beijing have dramatically improved in all spheres and on all

FIGURE 9.2. The state gates of China and Russia between Manzhouli and Zabaikalsk, 2009. Their different sizes symbolize the new power relationship between Beijing and Moscow.

levels. On the diplomatic level the relationship progressed from a constructive partnership toward friendship. With Russia transferring to China a part of Abagaitui Island on the upper Argun as well as the entire Tarabarov Island and about a half of Bolshoi Ussuriiskii Island at the confluence of the Ussuri and Amur rivers in October 2008, the two countries officially settled the last of their decades-old border disputes.[4]

Despite this new level of cordiality the Chinese-Russian relationship is becoming increasingly asymmetrical. Perhaps the most pressing question of our time for the China-Russia borderland is whether Chinese influence will reduce the region and its surroundings to a state of virtual economic and even political dependency. While the economic outputs of the People's Republic of China and the Soviet Union were roughly equal in 1991, China's gross domestic product is now about eight times the size of Russia's. With a dwindling population in the eastern regions of the Russian Federation and increasing numbers across the Argun, Amur, and Ussuri rivers, the population of China's Northeast today is about ten times that of the Russian Far East.[5]

This demographic imbalance and the inexorable spread of Chinese economic clout spurred a revival of old xenophobic fears among Russians, particularly those living near the Chinese border. In Moscow, and even more so in Russia's eastern provinces, skepticism about Beijing's motivations is growing even though China's politicians are doing everything they can to dispel this specter of fear and suspicion. A wave of public outrage against Chinese economic expansion gripped Transbaikalia in the summer of 2015, when the provincial government in Chita announced that a Chinese agriculture company secured a forty-nine-year contract, leasing 115,000 hectares of pastures and uncultivated land along the Argun at a symbolic price in a bid to farm poultry and livestock as well as raise crops for animal fodder. The public feared a sellout of Russia's natural resources to Chinese companies through this lease of an area approximately the size of Hong Kong. What terrified the Russian borderlanders even more, however, was the prospect of an increased influx of Chinese migrants, which is often associated with an expression of China's creeping territorial expansion.[6] Fears of a demographic time bomb may be unsubstantiated, at least at present, with rather low growth rates of the Russian economy and with China itself having vast underdeveloped areas and rapidly increasing wages. Yet many Russians remain wary of the Chinese.[7]

Manzhouli is a good place to hear how ordinary people from both countries talk about each other today. Suspicions lurk everywhere below the official narrative of good neighborliness and the public display of friendship. Russian visitors harbor deep distrust of the Chinese, and for many of them Manzhouli epitomizes China's unfathomable and dangerous nature.[8] Chinese views on Russians are no less colored by cynicism. For many Russia embodies a bygone hero with an inferior economy and a shrinking, complacent population.[9]

Nowadays, although there is evidence of numerous new transborder networks the international border along the Argun, Amur, and Ussuri rivers has not wholly withered away. It continues to exist as an economic, political, ethnic, social, and cultural line of division between China and Russia, with many barriers still visible on the ground or engraved on the minds of the borderlanders. While there is no closed zone on the Chinese side of the international border at present, access to Zabaikalsk became restricted again in April 2014, when the settlement was reincluded in the border zone. Ever since the local branches of the security organs have set up special road signs and checkpoints. Despite a renaissance of security mania, punishments for apprehended offenders are certainly less severe than they were under Stalin. Entrance and movement regulations are nevertheless reminiscent of Soviet-era border zone regulations.[10]

Even today not every visitor and border resident commutes freely back and forth between the two Argun banks, as the Cossacks and nomads did one hundred years ago. Absent an economic interest and still suspicious about the alien neighbor, many people would simply rather stay at home. Liudmila I. Mashukova, the former people's militia member and stationmaster, for instance, has never been to Manzhouli: "To be honest, I'm not interested in going there. Everything I need I can purchase here. And if I really want to see what Manzhouli looks like, I can turn on my television."[11]

Thus, despite a proliferation of cross-border human mobility in the post–Cold War era that largely stems from tourism and trade (and is not to be confused with immigration) there continues to be a considerable indifference and prejudice on both sides. The psychological alienation on a personal level, regardless of the close physical proximity, derives from decades of military confrontation, population exchange, and two very different systems of values and beliefs formed in the schools and by the media of two closed but very distinct countries. These legacies will have a lasting impact on the future of the border region, no matter how diplomatic relations, bilateral trade balances, or border management policies between China and Russia develop in the years to come.

————

More than three centuries of Sino-Russian encounters exert a powerful force in shaping present-day attitudes and perceptions of people on the Amur, Ussuri, and Argun rivers. The history of the vast Sino-Russian frontier and borderland has been exceptional in many ways. This region not only divided the two largest Eurasian empires but was also the place where European and Asian civilizations met, where nomads and sedentary people mingled, where the imperial interests of Russia and later the Soviet Union clashed with those of Qing and Republican China and Japan and where the world's two largest communist regimes went from allies to enemies.

Within just a few decades' time the Argun borderland changed from a territory with striking similarities to other porous borderlands on the margins of empires into a borderland with substantial analogies to tightly sealed borders between nation-states, although such comparisons always remain crude approximations. In the early twentieth century the Argun basin shared some basic commonalities with frontiers across different types of imperial states, land empires, and overseas empires alike, where logistical difficulties presented formidable obstacles for the metropoles, loyalties of frontier societies were unpredictable, and border crossing was a way of life. Beginning in the mid-twentieth century the Argun basin yielded a multitude of analogies with Cold War Europe, where state borders between the socialist and capitalist blocs became perimeters of military installations and ideological competition. In light of growing disconnections and escalating propaganda, projections of the neighboring side and its people became increasingly one-dimensional and depersonalized.

During the dramatic transformation of the Argun basin toward a more sharply defined boundary the imperial regimes faced a dilemma common to borders everywhere in the world: ambiguity. One and the same border can mean different things to various actors and observers. The clarity of a shadow-free line on a map is fiction. To understand the ambiguities of borders, the different shifts and turns in boundary production and various forms of border transgression, one must pay attention to multiple perspectives from the metropoles and the locality itself, no matter whether we study an arbitrary and diffuse imperial frontier, where state authority has not made inroads yet, or a tightly controlled and symbolically charged border between geopolitical adversaries. Therefore, this book has reconciled old empire-centered narratives with indigenous and local notions of territoriality and has told the micro-history within the macro-history of what was once the longest land border in the world. It is a space-centered history that zoomed in on one section of the vast borderland, looking outward and inward from the vantage point of the Argun River basin. By capturing the internal logic of the area near what today is the eastern Sino-Russian-Mongolian border triangle, this book not only spotlighted government policies devised to establish and maintain the Sino-Russian border in its various spheres but also focused on the borderlanders, an array of individual actors with various experiences and agendas, who have hitherto, if at all, appeared only at the fringes of historical scholarship.

Through the autobiographical lens of Russian, Chinese, and indigenous people and visiting foreigners and the stories they have to tell, the book challenges the great picture of diplomatic histories and top-down interpretations of this frontier and borderland. Listening to the voices of the nomadic herdsmen, artisans, merchants, and border guards, acknowledging them as historical actors and juxtaposing their narratives with the stories of the metropolitan elites, makes evident that the fate of the imperial frontiers and borderlands was never solely decided in the metropoles. The transformation of the Argun frontier into a borderland, where the nation-state concept of a boundary emerged triumphant, often took unexpected turns.

The networks, strategies, and social identities of the border people map complicated patterns that stretched across the border. Cossacks, for instance, sought self-determination, became brigands, or emigrated. Customs officials worked part-time as traders, selling commodities confiscated from smugglers in contraband bazaars. Native nomadic herders responded to metropolitan incursions by practicing cross-border migration or strategic naturalization.

To be sure not everybody was an active supporter or opponent of the state. Yet even the vast majority of those who were passive or indifferent helped to create, maintain, and destroy the border regimes. Through their stories it becomes clear that frontiers and borderlands have always been areas from which both support and subversion of the metropolitan center emanated. In this way the Argun basin represents a distinct constellation of developments that affected the entire Sino-Russian border.

Although China and Russia sketched the boundary approximately three hundred years ago, their executive bodies did not efficiently control flows of people and commodities on their shared frontier. In many ways the Argun basin remained a permeable imperial frontier where social and cultural identities of peoples of different ethnic and linguistic roots merged and shifted. The people of this liminal space often remained more attached to their immediate surroundings than to any national ideal, as did people elsewhere in remote areas of both empires. The principal reason for failing to establish imperial hegemony and efficient surveillance was an overextension of military and bureaucratic resources such actions would have required. Spheres of control stayed largely confined to a few scattered outposts. Most parts of this imperial frontier space thus remained porous, with people and commodities continuing to flow freely.

The mobility of hunting and gathering Tungus and livestock-breeding Mongols was a constant concern for the imperial authorities. The autochthonous frontier people recognized neither the Sino-Russian boundary nor imperial authority, unless they were forced to do so. Their traditional cultures, religions, and economies continued as the metropoles erected increasingly rigid border regimes. For the Mongols the Ganchzhur Fair remained a crucial site of cross-border sale for products of the local pastoral economy well into the twentieth century. The centrality of Buddhism for the nomadic herdsmen in both Russia and China and their common clan names are testaments to their common religion and kinship ties.

Imperial abilities to construct, strengthen, and maintain international boundaries grew over time, partly because of advancements in technology and organization but also because growing investments allowed resources to control even the remotest peripheries. Only by being able to install telegraphs, railroads, and other sorts of mechanisms into frontier landscapes did the empires succeed in expanding control and drawing peripheries closer to metropoles. Once the imperial policies became more assertive, nomads and herders resisted the conquest of their lands and the destruction of their mobile way of life. While Tokhtogo, the Mongol warlord, openly fought the Chinese forces during the 1900s, killing people and agitating among his peers, other nomadic herdsmen stayed silent, mainly concerned with the well-being of their families and their livestock during the same period.

By introducing modern infrastructure states authorized a particular form of border crossing and in doing so fostered outgrowths accelerating formal border making. New transit hubs replaced traditional routes and transport on horses, camels, and barges. Such infrastructure projects were built to facilitate trans-border communications as well as the flow of goods, people, and ideas through the borderland corridor in a manner suited to their political creators.

Colored by the prime operational institutions of empire these modern borderlands emerged in strategically important regions, while older, more penetrable styles of frontiers continued to exist elsewhere.

Modern means of transportation did not, however, perfectly serve the state. In fact railroads actually increased uncontrolled movement across borders, fostering new and subversive kinds of contact between people of different political, ethnic, economic, religious, and social backgrounds. For instance, Aleksei N. Nikitin, Manzhouli's municipal council chairman in the 1910s, was in theory entrusted with promoting Russian rule in this railroad town on Chinese territory. In practice, however, he was a corrupt official aligning himself with local Chinese merchants and working mainly for his personal gain. Although the Russians and Chinese of the frontier never developed a common cultural code, they had exposure to one another through trade and found limited ways of dealing with one another. Many others also adapted quickly to changing border situations over time. Yet their successors had fewer options available to them in adapting to new milieus taking shape on both sides of the boundary. They could abide by the rules now established by their states or leave.

On the Argun River the metropoles would succeed in tightening their control over the entire borderland significantly in the 1930s. They did so by applying more severe penalties to border transgression and by installing a much stronger military presence on state perimeters. No longer was just the external state boundary monitored. The borderland had become isolated from the inside and outside, with border zones in which communities and their members were subject to special supervision and individuals' movement into them restricted. Traditional life patterns, if they continued to exist, became encapsulated in new national cultures. Long-lived kinship and economic networks began to adopt the contours of the formal international border, and new networks emerged based on its full acceptance.

An entirely new demographic fabric supplanted the native population. The deportation of unreliable natives and early colonists and the immigration of people servile to state authority into the borderland left lasting effects ranging beyond individual fates. Born in central provinces of Russia and China and unfamiliar with the traditional frontier culture, they were probably the archetypical borderlanders of their time. One of them was Mikhail I. Sladkovskii. A native of the Krasnoiarsk province, some twenty-five hundred kilometers west of the Argun, he was made head of the Soviet border guard's Special Purpose Service at the border station of Otpor at the age of twenty-six. Sladkovskii was clearly a loyal agent of the Bolshevik regime, willing to enforce a new set of strict rules with a gun. Though Sladkovskii spoke Chinese (which he had learned in college) he was no longer able to pass to the Chinese side of the border, as would have been possible just a few years before. Other bureaucrats, like Petr P. Purin, a former consular official in Hailar in the 1920s and head of the technical department of the intelligence division in the Transbaikal Military District in the 1930s, suffered because they had once lived in the Chinese borderland. Accused of spying for the Japanese, Purin was arrested and shot years later under Stalin.

Purin and Sladkovskii represent two different types of border dwellers new to the Argun and illustrate its changes. Both men were agents of the state. Purin, though, arrived earlier, when the international border was still poorly guarded and undermanned. His "crime" was his prior contact with Chinese, Japanese, and other people from across the border. This cosmopolitan experience would be the final nail in his coffin. Sladkovskii, for his part, failed to get in touch with foreign nationals beyond his obligatory professional duties. With the international border firmly sealed, the Soviet party-state—and, to a lesser degree, the Manchukuo government—deported or killed locals holding ties across the perimeter. Reliable citizens gradually replaced such allegedly disloyal people—even if definitions of the category "reliable" constantly shifted.

Reciprocity between the metropole and a partially replaced borderland population further strengthened the legitimacy of a coherent bounded space and welded subjects and ruler closer together. In Manzhouli there were no longer Russian waiters who served Japanese customers speaking Chinese to each other. People who spoke only either Russian or Chinese and who had never before visited the neighboring country came to outnumber those with transcultural backgrounds. The overwhelming majority of the new residents would never cross the international border in their lives. It was during this troubled time that the border also rose in an ideological sense, fraught with new meaning and new legitimacy. The new, relatively close-minded borderlanders were more easily convinced by state propaganda, which portrayed the land beyond the river as alien and enemy territory and metaphorically reproduced it via the notion of a "sealed" and "sacred" border.

In many ways the postwar decades saw further separation. The party-state bureaucracies in Moscow and Beijing, thousands of kilometers away from the state border, succeeded in eliminating a cross-boundary "border culture" that went beyond physical disentanglement and in many ways turned the border into a psychological wall firmly implanted in the minds of residents and visitors alike. Compared to the Manchukuo years, cross-border ties in the Sino-Soviet borderland had certainly regained some strength during the alliance period, but these were almost exclusively on the state level, regulated by Beijing and Moscow. The 1950s were the heyday of bilateral friendship societies, youth delegations, and song and dance ensembles, often performing merely hollow rituals and massive peace propaganda in state media, but not the time of locals passing through the "border of peace" on a daily routine. This contradiction reveals discrepancies between allegedly open borders that are in fact closed and between allegedly sealed barriers that always remain surmountable for certain individuals and groups. The central governments in Beijing and Moscow succeeded in suppressing informal cross-border contacts and keeping economic, social, and cultural exchange under firm state command. When the Sino-Soviet conflict escalated in the late 1960s friendship rhetoric was replaced by hostile propaganda, which in many ways resembled enemy images propagated during the Manchukuo years. Yet with a border that had been under lock and key for four decades and a population no longer familiar with its neighbor, such messages were arguably more effective than ever before.

Even as it took on an extremely high degree of isolation, the Sino-Soviet borderland was also a product of the locals who lived inside it. Residents furnished with insider knowledge of the border's physical infrastructure and the personal characteristics of those who ran it possessed the means to keep the regime strong for outsiders or weak for insiders. Vera P. Zolotareva, for instance, cleared goods trains to China. The Soviet shunter belonged to a very small group of Soviet citizens allowed to travel to Manzhouli on duty during the Sino-Soviet split, in her case to couple and uncouple train carriages. Her passages were tightly overseen and confined to her professional duties. Though she recalled having amiable workmates among the Chinese railroad men, she never questioned the Soviet border regime. Zolotareva knew exactly where the red lines of the apparatus of extreme border surveillance were drawn. She enforced the control regime out of loyalty to her state. In the end the ordinary denizens in the restricted zones on the Argun may not have been able to thwart the implementation of rigid control mechanisms any longer. Even by the time, however, when locals were not playing an equal role in shaping the nature of the Sino-Soviet border anymore, they still had the choice of volunteering or passive resistance.

Thus, we cannot assume the complete remaking of any borderland or borderland denizen within just one or two generations' time. This book has provided some counterexamples disrupting a linear and teleological course from an open and vaguely demarcated interimperial frontier to a tightly patrolled borderland, alongside a continuous and cumulative vanishing of contact zones. Russian Cossacks in Trekhreche, for instance, continued to interact with Chinese borderlanders even when the border had been locked for several decades. Some Russians stayed within Chinese territory, though the vast majority of this rural diaspora had been repatriated to the Soviet Union or had emigrated to Australia or the Americas after the war. Though not allowed to speak Russian anymore, those who had lingered, like the mixed-blood Cossack

Yang Yulan, unintentionally displayed fragments of Russian life to newly arrived Chinese farmers in the Trekhreche delta. Those who returned "home"
across the Argun to the Soviet bank exposed their new Soviet environment,
peopled by state farm workers, to unfamiliar things. Bearers of a prerevolutionary rural culture, they brought back pieces of the old Russia to the new Soviet
lebenswelt: a handed-down way of making cheese or the old Russian accent
and grammar in addition to some pidgin phrases, also importing some elements of a Chinese way of life they themselves had adopted over the years. Yet
Yang and others remained exceptional in that they, in different ways, never
quite converted to become fully Russian or Chinese.

NOTES

Introduction

1. Paine, *Rivals*, in particular. While literature on the history of Inner and Northeast Asia and the imperial rivalry in the macro region is growing, scant attention has been given to regional lenses on the borderlands, and even less so to research involving both sides. Cf. Urbansky, "Subalternity." Two notable exceptions have recently been published: The first, by Victor Zatsepine, offers a broad-brush approach to examining Northeast Asia as a meeting place between the Russian and Chinese empires during the late tsarist period, though the perspective of the ordinary women and men from the fading frontier remains somewhat colorless. Cf. Zatsepine, *Amur*. The second is David Brophy's excellent study of nation building processes within Muslim communities in Central Asia during the late nineteenth and early twentieth centuries that embraces a transnational bottom-up perspective through which the shifting loyalties among the local frontier population can be understood. Cf. Brophy, *Nation*.

2. Pioneering works are those of Frederick Jackson Turner, *Frontier*, and his student Herbert Eugene Bolton, *Borderlands*. For all of its continuing resonance in popular culture, Turner's seminal essay has been thoroughly criticized in recent decades. While Bolton did not completely reject Turner's philosophy, the New Western Historians have taken a revisionist's stance against the image of a line separating "savagery" and "civilization." With their anti-Turnerian interpretation of the American West they offered historians a provocative new way to understand frontiers that has now become the new orthodoxy in the field. Cf., e.g., Limerick, *Legacy*, 20–23; White, *Ground*, ix–xvi, 50–60; Worster, *Skies*, 3–33 passim. A classic work on the notion of "opening" and "closing" frontiers is Lamar and Thompson, *Frontier*, esp. 23–26, 35–39. Turner's frontier thesis also tremendously influenced the earlier scholarship on the history of Inner and Northeast Asia, most prominently Owen Lattimore, *Studies*, esp. 134–159, 165–179, 469–491, although his notion of the frontier resembles a zone much more than a line.

3. Cf. Adelman and Aron, "Borderlands"; Baud and van Schendel, "History"; Hämäläinen and Truett, "Borderlands." This trend can also be observed in emerging scholarship on borderlands focused on human agency edging China (e.g., Giersch, *Borderlands*; Shao, *Homeland*; Song, *Borders*) and Russia (e.g., Adelsgruber, Cohen, and Kuzmany, *Getrennt*; Boeck, *Boundaries*).

4. Prescott, *Frontiers*, 1–14 passim, esp. 12–14.

5. This distinction was first made by the historian Geoffrey Hosking, "The Freudian Frontier," *Times Literary Supplement*, 10 March 1995, 27.

6. Essential features of the Chinese and Russian empires and their territorial expansion are scrutinized in Burbank and Cooper, *Empires*, 185–218 and Rieber, *Struggle*, 31–41, 49–58, 415–423.

Important historical studies of the empires are Kappeler, *Rußland*; Hosking, *Russia*; Lieven, *Empire*; Sunderland, *Taming* on Russia, and synthetic analyses of the Chinese Empire by Crossley, *Manchus*; Elliott, *Manchu*; and Perdue, *China*.

7. Lattimore, *Manchuria*, esp. 77–78, 99.

8. Cf. the classic works by Anderson, *Communities*; Hobsbawm and Ranger, *Invention*, esp. the introduction by Hobsbawm on 1–14; and Sahlins, *Boundaries*. See McKeown, *Order*, for increased border control and identity documentation.

9. Maier, *Borders*, 1–6. Cf. also Sassen, *Territory*.

10. Recent scholarship suggests that a nation-empire dichotomy is hard to maintain in the multiethnic settings of the Russian and Chinese empires. Those empires were not necessarily less able to deal with challenges posed by regional diversity, than ethnically or culturally more homogeneous national states. Cf. Burbank and Cooper, *Empires*, 251–459 passim and Rieber, *Struggle*.

11. Rieber, *Stalin*, 129–139; Martin, *Empire*, esp. 311–343 passim, on the interwar period.

12. Cf. Sahlins, *Boundaries*, esp. 7–9.

13. Mobility, in this context, has often been misconceived as the inclination of locals to challenge borders, as if borders came first and mobility second. But, as we know, the relationship works exactly the other way around. Ludden, "Address," 1061–1065.

14. Cf. Billé, "Ideas," 28; Michael Wines, "Behold! The Lost Great Wall," *New York Times*, 21 September 2001, A4.

15. Until the collapse of the Soviet Union this border was even longer and comprised three large sections rather than one. In addition to the eastern segment, the Mongolian border represented a second. Prior to the demise of the Qing in 1911, Outer Mongolia was an integrated yet autonomous part of China, the northern limits of which marked the boundary between the Qing and Romanov empires. With the founding of the People's Republic of Mongolia in 1924, becoming the first satellite state of the Soviet Union, this territory came under Moscow's control. The border of communist Mongolia with China represented the outer edge of Soviet power for more than half a century. The third and westernmost portion was China's northwestern mountainous frontier with Russia, later to become Soviet Central Asia (today Kazakhstan, Kyrgyzstan, and Tajikistan).

16. Cf. Park, *Sovereignty Experiments*, for the unprecedented mobility of Koreans across China and Russia during the late nineteenth and early twentieth centuries.

17. For the population dynamics of Siberian settlement from European Russia before 1917, see Coquin, *Sibérie* and Treadgold, *Migration*.

18. Although the toponym Manchuria was by no means unknown in the Chinese and Manchu imagination, it sounds inaccurate and offensive to Chinese ears today, carrying imperialist associations implicating both Russian and Japanese incursion. The present-day term for this political and geographic region is the Northeast (Dongbei), which comprises the three provinces of Heilongjiang, Jilin, and Liaoning. Elliott, "Limits," 604–607; Janhunen, *Manchuria*, 8–11. For the sake of simplicity I refer to it as both Manchuria and the Northeast.

19. For the great migration of Han Chinese from China proper to Manchuria, see Gottschang and Lary, *Swallows* and Reardon-Anderson, *Pioneers*.

20. With the earliest border agreement, the Treaty of Nerchinsk, in 1689—and renegotiated in much greater detail at Kiakhta in 1727—both empires had reached a regional military power

balance and agreed to delimit their spheres of interest. Although the line of delimitation has not shifted significantly during the last centuries, it nevertheless has not been acknowledged as a completely fixed boundary until recently. The last disputes between Moscow and Beijing over rights to some islands were settled only in the post-Soviet period. Iwashita, *4,000 Kilometer*, 160–164.

21. The name is pronounced "ergün" in Mongolian and means "wide."

22. Transbaikalia, the area to the east of Lake Baikal, is part of Eastern Siberia, whereas the Russian Far East refers to all land east of Transbaikalia, encompassing the Amur and the Maritime regions plus Sakhalin Island and Kamchatka. Before 1884 Transbaikalia was part of the East Siberian Governor Generalship. Between 1884 and 1906 the region belonged to the Amur province and was incorporated into the Irkutsk Governor Generalship in 1906. In the Soviet period Transbaikalia was divided into western and eastern halves. Its eastern part, Chita region (*oblast'*), was formed in 1923.

23. Traditionally, Hulunbeir belonged to Mongolia. During the late Qing and the Republican periods the region was part of the Heilongjiang and Xingan provinces (*sheng*). After the Communist revolution in 1949 Hulunbeir was absorbed into the newly created Inner Mongolia Autonomous Region, to which it has belonged since (barring a brief interregnum from 1969 to 1979, when it was again folded into Heilongjiang).

24. The nomadic people of this region had been called "Bargut" (meaning "unenlightened" or "dark") by the Mongols because they were the last to convert to Lamaist Buddhism, clinging to their ancient shamanistic rites. Cf. Lattimore, *Mongols*, 156; Lindgren, "Manchuria," 521.

25. Urbansky, "Diplomacy."

Chapter 1: Cossacks and Bannermen on the Argun Frontier

1. Giller, *Opisanie*, 10.

2. Kashin, "Vykhod," 567–582 passim, quotation on 573–574.

3. Mancall, *Russia*, 35–37. Cf. Beckwith, *Empires*, for an ambitious account of the transformations of societies in Eurasia from the Bronze Age to the present.

4. Mancall, *Russia*, 9–20; *Aziatskaia Rossiia*, 5–11, 361–367 passim.

5. Crossley, *Manchus*, 78–101 passim; Perdue, *China*, esp. 94–129.

6. In a diplomatic sense, the commercial caravans often failed since the Chinese imperial court regarded Russian commercial caravans as nothing more than tribute-paying barbarians. Economically, however, quite a number of these missions were successful. Cf. Mancall, *Russia*, 41–110, 163–207 passim, for the early caravan trade.

7. The epic publication by Aleksandr P. Vasil'ev, a Transbaikal Cossack army officer, remains the most comprehensive and accurate account to this day. For the early history of Cossack explorers in Transbaikalia, cf. Vasil'ev, *Kazaki*, esp. 1:47–51, 70–74, 102–116, 130, 144–145, 191–195.

8. Cf. Mancall, *Russia*, 20–32, 111–140 passim and Vasil'ev, *Kazaki*, 1:178–188, for the Russian clashes with the Manchu in the Amur basin.

9. Mancall, *Russia*, 141–162 passim and 280–283 for the wording of the treaty; Vasil'ev, *Kazaki*, 1:196–201, Miasnikov and Stepanov, *Granitsy*, 84–89.

10. Foust, *Muscovite*, 24–43 passim; Vasil'ev, *Kazaki*, 2:18–20; Miasnikov and Stepanov, *Granitsy*, 89–94. Mancall, *Russia*, 236–249 and 302–310, for the English translation of the treaty.

11. Foust, *Muscovite*, 44–52; Mancall, *Russia*, 249–255; Widmer, *Mission*; Meng, "E-lo-ssu Kuan."

12. For the Ides mission, Mancall, *Russia*, 188–194, and Brand, *Beschreibung*, 148–151, for the border crossing at the lower Argun. Nikolai G. Spafarii, *Puteshestvie*, 140–150, describes the difficulties his ambassadorial delegation faced when crossing the Argun in the winter of 1675.

13. Foust, *Muscovite*, 46–48.

14. In the Kiakhta stretch of the Qing-Russia frontier no one was able to roam at will from the time that the boundary had been fixed. Existing rules were more strictly enforced along this crucial section than elsewhere; penalties for crossing the border illegally or deviating from assigned trade routes were severe. Cf. Natsagdorzh, "O prichine."

15. Foust, *Muscovite*, here 73–82, 91–96, 330–342. Even in 1892 Kiakhta remained the key hub for China trade in Russia, accounting for about 99 percent of the official bilateral trade carried out in Transbaikalia. *Obzor Zabaikal'skoi oblasti za 1892 god*, statistics on 7–8. Cf. Ptitsyna, *Dauriia*, 149–163 passim, on Kiakhta's economic decline.

16. Foust, *Muscovite*, 83–85, 233–234, 342–344; Vasil'ev, *Kazaki*, 2:26–28.

17. As early as 1698 Tsar Peter had issued a decree according to which goods of private merchants were no longer to be inspected at each and every city but only at the terminal point of Nerchinsk. The furthest-reaching amendment under Catherine the Great was the abolition of internal customs borders in the 1750s; by contrast, in the same period tariffs levied at the external borders on foreign goods were raised. Foust, *Muscovite*, 8–9; 223–225.

18. Only after the First Opium War (1838–1842), as Western notions of international systems expanded into China, was a modern system of customs control introduced. On the origins, principles, and purpose of this customs authority, cf. Little, "Introduction," 3–34; Brunero, *Cornerstone*, 10–21; and van de Ven, *Breaking*, 22–102 passim.

19. Cf., e.g., the account of illicit tea and gold trade in the Kiakhta region during the 1860s, Stakheev, *Kitaia*, 35–68.

20. *Vysochaishe uchrezhdennaia*, 5:5–18 passim.

21. *Aziatskaia Rossiia*, 123–130, 132–143; *Vysochaishe uchrezhdennaia*, 5:19–52 passim; *Entsiklopediia Zabaikal'ia*, 1:152–156, 167–171, 182–187, 204–208.

22. In particular in Eastern Transbaikalia (Nerchinsk region) the vast majority were tribute paying indigenous (22,627) and peasants (15,251). Of the 1,890 Russians, 2,353 Khori Buriats, and about 500 Tungus Cossacks, only about half lived along the border. Vasil'ev, *Kazaki*, vol. 2, appendix, 2; *Entsiklopediia Zabaikal'ia*, 1:212–214.

23. *Vysochaishe uchrezhdennaia*, 6:28–56 passim, esp. tables on 49 and on 54–55; Epov, *Voisko*, table on 22.

24. *Entsiklopediia Zabaikal'ia*, 1:166–171.

25. The same decree initiated far-reaching agrarian reforms. Cf. Ascher, *Stolypin*, 155–164; Pallot, *Reform*, passim.

26. *Obzor Zabaikal'skoi oblasti za 1910 god*, 80–81. For a general overview and comparison with other regions, *Aziatskaia Rossiia*, 466–492 passim (esp. the map on 490).

27. Kruberom, *Rossiia*, 463–469, offers a brief, popular narrative of the Aga Steppe and its inhabitants around 1900.

28. Golovachev and Soldatov, *Trudy*, 10–11.

29. Ibid., 69–70; Peterson, *Vozmozhnost'*, 1–13.

30. Vasil'ev, *Kazaki*, vol. 2, appendix, 2 (for 1784); *Aziatskaia Rossiia*, table on 82–85 (for 1897).

31. GAChO/19/1/91/205–2070b.

32. Lattimore, *Mongols*, 156 (for 1808); Meshcherskii, *Barga*, 15 (for 1912).

33. The districts of Aksha and Nerchinskii Zavod, both bordering Hulunbeir, combined had roughly the size of the Chinese border region. According to the 1897 census, 107,968 people lived in both Russian districts combined. *Vysochaishe uchrezhdennaia*, 6:30.

34. Strel'bitskii, "Otchet," 222. Cf. Pozdneev, *Opisanie*, 235–249, on the early colonization of Manchuria with Han Chinese in the nineteenth century.

35. Cf. Lee, *Frontier*, 24–40. Banners (*khoshun* or *hoshuu*, Chinese *qi*) were medium-sized administrative units, usually ruled by hereditary princes, and subdivided into a number of smaller districts called (*sum* or *somon*, Chinese *zuoling*). Banners formed part of leagues (*aimagh* or *aimak*, Chinese *meng*). Cf. Shao, *Homeland*, 25–67 passim, for a general introduction to the Manchu banner system.

36. Meshcherskii, *Barga*, 15 (for the 1912 census); Pozdneev, *Opisanie*, 223–227, 232–233; Kormazov, *Barga*, 45–47; Lattimore, *Mongols*, 155–169 passim; Janhunen, *Manchuria*, 55–56, 68–72; Atwood, "Service," 6–7.

37. The Buriats had eight banners, Solon and Chipchin four banners each, and the Ölöt one. The Oroqen were not included in the banner structure. "Hulunbei'er gaiyao," 82–85 (original pagination); Borzhimskii, *Opisanie*, 14–25. With the emigration of Khori Buriats from Transbaikalia to Hulunbeir during the Russian Civil War, the number of banners increased to 18. Yet the Buriat refugees remained legally and socially separate from their Barga hosts. On the administrative division during the 1920s, see Kormazov, *Barga*, 59–66 passim.

38. The Russians divided this border into three sections; the Tsurukhaitui section in the east—including the area under study here—measuring roughly two thousand kilometers, was the longest and most difficult to monitor.

39. Foust, *Muscovite*, 97; Dabringhaus, "Grenzzone," 579–580; Kim, "Constituencies," 150.

40. Kim, "Constituencies," esp. 143–149, 190–191. Cf. also Zhang, *Hulunbei'er zhilüe*, 71, 107; Xu, *Dongsansheng zhenglüe*, 352–353; Wan, *Heilongjiang zhigao*, 1149–1151, 1458–1474 passim.

41. Manakin, "Opisanie," 4.

42. Similar to the Chinese borderland, the actual presence of Cossack troops was very low. There were just 891 Cossack soldiers in the entire Transbaikal area in 1725. Vasil'ev, *Kazaki*, 1:227 and 2:1–8. For a general introduction to the history of Cossacks in the Russian Empire, see O'Rourke, *Cossacks*.

43. The word *karaul* comes from the Buriat word *kharuul*, which means "sentry" or "guard post."

44. Known as *karun* in Manchu.

45. Foust, *Muscovite*, 82–83; Vasil'ev, *Kazaki*, 2:20–24.

46. Vasil'ev, *Kazaki*, 2:170–171, appendix, 3.

47. The number of Cossacks—roughly 2,400 Buriats, 500 Tungus, and 900 Russians—serving along the border remained stable until the mid-nineteenth century. Vasil'ev, *Kazaki*, 2:56–68, 106–111, 138–163, 255 passim.

48. Vasil'ev, *Kazaki*, vol. 2, appendix, 9, 14. A list of the sentry posts can be found in Kashin, "Neskol'ko slov," 102–103.

49. Vasil'ev, *Kazaki*, 2:255–257. A brief description of the reform of Graf Mikhail M. Speranskii can be found in Naumov, *History*, 95–98. The reform's impact on the indigenous people of Transbaikalia is discussed in chapter 3.

50. Though the tribute commission and other state bodies recognized the policies' negative impact on the indigenous population in the region, no reforms were carried out. Vasil'ev, *Kazaki*, 2:255–267, appendix, 10–15.

51. Paine, *Rivals*, 28–106 passim; Miasnikov and Stepanov, *Granitsy*, 95–118; Bassin, *Visions*.

52. Vasil'ev, *Kazaki*, 3:34–35; *Entsiklopediia Zabaikal'ia*, 1:159–160. Cf. Matsuzato, "Creation," for the establishment of the Priamur Governor Generalship.

53. *Aziatskaia Rossiia*, 370–376; Epov, *Voisko*, 9–19; Vasil'ev, *Kazaki*, 3:169–175.

54. RGVIA/404/2/444/109–122, quotation on 1210b.–122.

55. Beliaeva, *Porto-franko*, 9–37; Quested, "Matey," 74–77.

56. Krapotkin, "Poezdki," 2–7, quotation on 6. Nikolai A. Khilkovskii describes a similar experience of crossing at Starotsurukhaitui by a trade caravan in August 1862. Khilkovskii, "Zapiska," 149–150.

57. Manakin, "Opisanie," 5.

58. E.g., Butin, *Ocherk*, 40–45. Nevertheless, even by the late 1880s, approval for passage through Chinese territory was preceded by lengthy correspondences between the Chinese and Russian bureaucracies. Cf., e.g., RGIA DV/704/1/695/2–5.

59. Versta is a Russian measure of length; 1 versta is about 1.067 kilometers.

60. RGIA DV/702/1/356/18–19; *Tamozhennaia politika*, 13–17; Beliaeva, *Porto-franko*, 89–98; Pozdneev, *Opisanie*, 550–552.

61. Cf. Kormazov, *Barga*, 95–103; Tret'iak, "Dnevnik," 33–43; Strel'bitskii, "Otchet," 224–227, for very vivid and detailed descriptions of the monastery and fair.

62. "Po reke Arguni," *Kharbinskii Vestnik*, 14 October 1903 (27 October 1903), 2.

63. Manakin, "Opisanie," 4–5.

64. Pozdneev, *Opisanie*, 371–372; Strel'bitskii, "Otchet," 227–230.

65. Strel'bitskii, "Otchet," 211–216, quotation on 214–215. Dombrovskii and Voroshilov, *Man'chzhuriia*, 26, speak of up to two thousand residents, predominantly Han Chinese.

66. Khilkovskii, "Zapiska," 151–152, quotation on 151; cf. also Pozdneev, *Opisanie*, 303–304.

67. Vasil'ev, *Kazaki*, 2:146 (for 1759); *Materialy*, 7 (for 1883); *Otchet zabaikal'skogo kazach'ego voiska za 1912*, 132–133 (for 1912). In 1912, only eighteen residents were not classified as Cossacks.

68. Kriukov, *Zabaikal'e*, 142–143.

69. "Po reke Arguni," *Kharbinskii Vestnik*, 11 October 1903 (24 October 1903), 2.

70. Cf. Lindgren, "Example," for ethnographic evidence that there was long-lasting economic cooperation and a more general peaceful coexistence between Tungusic tribes and Cossack settlers on the Argun.

71. Quasi-indigenousness is attained when former migrant communities become biologically and culturally connected with indigenous inhabitants of a region. Peshkov, "Politicisation," 166. On the ambiguities of Russian colonization, Sunderland, "Empire."

72. Orlov, "Vdol granitsy," 11.

73. Aleksandrov, "Argun'," 293.

Chapter 2: Railroads, Germs, and Gold

1. Schivelbusch, *Journey*, 45. Cf. also Maier, *Borders*, 188–200 passim.

2. Cf. Marks, *Road*, on the construction of the Trans-Siberian Railroad.

3. Ablova, *KVZhD*, 48–53 and Paine, *Rivals*, 178–194 discuss diplomatic matters as well as the construction of this railroad.

4. Chinese and Russians disputed whether the line, officially a Sino-Russian joint venture, should serve as a commercial enterprise or an instrument of Russian colonization. Cf., e.g., Urbansky, *Wettstreit*, 37–43.

5. Paine, *Rivals*, 209–225; Paine, "Railway," esp. 21–24; Quested, *"Matey,"* 155–159; Urbansky, *Wettstreit*, 48–53.

6. Geyer, *Imperialismus*, 144–159 passim.

7. Despite the self-perception of some members of the tsarist elite, the main goal behind Russia's penetration remained strategic. Paine, *Rivals*, 194–197; Paine, "Railway," 26–29.

8. See the two-volume project by Steinberg, Wolff, et al., *War* and Paine, *Rivals*, 240–247, for the course of war and its consequences in Manchuria.

9. Quested, *"Matey,"* 197–208.

10. RGVIA/404/2/388/52–580b., here 52–520b. Wolff, *Harbin*, 21–25, on surveys of the Chinese Eastern Railroad route in general.

11. Ministerstvo putei soobshcheniia, Upravlenie po sooruzheniiu zheleznykh dorog, *Otchet*, 5–6. On the railroad construction works, see Wolff, *Harbin*, 30–34; Urbansky, *Wettstreit*, 40–48.

12. Soldatov, *Poselki*, 86.

13. RGIA/323/1/1214/65–660b., quotation on 66.

14. RGIA DV/702/1/312/2–4.

15. Orlov, *Zabaikal'tsy*, 3–35; Vasil'ev, *Kazaki*, 3:274–279, 334–337; Aleksandrov, "Argun'," 283–284; Golitsyn, *Ocherk*, 114–125.

16. GAChO/1/2 st./97/1–20b.

17. *Putevoditel'*, 265–266.

18. Regularly mentioning Manzhouli, e.g., Goebel, *Sibirien*, 136–138 and Taft, *Siberia*, 87–89.

19. Soldatov, *Poselki*, 296–309. Cf. also "S Arguni," *Zabaikal'skaia Nov'*, 26 August 1909 (8 September 1909), 3 and "Budushee st. Dauriia," *Zabaikal'skaia Nov'*, 14 August 1913 (27 August 1913), 3.

20. Even into the early 1930s, there were no paved roads in Hulunbeir at all. Tesler, "Dorogi," 63–66.

21. GAChO/1/1 st./165/1–5, 30–310b., 36–380b., quotation on 37. Later attempts failed due to lack of resources, lack of interest, and other obstacles. RGIA DV/702/2/967/1–10b., 47–550b., 85–860b.

22. Liubimov, "Transport," 15–16; "S beregov Arguni," *Zabaikal'skaia Nov'*, 1 February 1908 (14 February 1908), 4.

23. "Tsagan-Oluevskaia stanitsa," *Zabaikal'skie Oblastnye Vedomosti*, 19 March 1898, 3; "Izyskaniia i izbrannoe napravlenie vetvi Zabaikal'skoi zhelez. dorogi k kitaiksoi granitse," *Zabaikal'skie Oblastnye Vedomosti*, 19 November 1898 (1 December 1898), 3; Romanov, *Man'chzhuriia*, 68 and map "Karta Man'chzhurii."

24. "St. Man'chzhuriia (Kak voznik i ros poselok)," *Zabaikal'skaia Nov'*, 25 March 1908 (7 April 1908), 3; "Izyskaniia i izbrannoe napravlenie vetvi Zabaikal'skoi zhelez. dorogi k kitaiksoi granitse," *Zabaikal'skie Oblastnye Vedomosti*, 19 November 1898 (1 December 1898), 3.

25. "Ot Irkutska," 10; "Ot Chity do st. Man'chzhuriia," *Zabaikal'e*, 23 June 1902 (6 July 1902), 3; "St. Man'chzhuriia," *Zabaikal'e*, 31 October 1903 (13 November 1903), 2–3.

26. Hawes, *East*, 436–441, quotation on 437–438. For a similar account of Manzhouli as being overcrowded with passengers in late 1901, Vereshchagin, *Kitae*, 22–24.

27. Krasnov, *Azii*, quotations on 46, 48.

28. "St. Man'chzhuriia," *Zabaikal'e*, 16 July 1903 (29 July 1903), 3.

29. "St. Man'chzhuriia," *Zabaikal'e*, 31 October 1903 (13 November 1903), 2–3.

30. "Iz Man'chzhurii," *Zabaikal'e*, 10 January 1903 (23 January 1903), 2; "St. Man'chzhuriia," *Zabaikal'e*, 7 March 1903 (20 March 1903), 3; "St. Man'chzhuriia," *Kharbinskii Vestnik*, 9 October 1903 (22 October 1903), 2; "Zabaikal'ia. St. Man'chzhuriia," *Zabaikal'e*, 27 April 1905 (10 May 1905), 2.

31. Kavakami, "Promyshlennost'," 91. For a topographical description of the alienated zone's borders: "Dongsansheng guofang shiyi diaocha baogao," 183–189 passim (map on 185). On the Chinese Eastern Railroad alienated corridor in general, Wolff, *Harbin*, 28.

32. Soldatov, *Poselki*, 309–312, quotations on 310–311.

33. "Man'chzhurskie mysli," *Zabaikal'skaia Nov'*, 3 June 1914 (16 June 1914), 2.

34. According to Minzheng bu jingwu si, *Hukou*, 1, as late as 1936 the male to female sex ratio was still 1.6:1.

35. Soldatov, *Poselki*, 311–312. In 1909, 2,001 people lived at Lubin, among whom 1,945 were of Han ethnicity. "Heilongjiang zhilüe," table on 161–162.

36. "St. Man'chzhuriia," *Zabaikal'skaia Nov'*, 2 March 1908 (15 March 1908), 3.

37. "St. Man'chzhuriia," *Zabaikal'skaia Nov'*, 26 January 1908 (8 February 1908), 3.

38. RGIA/323/1/1026/278–280ob., here 278ob.–279ob.; "O novom karavan-sarae na st. Man'chzhuriia," *Novaia Zhizn'*, 6 October 1911 (19 October 1911), 2.

39. "St. Man'chzhuriia," *Zabaikal'skaia Nov'*, 10 January 1914 (23 January 1914), 3.

40. "St. Man'chzhuriia," *Novaia Zhizn'*, 16 January 1914 (29 January 1914), 5.

41. The turmoil of the Mongolian independence movement and unfavorable customs regulations coupled with competitively priced imports from Japan affected these plans. The market, which was first held in 1912, was soon excluded by more favorable trade routes. "Poselok Man'chzhuriia," *Dumy Zabaikal'ia*, 17 March 1911 (30 March 1911), 3; "Russkaia tamozhnia," *Zabaikal'skaia nov'*, 31 March 1913 (13 April 1913); "Pos. Man'chzhuriia," *Kharbinskii Vestnik*, 5 May 1915 (18 May 1915), 2.

42. RGIA/323/1/1028/14–150b.; RGIA/323/1/1031/165–166; "Novyi Bank," *Zabaikal'skaia Nov'*, 9 July 1914 (22 July 1914), 3; *Doklad*, 17–39; *Nachal'noe obrazovanie*, 188–190; "St. Man'chzhuriia," *Zabaikal'skaia Nov'*, 24 June 1914 (7 July 1914), 2.

43. RGIA/323/1/1030/134–134ob.

44. Ibid., 38–43 (here 39ob.), 57–60ob. (here 59–59ob.); "Poselkovaia zhizn'," *Man'chzhurskaia Gazeta*, 16 September 1911 (29 September 1911), 1.

45. With the exception of the northern territories of the Maritime region. Beliaeva, *Porto-franko*, 53–57, 64–68.

46. GARF/543/1/182/1–42, quotations on 38ob.–39 and 41ob.

47. GAIO/29/1(2)/348/137–138.

48. RGIA/323/1/1264/10; RGIA DV/702/1/348/19, 31; RGIA DV/702/1/411/30.

49. Taft, *Siberia*, 87–89.

50. The number of employees of Manzhouli's customs house rose from just 11 in 1902 to 159 in 1914 and declined after 1917 to 105 in 1919 and just 26 in 1923. Cf. GAChO/107/1/2/44–45, 248–248ob.; GAChO/R-404/1/110/427; GAChO/R-404/1/160/7–70b. The head of Manzhouli customs complained regularly about a severe shortage of employees. Cf., e.g., GAChO/107/1/125/58–61ob.

51. RGIA/323/1/1264/64–65.

52. The exception to this rule was alcohol. Beliaeva, *Porto-franko*, 116–139 passim.

53. Beliaeva, *Porto-franko*, 139–153; RGIA DV, *Tamozhnia*, 82–85.

54. RGIA DV, *Tamozhnia*, 73–80, 85–87.

55. Departament Tamozhennykh Sborov, *Obzor*, table III, 16; for a detailed record of all exported and imported goods through Manzhouli customs in 1914, ibid., table XVII, 753–756.

56. Prior to 1913, only commodities bound for destinations beyond this border zone had to be registered at sentry posts. Cf. Shteinfel'd, "Kupechestvo," 1–9, on the consequences for the borderland economy.

57. GAChO/107/1/43/140–141ob.

58. Even the plan to deploy the Dauriia unit closer to the border at Abagaitui or Matsieevskaia was abandoned, as appropriate infrastructure did not exist. GAChO/78/1/29/20–26, quotation on 22. Cf. also RGIA DV, *Tamozhnia*, 92–94, 130–134.

59. Land for the customs houses had already been allocated in 1902. RGIA/323/1/1264/25–26.

60. RGIA/560/28/126/183–186.

61. Foreigners were hired to prevent corruption of Chinese customs officials, thereby safeguarding not only the imperialists' trade but also the revenue to the Chinese state. Ladds, *Careers*, in particular 52–58, on the politics of nationality in the Chinese Maritime Customs Service. Cf. also van de Ven, *Breaking*. Yet the Russian side further torpedoed the commencement of duty collections. RGIA/323/1/456/104–105, 122–122ob., 171–173.

62. RGIA/323/1/457/13, 45; NARA/RG 84/U.S. Consulate, Harbin, China/vol. 5/241–252, here 241–242; *Vremennyia Pravila*, 1–20; Kantselariia Pravlenii Obshchestva Kitaiskoi Vostochnoi zheleznoi dorogi, *Sbornik*, 68–72. Cf. Goebel, *Volkswirtschaft*, 193–194, for a comprehensive summary of the complex system of custom tariffs on the Russo-Chinese border after 1908.

63. The Manzhouli customs station was initially under the supervision of the commissioner of customs stationed in Harbin—the Russian national N. A. Konovalov. Soon, however, Russian influence in the Chinese customs authority declined. NARA/RG 84/U.S. Consulate, Harbin, China/vol. 3/173–175, here 175. In 1914, throughout China less than 5 percent of the Chinese Maritime Customs' management ("indoor staff") were Russian nationals. In the Harbin, Manzhouli, Suifenhe, and Heihe customs offices only five employees, lower-ranking customs assistants at that, were Russians. RGIA/323/1/458/166–167ob. Cf. also Ladds, *Careers*, 54 (table 3.1).

64. Chinese customs agents just collected charges but did not inspect passengers and freight. "Kitaiskie tamozhni," *Zabaikal'skaia Nov'*, 31 January 1908 (13 February 1908), 3.

65. GAChO/107/1/37/35–350b., 43–430b., 47–470b., quotations on 350b.

66. In 1908, just twenty employees worked for the Chinese Maritime Customs at Manzhouli. *Manzhouli haiguan zhi*, 5–6.

67. GARF/818/1/187/3–44, quotation on 280b.

68. Distilled spirits that contain at least 40 percent alcohol.

69. Only during the Russian Revolution did opium trafficking became a serious problem in Manzhouli, as armed gangs got involved in the business, sometimes attacking the poorly protected officers of the Chinese Maritime Customs. RGIA/323/1/459/2–20b. Yet even during the turmoil of civil war, relative to gold or liquor the scale of opium smuggling was low.

70. Methodologically, the most inspiring study on the nature, practice, and extent of various forms of contrabandism in the Asian context is Tagliacozzo, *Trades*, esp. 5–9.

71. Appadurai, "Introduction."

72. "Po oblasti. St. Man'chzhuriia," *Zabaikal'skaia Nov'*, 5 March 1908 (18 March 1908), 3.

73. A vedro ("bucket") is an old Russian measure of liquid volume. One vedro equals 12.3 liters.

74. RGIA/560/45/59/60–810b., here 72–73 obl; RGIA/323/1/1027/16 obl, 46–48.

75. "St. Man'chzhuriia," *Novaia Zhizn'*, 8 February 1910 (21 February 1910), 3.

76. In 1916, Manzhouli still accounted for almost 30 percent of the total annual production of liquors in the alienated railroad corridor (111,000 vedro). This was a decline of only 13 percent in five years. Chinese distilleries outside the alienated railroad territory were not included in the statistics. RGIA/560/45/59/60–810b., esp. 700b.–71.

77. RGIA DV/R-2422/1/838/8–20, here 15; GAChO/78/1/22/3–4; GAChO/78/2/37/60–600b.; GAChO/107/1/125/386–3880b.; GAChO/R-404/1/134/164–1640b., 172–1720b.; "Kontrabandisty," *Rupor*, 28 June 1922, 3.

78. GAChO/78/1/15/37–420b., esp. 40–410b.; Shteinfel'd, "Kupechestvo," 11–12; "E'erguna he yan'an shangye tan," *Yuandong Bao*, 30 August 1910, no pagination.

79. "Trade and Smuggling in Manchuria," *Economist*, 9 October 1909, 691–692, quotation on 692.

80. GAIO/25/11/16/104–105, quotations on 104–1040b.

81. "S beregov Arguni," *Zabaikal'skaia Nov'*, 1 March 1911 (14 March 1911), 2. On the consequences for public discipline and public health, Urbansky, "Kosake," 320–322.

82. "Kontrabanda na Arguni," *Zabaikal'skaia Nov'*, 25 March 1908 (7 April 1908), 3 (quotation); "Eshche o kitaitsakh v pogranoichnoi polose," *Kharbinskii Vestnik*, 20 November 1910 (3 December 1910), 2.

83. RGIA/323/1/2937/1–90b., quotation on 20b.

84. For the full text of the agreement on the prohibition of alcohol trade in the 50 versta zone: GAAO/I-53/1/12/15–16. On the prohibition of alcohol in Russia at the start of the war, see Herlihy, *Empire*, 64–67; Quested, "Matey," 291–292.

85. Cf. table 2.2 and GAChO/78/1/22/3–4, 69–710b.; GAChO/107/1/125/386–3880b.

86. GAChO/78/1/12/59–60, quotation on 60; Shirokogorov, *Man'chzhuriia*, 5–6. In 1913, pressured by Saint Petersburg, Mongol rulers forbade the sale of liquor on the right bank of Argun. In 1914 they allowed the Russian border authorities to monitor the liquor ban and, jointly with Mongolian officials to confiscate the spoils. Urbansky, "Kosake," 316–319; Quested, "Matey," 292–293. Cf. also Sorokina, "Soglashenie," 242–251.

87. In the 1880s, the "Zheltuga Republic" in the northernmost part of Heilongjiang attracted several hundred Russians. On its history and mythological afterlife: Gamsa, "California," 236–266; Torgashev, "Zoloto," 47–48; Zatsepine, *Amur*, 62–67.

88. Torgashev, "Zoloto," 47–52; Kormazov, "Zolotopromyshlennost'," 41–44; *Obzor Zabaikal'skoi oblasti za 1910 god*, 63–70; Kommisiia, *Perechen'*, 140–148.

89. Compared to 4,686 workers in 1897 and 7,710 in 1901. *Obzor Zabaikal'skoi oblasti za 1910 god*, 69–70. In 1917, 79 percent of the Transbaikal gold mine toilers came from China. Lezhnin, *Vostok*, 29. For economic reasons, Russian mine owners had a strong interest in Chinese migrant diggers. Siegelbaum, "'Peril,'" 324–327.

90. E.g., Garin, *Koree*, esp. 25–29; "K voprosu o zheltom trude v Zabaikal'e," *Zabaikal'skoe Obozrenie*, 25 January 1916, 3 and 8 February 1916, 2–3.

91. Kormazov, "Zolotopromyshlennost'," 46; GAChO/334/1/68/19–210b., 84, 85–850b.; Popenko, *Opyt*, 114.

92. GAChO/107/1/125/365.

93. Funt and zolotnik are old Russian units of measurement. One funt equals 409.5 grams, and one zolotnik is 4.26 grams.

94. GAChO/13/2/55/2–20b., 31–37. Train passengers caught smuggling gold from Russia to China hid their contraband in more or less creative ways. See, e.g., GAChO/78/2/75/7, 14, 20–200b., 22, 25, 28, 30, 38, 49–490b., 89–890b.; GAChO/78/3/77/2, 12–13, 15, 18–19, 21–22, 24–25, 137, 139, 173, 180–1800b., 185–186, 196, 222, 235, 241.

95. GAChO/13/2/56/142–142 ob., 144; RGIA DV, *Tamozhnia*, 105–108.

96. Cossacks from Abagaitui, for instance, chopped wood on the Chinese Argun bank. RGIA DV/704/1/558/1–3, 7–80b. On climate and soil, flora and fauna, and the Russian rural economy of this region, see, e.g., Zhernakov, *Trekhrech'e*, 6–15.

97. Raiskii, "Snosheniia," 586–591; Baranov, *Barga*, 50–51; Giller, *Opisanie*, 7.

98. On Russian colonization plans for Manchuria in general, see Wolff, *Harbin*, 79–90, 109–114.

99. Raiskii, "Snosheniia," 591–592.

100. Ibid., 593–594; GARF/543/1/185/1–24, esp. 150b.–20.

101. RGIA/560/28/164/102–107, esp. 1020b.

102. RGIA/560/28/867/89–147, quotations on 1200b. and 1220b.

103. RGIA/560/28/1083/2–20b./6–7 and 21–240b. Correspondence between the governor of Heilongjiang province and the Transbaikal military governor suggests that Chinese provincial authorities were not amused by this practice. Cf. GAIO/25/11/16/92–93.

104. RGIA/560/28/1083/240b.–26; GAIO/25/11/16/90–91.

105. RGIA/560/28/1083/26–29. On the Russian inns along the Starotsurukhaitui-Hailar road, Kondratev, *Kitai*, 37–38.

106. Davidov, *Kolonizatsiia*, 72–76. As early as the summer of 1908, Russian diplomats in Hailar and the Hulunbeir fudutong had agreed on rules for land use on the Chinese Argun bank by Russian subjects. The wording of the agreements of 1908 and 1910 was almost identical. GAIO/25/11/16/115–124; Song, "Hulunbei'er," 79–92; Xu, *Dongsansheng zhenglüe*, 372–375.

107. GAChO/13/2/29/128–1280b., 137.

108. Cf. Tesler, "Gan'chzhurskaia iarmarka 1933 goda," 82–83; Smol'nikov, *Iarmarka*, 3–4; Kitaiskaia Vostochnaia zheleznaia doroga, *Man'chzhuriia*, 287–289.

109. Smol'nikov, *Iarmarka*, 4–19 passim.

110. Kormazov, *Barga*, 103–105, quotation on 105. Cf. also Tesler, "Gan'chzhurskaia iarmarka 1933 goda," 82–88 passim.

111. Lan, "Movement," 39–59 passim. Cf. Sanjdorj, *Manchu*, 40–82, for an excellent analysis of the spread of Chinese trade in Outer Mongolia and its consequences for the Mongols.

112. Shan, *Wilderness*, 47–68 passim, for the transition of land from state to private ownership in North Manchuria (including Hulunbeir). On developments in Inner Mongolia, see Lan, "Movement," 53–73 passim.

113. Also referred to as "New Administration," this set of radical initiatives was nothing less than an attempted revolution from above. Cf., e.g., Ichiko, "Reform," 375–415.

114. Dobrolovskii, *Provintsiia*, 137–139.

115. Baranov, *Barga*, 54; Men'shikov, *Otchet*, 10–11; Meshcherskii, *Barga*, 5.

116. Baranov, *Barga*, 50; Lan, "'New Administration,'" 45.

117. Baranov, *Barga*, 54–58.

118. Davidov, *Kolonizatsiia*, 119–123; "Kitaitsy i mongoly," *Kharbinskii Vestnik*, 2 April 1909 (15 April 1909); Lan, "Movement," 63–64. Land surveying was often carried out by Japanese topographers under the supervision of Chinese officers. GAChO/13/2/29/10–11.

119. GARF/R-6081/1/131/1–99, quotations on 51, 98. As a consequence of the Russian expansion, the new principle was applied to the entire land border of Russia after the Russo-Japanese War. Glavnoe upravlenie general'nogo shtaba, *Obzor*, 228–230.

120. Zhang, *Hulunbei'er zhilüe*, 71; Song, "Hulunbei'er," 67–70; Kotvich, *Obzor*, 29–31. Cf. also "Heilongjiang quan sheng sizhi ditu quanji," 233–242 with a detailed description of the *kalun* locations.

121. Baranov, *Barga*, 51–53; Davidov, *Kolonizatsiia*, 69–72; Zhang, *Hulunbei'er zhilüe*, 72. RGIA/323/2/43/93–930b.

122. A translation of this reform project appeared in Men'shikov, *Otchet*, 204–210. For descriptions of Chinese and Russian border villages, cf. Glavnoe upravlenie general'nogo shtaba, *Obzor*, 232–233 and Song, "Hulunbei'er," 101–102.

123. Men'shikov, *Otchet*, 210–212. After the separation of Hulunbeir in 1912 the number of border posts along the border with Russia was reduced to twelve, each manned with five to six Mongols. Cf. Baranov, *Barga*, 35.

124. Lan, "Movement," 166; Baranov, *Barga*, 53–54; Davidov, *Kolonizatsiia*, 122.

125. GARF/R-6081/1/131/1–99, quotation on 99.

126. Quested, *"Matey,"* 200–201.

127. Previous scholarship on the 1911 border Treaty of Qiqihar has concentrated primarily on the outcome of those negotiations, but not the actual border inspections in situ, the negotiation process itself, and the surrounding public discussions. Cf., for instance, Zhao, *Qingji*, 166–192 passim; Lü, *Zhongguo*, 192–212 passim; and Wu, "'Manzhouli,'" 1–17 passim. For a compact collection of published Chinese sources on the negotiations and the treaty, Meng, *Zhong*, 687–711.

128. "Neskol'ko slov o nashei estestvennoi granitse s Kitaem (r. Arguni)," *Zabaikal'skaia Nov'*, 23 April 1909 (6 May 1909), 3.

129. *Novoe Vremia*, 21 February 1910 (6 March 1910), quoted from a translation in NARA/RG 84/U.S. Consulate, Harbin, China/vol. 12/37–39, quotation on 38.

130. GAChO/107/1/70/7–90b., quotation on 9.

131. The Chinese proposed talks to the Russians because they had discovered old beacons marking the land boundary in their favor. The Russians later countered that the two-hundred-year-old frontier markers were ordinary piles of stones erected by Buddhist lamas for religious purposes. Quested, *"Matey,"* 201–203.

132. RGIA/1276/10/853/3–5, here 3.

133. "Pogranichnye stolknoveniia," *Zabaikal'skaia Nov'*, 11 July 1909 (24 July 1909), 3; "S beregov Borzi i Arguni. K kharakteristike pogranichnykh otnoshenii," *Zabaikal'skaia Nov'*, 5 January 1911 (18 January 1911), 3; "Kitaiskie topografy," *Zabaikal'skaia Nov'*, 23 March 1911 (5 April 1911), 2–3; Quested, *"Matey,"* 205–206, for rumors of an impending war.

134. "Pogranichnaia komissiia," *Zabaikal'skaia Nov'*, 24 October 1910 (6 November 1910), 3 (quotation). Quite in contrast to such nationalistic reports in the Russian press, the coverage in *Yuandongbao* (Far Eastern Journal) was much milder in tone and evenhanded. This difference is explained by the fact that the first Chinese-language newspaper in Northern Manchuria was written by Chinese editors but financed by the Russian government. "Zhong E huajie qingxing," *Yuandong Bao*, 6 October 1910, no pagination; "Diaocha bianjie wenti," *Yuandong Bao*, 3 December 1910, 2.

135. "St. Man'chzhuriia," *Zabaikal'skaia Nov'*, 4 June 1911 (17 June 1911), 3.

136. RGIA/1276/7/444/3–4 obl and 7–80b., quotation on 70b.

137. The Chinese had discovered that the Russians were bluffing. They did not have any of the 1727 maps they insisted would support their position. In fact, no maps had been exchanged when the boundary was drawn in 1727. Quested, *"Matey,"* 203. For early Russian mapping of the Chinese frontier, see Tolmacheva, "Exploration," esp. 51–52.

138. RGIA/1276/7/444/13.

139. GAKhK/I-286/1/24/2–6, 10–130b., quotations on 4.

140. Ibid., 111–112, quotation on 1110b.; cf. also ibid., 35–350b., 37–38, 42–420b., 44–450b., 57–570b., 64–640b., 108–1090b.

141. "Pogranichnyi vopros," *Zabaikal'skaia Nov'*, 3 April 1913 (16 April 1913), 3.

142. GAKhK/I-286/1/24/75–760b., 193–1930b.; RGIA/1276/10/853/3–5.

143. "Pogranznak 1886 goda ostaetsia na meste," *Komsomolets Zabaikal'ia*, 18 September 1993, 1; Iwashita, *4,000 Kilometer*, 157–161.

144. Cf. Summers, *Plague*, for the most recent overview of the plague's origins and development and the Chinese, Japanese, and Russian responses to it. See also Lynteris, *Plague*, on the Russian interpretations of who was responsible for the infection. Hsu, "Railroad," 231–400 passim, examines the epidemic both in terms of Russian colonial policies and Chinese resistance to these Russian policies as part of a broader nation-building project. Somewhat in contrast, Marc Gamsa follows Rosemary Quested's early interpretations stressing the close cooperation between the Chinese and Russian administrations that succeeded in containing the epidemic. Cf. Gamsa, "Epidemic," 147–183.

145. E.g., Echenberg, *Plague Ports*; Osterhammel, *Verwandlung*, 279–283.

146. RGIA/323/1/1212/80–81.

147. Ibid., 148–157 passim (quotation on 153–1530b.), 302–304.

148. During the next three years there were no cases of plague at Manzhouli or in the railroad territory, but cases were reported in Transbaikalia and Mongolia in 1907 and 1908. Cf. *Report*,

218–220; "Tarabagan'ia bolezn'," *Kharbinskii Vestnik*, 19 October 1910 (1 November 1910), 2–3; Khmara-Borshevskii, *V stepiakh*, 4–5.

149. *Report*, 35–36. Cf. also Hsu, "Railroad," 364–392 passim, on the range of opinion about the origin of the epidemic.

150. Soldatov, *Poselki*, 42–43, 311–312 and "Tarabagan'ia bolezn'," *Kharbinskii Vestnik*, 19 October 1910 (1 November 1910), 2–3.

151. RGIA/1298/1/2290/9–18, here 90b.

152. *Report*, 20–21; Soldatov, *Poselki*, 42, 311–312.

153. *Report*, 28. Cf. also RGIA/1298/1/2290/9–18, here 10.

154. "Chuma," *Novaia Zhizn'*, 19 October 1910 (1 November 1910), no pagination.

155. In 1908, about 4,822 Chinese settled in Transbaikal province, mainly working in the gold mines. RGIA/560/28/1083/59. Most Chinese coolies sought work in the Amur and Maritime territories. Compared to other migrant routes, train travel via Manzhouli to Transbaikalia was the most expensive and least popular route. GARF/102/dp. "osobyi otdel"/1908 g./457/9–12, here 100b.

156. Cf. Lynteris, *Plague*, 89–141 passim. The interrelation between epidemics and ethnic or class discrimination during times of plague was of course not a unique phenomenon limited to Russian spectators and authorities. For instance, in the United States, a high concentration of Chinese was also often suspected to be the hotbed of the disease. Cf. McClain, *Search*, 234–276.

157. "Chuma," *Novaia Zhizn'*, 19 October 1910 (1 November 1910), no pagination.

158. NARA/RG 84/U.S. Consulate, Harbin, China/vol. 6/56–60; "K bor'be s chumoi," *Novaia Zhizn'*, 28 October 1910 (10 November 1910), no pagination. Chinese epidemiologists also saw Chinese migrant laborers as a carrier of the disease. Lynteris, "Natives."

159. *Report*, 218–219.

160. RGIA/1298/1/2290/9–18, here 110b.–12 and 15–150b., quotation on 150b. Cf. also NARA/RG 84/U.S. Consulate, Harbin, China/vol. 5/657–660, here 658–659.

161. The expulsion of seasonal Chinese residents from the railroad zone soon became common practice during the epidemic. Hsu, "Railroad," 348–350.

162. Wu, *Plague*, 15; NARA/RG 84/U.S. Consulate, Harbin, China/vol. 5/717–722, here 717. Elsewhere the death toll was much higher. By the end of March 1911, in other parts of Manchuria and northern China between 42,000 and 60,000 people had died. Fisher, "Plague," 98.

163. RGIA/1298/1/2290/9–18, quotation on 17–170b.

164. Ibid., 204–2130b., here 204–207.

165. Wu, *Plague*, 1–5; Nathan, *Plague*, 42–62. The senior physician in charge of the hospital and quarantine appointed by the Chinese government was the American-born Chinese and Berkeley graduate Dr. M. Jee. NARA/RG 84/U.S. Consulate, Harbin, China/vol. 6/394–398.

166. NARA/RG 84/U.S. Consulate, Harbin, China/vol. 7/no. 27; "Zasedanie glavnoi sanitarnoi-ispolnitel'noi kommisii," *Kharbinskii Vestnik*, 11 October 1911 (24 October 1910), no pagination. For the 1920–1921 pneumonic plague with a particular high death toll in Manzhouli, cf. Wu, *Plague*, 51–78 passim; *Doklad*, 39–42.

167. NARA/RG 84/U.S. Consulate, Harbin, China/vol. 7/no. 30.

Chapter 3: Revolutions without Borders

1. Chang, *Rise*, 177–180, quotation on 178–179.

2. Suleski, *Government*, 5–10, 20–32.

3. Cf. Naumov, *History*, 155–185 and Stephan, *East*, 117–155. On peculiarities of developments in Transbaikalia, see Snow, "Revolution," 201–215.

4. Cf. Rupen, "Intelligentsia," 383–398. In spite of the rise of nationalism, a political identification with Russia prevailed not least because the empire's protection of their culture from the Chinese was seen as beneficial to the Buriat community. Cf. Skrynnikova, "Identichnosti," 395–420 passim.

5. In 1897, over 99 percent of the Aga Steppe Buriats were Buddhist. Golovachev and Soldatov, *Trudy*, 54; see also *Vysochaishe uchrezhdennaia*, vol. 6, table on 44–45. For Buddhism in Buriatia *Aziatskaia Rossiia*, 133–137.

6. GAChO/1/2p.o./267/5–70b. and 97–980b., quotation on 5. Cf. Bernstein, "Pilgrims," on the history of Buriats' engagement with greater Eurasia.

7. Golovachev and Soldatov, *Trudy*, 55–61.

8. *Vysochaishe uchrezhdennaia*, 6:107–116, on the Statute of 1822 and the reasons why it had been considered to be obsolete by the state. Cf. also Remnev, *Sibir'*, 95–105, 230–243 passim.

9. GAChO/1/1p.o./1198/12–160b. passim.

10. Peterson, *Vozmozhnost'*, 15–20, quotation on 19.

11. Golovachev and Soldatov, *Trudy*, 35; Peterson, *Vozmozhnost'*, viii–ix; GAChO/1/1p.o./1198/12–160b.

12. Golovachev and Soldatov, *Trudy*, 96–115.

13. GAChO/13/2/54/1–4, 8–9, 26–350b.

14. For an introduction to the Mongolian independence movement, Lan, "Movement."

15. For Chinese scholarship on the indigenous independence movement in Hulunbeir during the early twentieth century, see, e.g., Cui, *Haila'er*, esp. 1:74–104.

16. Lan, "Movement," 74–77.

17. Lan, "'New Administration,'" 49–50.

18. Different spellings occur in the sources: Tokhtogo, Toktokho, Tokhtokho, Toghtakhu.

19. For the opening of bannerland in Jirim league, see Baranov, *Khalkha*, 42–43; Lan, "Movement," 72–73.

20. GAChO/14/1/23/215–2170b.; cf. also RGVIA/1482/1/54/46–470b.; LOC/Lattimore/box 25/folder 13 "Inner Mongolia—History Notes" (undated)/7–8. Another version of the story about Tokhtogo was told to the Russian woman Kornakova who lived with her family in Mongolia near the Russian border. Her informants were Mongol visitors. According to this account, the death toll was lower, with Tokhtogo and his comrades killing more than one hundred Chinese soldiers, shopkeepers, and officials. Kornakova, "Po povodu," here 25–27.

21. GAChO/14/1/23/2–30b., quotation on 20b.–3.

22. Ibid., 17–170b. and 59–60.

23. Ibid., 216. For a similar account, see "Uchenie Tokhtokho-Taizhi," *Zabaikal'skaia Nov'*, 12 June 1910 (25 June 1910), 3–4, here 3.

24. GAChO/14/1/23/160–1600b. and 205–2050b.; see also RGIA/1276/6/509/1–10b.

25. "V poiskakh Tokhtokho," *Zabaikal'skaia Nov'*, 3 June 1910 (16 June 1910), 3.

26. GAChO/14/1/23/189–1890b., quotation on 189.

27. "Uchenie Tokhtokho-Taizhi," *Zabaikal'skaia Nov'*, 12 June 1910 (25 June 1910), 3–4.

28. GAChO/14/1/23/246–2470b.; cf. also RGVIA/1482/1/54/47, 49–50 and RGVIA/1482/1/89/129–1320b.

29. Cf. Humphrey, "Detachable Groups," esp. 53–57.

30. GAChO/13/2/29/10–11. In August 1911, the Kiakhta border commissioner reported that Mongol princes summoned all men capable of bearing arms for mobilization. Cf. GAChO/13/2/29/114–1150b.

31. Nakami, "Diplomats," 70–73.

32. Great Britain and the Russian Empire concluded several agreements between 1895 and 1907 solidifying spheres of interest in Asia. The Anglo-Russian agreement of May 1899 greatly strengthened Russia's claim to a Mongolian and Manchurian stake. After Russia's defeat in the Russo-Japanese War, Saint Petersburg concluded similar diplomatic agreements with Tokyo between 1907 and 1916. In 1907 both sides signed a secret treaty splitting Mongolia and Manchuria into, respectively, a northern Russian and a southern Japanese sphere of interest. In 1912, Russia was granted all of Outer Mongolia and Hulunbeir. Cf. Paine, *Rivals*, 272–276. For the entire agreement text, Woodhead, *China Year Book*, 630–633.

33. On the relation between the Chinese Revolution of 1911 and Mongolian independence, see Lan, "Movement," 106–107; on anti-Manchuism and the 1911 revolution in Northeast China, Shao, *Homeland*, 68–88 passim.

34. Lan, "Movement," 78–95. Russia's role in the independence of Outer Mongolia is discussed in Paine, *Rivals*, 287–295.

35. Guo, *Hulunbei'er*, 18.

36. LOC/Lattimore/box 25/folder 13 "Inner Mongolia—History Notes" (undated)/8; Lan, "Movement," 234.

37. For answers to the question of why Inner Mongolian banners never proclaimed independence or attempts to become independent failed, Lan, "Movement," 152–164.

38. Baranov, *Barga*, 55–56; Men'shikov, "Ocherk," 37–38; Woodhead, *China Year Book*, 622; RGIA/323/1/769/62–620b.; Meshcherskii, *Barga*, 5–6.

39. RGIA/323/1/769/47–480b., quotation on 480b.

40. RGIA/323/1/769/55–550b., 58; "Mongoly v Khailare," *Dumy Zabaikal'ia*, 12 January 1912 (25 January 1912), 2.

41. Officially, only 150–200 cavalry soldiers were stationed at Lubin. Observers, however, estimated the number at about 500 men. NARA/RG 84/U.S. Consulate, Harbin, China/vol. 7/no. 66; RGIA/323/1/769/58–580b.

42. RGIA/323/1/769/620b.; cf. also "Mongoly u st. Man'chzhuriia i v Khailare," *Dumy Zabaikal'ia*, 29 January 1912 (11 February 1912), 2.

43. NARA/RG 84/U.S. Consulate, Harbin, China/vol. 7/no. 69.

44. Ibid., nos. 40, 47.

45. Tang, *Policy*, 83. The Russian Ministries of Finance and Foreign Affairs both denied to have backed the support of Mongol insurgents in Hulunbeir by the Transamur Border Guards. RGIA/1276/7/463/115–118.

46. Cf. Urbansky, "Mission," 77–79.

47. "Zhizn pos. Man'chzhuriia," *Dumy Zabaikal'ia*, 23 February 1912 (7 March 1912), 2.

48. NARA/RG 84/U.S. Consulate, Harbin, China/vol. 36/no. 250.

49. NARA/RG 84/U.S. Consulate, Harbin, China/vol. 7/no. 62.

50. "Mongoly v Khailare," *Dumy Zabaikal'ia*, 3 April 1912 (16 April 1912), 2.

51. NARA/RG 84/U.S. Consulate, Harbin, China/vol. 7/no. 90.

52. Ibid., no. 100/1–10, quotation on 8. Cf. also RGIA/1276/7/463/144–147, 185–203, esp. 2010b.

53. Tang, *Policy*, 84–86.

54. Lattimore, *Mongols*, 119.

55. Woodhead, *China Year Book*, 622; Lattimore, *Mongols*, 167–168.

56. "Mongoliia," *Vestnik Azii*, no. 14 (February 1913), 15.

57. The critical question of China's borders, that is, whether the ethnic frontiers should be allowed to decide their own fate, was widely debated among scholars in Republican China. The position of the Chinese state, however, was a minority viewpoint, as many feared that the loss of the frontier territories would threaten the Chinese core by increasing its vulnerability to the Great Powers. Esherick, "Qing," esp. 233–238, 243–248.

58. RGIA/323/1/769/110–1110b., quotation on 111.

59. "Ugroza Barge," *Kharbinskii Vestnik*, 10 October 1912 (23 October 1912), 2.

60. Cf. Paine, *Rivals*, 295–298. Woodhead, *China Year Book*, 633–635 has the full content of the agreement.

61. RGIA/323/1/770/100–1010b., 135–1350b. and 155–1560b., quotation on 155–1550b.; "Khailar," *Zabaikal'skaia Nov'*, 19 April 1914 (2 May 1914), 3.

62. According to the eleventh article of the treaty, Hulunbeir remained outside the scope of autonomous Outer Mongolia. On the outcomes of this conference, see Lan, "Movement," 209–218; Nakami, "Diplomats," 75–76; Paine, *Rivals*, 298–305.

63. "Mongoliia," *Vestnik Azii*, nos. 35–36 (1915), quotation on 112.

64. Lan, "Movement," 218–223; Tang, *Policy*, 87–90. The entire agreement is published in "Hulunbei'er gaiyao," 59–63 (original pagination) and Kantselariia Pravlenii Obshchestva Kitaiskoi Vostochnoi zheleznoi dorogi, *Sbornik*, 250–254.

65. Also referred to as Babuujab.

66. LOC/Lattimore/box 25/folder 13 "Inner Mongolia—History Notes" (undated)/8.

67. Lan, "Movement," 239–249; Nakami, "Babujab" and Cui, *Haila'er*, 1:205–213, on the resistance of Babuzhab.

68. Meshcherskii, *Barga*, 7–12 and "Khailar 12 maia," *Kharbinskii Vestnik*, 25 May 1917 (7 June 1917), 3. Cf. also Cui, *Haila'er*, 1:204–217.

69. Restoration of the Chinese border post system began in 1917. Cf. Cheng, *Hulunbei'er zhilüe*, 107.

70. "Hulunbei'er gaiyao," 64–67 (original pagination); Cheng, *Hulunbei'er zhilüe*, 370–375; Kormazov, *Barga*, 59–62; Baranov, "Ustroistvo," 23–26. Lubin prefecture was renamed Lubin district and Jilalin prefecture was renamed Shiwei district. Some of the administrative reforms were partially reversed in 1925, placing Hulunbeir once again under tighter control of Heilongjiang province. Nan manzhou tiedao zhushi huishe, *Hulinbei'er*, 19–25.

71. GARF/102/dp.4/1908 g./21/ch.6/69–71 and 74–81 (quotation on 760b.); RGIA/323/1/1027/101–1010b.

72. "St. Man'chzhuriia," *Zabaikal'e*, 13 February 1904 (26 February 1904), 3; "St. Man'chzhuriia," *Zabaikal'e*, 20 November 1905 (3 December 1905), 2; "St. Man'chzhuriia,"

Zabaikal'e, 16 December 1905 (29 December 1905), 3; "St. Man'chzhuriia," *Dal'*, 3 June 1906 (16 June 1906), 1.

73. "Neprostitel'naia ekonomiia," *Zabaikal'skaia Nov'*, 16 March 1911 (29 March 1911), 3; "St. Man'chzhuriia (Dikost' nravov)," *Zabaikal'e*, 1 July 1903 (14 July 1903), 3.

74. GARF/102/dp.4/1908 g./21/ch.6/69–71, here 700b.

75. "St. Man'chzhuriia," *Zabaikal'skaia Nov'*, 4 June 1911 (17 June 1911), 3. Official statistics gave slightly lower numbers of liquor stores. Soldatov, *Poselki*, 1986–1991.

76. RGIA/323/1/1027/101–101 obl; Soldatov, *Poselki*, 311.

77. RGIA/323/1/1028/179–182ob., here 181.

78. "Pos. Man'chzhuriia," *Kharbinskii Vestnik*, 6 January 1915 (19 January 1915), 3.

79. Chiasson, *Administering*, 30–32.

80. *Doklad*, 1–4; RGIA/323/1/1026/1–20b.

81. Soldatov, *Poselki*, 336–343. After 1908, the regulations have been changed only slightly. Kantselariia Pravlenii Obshchestva Kitaiskoi Vostochnoi zheleznoi dorogi, *Sbornik*, 201–216. See also Chiasson, *Administering*, 32–35.

82. The Chinese commercial society, for instance, had the right to appoint two candidates to the municipal council of Manzhouli. The Chinese only once exerted this right, in 1908, and afterward no longer appointed candidates. In addition, foreign residents could not have a representative on the municipal council—also on the ground that foreigners refused to pay taxes and only taxpayers could be elected. RGIA/323/1/1030/48–49ob., quotation on 49. Only in 1914 did foreigners gain rights equal to those of the Russians in the municipal council. Kantselariia Pravlenii Obshchestva Kitaiskoi Vostochnoi zheleznoi dorogi, *Sbornik*, 168–171.

83. RGIA/323/1/1029/6–14; Klark, *Adres-kalendar'*, 181.

84. RGIA/323/1/1030/153–153ob.; "Zhizn' pos. Man'chzhuriia," *Dumy Zabaikalia*, 15 February 1912 (28 February 1912), 3.

85. "Zhizn' pos. Man'chzhuriia," *Dumy Zabaikalia*, 27 July 1912 (9 August 1912), 2.

86. "Zhizn' pos. Man'chzhuriia," *Dumy Zabaikalia*, 28 July 1912 (10 August 1912), 2–3.

87. RGIA/323/1/1030/153–153ob., 176–177.

88. "Vybory upolnomochennykh," *Zabaikal'skaia Nov'*, 4 February 1916 (17 February 1916), 3.

89. *Doklad*, 4–5.

90. The Sino-Japanese Treaty, signed in Beijing in 1905, declared Manzhouli open to foreign trade. *Opisanie naselennykh punktov*, 194–196; Brunero, *Cornerstone*, table on 12–13.

91. NARA/RG 84/U.S. Consulate, Harbin, China/vol. 10/153–155; NARA/RG 84/U.S. Consulate, Harbin, China/vol. 12/506–513, quotation on 510; PAAA/Peking II/1024/181–183verso; RGIA/323/1/1026/156–156ob.

92. "K intsidentu s inostrantsami," *Zabaikal'skaia Nov'*, 29 June 1911 (12 July 1911), 3.

93. NARA/RG 84/U.S. Consulate, Harbin, China/vol. 6/250–259, here 250–252, quotation on 251; PAAA/Peking II/1024/120–121verso, 178–179.

94. "K intsidentu s inostrantsami," *Zabaikal'skaia Nov'*, 29 June 1911 (12 July 1911), 3 (quotation); PAAA/Peking II/1024/145–147.

95. PAAA/Peking II/1024/120–121, 161–161verso, 166–168, 202–207verso, 209–210.

96. NARA/RG 84/U.S. Consulate, Harbin, China/vol. 6/402–409, here 402–403; PAAA/Peking II/1024/209–210.

97. Semenov, *O sebe*, 63–73, quotations on 71 and 72.

98. Semenov's military strength began to wane in the summer of 1920, when the Japanese began to withdraw from Siberia. Bolshevik troops exploited his weakened position, forcing his army to retreat to the Maritime region. From the eastern edge of the collapsing empire, Semenov finally fled into exile in China in September 1921. Cf. the highly subjective accounts by Semenov, *O sebe*, 92–99, 110–117; Sergeev, *Ocherki*, esp. 33–57; and Serebrennikov, *Otkhod*, 45–54.

99. Sunderland, *Baron's Cloak*, esp. 151–163. Serebrennikov, *Otkhod*, 91–102 passim, offers a not quite accurate narrative of victimhood. For fears among Manzhouli's merchants, cf. RGASPI/372/1/111/700b.

100. As early as 1907 Cossacks were campaigning against custom controls on the lower Argun. GAIO/25/11/16/43–45, here 44ob. The public excoriated customs officers from the Abagaitui post for their alleged corruption and arbitrariness. Cf., e.g., a letter to the editor "Abagaituevskii tam. post," *Zabaikal'skaia Nov'*, 4 January 1914 (17 January 1914), 3.

101. GAChO/334/1/68/4–50b., 13–14, quotation on 4.

102. RGVIA/1553/2/26/37–370b., 39–400b.

103. Cf. the autobiographical notes by Semenov, *O sebe*, 63–126 passim. Cf. also "Po vostoku. Dorozhnye vpechatleniia," *Zabaikal'skaia Nov'*, 1 December 1918, 3; "Man'chzhuriia. V pogranichnom gorode," *Zabaikal'skaia Nov'*, 31 January 1919, 3.

104. On the history of Russian emigration to China, and Harbin in particular, cf., e.g., Ablazhei, *Vostok*; Ablova, *KVZhD*; Bakich, "Charbin"; Lahusen, "Harbin"; Ristaino, "Shanghai"; Taskina, *Kharbin*; Shi, Liu, and Gao, *Ha'erbin*.

105. Krol', *Stranitsy*, 524.

106. Kazakov, *Svideteli*, 34.

107. Bancroft/Sharov/part 2/285–287, quote on 286.

108. Daurets, *Zastenki*, 75–76.

109. By 1925 it had fallen again to about twelve thousand people. Kitaiskaia Vostochnaia zheleznaia doroga, *Man'chzhuriia*, appendix no. 5; Kormazov, *Barga*, 90.

110. "O kvartirakh v Man'chzhurii," *Man'chzhuriia*, 4 October 1921, 3; "Otkrytie bezplatnoi stolovoi," *Man'chzhuriia*, 13 December 1921, 3; "Pis'mo v redaktsiiu," *Nash Put'*, 19 July 1922, 3.

111. Between fall 1920 and spring 1921, for instance, the border town was exclusively supplied over waterways and dirt roads. Kitaiskaia Vostochnaia zheleznaia doroga, *Man'chzhuriia*, 603.

112. GAKhK/R-18/3/6/35–37.

Chapter 4: The Soviet State at the Border

1. The Soviet diplomat Lev M. Karakhan offered to relinquish all Bolshevik claims to the special rights won by the tsarist government in China. The proposal created a positive impression in China, as the first unilateral offer of equality from a European country. In the first Karakhan Manifesto (25 July 1919), Moscow promised to return the Chinese Eastern Railroad without compensation. But in the second Manifesto (27 September 1920) the promise to return the railroad was not repeated. Elleman, "Tensions," 59–70 passim.

2. RGIA DV/R-2422/1/779/2–5; RGIA DV, *Tamozhnia*, 149–164.

3. Manzhouli's daily newspaper *Nash Put'* (Our Way), however, downplayed those rumors, referring to the skeptical observations of recently emigrated Russians about the situation in Transbaikalia. "Ocherednaia provokatsiia," *Nash Put'*, 30 April 1922, 3; "Komu eto nuzhno," *Nash*

Put', 3 May 1922, 2; "Spokoistvie—zalog poriadka," *Nash Put'*, 6 May 1922, 2; "'Saryn' na kichku!'," *Nash Put'*, 9 July 1922, 3.

4. RGASPI/159/2/52/11–12, quotation on 11.

5. "K sud'be russkoi tamozhni," *Man'chzhuriia*, 23 September 1921, 3; "Vopros o russkoi tamozhne na st. Man'chzhuriia," *Man'chzhuriia*, 28 October 1921, 3.

6. RGIA DV/R-2422/1/779/8–30, esp. 8–90b.

7. Soviet border guards allegedly forced two employees of Chinese customs and one Chinese soldier onto Soviet territory, where the three men were arrested. *Rupor* (Mouthpiece) and other Harbin Russian émigré newspapers covered the incident vociferously. E.g., "Chem zakonchitsia intsident na st. Man'chzhuriia," *Rupor*, 19 October 1923, 3; "Intsident na st. Man'chzhuriia na puti k likvidatsii," *Rupor*, 22 October 1923, 3; "Man'chzhurskii intsident oslozhniaetsia," *Rupor*, 19 October 1923, 3; "Otvet marshala Chzhan-tszo-lina na pis'mo osoboupolnomochennogo SSSR Karakhana," *Rupor*, 4 November 1923, 5. Cf. also *Sovetsko-kitaiskie otnosheniia*, 66–67.

8. RGASPI/159/2/52/28, 37.

9. PAAA/R 85573/no pagination.

10. "K napadeniiu na s. Abagaitui," *Nash Put'*, 13 October 1922, 3; "Podrobnosti naleta belykh na Abagaitui," *Nash Put'*, 14 October 1922, 3.

11. For the wording of the agreement signed in September 1924 in Mukden (Shenyang), see "Soglashenie," 88–89; *Sovetsko-kitaiskie otnosheniia*, 94–98. See also Elleman, "Tensions," 70–74; Urbansky, *Wettstreit*, 106–109.

12. RGASPI/372/1/758/71–79, here 72.

13. Ablova, *KVZhD*, 145–177 and Urbansky, *Wettstreit*, 106–114.

14. The Special District was created in 1920 to replace the Russian-controlled Chinese Eastern Railroad concession. Chiasson, *Administering*, 38–97 and 151–183 passim, esp. 48–49. The administrative structure of this district is outlined in Baranov, "Ustroistvo," 17–23.

15. *Doklad*, 42–56.

16. GAChO/P-81/1/214/2; GAChO/P-81/1/860/38–39; GAChO/P-81/1/1361/28–280b.; GAChO/P-81/1/1362/1; RGASPI/372/1/758/71–79 (here 71) and 112–119 (here 118–1180b.); RGASPI/372/2/15/23–260b.

17. "Prazdnovanie 5-i godovshchiny Oktiabr'skoi revoliutsii," *Nash Put'*, 11 November 1922, 2.

18. Several days later, the Chinese diplomatic commissar apologized to the Soviet Russian government commissioner for the unpleasant incident. "'Vasilii Ivanovich' st. Man'chzhuriia," *Novosti Zhizni*, 9 February 1923, 3.

19. RGASPI/372/1/758/202–221, here 216–217.

20. GAChO/P-81/1/860/64–640b.

21. "Razvernuli krasnoe znamia," *Zabaikal'skii Rabochii*, 18 July 1924, 7.

22. Cf., e.g., "1-oe maia v g. Man'chzhuriia," *Novosti Zhizni*, 6 May 1926, 3.

23. Shishkin, *Bol'shevizm*, 60–61, 114 (quotation). According to a record of party members in the railroad zone, Manzhouli was second only to Harbin as a hive of Communist activity; ibid., table 2 on 130.

24. *Haila'er tielu fenju zhi*, 972–977.

25. *Manzhouli shi zhi*, 151–154.

26. Kormazov, "Dvizhenie," 53.

27. Cargo and passenger traffic increased remarkably throughout the 1920s. Urbansky, *Wettstreit*, table on 102. There was a nearly fourfold increase in international passenger traffic between 1926 and 1928 at Manzhouli. Sokolov, "Liniia," 49.

28. Ekonomicheskii biuro KVzhd, *Spravochnik*, 484–486; Kormazov, *Barga*, 88–95.

29. "Kak Akim Nikiforov loshadei voroval," *Nash Put'*, 4 May 1922, 3.

30. GAKhK/P-2/2/166/16–22; RGIA DV/R-2422/1/670/22–240b., here 22–230b.; RGIA DV/R-2422/1/838/8–20, here 110b.–13.

31. Larin, *Migranty*, 119–140 passim. The 1959 Soviet census listed 1,155 Chinese in Chita region. GAChO/R-1645/6/182/2. By 1968 their number had fallen to just 172 people. GARF/A-612/1/147/8.

32. For example, prevailing chaos at Manzhouli's customs inspection hall. GAChO/R-404/1/134/56–560b.

33. Baranov, "Ustroistvo," 15–16. On the structures and regulations of the Customs Service during the Republican era, see Brunero, *Cornerstone*, 22–37 passim.

34. RGIA DV/R-2422/1/670/22–240b., quotation on 22; RGIA DV/R-2422/1/838/8–20; GAKhK/P-2/2/166/16–22, here 17.

35. GAKhK/P-2/2/166/16–22, quotation on 16.

36. Paine, *Rivals*, 194–195; Geyer, *Imperialismus*, 161–163.

37. If true, this trend was, of course, due to administrative restrictions, but not economic strength. Popenko, "Deiatel'nost'," 112–116. Ol'ga V. Zalesskaia argues that even in formal trade relations during the mid and late 1920s the Soviet Union still ran a deficit with northern Manchuria. Zalesskaia, "Torgovlia," esp. 54.

38. Tsybin, "Rol'," 119.

39. Cf. Khitin, "Okhrana," for the border control structures during the Far Eastern Republic.

40. RGIA DV/R-2422/1/333/7. For instance, the number of guards at the Matsievskaia customs lookout was reduced from seven (in 1922) to four men (in 1924). GAChO/R-79/2/67/5; GAChO/R-251/3/70/6–7 and 27–31, here 6, 27.

41. Khinganskii Krasnoznamennyi pogranichnyi otriad, *80 let*, 7.

42. RGIA DV/R-2422/1/838/8–20, quotation on 18. Cf. also Chandler, *Institutions*, 57–63.

43. RGIA DV/R-2422/1/670/22–240b., here 24–240b. By the mid-1920s, the government reluctantly accepted some of these proposals. Taxes and prices on alcoholic beverages and several goods in the borderlands were cut. Yet retail prices still trumped those on the Chinese side. RGIA DV/R-2422/1/838/8–20, here table on 90b.

44. Cf. Ball, "Trade," on private trade during the NEP. Between 1927 and 1930, the ranks of smugglers at the Sino-Russian border decreased to a quarter of their previous volume. Tsybin, "Rol'," 120–124; Popenko, *Opyt*, 117–118.

45. GAKhK/P-2/1/66/37–39, quotation on 38–39; GARF/R-1235/140/714/18.

46. With no immediate threat of a major war on the horizon, the battle against contraband along the Soviet Union's Central Asian international border did not progress noticeably in the 1930s, contrary to the Soviet-Manchukuo border. Shaw, "Friendship," 340–342.

47. During the 1930s customs authorities still made note of hideouts on freight trains, in passenger compartments, and in automobiles. Documents do not make any further mention of

mounted Cossacks who crossed borders without restriction. Cf., e.g., GAChO/R-1243/2/114/8–9. In the early 1940s, the files list only isolated cases of attempts to cross the border outside of official crossings to transport commodities illegally. Between 1941 and 1945 the accessible archive records of the customs station Otpor (the former Railroad Siding 86) list fewer than a dozen offenses. GAChO/R-1243/2/219/52–520b., 57–580b., 66.

48. Typical were smuggling parties such as the two armed Cossacks in their thirties who in the spring of 1913 transported for resale on a horse carriage around 250 liters of liquor from Manzhouli to the Cossack village of Klinovsk. GAChO/78/2/14/31–320b.

49. During the early 1930s, half of those apprehended by the Soviet authorities were Chinese smugglers and the other half were Russians and Buriats. My estimates from the listed files in GAChO/R-1243/1.

50. GAChO/R-1243/2/8/7, 30–310b., 51–520b.

51. GAChO/R-1243/2/8/5, 6.

52. GAChO/R-1243/2/8/7 (quotation) and 21.

53. Lattimore, *Manchuria*, 247.

54. With the Soviet consul at Manzhouli being involved in this form of smuggling, "Kontrabanda v avtomobile sov. konsula," *Kharbinskoe Vremia*, 8 April 1933, 4.

55. "Nazi Trade in the Far East," *Economist*, 3 May 1941, 588.

56. GARF/R-8131/37/1114/1–7, 20–25.

57. "Hulunbei'er gaiyao," 27–28 (original pagination); GAChO/13/2/29/8–80b., 139–141.

58. Ho, *Population*, table on 26 (table); Iashnov, *Kolonizatsiia*, 244–249.

59. Lattimore, "Setting," 401–402. Cf. Urbansky, *Wettstreit*, 123–131, on the impact of railroads on migration patterns in Manchuria.

60. The status of Outer Mongolia was not yet fixed. With the Russian Revolution and the turmoil of Civil War, the Holy Khan lost the backing of Saint Petersburg. Outer Mongolia was then occupied by Chinese troops in 1919. What followed was a period of disorder and confusion, fueled by the echoes of the Civil War in Russia. On 25 November 1924, the Mongolian People's Republic was founded. It became the first communist country outside the Soviet Union. Elleman, "Negotiations," 539–563 passim; Paine, *Rivals*, 314–342 passim.

61. In 1930 Moscow lured Gobol Merse into the Soviet consulate in Manzhouli, where he was kidnapped and taken to Moscow. He died in prison in 1934. A detailed course of events is given by Atwood, *Mongols*, 2:821–920 passim. On Merse's life see Humphrey and Onon, *Shamans*, 343–352.

62. Lattimore, "Setting," 405.

63. For the independence movement in Inner Mongolia during the late 1920s to mid-1930s and its relations with Moscow, Nanjing, and Tokyo, see Bulag, *Nationalism*, 86–163 passim.

64. Walker, "Road," 306–323 passim and Suny, *Revenge*, for a general analysis on nationalism in the Soviet Union. Unlike in other non-Russian-dominated peripheries of the Soviet Union, there were no effective challenges to the creation of a single Soviet people in this particular borderland. For Transbaikalia, generally in line with Suny, Pavel K. Varnavskii has argued even under the policy of *korenizatsiia*, indigenous self-determination was limited. Varnavskii, "Granitsy," 149–176. Cf. Sablin, "Autonomies," 450–453, for the origins of Buriat territorial autonomy during the Far Eastern Republic.

65. Tesler, "Buriaty," 30–32; Kormazov, "Kochevaia Barga," 51–53; Baldano, "People," 183–189.

66. GAChO/R-15/1/56/2–30b., 36. Similar reports of robberies by People's Revolutionary Army soldiers, in GAKhK/R-18/3/6/120–121.

67. GAKhK/R-18/3/5/14–15, 17–20, 40.

68. GAChO/R-1077/1/40/34–340b., 113–114.

69. From 1925 onward, the Outer Mongolian government allowed Soviet authorities to confiscate cattle on its territory. GARF/P-1235/140/481/40–41, 49–51.

70. GAChO/R-1243/2/369/139–145; GAChO/R-1243/1/1469/1–20b., 18–19, 22, 37–370b.

71. Cf., e.g., GAChO/R-1243/1/830/1–9; GAChO/R-1243/1/1090/1–3; GAChO/R-1243/2/4/1–2, 60–62. Soviet subjects escaped collectivization also in other sectors of the Sino-Soviet borderland; most notable perhaps were the nomads who fled from Kazakhstan to Xinjiang. Cf. Kindler, *Nomaden*, 215–218; Chandler, *Institutions*, 64.

72. The Soviet customs office at Otpor lists about 1,700 cases of detained smugglers between 1930 and 1937, of which the majority were arrested through 1932. Buriats accounted for the majority of cases that involved the smuggling of animals. GAChO/R-1243/1. Yet many Cossacks also fled to Mongolia in order to evade state control over their cattle and the tax payments that followed. See, e.g., the escape of 14 Cossacks with their 23,083 cattle to Outer Mongolia in 1926. GARF/P-1235/140/481/40–41, 49–51. Some Han Chinese were also among livestock smugglers. See, e.g., GAChO/R-1243/1/1426/26, 39, 46–460b.

73. GAChO/R-1243/1/1361, esp. 1–2, 23, 38. Cf. GAChO/R-1243/2/12/1–15, 22, 26 for similar cases.

74. When a group of about one hundred Buriats fled across the border near Manzhouli in early September 1931, for instance, Soviet soldiers killed four women and two men. Haila'er/1/1/121/1–5.

75. A classic book on strategies of everyday survival taken up by the peasants in the 1930s is Fitzpatrick, *Peasants*. For policies and consequences of collectivization in the Soviet periphery, Baberowski, *Feind*, 669–752; and Hughes, *Stalinism*.

76. *Ocherki istorii Vostochnogo Zabaikal'ia*, 45–51; *Entsiklopediia Zabaikal'ia*, 1:193 and Zherebtsov, *Vosstaniia*, on peasant uprisings in Chita region.

77. *Natsional'nyi somon* is a national self-administration equivalent to the *sel'sovet*.

78. GAChO/R-251/3/63/118–119; GAChO/R-1077/1/40/108. For an uncritical approach to collectivization in the Aga Steppe, see Zhamtsarano, "Kollektivizatsiia," 36–44.

79. GAChO/R-1077/1/142/4–7. Not only in Novaia Zaria was the schooling situation unsatisfactory: in 1927 less than 50 percent of children in that vast and sparsely populated Borzia district, nomad and sedentary offspring alike, attended school. GAChO/P-75/1/398/131–134.

80. GAChO/R-1077/1/142/56–590b.

81. GAChO/R-1077/4/6/6–11, esp. 10–11, and 12–13; GAChO/R-1077/4/14/5–6 and 12–13; Haila'er/1/1/67/1–2. "Man'chzhurskie melochi," *Russkoe Slovo*, 18 May 1929, 2; "Na zabaikal'sk. granitse," *Russkoe Slovo*, 21 May 1929, 3.

82. GAChO/R-1257/1/75/13. Collective farms in the Argun borderland remained in dire straits throughout the 1930s and 1940s. GARF/R-5446/24a/949/2–7. Cf. Sibiriakov, "Konets," 228–241, on the fate of those who remained in the Soviet Union after collectivization.

83. From 959 people in 1912 the population dropped to 776 people in 1923, declining further to 618 people in 1935. GAChO/R-1257/1/27/97–100, here 97 (for 1935); Dal'ne-Vostochnoe Oblastnoe Statisticheskoe Upravlenie, *Perepis'*, 90–91 (for 1923); figures for 1912 in chapter 1.

84. GAIO/25/11/213/20–200b.

85. GAKhK/P-2/2/181/98–99, 101–103, 107–111.

86. Kormazov, *Barga*, 50–51 (for 1927); Anuchin, *Ocherki*, 179 (for 1933); Argudiaeva, "Naselenie," 126 (for 1945).

87. Cf. Argudiaeva, "Naselenie," 123–126; Shestakov, "Trekhrech'e," 193; Zhernakov, *Trekhrech'e*, 16–17 for a description of Dragotsenka and other villages.

88. On the preservation of religion, education, dresses, architecture, and traditions, cf. Zhernakov, *Trekhrech'e*, 17–21; *E'erguna youqi zhi*, 128–134; Anuchin, *Ocherki*, 179; "Ugolok Rossii v Kitae," *Rupor*, 5 August 1927, 8, 15.

89. Anuchin, *Ocherki*, 185.

90. GAKhK/R-1128/1/71/50–57, here 50–52; Kormazov, *Barga*, 65–66.

91. Cf. Matsusaka, *Manchuria*, 312–348 passim, for an analysis of deteriorating relations between Zhang and Japan.

Chapter 5: An Open Steppe under Lock and Key

1. "Na granitse russkoi zemli," *Zaria*, 6 September 1931, 5.

2. This form of imperialism seeks not primarily subordination by military rule and pure economic exploitation but rather to create a "sovereign" nation-state similar in structure, culture, and ideology to the metropole. Duara, "Nationalism," 48–49. The history of this Japanese-created entity has been thoroughly researched, esp. from angles foregrounding imperial politics and economy, the chimera and actual structure of the colonial government, Chinese nationalism, resistance, and collaboration, as well as the production of pan-Asianism and imperial nationalism. Cf. in particular Duara, *Sovereignty*; Mitter, *Myth*; Yamamuro, *Manchuria*; and Young, *Empire*. At present there is only Chinese scholarship, without accurate source references and with patriotic overtones, on the crimes of the Japanese against the civilian population and the resistance against the foreign rule in Hulunbeir during the Manchukuo period. Cf. Cui, *Haila'er*, passim, esp. 2:185–199, 236–258.

3. Russian and Western historians have produced a massive body of historical research on Stalinism and the Great Terror that is beyond summary here. To head a short list of the classics in this field, Baberowski, *Feind*; Baberowski, *Terror*, esp. 135–208; Martin, *Empire*, esp. 311–461 passim; Fitzpatrick, *Stalinism*.

4. Osobaia Dal'nevostochnaia armiia (ODVA), later renamed the Special Far Eastern Red Banner Army (OKDVA).

5. Patrikeeff, *Politics*, 80–103; see also Ablova, *KVZhD*, 198–221; Tang, *Policy*, 218–259; Urbansky, *Wettstreit*, 136–143. On the role the conflict played in Stalin's quest for supremacy in the Kremlin, see Elleman, *Moscow*, 192–205. For the general course of military interactions, cf. Walker, *War*, 144–253, passim; Erickson, *Command*, 240–246.

6. GAKhK/P-2/1/165/60–61, 64–65, 73, 167, 345; Haila'er/1/1/30/27.

7. "Su E rao bian qingbao hui zhi," *Guo Wen Zhoubao*, 10 November 1929, 1–7 passim and 24 November 1929, 1–6 passim. Cf. also "Sovetskaia operatsiia na zapade," *Zaria*, 27 September 1929, 5;

"Voennaia obstanovka v Man'chzhurii," *Rupor*, 29 September 1929, 1; "Zhestkaia bombardirovka Man'chzhurii," *Rupor*, 3 October 1929, 3; "Krasnye ugrozhaiut Man'chzhurii novoi bombard-irovkoi," *Zaria*, 5 October 1929, 5.

8. RGVA/33879/1/4/1–23, quotations on 13–14.

9. In 1934 the GPU was absorbed into the new People's Commissariat of Internal Affairs or NKVD.

10. GAChO/P-75/1/853/18, 34, 50–51; GAKhK/P-2/1/167/5–6; NARA/RG 59/Records relating to the activities in Manchuria and the Japanese military potential, 1930–1933/box 2/32–34; PAAA/R 85585/no pagination; "Chto bylo v Man'chzhurii," *Zaria*, 18 December 1929, 5.

11. GAChO/P-75/1/853/37; Patrikeeff, *Politics*, 83–85; Walker, *War*, 241–253.

12. "War Paralyzes North Manchuria," *New York Times*, 15 September 1929, E6. Cf. also "Gorod Man'chzhuriia," *Gun-Bao*, 1 October 1929, 2.

13. Kormazov, "Dvizhenie," 53 (for 1929); and "Zakat goroda Man'chzhurii," *Rupor*, 20 August 1931, 3 (for 1931). Cf. also "Krasnye ugrozhaiut Man'chzhurii novoi bombardirovkoi," *Zaria*, 5 October 1929, 5; "Zakat goroda Man'chzhurii," *Rupor*, 20 August 1931, 3.

14. GAChO/P-81/1/1422/2–16.

15. GAChO/P-75/1/853/6–8.

16. GAKhK/P-2/1/242/29–40.

17. GAChO/R-1077/1/142/113.

18. GAKhK/P-2/1/242/19–26, quotation on 19.

19. E.g., GAKhK/P-2/1/115/29–30; NARA/RG 59/Records relating to the activities in Manchuria and the Japanese military potential, 1930–1933/box 2/24–25.

20. Also Chinese civilians died in Soviet punitive raids in the borderlands. See, e.g., the attacks on Chinese villages further upstream Argun with many casualties. Cf. E'erguna/1/1/7–23/1–25 passim.

21. "Napadenie krasnykh vsadnikov na Trekhrech'e," *Zaria*, 28 September 1929, 5.

22. GAKhK/R-1128/1/29/135–135ob.

23. Ibid., 136–138ob., quotation on 137.

24. GAKhK/R-1128/1/71/98–99.

25. The Chinese army leadership suspected that a number of communists among the Russians in Trekhreche who were arming traitors would pose an immediate threat to the security of the border. GAKhK/R-1128/1/29/172–173ob.

26. "U bratskoi mogily v Trekhrech'e," *Zaria*, 22 October 1929, 5.

27. "Zverskaia rasprava krasnykh s mirnym poselkom v Trekhrech'e," *Zaria*, 8 October 1929, 5. The facts in this article are consistent with later reports from the same paper by special cor-respondent Boris Shilov, who visited Tynykha and interviewed the only male survivor, Ivan Volgin. "U bratskoi mogily v Trekhrech'e," *Zaria*, 22 October 1929, 5; "Trekhrech'e posle naleta krasnykh," *Zaria*, 24 October 1929, 5; "Kogo ubivali v Trekhrech'e?," *Rupor*, 9 October 1929, 2. German and American diplomats confirmed these death counts, referring to other "credible" sources. NARA/RG 59/Records relating to the activities in Manchuria and the Japanese mili-tary potential, 1930–1933/box 2/21; PAAA/R 85583/no pagination. Cf. also the account of Si-biriakov, "Konets," 216–219.

28. "Sto dvadtsat' novykh zhertv krasnago naleta na Trekhrech'e," *Zaria*, 15 October 1929, 5.

29. "Krovavye koshmary Trekhrech'ia," *Zaria*, 18 October 1929, 5. Nadezhda E. Ablova, referring to the "emigrant press," estimates the number of victims much lower at approximately 150 people. Ablova, "Deiatel'nost'," 147. Contemporary émigré sources agree with that number. See, e.g., Serebrennikov, *Otkhod*, 251.

30. "Den' traura po ubitym v Trekhrech'i," *Zaria*, 13 October 1929, 7.

31. PAAA/R 85583/no pagination.

32. On 10 October, a Chinese general expressed condolences, via *Zaria*, to the Russian community. A *Zaria* journalist informed consuls and foreign correspondents about the incident. Cf. "Gen. Chzhan Tszin-kui o krasnoi rasprave v Trekhrech'i," *Zaria*, 11 October 1929, 5. Cf. also "Bai'E fan hongdang xuanyan neirong," *Binjiang Shibao*, 17 October 1929, 3.

33. GARF/R-5963/1/39/25–26, 55, quotations on 55.

34. PAAA/R 85588/no pagination; cf. also "7 smertnykh prigovorov v Khailare," *Rupor*, 16 November 1930, 6.

35. "Polozhenie na zapadnoi linii," *Zaria*, 1 August 1930, 5.

36. GAKhK/R-1128/1/71/121–122, quotation on 122.

37. Soviet border troops carried out punitive raids in other areas of the Soviet-Chinese borderlands as well, for instance against Kazakh emigrants in Xinjiang. Cf. Kindler, *Nomaden*, 209–215.

38. It was the escalating Sino-Soviet conflict in the late 1920s that attracted attention not only among Chinese scholars (such as the historian Chen Dengyuan, *Zhong E*, esp. 35–43), but also among a wider Chinese audience for the first time around border issues and imperial policies of the northern neighbor in China's Northeast. See, for instance, Hollington Tong's book on the Sino-Soviet dispute over the Chinese Eastern Railroad: Dong, *Dong lu*. Chinese media also covered the conflict extensively. *Dongfang Zazhi* (Eastern Miscellany), for instance, a popular magazine that was the flagship of the periodicals published by Shanghai's Commercial Press, ran several comprehensive stories. E.g., "Dongbei bianfang zhi weiji," *Dongfang Zazhi* 26, no. 4 (February 1929): 1–2 and Yu Gan, "Sulian daju qinlüe bianjing," *Dongfang Zazhi* 26, no. 16 (August 1929): 1–3.

39. GARF/R-3316/23/1125/1–3.

40. GARF/A-385/17/2399/9.

41. Cf. "Kak Zabaikal'sk nachinalsia," *Zabaikal'skaia Magistral'*, 31 March 1995, 7.

42. "Sulian jundui gushou bianjiang," *Binjiang Shibao*, 2 October 1931, 3.

43. "Bliukher prodolzhaet pugat' belogvardeitsami," *Zaria*, 21 March 1932, 5.

44. RGASPI/514/1/773/1a, 29–290b., 36, 520b.; China, *Documents*, 148–161, esp. 159.

45. "Chto proizoshlo v gor. Man'chzhuriia," *Zaria*, 30 September 1932, 5; "Iaponskie rezidenty evakuiruiutsia na sov. territoriiu," *Zaria*, 2 October 1932, 8. Cf. also "Manzhouli zhi hulujun quanti huabian jiang chezhan zhanling jinzhi lieche chufa," *Binjiang Shibao*, 29 September 1932, 2; "You Manzhouli zhi Fula'erji jian yanxian bingbian zhenxiang zai zhi," *Binjiang Shibao*, 1 October 1932, 2; "Disorder in the Far East," *Economist*, 679–680; and Su's recollections in Cui, *Haila'er*, 2:24–34, esp. 24–29.

46. "Iaponskaia delegatsiia vyletaet 6 noiabria na st. Matsievskaia," *Zaria*, 1 November 1932, 2; "Vstrecha na Matsievskoi ne sostoialas'," *Zaria*, 25 November 1932, 3; "Iapontsy ustanavlivaiut radio-stantsiiu v Matsievskoi," *Rupor*, 26 November 1932, 5. Cf. also PAAA/Peking II/2388, 90–90verso.

47. "Peregovory proizodut v Khailare," *Zaria*, 2 December 1932, 5.

48. See the memoirs by eyewitness Sladkovskii, *Znakomstvo*, 181–188. Cf. also RGASPI/514/1/773/52–520b.; "Khailar pal—avantiura miatezhnikov konchena!," *Zaria*, 7 December 1932, 5; Cui, *Haila'er*, 2:31–32.

49. RGVA/32114/1/15/155–157, quotation on 155.

50. By June 1933, the majority of the Chinese internees had been sent, via Siberia and Kazakhstan, to Xinjiang. RGASPI/514/1/1076/2, 3, 6–7, 17, 60.

51. RGVA/33879/1/509/91–92; "Pervyi poezd iz Kharbina v Man'chzhuriiu," *Rupor*, 9 December 1932, 7.

52. "Polovina st. Man'cuzhurii 'uezzhaet' v SSSR," *Rupor*, 14 December 1931, 3. Soviet customs at Manzhouli was officially closed in May 1933. *Manzhouli shi zhi*, 243.

53. Lensen, *Inheritance*, 212–334 passim; Urbansky, *Wettstreit*, 147–153.

54. GAChO/P-75/1/65/1–29, 32–38.

55. Fleming, *Travels*, 50.

56. Cf. table 2.1 for the census of Manzhouli.

57. Cordes, *Kaiserreich*, 18–24.

58. Barber, *Trans-Siberian*, 41–42.

59. The numbers of Soviet railroad workers in Manzhouli even rose slightly, to about sixty in 1940, when cargo traffic increased due to a brief prewar spike in soybean exports to Germany. GARF/R-5446/24a/3163/4–7.

60. Cf. the report by Luosaier (Russel) for *Xuelu* (Bloody Road), a widely read Hankou weekly journal. Luosaier, "Wuren zhijing—Manzhouli," *Xuelu*, no. 35 (1938): 563.

61. Cf. Sladkovskii, *Znakomstvo*, 183–184.

62. These figures excluded perhaps military personnel. GAChO/R-1257/1/111/220b.

63. GAChO/R-1243/2/229/1.

64. Cf. Murphy, *Stalin*, for an excellent introduction to the abundant literature.

65. NARA/RG 165/Military Intelligence Division "Regional File," 1922–1944, Manchuria/box 2432/folder 3. Soviet soldiers included regular, NKVD, and Kolkhoz Corps troops. Cf. United States, *Peculiarities*, 60–66.

66. Cf. Erickson, *Command*, esp. 349–357, 397–401 and 449–561 passim.

67. Plaetschke, "Mandschurei," 821.

68. GAChO/R-1077/1/249/78, 95; GAChO/P-3/1/861/5–7, 98–99, 110–114.

69. RGVA/33879/1/51/1–8.

70. United States, *Operational Planning*, 121–124.

71. "Bliukher prodolzhaet pugat' belogvardeitsami," *Zaria*, 21 March 1932, 5.

72. Hidaka, *Issues*, 98.

73. United States, *Peculiarities*, 30, 48, 95, 101–102, 104–107; United States, *Intelligence Planning*, 28–29. Cf. also NARA/RG 165/Military Intelligence Division "Regional File," 1922–1944, Manchuria/box 2432/folder 4; "K chemu gotoviat krasnuiu armiiu v Zabaikal'e," *Kharbinskoe Vremia*, 23 July 1933, 6; "SSSR vedet podgotovku k voine," *Kharbinskoe Vremia*, 16 August 1933, 4.

74. GAChO/R-1077/1/289/29.

75. Sorge, *Mandschukuo*, 201.

76. See the 1936 census of Northern Xingan Province (Hulunbeir) in Cui, *Haila'er*, 2:72.

77. Fleming, *Peking*, 142.

78. Immediately after the occupation the Guandong Army stationed about 900 soldiers in Manzhouli and about 1,500 soldiers in Hailar. RGVA/33879/1/509/99. Cf. also Federal'naia sluzhba Kontrrazvedki Rossiiskoi Federatsii, *Organy*, 42–43; IV Otdel Shtaba Osoboi Krasnoznamennoi DV armii, *Zakhvat*, 129–131.

79. NARA/RG 165/Military Intelligence Division "Regional File," 1922–1944, Manchuria/box 2427/folder 5 and box 2430/folder 7. Guidebooks warned travelers of "must-nots" for photographers. E.g., *Travel in Manchoukuo*, 5–6. In 1940, the Soviet Union set up a similar no-fly zone along its border with Manchukuo. Cf. Federal'naia Sluzhba Bezopasnosti, *Pogranichnaia Sluzhba Rossii*, 127.

80. GARF/R-5446/13a/1271/1–3, quotation on 1.

81. United States, *Peculiarities*, 32; NARA/RG 165/Military Intelligence Division "Regional File," 1922–1944, Manchuria/box 2432/folder 4.

82. RGVA/25871/2/486/61–610b.

83. Federal'naia Sluzhba Bezopasnosti, *Pogranichnaia Sluzhba Rossii*, 150–155; Martin, *Empire*, 312–316; GAChO/R-251/2/11/16. Historically the responsibilities for Soviet border control have been diffused throughout different government bodies. Cf. Chandler, *Institutions*, 68–75, for an overview.

84. A three-column article in a Harbin newspaper explains the particularities of this zone in great detail. "Zapretnaia zona," *Gun-Bao*, 19 May 1932, 2. In the western borderlands this new regime of control was only formulated in 1934. Cf. Martin, *Empire*, 329–330.

85. GARF/R-5446/3as/1/151–154.

86. Matthews, *Passport*, 27–30.

87. "Zapretnaia zona," *Gun-Bao*, 19 May 1932 2; GARF/R-3316/28/189/2–20b.; GARF/R-3316/29/243/1. Cf. also Chandler, *Institutions*, 65–66.

88. GAChO/R-1077/1/165/63.

89. GAAO/R-81/1/161/44–47 (quotation on 44); GAAO/R-81/1/188/15–17.

90. *Zakon*, 1–3. An English translation of the law is in NARA/RG 165/Military Intelligence Division "Regional File," 1922–1944, Manchuria/box 2430/folder 11/105–106; cf. also ibid., box 2426/folder 3.

91. Sladkovskii, *Znakomstvo*, 189–191, quotation on 190.

92. United States, *Intelligence Planning*, 11–15; RGIA/323/1/575/27–29; "Shpiony," *Zabaikal'skaia Nov'*, 1 August 1912 (14 August 1912), 3.

93. These labor-intensive expeditions involved up to 120 people in topographical survey works around Manzhouli in November 1933 alone. Surveying continued over the following years. RGVA/33879/1/511/132–137, esp. 135–136. Cf. also later reports, e.g., RGVA/33879/1/512/160; United States, *Intelligence Planning*, 30–31. Soviet planes took aerial photos of the boundary as well. PAAA/Peking II/2388/71.

94. For a summary of Manchukuo intelligence work in the Soviet border areas, see United States, *Intelligence Planning*, 25–117 passim. On both sides, espionage often went hand in hand with sabotage. The Japanese strategy focused mainly around sabotage operations against the Trans-Siberian Railroad in case of a war with the Soviet Union. Soviet sabotage is said to have centered on Harbin as well as on strategic border settlements and the railroad lines. For Soviet subversive activities in Manchukuo, see the obviously sensationalized émigré Russian pamphlet by Groza, *Podzhigateli*, 179–196.

95. United States, *Intelligence Planning*, 41, 68, 82.

96. E.g., RGVA/25871/2/486/47–48.

97. RGASPI/613/3/51/31–32.

98. "Tainye dokumenty obnaruzheny na st. Man'chzhuriia," *Rupor*, 22 September 1932, 5.

99. IV Otdel Shtaba Osoboi Krasnoznamennoi DV armii, *Zakhvat*, 166–168.

100. Federal'naia sluzhba Kontrrazvedki Rossiiskoi Federatsii, *Organy*, 104.

101. No later than 1933, the Japanese are said to have established White Russian sabotage and intelligence groups in Manzhouli, charged with penetrating the areas surrounding defensive structures north of Borzia in order to gather information. Cf. Sladkovskii, *Znakomstvo*, 194–197.

102. Federal'naia sluzhba Kontrrazvedki Rossiiskoi Federatsii, *Organy*, 102–107.

103. United States, *Intelligence Planning*, 35–36; Burds, "Soviet War," 273–274. Cf. also "Kak ia zaderzhala shpiona," *Pravda*, 8 July 1938, 3. Cf. Perminov, *Nakazanie*, 54–62, for recollections of two émigré Russians sent by the Japanese Military Missions across the Argun to gather intelligence on the Soviet Union.

104. Solov'ev, *Budni*, 203–208; "So st. Iablonia v SSSR bezhali tri krasnykh shpiona," *Rupor*, 28 August 1934, 3. In August 1936 alone, Japanese authorities arrested several hundred Trekhrech'e Cossacks, accusing them of spying for the Soviet Union. At least forty men were executed. "Rasstrely russkikh belogvardeitsev v Man'chzhurii," *Pravda*, 30 August 1936, 1.

105. Liushkov, *Pochemu*, 3–15, quotation on 7; Jansen and Petrov, *Executioner*, 143–146.

106. "Ne uznat' teper zabaikal'tsu svoei privol'noi rodiny," *Rupor*, 6 February 1935, 7. Cf. also, e.g., "Krasnye provokatory v prigranichnykh raionakh na Man'chzhurskoi zemle," *Kharbinskoe Vremia*, 3 January 1937, 4; "Svezhii razskaz novogo bezhentsa iz SSSR," *Kharbinskoe Vremia*, 13 February 1937, 4. Cf. also interview Iakimov.

107. Already during World War I, the tsarist regime had dropped its ambivalence about Russian nationalism, but victims were primarily of Jewish, Muslim, and German backgrounds. Cf. Lohr, *Nationalizing*.

108. The Koreans were deported to other areas of the Soviet Union, whereas the Chinese were repatriated to China. Cf. Martin, *Empire*, 319–343 passim; Chernolutskaia, "Vytesnenie"; Polian, *Will*, 92–93, 98–102; Shulman, *Stalinism*, 57–63. During the late 1930s, the entire Buriat elite of the Communist Party was purged. Many Buriat families were moved from the steppes near Borzia, deeper into the territory of Chita region. A plan to remove Buriats from border regions completely, however, was averted by the local Buriat party boss Namsarai B. Badmazhabe. Some people were arrested, but the main body of inhabitants were then classed as "loyal" and allowed to stay in their new collective farms. Cf. interview Namsaraeva.

109. Fitzpatrick, *Stalinism*, 199–209; Kuromiya, *Voices*, 126–128; Chandler, *Institutions*, 76–77.

110. Burds, "Soviet War," 271–273.

111. GAChO/P-3/1/137/112–117.

112. Hiroaki Kuromiya bases his study of Stalinist repression on NKVD case files of victims in Kiev. For a profound criticism of these sources, see Kuromiya, *Voices*, 6–12.

113. GAChO/P-3/1/137/98–109.

114. For a similar case of a Korean victim in Soviet Ukraine, see Kuromiya, *Voices*, 128–132.

115. In 1933, approximately 29,700 people out of Hulunbeir's total population of 60,900 were categorized as "nomadic" or "seminomadic." Kormazov, "Provintsiia," 37–38.

116. For Mongol attitudes toward Japan, see U.S. Department of State, *Conditions*, 20–22; Lattimore, *Studies*, 404–405; NARA/RG 59/Decimal File, 1930–1939/box 7162/no pagination.

117. Kormazov, "Provintsiia," 31–32; for data on the economy, agriculture, population, etc. of the remaining three sub-provinces (Eastern, Southern and Western), see ibid., 51–73 and the study by the German consular officer Heissig, *Kulturwandel*.

118. NARA/RG 165/Military Intelligence Division "Regional File," 1922–1944, Manchuria/box 2426/folder 10; Kawakami, *Manchoukuo*, 211–212.

119. RGVA/33879/1/510/129, 277; "Potomki Chingis-khana—na okhranu granits," *Zaria*, 3 January 1933, 3.

120. Fleming, *Peking*, 155–156.

121. NARA/RG 165/Military Intelligence Division "Regional File," 1922–1944, Manchuria/box 2432/folder 4.

122. As will be shown on the following pages, Mongol units participated in the Khalkhyn-Gol battle of 1939. And by 1940 they joined the battles against communist guerrilla forces in Manchuria. Cf. RGASPI/514/1/943/4–107, here 97–98.

123. Bulag, "Clashes," 363–367.

124. NARA/RG 165/Military Intelligence Division "Regional File," 1922–1944, Manchuria/box 2432/folder 4.

125. As will be shown on the following pages, Mongol units participated in the Khalkhyn-Gol battle of 1939. And by 1940 they joined the battles against communist guerrilla forces in Manchuria. Cf. RGASPI/514/1/943/4–107, here 97–98.

3; Sneath, *Mongolia*, 69–70.

126. NARA/RG 165/Military Intelligence Division "Regional File," 1922–1944, Manchuria/box 2426/folder 10.

127. Fleming, *Peking*, 155.

128. Cf., e.g., Kaplonski, "Prelude."

129. For a diplomatic history of the relations between Outer Mongolia and the Soviet Union in 1929 to 1939, Boikova, "Aspects," 107–121.

130. Cf. U.S. Department of State, *Conditions*, 23, for attitudes among the Russians of Manchukuo toward Japan.

131. Official statistics state in 1930 about 4,619 ethnic Russians in Trekhreche. GAKhK/R-830/1/218/1–27, here 17.

132. RGASPI/514/1/773/560b.

133. Cf. Urbansky, "Lehrer," 103–105, 116–121.

134. E.g., "Kusochek staroi Rossii v Man'chzhu-Di-Go," *Vremia*, 7 June 1944, or the periodic stories in *Rubezh* (*Frontier*), an illustrated Harbin Russian-language weekly journal, about the calm and peaceful life of the Transbaikal Cossacks in Trekhreche, e.g., "Russkie derevni za rubezhom," *Rubezh*, 6 May 1933, 12–13; "V prostorakh tsvetushchego Trekhrech'ia," *Rubezh*, 27 September 1941, 8–9.

135. For the mission of BREM, see Breuillard, "General," 128–131; Ablova, *KVZhD*, 305–320; NARA/RG 165/Military Intelligence Division "Regional File," 1922–1944, Manchuria/box 2427/folder 4.

136. GAKhK/R-830/2/32/37–39 and GAKhK/R-830/1/56/122–1220b.

137. GAKhK/R-830/2/32/18.

138. GAKhK/R-830/2/13/136–137.

139. GAKhK/R-830/1/204/11–12; GAKhK/R-830/1/270/81.

140. RGVA/33879/1/510/51–60, here 59–60.

141. GAKhK/R-830/2/13/87–90.

142. "Manzhouli juxing pai gong dahui," *Binjiang Shibao*, 23 December 1936, 3.

143. GAKhK/R-830/1/56/196–201.

144. "Vecher kazach'ei molodezhi," *Vremia*, 24 March 1944; "Gastrol'naia poezdka Kruzhka Russkoi Molodezhi v Man'chzhuriiu," *Zakhinganskii Golos*, 3 July 1945.

145. GAKhK/R-830/1/189/105–110, here 106–108. See also "Vesti iz Man'chzhurii," *Vremia*, 6 March 1943; Kio-va-kai, *Imperiia*, 404.

146. GAKhK/R-830/1/56/150–1500b., quotation on 1500b.

147. "Gen. F. Vlas'evskii v gor. Man'chzhuriia," *Zakhinganskii Golos*, 24 October 1944, 2.

148. Kyōwakai (translated into English as Concordia Society) was created as part of the strategy to eliminate resistance to the Manchukuo regime and extend its political control over people living in Manchuria. Young, *Empire*, 287–290.

149. "Prazdnik georgievskikh kavalerov v Man'chzhurii," *Vremia*, 16 December 1943, 3; "Segodnia—protivovozdushnaia oborona," *Zakhinganskii Golos*, 18 July 1944, 2; "V gorodakh i na linii. G. Man'chzhuriia," *Vremia*, 27 February 1945, 3.

150. GAKhK/R-830/1/189/105–110 (here 109), 141–1410b.; GAKhK/R-830/1/56/152–1520b.; "Voennaia podgotovka v Zakhingan'i proshla blestiashche," *Zakhinganskii Golos*, 1 August 1944, 2; "Organizovan Soiuz rezervistov," *Vremia*, 6 February 1945, 3.

151. RGVA/25871/2/489/1–2. This file notes dozens of further incidents along the upper Argun alone, such as two engagements in February 1939 near Starotsurukhaitui between Soviet and Manchukuo soldiers. Cf. ibid., 5–6, 32–33. For the violation of Soviet airspace, see, e.g., RGVA/33879/1/512/80. Cf. also the documentation of incidents along the Soviet-Manchukuo border by Chinese diplomats: Waijiao bu, *Dang'an*, 178–184.

152. Hidaka, *Issues*, 7–8.

153. Moore, *Policy*, 54–58. For contemporary Japanese perspectives, see the "thoughts" of Tanehide Furujo, a high-ranking military officer, in Hidaka, *Issues*, 243–261 and *Japan-Manchoukuo Year Book*, 714–715.

154. RGASPI/17/166/543/87–91. For several weeks the Soviets refused to release some of the border violators, further straining relations with Japan. RGASPI/17/166/544/88–90.

155. The Soviet Union did not have diplomatic representation in Xinjing and Hailar and refused to let Japanese into Ulaanbaatar. RGASPI/17/166/543/32–33. Cf. also *Japan-Manchoukuo Year Book*, 711–712; Cui, *Haila'er*, 2:172–175. A vivid description of the negotiations is given by Sorge, *Mandschukuo*, 132–136.

156. Manchukuo soldiers were said to have provoked a violent encounter with Soviet border guards near Manzhouli on 12 October 1935. Moscow's highest political circles debated this incident. RGASPI/558/11/92/33, 37, 39, 46–50. For the failed Soviet-Japanese diplomatic negotiations on the Manchukuo-Mongolian border issue between 1932 and 1939, see Luzianin, "Diplomaticheskaia istoriia," 41–51; *Japan-Manchoukuo Year Book*, 715–717. Talks resumed in 1939, Waijiao bu, *Dang'an*, 260–265.

157. It was even decided by the Communist Party of the Soviet Union's Central Committee whether or not the corpse of a single Manchukuo police officer, shot by Soviet border guards, should be returned to the Manchukuo authorities. RGASPI/17/166/575/5.

158. The so-called Zhanggufeng Incident (Chōkohō Jiken), where the Soviet performance, for an army that had just undergone drastic purging, was surprisingly good. See, e.g., Erickson, *Command*, 492–499; Coox, *Nomonhan*, 1:120–141.

159. Casualty estimates vary widely. According to a recent study by Russian historian Tat'iana S. Bushueva, casualties during the Khalkhyn-Gol clashes on the Soviet side were 9,695 dead or missing and 15,521 wounded. On the Japanese side, the number of victims was even higher, with about 25,000 dead and 36,000 wounded or prisoners of war. Bushueva, "Khalkhin-Gol," 41–47. For the history and consequences of this battle in general, see the works by Coox, *Nomonhan*, on the course of war esp. 1:200–590, 2:663–919 and Goldman, *Nomonhan*.

160. Cf. Namsaraeva, "States," 416–419.

161. Cf. Moore, *Policy*, 200–201, for the exact wording. On Soviet-Japanese negotiations after Khalkhyn-Gol, see Elleman, "Consolidation," 126–129. Cf. also Lensen, *Neutrality* and Krebs, "Japan."

162. Moscow experienced a reversal in relations not just with China but also with Britain. This setback fueled fears that Western powers, too, were attempting to isolate, weaken, and destroy the Soviet state, inspiring a crudely manipulated war-scare campaign that swept the Soviet Union. Sontag, "Soviet," 66–77. Cf. Hughes, *Stalin*, 117–119, on the "war scare" and its local factors in Siberia.

163. For borders as ambiguous symbols in Soviet mass consciousness, see Guseinov, *Karta*, esp. chaps. 2–4; Günther, "Motherland," 77–92; and Dobrenko, "Navigation," esp. 185–188.

164. Cf. Fitzpatrick, *Stalinism*, 71–75.

165. Kostarev, *Granitsa*, quotations on 5, 18.

166. The first edition had a circulation of only 7,100 copies, but numerous editions followed, the second already in 1931 in Kostarev, *Dnevniki*, 235–316.

167. Peshkov, "Politicisation," esp. 173–177; Peshkov, "Shadow."

168. To name just three Manchukuo and Soviet examples: "24 intsidenta na granitse," *Rupor*, 22 August 1934, 2; "Obstrel sovetskikh pogranichnikov s Manchzhurskoi storony," *Otpor*, 22 December 1934, 4; "Protest polpreda SSSR v Tokio tov. Iureneva protiv novykh narushenii sovetskoi granitsy," *Otpor*, 4 July 1935, 3.

169. Japanese and Manchukuo publishers issued numerous English-language pamphlets on the theme. Cf., e.g., Hidaka, *Issues*; Foreign Affairs Association of Japan, *Questions*.

170. See, e.g., Peter Paul Devlin, "Japan Is Headed for Military Doom!," *Los Angeles Times*, 1 April 1934, G12.

171. *Nomonhan Incident*, 1–13, quotation on 13.

172. Cf. the "diary" of Reuters' representative Maurice D'Alton and the account of Johann Newel, a newspaperman of the *Deutsche Allgemeine Zeitung*, in *Nomonhan Incident*, 31–47.

173. Hidaka, *Issues*, 5–6. See similar statistics in the Japanese-controlled Russian Harbin press, e.g., "Sinodik sovetskikh bezzakonii na granitse," *Kharbinskoe Vremia*, 7 September 1935, 4. Cf. Hidaka, *Issues*, 98–105, for a complete list of border violations allegedly done by the Soviet military along the western border section between 1932 and 1938.

174. Alleged attacks by Soviet troops on Japanese patrols were the favorite theme of often page-long articles in the Russian-language papers. Just to mention a few: "Narushenie

suvereniteta Man'chzhu-Ti-Go," *Kharbinskoe Vremia*, 13 June 1935, 4; "Boi s krasnoarmeitsami," *Kharbinskoe Vremia*, 15 October 1935, 2; "Granitsy, mezhdunarodnye zakony—ne dlia Bol'shevikov!" *Zaria*, 17 October 1936, 4; "Krovavoe stolknovenie na granitse Man'chzhu-Di-Go i SSSR," *Zaria*, 6 April 1939, 1. From the mid-1930s onward, Manchukuo's Chinese-language papers ran similar stories. *Binjiang Shibao* reported every week on Soviet incursions, such as illegal border crossings of Soviet troops, e.g., "Dui Sulian bufa yuejing shijian," *Binjiang Shibao*, 11 September 1934, 3; aerial incursions: "Guanyu Manzhouli Sulian feiji yuejing shijian. Zhenxiang dabai yuanman jiejue," *Binjiang Shibao*, 3 October 1934, 2; kidnappings committed by Soviet men in uniform on Manchukuo territory: "Manzhouli beifang fujin. Sulian yuejing bang qu Eren," *Binjiang Shibao*, 7 May 1936, 3; shootouts between Red Army and Manchukuo troops: "Sulian bing bufa yuejing shijian. Waijiao dangju tichu kangyi," *Binjiang Shibao*, 4 February 1937, 2; or the paper simply made listings of alleged Soviet border violations: "Zui jin sange yue lai Man Su guojing fangmian. Sulian bufa shijian zhi diaochao," *Binjiang Shibao*, 7 March 1935, 2.

175. For Manchukuo propaganda among Manchukuo's Russian community, see the early analysis by British newspaper correspondent Holmes, *Eye-Witness*, 41–48, quotation on 46.

176. E.g., a Soviet analysis of Manchukuo propaganda aimed for internal use only by Kara-Murza, *Poriadok*, pt. 2, 10–13.

177. In 1938, the number of regular radio listeners in the Soviet Union exceeded twenty million people. On the role of radio in the Soviet Union during the 1930s, see Schlögel, *Terror*, 289–295. The Manchukuo propaganda in the Soviet border areas is outlined in United States, *Intelligence Planning*, 87–95.

178. RGVA/25871/2/486/78.

179. GAKhK/R-830/1/189/105–110, here 105–106.

180. Original sources remain vague, however. The newspaper *Otpor* (Repulse), mouthpiece of the Political Department of Transbaikal Railroad, "translated" various texts. For plans of Japanese military aggression, see, e.g., for "Gazeta 'Simbun' o voennykh planakh Iaponii," *Otpor*, 20 March 1934, 4; "Kak my budem voevat'," *Otpor*, 1 August 1934, 3. For false propaganda to discredit the Soviet Union, see, e.g., "Novaia antisovetskaia kampaniia v manchzhuro-iaponskoi presse," *Otpor*, 15 August 1934, 4; "Krushenie poezda na KVZhD ispol'zuetsia dlia novoi antisovetskoi kampanii," *Otpor*, 8 September 1934, 4.

181. U.S. Department of State, *Conditions*, 28.

182. "Po radio mozhno slushat' tol'ko stantsii Man'chzhu-Di-Go, Nippon i Korei," *Zaria*, 22 November 1937, 5.

183. The heroic myth was already constructed during the conflict. See, e.g., the semiautobiographical recollections of Dmitrii A. Bakaev, who fought in both clashes, published in 1984. Bakaev, *V ogne*, 143. 15 February and 28 May, respectively, had been declared the Day of the Border Guard and were celebrated annually in the Soviet Union.

Chapter 6: Staging Friendship at the Barbed-Wire Fence

1. For the 1945 Soviet operation in Manchuria, the two volumes of pure military history by David M. Glantz: Glantz, *Soviet Operational and Tactical Combat*; Glantz, *Soviet Strategic Offensive*. For a popular Chinese perspective on the Soviet campaign and the defeat of the Japanese Guandong Army with a focus on Hulunbeir, Cui, Haila'er, 2:259–297 passim.

2. "Iaponskogo agressora zhdet besslavnyi konets," *Otpor*, 12 August 1945, 1; "Operativnaia svodka za 10 avgusta," *Otpor*, 12 August 1945, 1; "Na prifrontovoi stantsii," *Otpor*, 3 September 1945, 2; "Siuda prishli russkie . . . ," *Otpor*, 3 September 1945, 2. In 1951, just two Japanese residents were listed in the Manzhouli census. *Manzhouli shi zhi*, table on 219. For the Soviet "liberation" of Hailar, Ren, "1945," 54–61.

3. GAKhK/R-830/2/64/89–90, quotations on 89.

4. The Khori Buriats, who had fled from the Aga Steppe in Transbaikalia to Shenekhen region in Hulunbeir during the Russian Civil War, seem to have fared the worst among the émigrés from the Russian Empire. Cf. Sneath, *Mongolia*, 15.

5. *Zhonggong Manzhouli shi difang jian shi*, 16–25. On the origins of the Sino-Soviet alliance, e.g., Niu, "Origins," 47–89 passim.

6. On both sides there were reverberations from the war: a food supply in crisis and millions of men demobilized for whom neither jobs nor homes existed. For consequences of the Great Patriotic War in the postwar Soviet Union, Zubkova, *Russia*, esp. 11–50. On the social and economic impact of the Civil War in China, see Lary, *China*, passim.

7. Zubkova, *Russia*, esp. 151–170. Yet people still did fear saying the wrong thing and being the wrong category of person. Having a relative was also enough to get someone thrown out of the job or home. Gessen, *Babushkas*, 185–244 passim.

8. The treaty provided China with economic aid and security guarantees, but the Chinese delegation failed to restore sovereignty in Outer Mongolia and was forced to grant the Soviets temporary military and economic concessions in Manchuria and Xinjiang. For the alliance period, Westad, "Introduction," 1–46 passim. On the assistance of Soviet experts in China's struggle toward socialist modernity, Westad, "Struggles," 35–57 passim.

9. Shen and Li, *Leaning*, 138–140.

10. After 1945 the basic goals and assumptions of the Soviet control regime changed very little, even along borders with socialist states. Cf. Chandler, *Institutions*, 80–89.

11. *Manzhouli zhan zhi*, 53–54. For the negotiations around the Chinese Changchun Railroad's return and its impact on bilateral relations, Zhang, "Causes"; and Zhang, "Return."

12. Freight and passenger traffic along a new railroad link via Ulaanbaatar began on New Year's Day of 1956, thereby reducing the traveling distance between Moscow and Beijing by 1,141 kilometers. Yet the Trans-Manchurian Railroad and the twin border city Otpor-Manzhouli did not lose their significance even after the Trans-Mongolian Railroad had been completed. Petrov, "Railway."

13. *Manzhouli shi zhi*, table on 54.

14. For the "Resist America Support Korea" and other political campaigns of the 1950s and their impact on the border city of Manzhouli, *Manzhouli shi zhi*, 125–128.

15. On the specifics of the Chita region border districts, GAChO/P-3/4/1224/1–27, esp. 1–6. For a general structural economic analysis of the Soviet Far East of the first two postwar decades, Kirby, "Far East."

16. GARF/A-385/17/2251/2–3; GARF/A-385/17/2619/12.

17. GAChO/P-3/4/2354/9–17, here 16–17.

18. GAChO/P-3/4/1665/35–39; GAChO/P-3/4/2354/1–7, here 2–3.

19. GAChO/P-1710/1/32/16–31, here 31.

20. Interviews Valentina V. Kozlova (quotation); Iurii I. Kozlov; Zolotareva.

21. GARF/A-385/17/2399/2 (quotation), 9, 11.

22. GARF/R-7523/85/354/2–4, 6 (quotation).

23. Interviews Valentina V. Kozlova; Iurii I. Kozlov.

24. GARF/A-385/17/3385/2.

25. Interviews Valentina V. Kozlova; Iurii I. Kozlov.

26. This pronouncement was made, for instance, by Khrushchev in a speech at Leipzig in March 1959. Cf. "Rech' tovarishcha N. S. Khrushcheva," *Pravda*, 27 March 1959, 1–3, quotation on 2.

27. *Manzhouli zhan zhi*, 55; *Hulunbei'er meng waishi zhi*, 76–77; *Manzhouli shi zhi*, 217–219 (esp. table on 219) and 227–228; interview Zolotareva.

28. Semenov, *Tri goda*, 25.

29. "Novyi grafik dvizhenia poezdov," in *Otpor*, 10 May 1950, 1; *Manzhouli zhan zhi*, 159–160; RGANI/5/30/66/10–11.

30. "Poezd Pekin-Moskva," *Zabaikal'skii Rabochii*, 4 February 1954, 1 and "Poezd idet iz Pe-kina," *Zabaikal'skii Rabochii*, 5 February 1954, 3. Cf. also "Beijing-Mosike shouci zhida keche jinru Sulian guojing," *Renmin Ribao*, 4 February 1954, 2; "Zai Beijing-Mosike zhida keche shang," *Renmin Ribao*, 14 February 1954, 2.

31. By 1957, over 50 percent of China's foreign commerce was with the Soviet Union, while China's share in the overall total foreign trade of the Soviet Union was about one-fourth. For Sino-Soviet economic ties during the alliance period, e.g., Shu, "Cooperation," 189–225 passim; Scott, "Trade."

32. *Manzhouli shi zhi*, 125.

33. *Manzhouli zhan zhi*, 129–131 and tables on 137–140.

34. "Bol'she vnimaniia stantsii Otpor!," *Otpor*, 11 April 1951, 2.

35. GARF/R-8300/22/1090/4–9, here 4–6.

36. E.g., GAChO/P-3/4/2354/23–35; GAChO/P-1710/1/32/1–15, here 3; GAChO/P-1710/1/37/10–26, here 21.

37. Larin, *Otnosheniia*, 212.

38. As early as October 1945, the first cases of smuggling by Otpor rail and postal workers went on record. GAChO/R-1243/2/219/98.

39. E.g., GAChO/R-1243/2/237/50–51, 90–91, 206–208, 210, 213; GAChO/R-1243/2/276/3–6, 32, 37, 51, 67–68, 136, 155, 216; GAChO/R-1243/2/289/54, 109–110, 209, 260; GAChO/P-3945/1/1/37–40.

40. Transbaikal Railroad conductors and engine drivers who regularly commuted to Man-zhouli supplied employees in Borzia, Otpor, or elsewhere who were not allowed to travel with cognac, vodka, or pairs of shoes. GAChO/R-1243/2/242/20–210b., 23–24, 27–29, 61, 198, 221–222.

41. Between October 1958 and October 1959 Otpor customs discovered forty-six cases of smuggling, with a net loss of 82.321 rubles. In the following years the number of smuggling offenses declined further. GAChO/P-3945/1/18/31–34, 62–64.

42. Kapuściński, *Imperium*, 23.

43. Soviet-Chinese Friendship Societies were set up in major cities of the Soviet Far East, such as in Khabarovsk in 1958. These societies ratified twinning agreements with Chinese partner organizations. Frolov, "Razvitie," 114–118. Cf. Jersild, *Alliance*, 179–182, for the establishment of friendship societies in China after 1945.

44. On Soviet postwar presence in Dalian, Hess, "Brother." After 1949 the existing network of Sino-Soviet Friendship Societies in China was expanded further. For Hulunbeir, *Hulunbei'er meng waishi zhi*, 15–21.

45. GARF/R-5283/18/58/35–36.

46. GARF/R-5283/18/72/55–57, 126–127.

47. Xu, "Youyi gong," 217–219.

48. GARF/R-5283/18/72/81–82, 86–87 and 250–272, here 251, 254, 265–266.

49. GARF/R-5283/18/62/15–17.

50. Until the mid-1950s *Renmin Ribao*, like other papers, ran numerous stories that included the Otpor-Manzhouli border-crossing theme. E.g., "Sulian dianying yishu gongzuozhe daibiaotuan li Manzhouli fanhui Mosike," *Renmin Ribao*, 3 January 1953, 4; "Sulian hongqi gewutuan huiguo," *Renmin Ribao*, 12 January 1953, 1; "Baojialiya renminjun gewutuan daoda Manzhouli," *Renmin Ribao*, 1 September 1954, 1; and "Nansilafu 'keluo' minjian gewutuan guo Manzhouli lai jing," *Renmin Ribao*, 27 August 1955, 1, which all, like numerous further articles, report the greeting of Soviet and other foreign delegations at Manzhouli.

51. "Moskva–Pekin," *Pravda*, 10 February 1953, 3.

52. "Sulian yishu kexue gongzuozhe daibiaotuan he Sujun hongqi gewutuan di Manzhouli," *Renmin Ribao*, 1 November 1952, 1.

53. Interview Valentina V. Kozlova. Cf. also "Zaijian le, Sulian pengyoumen," *Gongren Ribao*, 4 February 1960, 1.

54. E.g., Wu, "Yinxiang," 12; Zuo, *Guojia*, 1–2; Zhong Su youhao xiehui zonghui, *Biji*, 3.

55. For the Soviet Far East, Frolov, "Razvitie," 81–107 passim.

56. "Shi E'erguna he wei liangguo fuwu," *Renmin Ribao*, 26 May 1957, 1.

57. "Heilongjiang jiang wei Su Zhong liang guo renmin fuwu," *Renmin Ribao*, 17 October 1956, 1; "Zai Zhong Su youyi jiaoliu de Heilongjiang shang," *Renmin Ribao*, 7 November 1956, 4.

58. GAChO/P-3/7/243/20. Earlier, in 1957, Soviet planes had saved a Chinese village from flooding. "E'erguna hepan de youyi," *Renmin Ribao*, 28 October 1957, 2.

59. GAChO/P-3/7/700/1–3, 9–16.

60. They numbered between eighteen and thirty. *Manzhouli zhan zhi*, 239–240; *Haila'er tielu fenju zhi*, 195; interview Zolotareva.

61. "Russkii s kitaitsem—brat'ia navek!" *Leninskii Put'*, 1 October 1959, 2. Similar reports appeared in Chinese newspapers. Under the florid headline "The Sino-Soviet Friendship Is Deeper Than the Sea" the national *Gongren Ribao* (Workers' Daily), for instance, devoted a whole page to the friendship between the people of Manzhouli and Zabaikalsk as late as February 1960: "Zhong Su youyi bi hai shen. Bianjing renmin xin lian xin," *Gongren Ribao*, 13 February 1960, 4.

62. In 1960, for instance, five meetings with participants from both railroads were held in Manzhouli and Zabaikalsk. GAChO/P-3/7/541/1–5.

63. "E'erguna hepan de youyi," *Renmin Ribao*, 28 October 1957, 2.

64. 1956: 98, 1957: 80, first half of 1958: 36 tourists. GAChO/P-3/7/239/20–21.

65. E.g., GAChO/P-3/7/243/21–22, 44–47. Cf. also *Manzhouli shi zhi*, 221–223.

66. Interview Zolotareva.

67. Interviews Iurii I. Kozlov (quotation); Valentina V. Kozlova. Though the Kozlovs spent more than half a century in Zabaikalsk, at the time of my interview they had never been to nearby Manzhouli, even after the border reopened in the late 1980s.

68. GAChO/P-3/7/243/32–41, quotations on 34 and 39.

69. "Zhong Su liang guo qingnian de youyi huaduo zai shengkai," *Neimenggu Ribao*, 16 October 1958, 3.

70. GAChO/P-3/7/243/40–41, quotation on 40.

71. Interviews Iakimov (quotation) and Qu. Cf. also Perminov, *Nakazanie*, passim; *Hulunbei'er meng waishi zhi*, 87–89; Argudiaeva, "Naselenie," 133; Zhernakov, *Trekhrech'e*, 4; *E'erguna youqi zhi*, 665–667. Cf. Ablazhei, *Vostok*, 150–231 passim, for a general overview of the repatriation of Russian emigrants to the Soviet Union after 1945.

72. *Hulunbei'er gong'an bianfang zhilüe*, 170–172.

73. Interview Sokolov.

74. Interview Yang.

75. Interview Sokolov.

76. RGASPI/17/128/1118/2–10; Atwood, "Diplomacy," 137–161 passim; Siri, "Hulunbei'er"; Wolff, "Border-Making," 281–290.

77. Bulag, "Mongolia," esp. 93–95.

78. Yanjing, *Neimenggu*, on interethnic relations before and after 1945, 130–138. For an excellent study of the integration and distinction of Mongols in the People's Republic of China, see Bulag, *Mongols*.

79. On post-1949 Chinese religious policy in Inner Mongolia, Sneath, *Mongolia*, 67–70.

80. "Cong yuanshi gongshe dao renmin gongshe," *Neimenggu Ribao*, 14 October 1960, 3 (quotation); Sneath, *Mongolia*, 70–96 passim; Clubb, *Development Programs*, 38–43; The local press praised the "success" of denomadization. E.g., "Ewenke zu zhubu zouxiang dingju," *Hulunbei'er Ribao*, 3 September 1957, 1.

Chapter 7: Invisible Enemies across the Frozen River

1. Kapuściński, *Imperium*, 21–26, quotation on 21–22.

2. Recent scholarship argues for seeing the collapse of the alliance as grounded in both ideology and clashing state interests. Important works up to the mid-1960s are Lüthi, *Split*, which focuses more on the Chinese side; and Radchenko, *Suns*, which privileges the Soviet side.

3. Lüthi, *Split*, 174–180.

4. More particularly, it precipitated a mass exodus of Kazak, Uigur, and other ethnic minority people from the Chinese borderland. Recent Chinese scholarship argues that this incident was provoked by profound Soviet influence in Xinjiang. Shen and Li, *Leaning*, 167–195 passim.

5. Wemheuer, *Famine*, 51–52.

6. Lüthi, *Split*, esp. 224–228, 246–260, 285–301.

7. For an overview of the views of Russian and Chinese researchers on the causes responsible for the conflict, Goldstein, "Island" and Robinson, "China," 261–265. For a sound account, based predominantly on Chinese sources, Yang, "Clash," 21–49, esp. 22.

8. The Chinese government pursued a dual strategy, making pragmatic offers on border issues while at the same time engaging in ideological polemics against Moscow's designs in the "disputed territories." Lüthi, *Split*, 275–277.

9. Chen, *China*, 238–276.

10. On Sino-Soviet border negotiations, Robinson, "China," 265–291 passim and Wishnick, *Fences*, esp. 37–48. For a contemporary Soviet account of attempts to settle the border, Prokhorov, *K voprosu*, 229–245.

11. For cases of serious infringement, the use of firearms was now expressly permitted in the border zone. GAAO/R-114/2/1311/14–19; GAAO/R-114/2/1718/29–36. On 5 August 1960 the Soviet Union Council of Ministers adopted an even more comprehensive border zone regime applying to residents, visitors, and laborers in the restricted zone adjoining nonallied neighbor states, esp. China. GAAO/R-114/2/1485/75–87. Cf. also Frolov, "Razvitie," 174–175.

12. E.g., "O sobliudenii pogranichnogo rezhima v zapretnoi pogranichnoi zone Chitinskoi oblasti," *Leninskii Put'*, 31 May 1956, 4. On sensitive matters, local authorities notified locals door-to-door. GAAO/R-114/2/2237/74–75, here 75.

13. Khinganskii Krasnoznamennyi pogranichnyi otriad, *80 let*, 79 and GAAO/R-114/2/2237/74–75, here 74.

14. Interview with Iurii I. Kozlov (quotation) and Valentina V. Kozlova.

15. GAAO/R-114/2/2237/74–83, here 74 and interview Mashukova.

16. *Hulunbei'er gong'an bianfang zhilüe*, 19, 135, 138, 172–176.

17. Ibid., 158–162. On the establishment and functions of the people's militia and the military police in Hulunbeir, *Hulunbei'er meng zhi*, 685–694; GAChO/P-3/27/51/1–30, here 9.

18. Khinganskii Krasnoznamennyi pogranichnyi otriad, *80 let*, 77–80; *Hulunbei'er gong'an bianfang zhilüe*, 54–55.

19. Robinson, "China," 291–301 (esp. the table on 299); Lüthi, *Split*, 340.

20. Kirby, "Far East," 77 and interview Sushkina.

21. Interview Zolotareva. Vasilii M. Iakimov and Klavdiia M. Sushkina had similar memories of the situation after the March 1969 events in Abagaitui. Interviews Iakimov and Sushkina.

22. *Hulunbei'er gong'an bianfang zhilüe*, table on 156–157.

23. These and other incidents are documented in Khinganskii Krasnoznamennyi pogranichnyi otriad, *80 let*, 84–86.

24. Accidental border crossings by foreigners in China were to be punished more leniently, while intentional border crossings were to be prosecuted to the full rigor of the law. *Hulunbei'er gong'an bianfang zhilüe*, 162–163, 168.

25. Cf. the tables on Soviet and Mongolian border violators in ibid., 164–167.

26. Ibid., 153–155. Already in 1957 the Chinse had erected a similar fence on this disputed territory, but removed the barrier after Soviet protests. *Manzhouli shi zhi*, 209.

27. GAChO/P-3/27/51/12, 36 and GAChO/P-3/36/72/4–8, here 5–6.

28. GAChO/P-3/27/51/68–74, quotations on 68–69.

29. GAChO/P-3/36/72/128–133, here 128–129.

30. Khinganskii Krasnoznamennyi pogranichnyi otriad, *80 let*, 87–89.

31. Members of the Soviet agricultural brigades repeatedly violated the border regime during the annual harvest in Mongolia. Conversely, Mongols violated border regulations allowing them to travel within a hundred-kilometer zone on Soviet territory in the vicinity of the Aga Steppe. GAChO/P-3/36/72/128–133, here 131–132, quotation on 132. Some of the restrictions were relaxed in the late 1960s, however, to increase Soviet-Mongolian cooperation in agriculture. GARF/A-612/1/112/28, 43–45, 89–93, 99–100.

32. GAChO/P-3/36/72/137–140 and 141–146, here 141.

33. GAChO/P-3/27/51/30–35, here 34; Federal'naia Sluzhba Bezopasnosti, *Pogranichnaia Sluzhba Rossii*, 418–419.

34. GAChO/P-3/36/72/119–122, here 120. Cf. also "My zhivem v pogranich'e," *Zabaikal'ets*, 15 November 1977, 3.

35. Interview Mashukova.

36. GAChO/P-3/27/51/35–40, here 37–38.

37. GAChO/P-3/36/72/141–146, here 143–146; Khinganskii Krasnoznamennyi pogranich-nyi otriad, *80 let*, 92.

38. GAChO/P-1710/1/58/6–7.

39. In Shelopuginsk district to the east of the Transbaikal region, for instance, the number of violations in 1978 was fifteen times lower than in 1969. GAChO/P-3/36/72/141–146, here 143. Similar reductions were achieved in other border districts. GAChO/P-3/36/72/76–77, 104–107 passim.

40. "Moglo byt' i luchshe. Vtoraia raionnaia konferentsiia DOSAAF," *Zabaikal'ets*, 16 January 1969, 4; "Vyigrala druzhba," *Zabaikal'ets*, 2 June 1984, 3; GAChO/P-3/36/72/90–91.

41. Interview Mashukova.

42. For an official narration of cooperation between the military and civilian borderlanders during the 1970s, Dvornichenko, *Na strazhe*, 194–209 passim, quotation on 195.

43. GAChO/P-6748/3/7/1–59, here 54–59, quotation on 55.

44. Population figures are for 1978, cf. GAChO/P-3/36/83/1–2, here 2.

45. GAChO/P-3/27/51/1–30, here 12.

46. GAChO/P-3/32/10/1–4, here 3.

47. Form and impact of such policies in the Soviet Far East are discussed in Kravchuk and Motrich, "Potentsial."

48. Wishnick, *Fences*, 49–50, 66–68.

49. E.g., 40 percent for workers in the livestock industry. GAChO/P-3/32/10/91–93.

50. Ibid., 5–16 and GAChO/P-3/36/83/1–2. In an interview for the local paper in June 1976, Zabaikalsk's chief planner Valerii E. Logunov euphorically envisioned the bright future of the border settlement. "Zabaikal'sk v budushchem," *Zabaikal'ets*, 10 June 1976, 2.

51. In the late 1960s and early 1970s, major roads were paved, two parks were refurbished, and residential houses and the outdoor cinema Dauriia were built. Cf. "Trebovat', dobyvat'sia," *Zabaikal'ets*, 13 May 1969, 2; "Khorosheet nash poselok," *Zabaikal'ets*, 4 June 1974, 2. In the mid-1970s, however, construction stagnated, blackouts were frequent, and residents waited for a swimming pool in vain. GAChO/R-2610/1/148/94–97, here 94–96; GAChO/P-1710/1/46/14–19, here 16; GAChO/P-1710/1/56/68–74, here 68.

52. All nine state farms and two collective farms in Zabaikalsk district suffered shortages of labor. E.g., "K nam, v Zabaikal'skii raion," *Zabaikal'ets*, 12 December 1967, 2; "My zhdem Vas, druz'ia," *Zabaikal'ets*, 23 November 1968, 2; "Priezzhaite zhit' i rabotat'," *Zabaikal'ets*, 14 September 1974, 2; "Priezzhaite v Zabaikal'e," *Zabaikal'ets*, 25 September 1982, 2.

53. For instance, the letter to the editor by the retired villager A. Gorshnov: "Zagliadyvaia vpered," *Zabaikal'ets*, 3 June 1969, 3.

54. "Priglashaem zemliakov," *Zabaikal'ets*, 25 September 1982, 3.

55. GAChO/P-3/32/10/1–4, here 3–4.

56. According to official pronouncements, 369 families had moved to villages in Zabaikalsk district in 1967–1969 and 593 families in 1971–1973. Newspapers however omitted those families who had left the district in the meantime. "Priglashaem, zhdem," *Zabaikal'ets*, 25 December 1969, 2; "Priglashaem zhit' v Zabaikal'e," *Zabaikal'ets*, 28 July 1973, 2.

57. Sneath, *Mongolia*, 102–125 passim.

58. Ibid., 96–101; Pasternak and Salaff, *Cowboys*, 14–15. On the demographic, cultural, and economic transformation of whole Inner Mongolia during the post-1949 period, Hurelbaatar, "Survey," 191–222 passim; Li, "Migration," 503–538 passim.

59. Pasternak and Salaff, *Cowboys*, 144–148, quotation on 147.

60. Xu, "Youyi gong," 219. Railroad employees caused most delays in international passenger traffic, by accident. E.g., GAChO/R-2610/1/134/93–94. Cf. *Zhonggong Manzhouli shi difang jian shi*, 119–143, for the impact of the Cultural Revolution on Manzhouli.

61. In 1970 and 1971, 97 percent of all international travelers were either Vietnamese or North Korean. Whereas the Vietnamese prevailed between 1970 and 1977, the share of North Koreans grew sharply, to about two-thirds of all passengers during 1979 and 1982. This increase was mainly due to the decline of Vietnamese travelers as relations between Hanoi and Beijing had deteriorated following the Vietnamese invasion of Cambodia and then after China's response, a punitive expedition.

62. Figures for exit and entry of railroad passengers on international trains no. 17 (Beijing-Moscow) and no. 18 (Moscow-Beijing), as well as on special trains for Vietnamese nationals between 1966 and 1982, are listed in the annual reports of the Transbaikal Railroad Administration on the operation of Zabaikalsk station. GAChO/R-604/25/88/1–3 (1966); GAChO/R-604/25/93/1 (1967); GAChO/R-604/25/102/1 (1968); GAChO/R-604/25/112/1, 6 (1969 and 1970); GAChO/R-604/25/136/2 (1971); GAChO/R-604/25/155/7 (1972); GAChO/R-604/25/166/6–7 (1973); GAChO/R-604/25/190/7–8 (1974); GAChO/R-604/25/214/5 (1975); GAChO/R-604/25/242/4–5 (1976); GAChO/R-604/25/263/6–7 (1977); GAChO/R-604/25/289/4–5 (1978); GAChO/R-604/25/298/6 (1979); GAChO/R-604/25/313/6 (1980); GAChO/R-604/25/334/4 (1981); GAChO/R-604/25/355/4 (1982).

63. GAChO/R-604/25/166/1–7, here 2.

64. Xu, "Aotebao'er," 133–134.

65. Gatti, *Sibérie*, 68; "Vokzaly—bliznetsy," *Zabaikal'skaia Magistral'*, 6 August 1988, 3.

66. GARF/R-8300/12/2309/249–263, here 252–254; GARF/R-8300/22/1090/65–67, here 65.

67. GAChO/P-1710/1/39/61–63; Fedotov, *Polveka*, 8.

68. GAChO/R-604/25/88/1–6, here 3, 10; GAChO/R-604/25/102/6–9, here 8; GAChO/R-604/25/121/1–5, here 4.

69. GAChO/R-604/25/93/1–3, here 2; GAChO/R-604/25/102/6–9, here 6 and 10–12, here 10–11.

70. GAChO/R-604/25/88/7–11, here 8; GAChO/R-604/25/121/1–5, here 3; GAChO/R-604/25/289/1–11, here 3; GAChO/R-604/25/102/1–5, here 4; GAChO/R-604/25/112/1–5, here 3–4. Conductors on the Beijing-Moscow were instructed on the peculiarities in handling international passengers and norms of behavior during their stay abroad. GAChO/R-604/25/214/2–4, here 3.

71. GAChO/R-604/25/112/1–5; GAChO/R-604/25/155/16–21, here 17; GAChO/R-604/25/190/1–6.

72. The Transbaikal Railroad annual report on the work the Zabaikalsk station of 1969 does not devote a word to the clashes in March on the Ussuri. GAChO/R-604/25/112/1–5. Subsequent reports also refer to the conflict, if at all, only between the lines.

73. GAChO/R-604/25/136/1–12, here 7.

74. GAChO/R-604/25/190/9–14, esp. 10.

75. GAChO/R-604/25/155/16–21, here 16–18; "S sessii possoveta. V kotoryi raz," *Zabaikal'ets,* 27 August 1968, 2; "Ser'eznyi razgovor," *Zabaikal'ets,* 21 October 1967, 1.

76. Though food shortages began to assume critical proportions during the three bitter years of the Great Leap Forward, Manzhouli's railroad workers provided proper standards of hospitality at regular meetings with delegations from Zabaikalsk. Soviet receptions of Chinese railroad men at Zabaikalsk were usually less opulent. GAChO/P-1710/1/42/1–6, here 5 and 43–50, here 48–50. At least as late as 1964, the majority of Chinese workers in the Chinese dormitory in Zabaikalsk were "maintaining good relations" with the local Soviet residents. GAChO/P-1710/1/45/60–64, quotation on 61.

77. Locals in Manzhouli, who had been greeting Soviet railroad employees with a smile, were now turning away their heads. Cf. interview Zolotareva.

78. See table 6.1 on annual international cargo shipment through Manzhouli. In spite of the bilateral conflict, the transport of Soviet aid and military equipment from the Soviet Union through China to North Vietnam continued. That is yet another indication that Beijing and Moscow could prove practical and strategic in their efforts to pursue diverse goals. Cf. Li, "Dispute," 304–311. In contrast to the international passenger service, cross-border freight traffic met difficulties more frequently, often caused by coordination problems and conflicts between the railroad companies or border guard agencies of the two countries. Cf. GAChO/P-1710/1/58/6–7, 23–24; GAChO/P-1710/1/45/60–64, here 60; GAChO/P-6748/3/6/2–40, here 4.

79. Number of employees for 1968. Cf. "Nashi veterany," *Zabaikal'ets,* 3 August 1968, 2.

80. Interview Zolotareva.

81. Ibid. Other incidents at the Manzhouli-Zabaikalsk railroad crossing during the Sino-Soviet rift are listed in *Hulunbei'er meng waishi zhi,* 58–60 and GAChO/P-3/27/51/41–42.

82. Cf. GAChO/P-1710/1/45/36–45, here 37–39 for the civil protection exercise.

83. GAChO/P-3/23/8/8–10, quotations on 9–10.

84. Throughout the Sino-Soviet split, the Chinese press widely reported on those ceremonies. E.g., *Renmin Ribao,* 24 February 1972, 3; 24 February 1973, 4; 24 February 1974, 2; 24 February 1975, 4; 4 September 1975, 2.

85. GAChO/P-3/29/8/1–2. Cf. also *Manzhouli zhan zhi,* 254–255.

86. Urbansky, "Foe," 271–275.

87. E.g., by portraying the indomitable spirit of Manzhouli's inhabitants and their vanguard role in fighting Russian and Soviet imperialism. "Fanxiu biancheng chuangxin pian," *Hulunbei'er Ribao,* 4 February 1968, 4.

88. Two examples are "Dadao xin shahuang!," *Heilongjiang Ribao,* 4 March 1969, 1 and *Doloi novykh tsarei!* In particular the domestic propaganda was quite effective in the mobilization of the masses. Mehnert, "Schüsse," 550–552.

89. RGANI/5/61/27/50–54, quotation on 50.

90. It was screened about 1,200 times, reaching 145,000 viewers in the Chita region. GAChO/P-3/27/51/1–30, here 17–18.

91. For a detailed look at the ideas and themes emanating from Moscow and Beijing, König, "Rundfunkkrieg," 566–574.

92. Stephan, *East*, 282–284; "V odnom stroiu," *Zabaikal'ets*, 27 May 1978, 3.

93. "Geroi ostrova Damanskii," *Zabaikal'skaia Magistral'*, 20 March 1969, 4. Portrayals of the Soviet border guards in the local and regional papers continued and intensified in fervor over subsequent years. For instance, the series of articles "Pogranichnyi al'bom" by Valerii Berezin, *Zabaikal'ets*, 7 February 1974, 2; 9 February 1974, 4; 12 February 1974, 4; 14 February 1974, 4 and 16 February 1974, 4; "Zhivut i sluzhat na granitse," *Zabaikal'ets*, 27 May 1976, 2; "Vstrecha s pogranichnikami," *Zabaikal'ets*, 27 May 1978, 3; "Naslednik Karatsiupy," *Zabaikal'ets*, 13 October 1983, 2; "60 let na okhrane vostochnykh rubezhei," *Zabaikal'ets*, 9 March 1984, 2.

94. "My sluzhbu nesem na granitse," *Zabaikal'skaia Magistral'*, 29 March 1969, 4.

95. Cf. *Bol'shaia Sovetskaia Entsiklopediia*, 259.

96. "'Ne khochu po svoei zemle khodit' sognuvshis'," *Zabaikal'skii Rabochii*, 26 March 1969, 1, 3.

97. "Tvoi soldat, Rossiia," *Zabaikal'skii Rabochii*, 23 March 1969, 4.

98. "Nash zemliak—geroi Damanskogo," *Na Boevom Postu*, 23 March 1969, 3. On 3 April, in a special issue of the same newspaper devoted to the March events, the headmistress of the twenty-ninth high school of Chita praised its former pupil Sergei. "Nash geroi," *Na Boevom Postu*, 3 April 1969, 2. In October, Gladyshev was posthumously decorated with the medal for bravery, which his mother, head of a nursery school, received on his behalf in an official ceremony. "Medal' geroia," *Zabaikal'skii Rabochii*, 4 October 1969, 2.

99. Nikolai N. Petrov from Ulan Ude had been killed in combat on 2 March 1969. "On srazhalsia na Damanskom," *Na Boevom Postu*, 22 March 1969, 3.

100. The party administration of the district of Zabaikalsk printed its own newspaper. Four pages long, *Zabaikal'ets* appeared three times a week beginning on 27 June 1967.

101. "V polnyi golos," *Zabaikal'ets*, 11 March 1969, 1.

102. "Vstrecha s geroiami Damanskogo," *Zabaikal'ets*, 24 July 1969, 4; see also interview Zolotareva.

103. E.g., "Zaiavlenie pravitel'stva SSSR," *Zabaikal'ets*, 17 June 1969, 1–3; "Provokatory po-luchili otpor," *Zabaikal'ets*, 22 March 1969, 3; "Rubezhi rodiny sviashchenny," *Zabaikal'ets*, 3 April 1969, 4; and "Zabaikal'tsy—geroi Damanskogo," *Zabaikal'ets*, 17 April 1969, 2. Another central component of the regional coverage of China in 1969 was reprints drawn from national newspapers, TASS articles on crimes perpetrated against the Chinese people by the "Maoist clique," and news of military clashes with China occurring in places other than Damanskii Island. Urbansky, "Foe," 265–266.

104. "Vozvratilis' s pobedoi," *Zabaikal'ets*, 30 October 1969, 2.

105. E.g., "Vrazhdebnost' Pekina k sotsialisticheskomu sodruzhestvu," *Zabaikal'ets*, 11 September 1973, 2–3; "Psikhoz v Pekine," *Zabaikal'ets*, 11 September 1973, 4; "O podryvnoi deiatel'nosti maoistov," *Zabaikal'ets*, 5 March 1974, 4; "Kitai: Strana v likhoradke," *Zabaikal'ets*, 30 March 1976, 4.

106. Residents of Zabaikalsk could read *Leninskii Put'*, a newspaper first published in 1930 by the district administration of Borzia, to which Zabaikalsk belonged until 1966.

107. "Russkii s kitaitsem—brat'ia navek!," *Leninskii Put'*, 1 October 1959, 2.

108. "SSSR-KNR: sviazi rasshiriaiutsia," *Zabaikal'ets*, 26 July 1986, 3.

109. "Delegatsiia g. Man'chzhurii KNR v Zabaikal'skom raione," *Zabaikal'ets*, 13 September 1986, 1.

110. "Sem' dnei v Kitae," *Zabaikal'ets*, 28 August 1990, 3, 11 September 1990, 3, 25 September 1990, 3.

111. On the origins and expansion of Chinese and Soviet radio propaganda, Urbansky, "Foe," 267–268.

112. GAChO/P-3/27/51/1–30, here 9.

113. RGANI/89/46/14/1–3. Moscow responded by establishing a fourth radio channel, subsequently dedicated to providing the regions between Sverdlovsk (Ekaterinburg) and Chita with evening news. Cf. ibid., 8–11, here 8.

114. RGANI/5/55/20/23–26.

115. König, "Rundfunkkrieg," 561–562. In the mid-1980s, thirteen wide-range and eighty-one regional jamming stations shielded one-third of Soviet territory and more than one hundred million citizens from hostile radio bombardment. Cf. RGANI/89/18/105/1–2, here 1.

116. GAChO/P-6748/7/9/31.

117. GAChO/P-3/27/51/85.

118. Ibid., 13–14, quotation on 14.

119. On the history of television in China, Lull, *China*.

120. On the spread of television and television culture in the Soviet Union, Roth-Ey, "Home," here 281–282.

121. GAChO/P-3/27/51/32–33.

122. Interview Tarasov.

123. GAChO/P-3/27/51/15–16; cf. also "Na boevykh i trudovykh traditsiiakh," *Zabaikal'ets*, 14 June 1969, 1.

124. GAChO/P-3/19/126/61–64, here 61–63.

125. GAChO/P-3/27/51/30–32.

126. Ibid., 47–49, 50 (quotation) and 72–73.

127. Rupen, "Mongolia," 75–85, quotation on 75.

128. Sanders, "Mongolia," Brezhnev's quotation cited on 66.

129. There were about forty radio and television broadcasts on the twinning relations with Mongolia in Chita's regional media within eleven months in 1968. Cf. GAChO/P-3/10/441/31–34; GARF/A-612/1/112/25–27. Friendship activities intensified in subsequent years, cf., e.g., "Gosti iz MNR," *Zabaikal'skii Rabochii*, 6 August 1972, 1; "Vstrechi na zabaikal'skoi zemle," *Zabaikal'skii Rabochii*, 15 June 1973, 1; "Teplye vetry Mongolii," *Komsomolets Zabaikal'ia*, 1 May 1977, 4; "Nairamdal—druzhba," *Zabaikal'ets*, 29 October 1981, 3.

Chapter 8: Watermelons and Abandoned Watchtowers

1. Michael Weisskopf and Howard Simons, "Surreal Tranquility Prevails along Critical Border Section," *Los Angeles Times*, 1 April 1981, 6–7, quotation on 6.

2. One of the last of such fatal incidents in the Argun borderland occurred on 5 October 1980, near Olochi. "Nota posol'stvu KNR," *Pravda*, 10 October 1980, 4; "Sulian zai Zhong Su bianjing zhizao liuxue shijian de jingguo," *Renmin Ribao*, 18 October 1980, 1.

3. A first volleyball match between the teams of the two border stations was organized on 1 August 1982. GAChO/P-6748/20/10/2–11.

4. RGANI/89/43/13/2.

5. The jamming of broadcasts by the BBC, Voice of America, and other enemy stations was halted as well. RGANI/89/18/105/1–2.

6. For Sino-Soviet diplomatic relations, see Vámos, "Handshake," 80–97; Wishnick, *Fences*, 73–113; Zubok, "Policy," 265–279 passim; Zubok, "Soviet Union." By December 1992, the Soviet Union had withdrawn its forces from Mongolia completely. Radchenko, "Withdrawal." During the 1990s the number of armed forces along the Sino-Soviet border was reduced significantly. Wilson, *Partners*, 48–50.

7. Wishnick, *Fences*, 79. First delegations from Chita region had visited Hailar and Harbin as early as 1983. *Zabaikal'skii Rabochii*, 22 December 1987, 3.

8. Cf. chapter 7.

9. GAChO/P-6748/34/89/2–4, here 4. There were a total of twenty-three local subdivisions in the Soviet Union in 1986. GAChO/P-6748/34/193/4–8, here 4. For a brief official history of the Zabaikalsk branch, see "Otnosheniiam krepnut', razvivat'sia," *Zabaikal'ets*, 29 October 1987, 3.

10. GAChO/P-6748/34/89/9–10, 37, 41–43.

11. GAChO/P-6748/34/145/1–26, 29–32, 34–35, 42–43 (quotations on 20, 30, 42); GAChO/P-6748/34/193/9–12; "Gorod na granitse," *Pravda*, 29 May 1987, 5.

12. GARF/R-9576/20/5099/1–4, here 1; GAChO/P-6748/34/193/23–27; "Delegatsiia g. Man'chzhurii KNR v Zabaikal'skom raione," *Zabaikal'ets*, 13 September 1986, 1.

13. GAChO/P-6748/34/246/8–11 and 13, quotation on 9; "Otnosheniiam krepnut', razvivat'sia," *Zabaikal'ets*, 29 October 1987, 3.

14. GAChO/P-6748/34/246/12–14; see also ibid., 25.

15. Wishnick, *Fences*, 84.

16. GAChO/P-1710/1/70/101–115, here 112. Dispatch coordination problems and a shortage of railroad staff remained problems well into the late 1980s. These caused continual holdups of international freight traffic. "Proizvoditel'nee ispol'zovat' oborot vagona," *Zabaikal'ets*, 3 August 1989, 2–3. For 1950s freight rates, see table 6.1.

17. Wishnick, *Fences*, 103, 117; Zubok, "Soviet Union," 134. Cf. also "Beijiang 'Shenzhen'—Manzhouli," *Renmin Ribao*, 2 May 1989, 5.

18. GAChO/P-6748/34/316/1–8, protocol on 1–3; "SSSR-KNR: Prigranichnaia torgovlia," *Zabaikal'ets*, 14 May 1988, 1; "SSSR-KNR: Vzaimnoe sotrudnichestvo," *Zabaikal'ets*, 23 July 1988, 1.

19. *Entsiklopediia Zabaikal'ia*, 4:360.

20. "Zamershie stroiki Zabaikal'ska," *Zabaikal'ets*, 12 August 1986, 2; "Nash obshchii dom," *Zabaikal'ets*, 31 May 1988, 3.

21. GAChO/P-6748/34/316/12–15. "Vzaimnoe sotrudnichestvo," *Zabaikal'ets*, 23 July 1988, 1. Positive reports on Chinese labor in Zabaikalsk appeared regularly in the regional press. Cf., e.g., "Kliuchi vruchili kitaiskie stroiteli," *Zabaikal'skii Rabochii*, 2 July 1989, 6; "Zabaikal'tsy dovol'ny pomoshch'iu," *Zabaikal'skaia Magistral'*, 12 December 1989, 2–3.

22. "Diplomacy Swords into Sample Cases," *Time*, 18 July 1988, no pagination. In 1989 Chinese construction workers erected some buildings in the state farm Krasnyi Velikan. A group of forty Chinese peasants arrived at the farm during the spring to assist during planting season. "Sviazi sovkhoza," *Zabaikal'skii Rabochii*, 26 February 1989, 3; "Rasschitalis' baranchikami," *Zabaikal'skii Rabochii*, 2 June 1989, 3.

23. "Zabaikal'sk—stantsiia prigranichnaia," *Izvestiia*, 4 May 1988, 1. Cf. also "2. mosty vzaimoponimaniia," *Zabaikal'skii Rabochii*, 22 April 1988, 4.

24. "Dialog 'Sverkh vsiakikh ozhidanii'," *Zabaikal'skii Rabochii*, 1 October 1989, 6.

25. GAChO/P-6748/34/246/16–18; GAChO/P-6748/34/316/26.

26. GAChO/P-6748/34/378/8–10, 15; GAChO/P-6748/34/452/2, 24; "Obmenialis' delegatsiiami," *Zabaikal'ets*, 28 November 1989, 3; "Vpervye posle voiny," *Komsomolets Zabaikal'ia*, 16 May 1990, 1; "V pamiati narodnoi," *Zabaikal'ets*, 8 September 1990, 3.

27. "Ne preryvaetsia sviaz'," *Zabaikal'skii Rabochii*, 1 October 1989, 6.

28. In the early 1990s, a return movement emerged, encouraging the return of Shenekhen Buriats to their original country, where they were meant to surprise everyone with their "pure" Buriatism. Since then several hundred Shenekhen Buriat families have moved back to Russia. Cf. Baldano, "People," 192–198; Baldano and Diatlov, "Buriaty," 183–188. For a Buriat family reunification, see Golorbueva, *Storony*, 113–139.

29. Interview Yang.

30. According to Soviet statistics, only two U.S. citizens had crossed the border officially by train at Zabaikalsk between 1966 and 1976. In the late 1980s they were counted in dozens and later hundreds. Cf. chapter 7.

31. *New York Times*, 10 August 1988. See also *New York Times*, 29 May 1988.

32. "O 'Vostochnom ekspresse'," *Zabaikal'ets*, 24 September 1988, 2.

33. "Tamozhnia. Svoi problemy," *Zabaikal'ets*, 26 June 1991, 1; *Manzhouli shi zhi*, 233–234.

34. Figures according to *Manzhouli shi zhi*, 673–674.

35. "Poselok u granitsy," *Zabaikal'ets*, 24 July 1990, 3.

36. Fetherling, *Year*, 98–99, quotations on 99.

37. "V Pekin bez peresadok," *Zabaikal'skii Rabochii*, 30 May 1991, 4; "Zabaikal'sk-Man'chzhuriia," *Zabaikal'skii Rabochii*, 3 August 1991, 3.

38. "V interesakh gosudarstva," *Zabaikal'ets*, 29 May 1990, 1 (quotation); "Poezd," *Komsomolets Zabaikal'ia*, 16 September 1990, 4; "Tamozhnia. Svoi problemy," *Zabaikal'ets*, 26 June 1991, 1.

39. "Kontrabandnyi zhemchug," *Zabaikal'ets*, 10 July 1990, 3; "Zhemchuzhnyi ulov," *Zabaikal'skaia Magistral'*, 28 July 1990, 3. For Berlin's bazaar, see Schlögel, "Polenmarkt," 259–266.

40. "Guowuyuan zuochu jueding dongbei sige bianjing chengshi jinyibu kaifang," *Renmin Ribao*, 12 March 1992, 4; Wishnick, *Fences*, 159–163; *Manzhouli shi zhi*, 620–621.

41. Although the Russian Federation reestablished a border strip of five kilometers in 1993, access to Zabaikalsk remained unrestricted. Cf. Kireeev, *Granitsa*, 302.

42. "Bespredel u kalitki v Rossiiu," *Zabaikal'skii Rabochii*, 9 April 1992, 4.

43. "Meniaem zoloto na . . . 'adidas'," *Zabaikal'skii Rabochii*, 23 June 1992, 4 (quotation); "Granitsa na zamke: Kliuch poteriali," *Komsomolets Zabaikal'ia*, 22 August 1992, 1.

44. "Ne vidat' Kitaia, kak svoikh ushei," *Zabaikal'skii Rabochii*, 8 August 1992, 2.

45. "Strel'ba na 'ulitse millionerov'," *Zabaikal'skii Rabochii*, 22 December 1992, 1.

46. "Nekotorye voprosy tamozhenno-tarifnogo regulirovaniia," *Zabaikal'ets*, 13 July 1989, 3; "Sklady na kolesakh," *Zabaikal'ets*, 28 November 1989, 2.

47. *Manzhouli shi zhi*, 230–232; "Vse 'ushli na vagony' no stantsiia ne zakryta," *Zabaikal'skaia Magistral'*, 1 March 1994, 2; "Besperedel u kalitki v Rossiiu," *Zabaikal'skii Rabochii*, 9 April 1992, 4; "Bitva na putiakh," *Zabaikal'skaia Magistral'*, 2 March 1993, 2.

48. "Meniaiu sovest' na 'adidas'," *Zabaikal'skii Rabochii*, 19 January 1993, 2 (quotation); "Strel'ba na 'ulitse millionerov'," *Zabaikal'skii Rabochii*, 22 December 1992, 1.

49. "O vremennom polozhenii spetsial'nogo rezhima vezda i propuska v Zabaikal'skii raion Chitinskoi oblasti," *Zabaikal'skii Rabochii*, 7 January 1993; "Vremennoe polozhenie," *Zabaikal'skaia Magistral'*, 12 January 1993, 2. Later, these regulations were lifted again but reestablished in late 2007. "Ob utverzhdenii pravil pogranichnogo rezhima," *Rossiiskaia Gazeta*, 24 November 2007, no pagination.

50. Schools, kindergartens, shops, and the regional hospital were shut down for weeks. The local newspaper *Zabaikal'ets* was not printed for months. "'Infarkt' po-zabaikal'ski," *Zabaikal'skii Rabochii*, 24 February 1993, 2.

51. E.g., *Zabaikal'skaia Magistral'* believes the losses to be about two billion rubles. "Vse 'ushli na vagony' no stantsiia ne zakryta," *Zabaikal'skaia Magistral'*, 1 March 1994, 2.

52. Other guesses were significantly higher, and there were other kinds of casualties elsewhere. According to *Zabaikal'skaia Magistral'* forty-eight people were killed in the Zabaikalsk district between November 1992 and March 1993. "Obstanovku v Zabaikal'ske mozhno smiagchit' . . . ," *Zabaikal'skaia Magistral'*, 22 May 1993, 1–2.

53. Meniaiu sovest' na 'adidas'," *Zabaikal'skii Rabochii*, 19 January 1993, 2; "Opasno dlia zhizni," *Zabaikal'skii Rabochii*, 13 May 1993, 1; "Oborotnaia storona medali," *Zabaikal'skii Rabochii*, 1 October 1993, 2.

Conclusion

1. Michael Wines, "Chinese Creating a New Vigor in Russian Far East," *New York Times*, 23 September 2001, 3.

2. Between the late 1950s and 1980s Manzhouli had a stable population of 25,000 to 35,000 inhabitants. Its population then multiplied to 153,571 people in 2002 and to roughly 300,000 in 2019. Cf. *Manzhouli shi zhi*, tables on 54–55, for 2002. There are no precise data available for years after 2002.

3. Author's own observations: Sören Urbansky, "Jenseits des Steppenhügels," *Neue Zürcher Zeitung*, 26 October 2007, B1–B3. Cf. also Fedorovna, "Trade," 116–118; Peshkov, "Manzhouli," 128–131.

4. Cf. Wilson, *Partners*.

5. Developments of the post-Soviet period in the borderlands cannot be reviewed in detail here. They have been studied by a number of scholars, e.g., Billé, Delaplace, and Humphrey, *Encounters*; Larin, *Otnosheniia*; Tarasov, "Chinese" and Urbansky, "Ebbe."

6. "Zemliu otdadim v arendu KNR," *Zabaikal'skii Rabochii*, 18 June 2015, 1; "Zemlia— kitaitsam, zaboty—krest'ianam?," *Zabaikal'skii Rabochii*, 19 June 2015, 1–2.

7. Cf. Humphrey, *Trust*, for an anthropological understanding of the historical legacy and current state of trust and mistrust in the Sino-Russian border regions.

8. Cf. Peshkov, "Manzhouli," 122.

9. Cf. Lo, *Chinese*, 20–22.

10. "Ne zabud'te oformit' propusk!," *Zabaikal'skii Rabochii*, 25 September 2015, 4.

11. Interview Mashukova.

BIBLIOGRAPHY

Primary Sources

Archival Sources

Bancroft Library (Bancroft), University of California, Berkeley (United States):
  Oral History Documents: *Lialia Sharov, Life in Siberia and Manchuria, 1898–1922. A Memoir*, Los Angeles, 1960
E'erguna youqi dang'anguan (E'erguna), E'erguna Right Banner Archives, Labudalin (China):
  q. 1: *Shiwei xian quanzong huiji*
Gosudarstvennyi arkhiv Amurskoi oblasti (GAAO), State Archive of Amur Region, Blagoveshchensk (Russia):
  f. I-53: *Blagoveshchenskaia tamozhnia* (1913–1917)
  f. R-81: *Blagoveshchenskii gorodskoi ispolnitel'nyi komitet* (1916–1962)
  f. R-114: *Amurskii oblastnoi ispolnitel'nyi komitet* (1916–1991)
Gosudarstvennyi arkhiv Chitinskoi oblasti (GAChO), State Archive of Chita Region, Chita (Russia):
  f. 1: *Zabaikal'skoe oblastnoe pravlenie* (1851–1917)
  f. 13: *Voennyi gubernator Zabaikal'skoi oblasti* (1851–1917)
  f. 14: *Osobaia kantseliariia voennogo gubernatora Zabaikal'skoi oblasti* (1866–1915)
  f. 78: *Inspektor Chitinskogo tamozhennogo uchastka* (1885–1920)
  f. 107: *Man'chzhurskaia tamozhnia* (1902–1916)
  f. 334: *Zabaikal'skii oblastnoi komissar Vremennogo pravitel'stva* (1917–1919)
  f. P-3: *Chitinskii obkom KPSS*
  f. P-75: *Chitinskii okruzhnoi komitet VKP(b)* (1926–1930)
  f. P-81: *Zabaikal'skii gubernskii komitet RKP(b)* (1921–1926)
  f. P-1710: *Pervichnaia organizatsia KPSS stantsii Zabaikal'sk* (1937–1990)
  f. P-3945: *Pervichnaia organizatsia KPSS tamozhni stantsii Zabaikal'sk* (1951–1964)
  f. P-6748: *Zabaikal'skii raikom KPSS* (1967–1991)
  f. R-15: *Ministerstvo vnutrennikh del DVR* (1920–1922)
  f. R-79: *Chitinskaia tamozhnia* (1917–1959)
  f. R-251: *Borzinskii uezdnyi ispolnitel'nyi komitet* (1923–1926)
  f. R-404: *Man'chzhurskaia tamozhnia* (1902–1930)
  f. R-586: *Matsievskaia tamozhnia* (1929–1930)
  f. R-604: *Upravlenie Zabaikal'skoi zheleznoi dorogi*
  f. R-608: *Upravlenie Chitinskoi zheleznoi dorogi* (1920–1925)

f. R-1077: *Borzinskii raiispolkom* (1926–1963)

f. R-1243: *Zabaikal'skaia tamozhnia* (1930–1958)

f. R-1257: *Borzinskaia raionnaia inspektura gosudarstvennoi statistiki* (1928–1963)

f. R-1645: *Chitinskoe oblastnoe upravlenie statistiki*

f. R-2610: *Borzinskoe otdelenie Zabaikal'skoi zheleznoi dorogi* (1973–1997)

Gosudarstvennyi arkhiv Irkutskoi oblasti (GAIO), State Archive of Irkutsk Region, Irkutsk (Russia):

f. 25: *Kantseliariia Irkutskogo general-gubernatora* (1887–1917)

f. 29: *Kantseliariia Priamurskogo general-gubernatora dlia upravleniia Zabaikal'skoi oblast'iu*

Gosudarstvennyi arkhiv Khabarovskogo kraia (GAKhK), State Archive of Khabarovsk Region, Khabarovsk (Russia):

f. I-286: *Kollektsiia dokumentov "Organy upravleniia Zabaikal'skogo, Amurskogo i Ussuriiskogo kazach'ykh voisk"* (1871–1928)

f. P-2: *Dal'nevostochnyi Kraevoi Komitet VKP(b)*

f. R-18: *Ministerstvo Inostrannnykh Del Narodno-Revoliutsionnoi Vlasti Dal'nevostochnoi Respubliki* (1918–1922)

f. R-424: *Osobyi otdel polnomochnogo predstavitel'stva otdela gospolitupravleniia DV oblasti* (1920–1924)

f. R-830: *Glavnoe Biuro po delam Rossiiskikh Emigrantov v Man'chzhurii*

f. R-1128: *Kharbinskii komitet pomoshchi russkim bezhentsam* (1923–1945)

Gosudarstvennyi arkhiv Rossiskoi Federatsii (GARF), State Archive of the Russian Federation, Moscow (Russia):

f. 102: *Departament Politsii Ministerstva Vnutrennikh Del* (1880–1917)

f. 543: *Kollektsiia rukopisei tsarskosel'skogo dvortsa* (1863–1916)

f. 818: *Planson Georgii Antonovich* (1869–1916)

f. A-385: *Verkhovnyi Sovet RSFSR* (1937–1990)

f. A-612: *Ministerstvo Innostrannych del RSFSR* (1944–1991)

f. R-1235: *Vserossiiskii Tsentral'nyi Ispolnitel'nyi Komitet Sovetov Rabochikh, Krest'ianskikh i Krasnoarmeiskikh Deputatov* (1917–1938)

f. R-3316: *Tsentral'nyi Ispolnitel'nyi Komitet SSSR* (1922–1938)

f. R-5283: *Vsesoiuznoe Obshchestvo Kul'turnykh Sviazei s Zagranitsei* (1925–1957)

f. R-5446: *Sovet Ministrov SSSR* (1923–1991)

f. R-5963: *Kazachii Soiuz v Shankhae* (1925–1939)

f. R-6081: *Upravlenie Kitaiskoi Vostochnoi Zheleznoi Dorogi, Kharbin* (1896–1945)

f. R-7523: *Verkhovnyi Sovet SSSR* (1937–1989)

f. R-8131: *Prokuratura SSSR* (1924–1991)

f. R-8300: *Ministerstvo Gosudarstvennogo Kontrolia SSSR* (1940–1957)

f. R-9576: *Soiuz Sovetskikh Obshchestv Druzhby i kul'turnoi sviazi s zarubezhnymi stranami* (1958–1992)

Hulunbei'er shi Haila'er qu dang'anguan (Haila'er), Hailar Municipal Archives (China):

q. 1 *Minguo wenjian*

Library of Congress (LOC), Washington, D.C. (United States):

Manuscript Collection: *The Papers of Owen Lattimore*

National Archives and Records Administration (NARA), College Park, Md. (United States):
RG 59: *Records of the Department of State*
RG 84: *Records of the Foreign Service Posts*
RG 165: *Records of the War Department General and Special Staffs*
Politisches Archiv des Auswärtigen Amts (PAAA), Political Archive of the Federal Foreign Office, Berlin (Germany):
Peking II: *Akten der Gesandtschaft/Botschaft in China*
R: *Auswärtiges Amt, Abteilung A and Politische Abteilung IV*
Rossiiskii Gosudarstvennyi arkhiv noveishei istorii (RGANI), Russian State Archive of Contemporary History, Moscow (Russia):
f. 5: *Fond apparata TsK KPSS (1935–1991)*
f. 89: *Kollektsiia rassekrechennykh dokumentov (1919–1992)*
Rossiiskii Gosudarstvennyi arkhiv sotsial'no-politicheskoi istorii (RGASPI), Russian State Archive of Socio-Political History, Moscow (Russia):
f. 17: *Tsentral'nyi komitet KPSS (1898, 1903–1991)*
f. 159: *Chicherin Georgii Vasil'evich (1872–1936)*
f. 372: *Dal'nevostochnoe biuro TsK RKP(b) (1920–1925)*
f. 514: *Kommunisticheskaia partiia Kitaia*
f. 558: *Stalin (nast. Dzhugashvili) Iosif Vissarionovich (1878–1953)*
f. 613: *Tsentral'naia kontrol'naia komissiia VKP(b) (1920–1934)*
Rossiiskii Gosudarstvennyi istoricheskii arkhiv Dal'nego Vostoka (RGIA DV), Russian State Historical Archive of the Far East, Vladivostok (Russia):
f. 702: *Kantseliariia Priamurskogo general-gubernatora (Khabarovka, Khabarovsk) (1861–1920)*
f. 704: *Kantseliariia voennogo gubernatora Amurskoi oblasti (Blagoveshchensk) (1858–1918)*
f. R-2422: *Dal'nevostochnyi revoliutsionnyi komitet (Chita, Khabarovsk) (1920–1926)*
Rossiiskii Gosudarstvennyi istoricheskii arkhiv (RGIA), Russian State Historical Archive, Saint Petersburg (Russia):
f. 323: *Pravlenie Obshchestva Kitaisko-Vostochnoi zheleznoi dorogi (1896–1935)*
f. 560: *Obshchaia kantseliariia ministra finansov (1811–1917)*
f. 1276: *Sovet Ministrov (1905–1917)*
f. 1298: *Upravlenie glavnogo vrachebnogo inspektora MVD (1897–1919)*
Rossiiskii Gosudarstvennyi voenno istoricheskii arkhiv (RGVIA), Russian State Military-Historical Archive, Moscow (Russia):
f. 404: *Voenno-topograficheskoe upravlenie Glavnogo shtaba i voenno-topograficheskie semki (1817–1919)*
f. 1482: *Voennyi gubernator Zabaikal'skoi oblasti (1900–1916)*
f. 1553: *Zabaikal'skoe kazach'e voisko (1881–1919)*
Rossiiskii Gosudarstvennyi voennyi arkhiv (RGVA), Russian State Military Archive, Moscow (Russia):
f. 25871: *Upravlenie Zabaikal'skogo voennogo okruga g. Chita (1921–1922, 1935–1941)*
f. 32114: *Upravlenie Zabaikal'skoi gruppy voisk Osoboi Krasnoznamennoi Dal'nevostochnoi Armii g. Chita (1929, 1932–1935, 1939)*
f. 33879: *Osobaia Krasnoznamennaia Dal'nevostochnaia Armiia g. Khabarovsk (1929–1938)*

Newspapers and Periodicals

Binjiang Shibao

Dal'

Dongfang Zazhi

Dumy Zabaikal'ia

Economist

Gongren Ribao

Gun-Bao

Guo Wen Zhoubao

Heilongjiang Ribao

Hulunbei'er Ribao

Izvestiia

Kharbinskii Vestnik

Kharbinskoe Vremia

Komsomolets Zabaikal'ia

Leninskii Put'

Los Angeles Times

Man'chzhuriia

Man'chzhurskaia Gazeta

Na Boevom Postu

Nash Put'

Neimenggu Ribao

Neue Zürcher Zeitung

New York Times

Novaia Zhizn'

Novosti Zhizni

Otpor

Pravda

Renmin Ribao

Rossiiskaia Gazeta

Rubezh

Rupor

Russkoe Slovo

Time

Times Literary Supplement

Vremia

Xuelu

Yuandong Bao

Zabaikal'e

Zabaikal'ets

Zabaikal'skaia Magistral'

Zabaikal'skaia Nov'

Zabaikal'skie Oblastnye Vedomosti

Zabaikal'skii Rabochii

Zabaikal'skoe Obozrenie

Zakhinganskii Golos

Zaria

Interviews

Vasilii M. Iakimov, 4 August 2009, Abagaitui (Russia)

Iurii I. Kozlov, 3 August 2009, Zabaikalsk (Russia)

Valentina V. Kozlova, 3 August 2009, Zabaikalsk (Russia)

Liudmila I. Mashukova, 3 August 2009, Zabaikalsk (Russia)

Sayana B. Namsaraeva, 27 November 2016, Cambridge (United Kingdom)

Ivan M. Sokolov, 4 August 2009, Abagaitui (Russia)

Klavdiia M. Sushkina, 4 August 2009, Abagaitui (Russia)

Aleksandr P. Tarasov, 16 August 2008, Chita (Russia)

Yang Yulan (Tamara V. Erekhina), 10 August 2009, Enhe (China)

Vera P. Zolotareva, 3 July 2007, Zabaikalsk (Russia)

Published Sources

Aleksandrov, V. "Argun' i Priargun'e. Putevye zametki i ocherki." *Vestnik Evropy* 39, no. 5 (1904): 281–310.

Anuchin, V. A. *Geograficheskie ocherki Man'chzhurii*. Moscow: Gosudarstvennoe izdatel'stvo geograficheskoi literatury, 1948.

Aziatskaia Rossiia: Izdanie pereselencheskogo upravleniia glavnogo upravleniia zemleustroistva i zemledeliia. Vol. 1. Saint Petersburg: Pereselencheskoe upravlenie, 1914.

Bakaev, Dmitrii A. *V ogne Khasana i Khalkhin-Gola.* Saratov: Privolzhskoe kn. izd-vo, 1984.

Baranov, A. *Barga.* Harbin: Tipo-lit. Zaamursk. Okr. Otd. Korpusa Pogran. Strazhi, 1912.

———. *Khalkha: Aimak Tsetsen-khana.* Harbin: Tipo-lit. Okhrannoi strazhi Kit. Vost. zh. d., 1919.

Baranov, I. G. "Administrativnoe ustroistvo Severnoi Man'chzhurii." *Vestnik Man'chzhurii* 11–12 (1926): 5–26.

Barber, Noel. *Trans-Siberian.* London: G.G. Harrap, 1942.

Borzhimskii, F. *Kratkoe istorichesko-geograficheskoe i statisticheskoe opisanie Khulunbuirskoi oblasti (k dnevniku puteshestviia po Mongolii v 1911 godu).* Irkutsk: Tipografiia T-va. Pechatn. Dela, 1913.

Brand, Adam. *Beschreibung der dreijährigen Chinesischen Reise: Die russische Gesandtschaft von Moskau nach Peking 1692 bis 1695 in den Darstellungen von Eberhard Isbrand Ides und Adam Brand* (Quellen und Studien zur Geschichte des östlichen Europa, vol. 53). Edited by Michael Hundt. Stuttgart: Steiner, 1999.

Butin (brat'ia). *Istoricheskii ocherk snoshenii russkikh s Kitaem i opisanie puti s granitsy Nerchinskogo okruga v Tian'dzin.* Irkutsk: n.p., 1871.

Chang, Kuo-t'ao. *The Rise of the Chinese Communist Party: The Autobiography of Chang Kuo-t'ao.* Vol. 1. Lawrence: University Press of Kansas, 1971.

Chen Dengyuan. *Zhong E guanxi shulüe.* Shanghai: Shangwu yinshuguan, 1929.

China (The Maritime Customs). *Documents Illustrative of the Origin, Development, and Activities of the Chinese Customs Service.* Vol. 5. Shanghai: Statistical Department of the Inspectorate General of Customs, 1939.

Cordes, Ernst. *Das jüngste Kaiserreich: Schlafendes, wachendes Mandschukuo.* Frankfurt a. M.: Societäts-Verlag, 1936.

Dal'ne-Vostochnoe Oblastnoe Statisticheskoe Upravlenie. *Sel'sko-khoziaistvennaia perepis' 1923 goda na Dal'nem Vostoke. Vypusk 3: Poselennye itogi.* Khabarovsk: n.p., 1925.

Daurets, N. *Semenovskie zastenki (Zapiski ochevidtsa).* Harbin: n.p., 1921.

Davidov, D. A. *Kolonizatsiia Man'chzhurii i S.-V. Mongolii (oblasti Tao-Nan'-Fu).* Vladivostok: Vostochnyi Institut, 1911.

Departament Tamozhennykh Sborov. *Obzor vneshnei torgovli Rossii po evropeiskoi i aziatskoi granitsam za 1914 god.* Vol. 1. Petrograd: Tipo-Litografiia M. P. Frolovoi, 1915.

Dobrolovskii, I. *Kheiluntszianskaia Provintsiia Man'chzhurii: Kratkii ocherk geografii, putei soobshcheniia, naseleniia, administratsii i ekonomicheskogo polozheniia.* Harbin: Tipo-lit. Shtaba Zaamursk. Okruga Pogranichnoi Strazhi, 1906.

Doklad Gorodskogo Soveta Man'chzhurskogo Obshchestvennogo Upravleniia po voprosu o zhizni i deiatel'nosti nazvannogo Upravleniia v periode trekhletiia 1919–1922 g.g. Harbin: Tipografiia T-va "Zaria," 1922.

Doloi novykh tsarei! Antikitaiskie zlodeianiia sovetskogo revizionizma na rekakh Kheiluntszian i Usulitszian. Beijing: Izdatel'stvo literatury na inostrannykh iazykakh, 1969.

Dombrovskii, A., and V. Voroshilov. *Man'chzhuriia.* Saint Petersburg: Tipografiia N.V. Vasil'eva, 1897.

"Dongsansheng guofang shiyi diaocha baogao." In *Qingdai Minguo diaocha baogao congkan,* vol. 30, edited by Guojia tushuguan gujiguan, 3–248. 190?. Beijing: Beijing yanshan chubanshe, 2007.

Dong Xianguang. *Dong lu Zhong E juelie zhi zhenxiang.* Shanghai: Zhenmeishan shudian, 1929.

Ekonomicheskii biuro KVzhd, ed. *Spravochnik po S. Man'chzhurii i KVzhd.* Harbin: Izdanie ekonomicheskogo biuro KVzhd, 1927.

Epov, N. I. *Zabaikal'skoe kazach'e voisko.* Nerchinsk: Tipografiia M.D. Butina, 1889.

Federal'naia sluzhba Kontrrazvedki Rossiiskoi Federatsii. *Organy gosudarstvennoi bezopasnosti SSSR v Velikoi Otechestvennoi Voine: Sbornik dokumentov.* Vol. 1: *Nakanune: Kniga pervaia (noiabr' 1938 g.-dekabr' 1940 g.).* Moscow: A/O Kniga i biznes, 1995.

Fedotov, Vladimir. *Polveka vmeste s Kitaiem: Vospominaniia, zapisi, razmyshleniia.* Moscow: ROSSPEN, 2005.

Fetherling, Douglas. *Year of the Horse: A Journey through Russia and China.* Toronto: Stoddart, 1991.

Fleming, Peter. *To Peking: A Forgotten Journey from Moscow to Manchuria.* London: Tauris Parke, 2009.

———. *Travels in Tartary: One's Company and News from Tartary.* London: Jonathan Cape, 1948.

Foreign Affairs Association of Japan, ed. *Manchoukuo-Soviet Union Border Questions.* Tokyo: Kenkyusba Press, 1938.

Garin, N. *Po Koree, Man'chzhurii i Liaodunskomu poluostrovu: Karandazhom z natury.* Saint Petersburg: n.p., 1904.

Gatti, Armand. *Sibérie—Zéro + L'Infini.* Paris: Du Seuil, 1958.

Giller, Agaton. *Opisanie Zabajkalskiej krainy w Syberyi.* Vol. 2. Leipzig: F.A. Brockhaus, 1867.

Glavnoe upravlenie general'nogo shtaba. *Dal'nii Vostok: Prilozhenie k vtoromu tomu: Marshruty i opisaniia putei Zabaikal'skoi oblasti.* No. 2. Saint Petersburg: Tipografiia A. Benke, 1911.

———. *Dal'nii Vostok*, vol. 3: *Voenno-statisticheskii obzor.* Saint Petersburg: Tipografiia A. Benke, 1911.

Goebel, Otto. *Über Sibirien nach Ostasien: St. Petersburg und Moskau, Tscheljabinsk-Mandschuria, Wladiwostok und Dairen.* Frankfurt a. M.: Hendschel, 1914.

———. *Volkswirtschaft des Ostbaikalischen Sibiriens ums Jahr 1909* (Berichte über Landwirtschaft, herausgegeben im Reichsamte des Innern, no. 19). Berlin: Paul Parey, 1910.

Golorbueva, Marina. *Po obe storony khrebtov.* Chita: Izd-vo ANO "Tsentr gigenicheskogo obuchenia," 2001.

Golovachev, D. M., and V. V. Soldatov. *Trudy Aginskoi ekspeditsii.* Chita: Parovaia Tip. Zab. T-va pech. dela, 1911.

Golitsyn, V. V. *Ocherk uchastiia okhrannoi strazhi KVzhd v sobytiiakh 1900 g. v Man'chzhurii.* Harbin: n.p., 1910.

Groza, B. *Podzhigateli mirovoi revoliutsii za rabotoi (Zagranichnaia rabota GPU).* Harbin: n.p., 1937.

Guo Daofu. *Hulunbei'er wenti.* Shanghai: Da dong shu ju, 1931.

Hawes, Charles. *In the Uttermost East: Being an Account of Investigations among Natives and Russian Convicts of the Island of Sakhalin, with Notes of Travel in Korea, Siberia, and Manchuria.* New York: Charles Scribner's Sons, 1904.

"Heilongjiang quan sheng sizhi ditu quanji." In Ou Benlin, *Diaocha weiyuan Ou Benlin fu ji jiang liang sheng diaocha yanwu li bi*, vol. 2. N.p., n.d.

"Heilongjiang zhilüe." In *Qingdai Heilongjiang guben fangzhi sizhong*, edited by Liu Chengde, 137–336. Harbin: Heilongjiang renmin chubanshe, 1989.

Heissig, Walter. *Der mongolische Kulturwandel in den Hsingan-Provinzen Mandschukos*. Vienna: Siebenberg-Verlag, 1944.

Hidaka, Noboru. *Manchoukuo-Soviet Border Issues*. Dairen: Manchuria Daily News, 1938.

Ho, Franklin L. *Population Movement to the North Eastern Frontier in China*. Shanghai: Thomas Chu & Sons, 1931.

Holmes, W. M. *An Eye-Witness in Manchuria: How Japan is Waging War in the Far East*. London: Martin Lawrence, 1932.

"Hulunbei'er gaiyao." In Zhongguo bianjiang shizhi jicheng, *Neimenggu shizhi*, vol. 41. 1930. Beijing: Quanguo tushuguan wenxian suowei fuzhi zhongxin, 2002.

Iashnov, E. E. *Kitaiskaia Kolonizatsiia Severnoi Man'chzhurii i ee perspektivy*. Harbin: Tipografiia Kitaiskoi Vostochnoi zheleznoi dorogi, 1928.

IV Otdel Shtaba Osoboi Krasnoznamennoi DV armii, ed. *Zakhvat i osvoenie Man'chzhurii iaponskim imperializmom*. Khabarovsk: Dal'partizdat, 1934.

The Japan-Manchoukuo Year Book. Tokyo: Japan-Manchoukuo Year Book Co., 1937.

Kantselariia Pravlenii Obshchestva Kitaiskoi Vostochnoi zheleznoi dorogi, ed. *Sbornik dokumentov otnosiashchichsia k Kitaiskoi Vostochnoi zheleznoi doroge*. Harbin: Tipografiia Kitaiskoi Vostochnoi zheleznoi dorogi, 1922.

Kapuściński, Ryszard. *Imperium*. New York: Vintage Books, 1995.

Kara-Murza, G. S. *"Novyi poriadok" v Manchzhurii*, vol. 4: *Ideologicheskaia obrabotka naseleniia Manchzhou-Go*. Chita: n.p., 1944.

Kashin, N. "Ezhegodnyi vykhod Mergentsev na r. Argun' dlia osmotra granitsy i dlia torgovli s zhiteliami Priargun'ia." In *Zapiski Sibirskogo otdela Imperatorskogo Russkogo geograficheskogo obshchestva*, vol. 9–10, 567–581. Irkutsk: Topografiia okr. shtaba, 1867.

———. "Neskol'ko slov ob Arguni: Ob istinnom istoke etoi reki." In *Zapiski Sibirskogo otdela Imperatorskogo Russkogo geograficheskogo obshchestva*, vol. 6, 97–104. Irkutsk: Topografiia shtaba voisk, 1863.

Kavakami Tosichiko, ed. "Promyshlennost' Severnoi Man'chzhurii." In *Materialy po Man'chzhurii, Mongolii, Kitaiu i Iaponii*, no. 33. Harbin: Tipo-lit. Shtaba Zaamurskago Okruga Pogranichnoi Strazhi, 1909.

Kawakami, K. K. *Manchoukuo: Child of Conflict*. New York: Macmillan, 1933.

Kazakov, Vasilii. *Nemye svideteli*. Shanghai: n.p., 1938.

Keizai Chōsakai Dai'ichibu. "Manshūri Charainoaru hōmen chōsa hōkokusho." 1940? In *Mantie diaocha baogao*, vol. 1, no. 2, edited by Heilongjiang sheng dang'anguan, 425–746. Guilin: Guangxi shifan daxue chubanshe, 2009.

Khilkovskii, N. "Putevaia zapiska o poezdke v Kitaiskii gorod Khailar." In *Zapiski Sibirskogo otdela Imperatorskogo Russkogo geograficheskogo obshchestva*, vol. 8, 149–156. Irkutsk: Topografiia shtaba voisk, 1865.

Khmara-Borshevskii, E. *V stepiakh Mongolii: Putevyia zapiski*. Harbin: Tipografiia Kitaiskoi Vostochnoi zheleznoi dorogi, 1915.

Kio-va-kai, Glavnoe Biuro po delam rossiiskikh emigrantov v Man'chzhurii, ed. *Velikaia Man'chzhurskaia Imperiia: K desiatiletnemu iubileiu*. Harbin: n.p., 1942.

Kitaiskaia Vostochnaia zheleznaia doroga. *Severnaia Man'chzhuriia i Kitaiskaia Vostochnaia zheleznaia doroga*. Harbin: Tipografiia Kitaiskoi Vostochnoi zheleznoi dorogi, 1922.

Klark, I. S. *Adres-kalendar' i Torgovo-Promyshlennyi ukazatel' Dal'nego Vostoka i Sputnik po Sibiri, Man'chzhurii, Amuru i Ussuriiskomu Kraiu*. Irkutsk: Parovaia tipo-litografiia P. Makushina i V. Posokhina, 1910.

Kommisiia dlia sobraniia i razrabotki svedenii o sibirskoi zolotopromyshlennosti i dlia sostavleniia programmy izsledovaniia zolotonosnykh raionov, ed. *Perechen' zolotopromyshlennykh raionov Sibiri i opisanie priiskovykh dorog*. Saint Petersburg: Tipografiia L. Smol'ianinova, 1901.

Kondratev, V. N. *Sovremennyi Kitai*. Blagoveshchensk: V.M. Butriakov i syn, 1908.

Kormazov, V. A. *Barga: Ekonomicheskii ocherk*. Harbin: Tipografiia Kitaiskoi Vostochnoi zheleznoi dorogi, 1928.

———. "Dvizhenie naseleniia v raione Zapadnoi linii KVzhd (Uchastok st. Man'chzhuriia-r. Petlia)." *Vestnik Man'chzhurii* 4 (1930): 51–57.

———. "Khinganskaia provintsiia (Sinan')." *Vestnik Man'chzhurii* 1 (1934): 31–73.

———. "Kochevaia Barga (Naselenie, religiia, legendy, zaniatiia)." *Vestnik Man'chzhurii* 8 (1928): 50–59.

———. "Zolotopromyshlennost' v Kheiluntszianskoi provintsii." *Vestnik Man'chzhurii* 3 (1927): 41–46.

Kornakova, A. D. "Po povodu provozglasheniia mongolami nezavisimosti." In *Trudy Troitskosavodsko-Kiakhtinskogo otdeleniia Priamurskogo otdela Imperatorskogo Russkogo geograficheskogo obshchestva*, vol. 15, no. 2, 17–37. Saint Petersburg: Senatskaia tipografiia, 1913.

Kostarev, Nikolai. *Granitsa na zamke*. Moscow: Molodaia gvardiia, 1930.

———. *Kitaiskie dnevniki*. Moscow: Gosudarstvennoe izdatel'stvo khudozhestvennoi literatury, 1931.

Kotvich, Vl. *Kratkii obzor istorii i sovremennogo politicheskogo polozheniia Mongolii: Prilozhenie k karte Mongolii sostavlennoi po dannym I. Ia. Korostovtsa*. Saint Petersburg: Kartograficheskoe Zavedenie A. Il'ina, 1914.

Krapotkin, P. "Dve poezdki v Man'chzhuriiu v 1864 godu: I. Opisanie puti iz Staro-Tsurukhaituevskogo karaula cherez g. Mergen na Aigun. II. Sungari ot Girina do ust'ia." In *Zapiski Sibirskogo otdela Imperatorskogo Russkogo geograficheskogo obshchestva*, vol. 8, 1–57. Irkutsk: Topografiia shtaba voisk, 1865.

Krasnov, P. *Po Azii: Putevye ocherki Man'chzhurii, Dal'niago Vostoka, Kitaia, Iaponii i Indii*. Saint Petersburg: Tip. Isidora Gol'dberga, 1903.

Kriukov, N. A. *Vostochnoe Zabaikal'e v sel'skokhoziaistvennom otnoshenii*. Saint Petersburg: Tipografiia V. Kirshbauma, 1895.

Krol', Moisei. *Stranitsy moei zhizni*. 1944. Moscow: Mosty kul'tury, 2008.

Kruberom, A., et al., eds. *Aziatskaia Rossiia: Illiustrirovannyi geograficheskii sbornik*. Moscow: Tipo-litografiia T-va I. N. Kushnerev i Ko., 1903.

Lezhnin, P. D. *Dal'nii Vostok (Bogatstva Priamur'ia i Zabaikal'ia)*. Chita: Tipografiia Zabaikal'skogo Obedin. Soiuza Kooperativ, 1922.

Liubimov, L. I. "Rechnoi transport severnoi Man'chzhurii." *Vestnik Man'chzhurii* 9–10 (1932): 11–25.

Liushkov, Genrikh. *Pochemu begut iz SSSR?* Shanghai: VEGA, 1939.

Manakin, M. "Opisanie puti ot Staro-Tsurukhaituevskogo karaula do g. Blagoveshchenska, cherez goroda Mergen i Aigun." In *Zapiski Chitinskogo otdela Priamurskogo otdela Imperatorskogo Russkogo Geograficheskogo Obshchestva*, vol. 3, 1–79. Chita: Tipografiia Torgovago Doma "N. A. Badmaev i Ko," 1899.

Materialy dlia statistiki naseleniia v Zabaikal'skom kazach'em voiske, sobrannye iz dannykh dostavlennykh perepis'iu proizvedennoiu 1-go ianvaria 1883 goda. [Chita]: Zabaikalsk. Obl. Tipografiia, 1884.

Meng Guangyao. *Zhong E guanxi ziliao xuanbian. Jindai Menggu bufen.* Huhehaote: n.p., 1976.

Men'shikov, P. N. "Kratkii istoricheskii ocherk Man'chzhurii." *Vestnik Azii* 9, no. 42 (30 September 1917): 27–44.

———. *Otchet kommercheskogo agenta Kitaiskoi Vostochnoi zheleznoi dorogi po obsledovaniiu Kheiluntszianskoi provintsii i chasti Chzherimskogo seima Vnutrennei Mongolii.* Harbin: Tipografiia Kitaiskoi Vostochnoi zheleznoi dorogi, 1913.

Meshcherskii, A. *Avtonomnaia Barga (Mongol'skaia Ekspeditsiia po zagotovke miasa dlia deistvuiushchikh armii: Vladivostoksko-Man'chzhurskii raion. Materialy k otchetu o deiatel'nosti s 1915 po 1918 g.g.,* vol. 12, appendix 3). Shanghai: Tipografiia "Russkago Knigoizdatel'stva," 1920.

Ministerstvo putei soobshcheniia, Upravlenie po sooruzheniiu zheleznykh dorog, ed. *Otchet po postroike soedinitel'noi vetvi ot Kitaiskogo razezda Zabaikal'skoi zh. d. do st. Man'chzhuriia Kitaiskoi-Vostochnoi zh. d. 1898–1901 g.g.* Saint Petersburg: Tipografiia Ministerstva putei soobshcheniia, 1904.

Minzheng bu jingwu si. *Hukou diaocha tongji biao.* N.p., 1936.

"Mongoliia." *Vestnik Azii* 4, no. 14 (February 1913): 12–16.

"Mongoliia." *Vestnik Azii* 7, nos. 35–36 (1915): 112–119.

Moore, Harriet L. *Soviet Far Eastern Policy, 1931–1945.* Princeton: Princeton University Press, 1945.

Nachal'noe obrazovanie na Kitaiskoi Vostochnoi zheleznoi doroge i Ussuriiskoi linii (1908/09 uch. g.). Vol. 3. Harbin: Tipografiia Kitaiskoi Vostochnoi zheleznoi dorogi, 1910.

Nan manzhou tiedao zhushi huishe, Ha'erbin shiwu suo diaocha ke, ed. *Cong zhengzhi fangmian kan Hulunbei'er.* N.p., 1927.

Nomonhan Incident: Manchoukuo-Outer Mongolia Border Clashes (Second Issue). Dairen: Manchuria Daily News, 1939.

Obzor Zabaikal'skoi oblasti za 1892 god. Chita: n.p., 1893.

Obzor Zabaikal'skoi oblasti za 1910 god. Chita: n.p., 1911.

Opisanie naselennykh punktov, rek, gor i prochykh geograficheskikh nazvanii Man'chzhurii i Vn. Mongolii (perevod s iaponskogo). Typescript, vol. 1, n.p., n.d.

Orlov, Nikolai. *Zabaikal'tsy v Man'chzhurii v 1900 g.: Ocherki iz pokhoda Khailarskogo Otriada Generala N. A. Orlova v Kitai v 1900 g.* Saint Petersburg: Sklad u V. A. Berezovskago, 1901.

Orlov, P. "Vdol granitsy s Kitaem po verkhnei Arguni (Zabaikal'e—1915 god)." *Izvestiia obshchestva izucheniia Zabaikal'skogo kazachestva* 5 (December 1916). Chita: Tipografiia Voiskovogo Khoziaistvennago Pravleniia, 1917, 9–31.

"Ot Irkutska do Pogranichnoi." In *Sputnik po Man'chzhurii, Amuru i Ussuriiskomu kraiu*, 1–20. Vladivostok: Tipografiia Primorskago Oblastnogo Pravleniia, 1906.

Otchet zabaikal'skogo kazach'ego voiska za 1912. Chita: n.p., 1913.

Perminov, Vadim V. *Nakazanie bez prestupleniia.* Chita: n.p., 2007.

Peterson, N. *Vozmozhnost' i usloviia pozemel'nogo ustroistva Zabaikal'skikh kochevykh inorodtsev: Dokladnaia zapiska po povodu komandirovki v Zabaikal'e letom 1900 goda.* Saint Petersburg: n.p., 1901.

Plaetschke, Bruno. "Die nordwestliche Mandschurei als Operationsgebiet." *Militär-Wochenblatt* 25 (4 January 1934): 819–821.

Pozdneev, Dimitrii, ed. *Opisanie Man'chzhurii.* Vol. 1. Saint Petersburg: Tipografiia Iu. N. Erlikh, 1897.

Ptitsyna, V. V. *Selenginskaia Dauriia: Ocherki Zabaikal'skogo kraia.* Saint Petersburg: Tipo-Litografiia B. Vul'fova, 1896.

Putevoditel' po Velikoi Sibirskoi zheleznoi doroge, 1901–1902. N.p., n.d.

Raiskii, D. "Snosheniia zabaikal'skikh krest'ian i kazakov s Mongoliei i Man'chzhurii." *Russkii Vestnik* 46, no. 274 (August 1901): 585–595.

Report of the International Plague Conference Held at Mukden, April 1911. Manila: Bureau of Printing, 1912.

RGIA DV, ed. *Zabaikal'skaia Tamozhnia (Tamozhnia na Tikhom okeane. Dokumenty i materialy,* vol. 5). Vladivostok: VF RTA, 2008.

Romanov (Digamma), F. *Man'chzhuriia i Kitaiskaia Vostochnaia zheleznaia doroga.* Tomsk: Parovaia Tipo-Litografiia P. I. Makushina, 1898.

Semenov, Ataman. *O sebe: Vospominaniia, mysli i vyvovody.* Harbin: Izdatel'stvo "Zaria," 1938.

———. *Tri goda v Pekine: Zapiski voennogo sovetnika.* Moscow: Nauka, 1980.

Serebrennikov, I. I. *Velikii otkhod: Razseianie po Azii belykh Russkikh Armii. 1919–1923.* Harbin: Izdatel'stvo M. V. Zaitseva, 1936.

Sergeev, Vs. L. *Ocherki po istorii belogo dvizheniia na Dal'nem Vostoke.* Harbin: n.p., 1937.

Shestakov, M. "Blagodatnoe Trekhrech'e." In *Vestnik Kazach'ei Vystavke v Kharbine 1943 g: Sbornik statei o kazakakh i kazachestve.* Harbin: n.p., 1943.

Shirokogorov, E. *Severo-zapadnaia Man'chzhuriia (Geograficheskii ocherk po dannym marshrutnykh nabliudenii).* Vladivostok: Tipografiia Oblastnoi Zemskoi Upravy, 1919.

Shishkin, P. *Bol'shevizm v Kitae: Chast' 1-ia: Obzor deiatel'nosti Severo-Man'chzhurskoi kommunisticheskoi partii.* Shanghai: Tipografiia Izdatel'stva "Vremia," 1930.

Shteinfel'd, N. "Mestnoe kupechestvo o posledstviiakh zakrytiia 50-verstnoi polosy." *Vestnik Azii* 4, no. 13 (January 1913): 1–19.

Sladkovskii, M. I. *Znakomstvo s Kitaem i Kitaitsami.* Moscow: Mysl', 1984.

Smol'nikov, P. N. *Mongol'skaia iarmarka v Gan'chzhure v 1912 godu.* Harbin: Tipografiia Kitaiskoi Vostochnoi zheleznoi dorogi, 1913.

"Soglashenie avtonomnogo provintsial'nogo pravitel'stva 3-kh Vostochnykh Provintsii Kitaiskoi Respubliki s pravitel'stvom SSSR." *Vestnik Man'chzhurii* 1–2 (1925): 88–89.

Sokolov, N. A. "Zapadnaia liniia KVzhd pered otkrytiem skvoznogo dvizheniia." *Vestnik Man'chzhurii* 1 (1930): 48–51.

Soldatov, V. V. *Zheleznodorozhnye poselki po Zabaikal'skoi linii: Statisticheskoe opisanie i materialy po perepisi 1910 goda: S predisloviem i pod redaktsiei D. M. Golovacheva*. Vol. 5, book 1. Saint Petersburg: Tipografiia "Slovo," 1912.

Solov'ev, Aleksei. *Trevozhnye budni zabaikal'skoi kontrrazvedki*. Moscow: Rus', 2002.

Song Xiaolian. "Hulunbei'er bian wu diaocha baogao shu." In *Qingdai Minguo diaocha baogao congkan*, vol. 8, edited by Guojia tushuguan gujiguan, 3–111. 1909. Beijing: Beijing yanshan chubanshe, 2007.

Sorge, Wolfgang. *Erlebtes Mandschukuo: Die Jugend eines altneuen Kaiserreiches*. Berlin: Kommodore Verlag, 1938.

Sovetsko-kitaiskie otnosheniia 1917–1957: Sbornik dokumentov. Moscow: Izdatel'stvo vostochnoi literatury, 1959.

Spafarii, Nikolai. *Puteshestvie cherez Sibir' ot Tobol'ska do Nerchinska i granits Kitaia russkago poslannika Nikolaia Spafariia v 1675 godu*. Saint Petersburg: Tipografiia V. Kirshbauma, 1882.

Stakheev, D. I. *Ot Kitaia do Moskvy: Istoriia iashchika chaiu*. Saint Petersburg: Izdanie Knigoprodavtsa M. O. Vol'fa, 1870.

Strel'bitskii. "Otchet o puteshestvii v 1894 g., po Man'chzhurii, chlena Priamurskogo otdela I. R. G. Ob. Strel'bitskogo." In *Zapiski Priamurskogo otdela Imperatorskogo Russkogo Geograficheskogo Obshchestva*, vol. 1, no. 4, 211–312. Khabarovsk: Tipo-litografiia kantseliarii priamurskago general-gubernatora, 1896.

Taft, Marcus Lorenzo. *Strange Siberia: Along the Trans-Siberian Railway: A Journey from the Great Wall of China to the Skyscrapers of Manhattan*. New York: Eaton & Mains, 1911.

Tamozhennaia politika Rossii na Dal'nem Vostoke, 1858–1917: Khrestomaniia. Vladivostok: Izd-vo Dal'nevostochnogo universiteta, 2003.

Tesler, E. L. "Buriaty v Barge." *Vestnik Man'chzhurii* 20 (1 November 1933): 30–34.

———. "Gan'chzhurskaia iarmarka 1933 goda." *Vestnik Man'chzhurii* 18–19 (15 October 1933): 82–88.

———. "Gan'chzhurskaia iarmarka 1934 goda." *Ekonomicheskii biulleten'* 9 (September 1934): 8–10.

———. "Gruntovye dorogi i gruzhevoi transport v Barge." *Vestnik Man'chzhurii* 23–24 (1933): 63–66.

Torgashev, B. "Zoloto v Man'chzhurii." *Vestnik Man'chzhurii* 8 (1927): 47–52.

Travel in Manchoukuo. Dairen: Manchuria Daily News, 1941.

Tret'iak, Iv. Aleksandr. "Dnevnik puteshestviia vorkug Khingana (Rezul'taty komandirovki v 1908 i 1909 g.g.)." In *Zapiski Priamurskogo otdela Imperatorskogo Russkogo Geograficheskogo Obshchestva*, vol. 8, no. 1, 1–175. Khabarovsk: Tipo-litografiia kantseliarii priamurskago general-gubernatora, 1912.

United States Army, Forces in the Far East. *Japanese Intelligence Planning Against the USSR* (Japanese Special Studies on Manchuria, vol. 10). N.p., 1955.

———. *Japanese Operational Planning Against the USSR* (Japanese Special Studies on Manchuria, vol. 1). N.p., 1955.

————. *Study of Strategical and Tactical Peculiarities of Far Eastern Russia and Soviet Far East Forces* (Japanese Special Studies on Manchuria, vol. 13). N.p., 1955.

U.S. Department of State, Office of Intelligence Research, Office of Strategic Services, Research and Analysis Branch. *Social Conditions, Attitudes, and Propaganda in Manchuria with Suggestions for American Orientation toward the Manchurians.* No. 295. 1942.

Vasil'ev, Aleksandr. *Zabaikal'skie Kazaki: Istoricheskii ocherk.* Vols. 1–3. Chita: Tipografiia Voiskovogo Khoziaistvennago Pravleniia Zabaik. kaz. voiska, 1916.

Vereshchagin, A. *V Kitae: Vospominaniia i razskazy 1901–1902 gg.* Saint Petersburg: V. Berezovskii, 1903.

Vremennyia Pravila dlia deistviia Kitaiskikh Tamozhen na stantsiiakh Man'chzhuriia i Pogranichnaia (Suifen'khe). Harbin: Russko-Kit. Tip. gaz. "Iuan'-dun-bao," 1908.

Vysochaishe uchrezhdennaia pod predsedatel'stvom stats-sekretaria Kulomzina: Kommisiia dlia izsledovaniia zemlevladeniia i zemlepol'zovaniia v Zabaikal'skoi oblasti. Materialy, vol. 5: *Istoricheskie svedeniia.* Edited by A. Shcherbachev. Saint Petersburg: Gosudarstvennaia tipografiia, 1898.

Vysochaishe uchrezhdennaia pod predseldatel'stvom stats-sekretaria Kulomzina: Kommisiia dlia izsledovaniia zemlevladeniia i zemlepol'zovaniia v Zabaikal'skoi oblasti. Materialy, vol. 6: *Naselenie, znachenie roda u inorodtsev i lamaizm.* Edited by N. Razumov and I. Sosnovskii. Saint Petersburg: Gosudarstvennaia tipografiia, 1898.

Waijiao bu, ed. *Waijiao bu dang'an congshu. Bianwu lei.* Vol. 1, *Dongbei juan.* Taibei: Waijiao bu, 2001.

Wan Fulin, ed. *Heilongjiang zhigao* (Hei shui congshu, no. 1). 1929. Harbin: Heilongjiang renmin chubanshe, 1992.

Woodhead, H. G. W., ed. *The China Year Book.* London: George Routledge & Sons, 1914.

Wu Han. "Fang Su yinxiang." In *Fang Su yinxiang,* edited by Zhong Su youhao xiehui zonghui. Beijing: Xinhua shudian, 1950.

Wu Lien-tieh, ed. *Manchurian Plague Prevention Service Memorial Volume, 1912–1932.* Shanghai: National Quarantine Service, 1934.

Xu Shichang. *Dongsansheng zhenglüe.* 1911. Changchun: Jilin wenshi chubanshe, 1989.

Yanjing, Qinghua, Beida 1950 nian shuqi Neimenggu gongzuo diaochatuan, ed. *Neimenggu Hunameng minzu diaocha baogao.* 1950. Huhehaote: Neimenggu renmin chubanshe, 1997.

Zakon o prigranichnoi zone. Harbin: n.p., 1937.

Zhang Jiafan, ed. *Hulunbei'er zhilüe.* 1924, Hailar: n.p., 2003.

Zhao Zhongfu. *Qingji Zhong E Dongsansheng jiewu jiaoshe* (Zhongyang yanjiu yuan jindaishi yanjiusuo, vol. 25). Taibei: Zhongyang yanjiu yuan jindai shi yanjiusuo, 1970.

Zhernakov, V. N. *Trekhrech'e.* Unpublished manuscript, Oakland, Calif., n.d. (courtesy of Olga Bakich, Toronto).

Zhong Su youhao xiehui zonghui, ed. *Fang Su biji.* Beijing: Shidai chubanshe, 1955.

Zuo Lin. *Zai xingfu de guojia li: Fangwen youji.* Beijing: Qingnian chubanshe, 1951.

Secondary Sources

Ablazhei, N. N. *S vostoka na vostok: Rossiiskaia emigratsiia v Kitae.* Novosibirsk: Izd-vo SO RAN, 2007.

Ablova, Nadezhda. "Deiatel'nost' beloemigrantskikh organizatsii v Kitae vo vremia obostreniia sovetsko-kitaiskikh otnoshenii (1929–1931 gg.)." *Problemy Dal'nego Vostoka* 4 (2005): 143–153.

————. *KVZhD i rossiiskaia emigratsiia v Kitae: Mezhdunarodnye i politicheskie aspekty istorii (pervaia polovina XX veka)*. Moscow: Russkaia panorama, 2005.

Adelman, Jeremy, and Stephen Aron. "From Borderlands to Borders: Empires, Nation-States, and the Peoples in between in North American History." *American Historical Review* 104, no. 3 (August 1999): 815–816.

Adelsgruber, Paulus, Laurie Cohen, and Börries Kuzmany. *Getrennt und doch verbunden: Grenzstädte zwischen Österreich und Russland, 1772–1918*. Vienna: Böhlau, 2011.

Anderson, Benedict. *Imagined Communities: Reflections on the Origin and Spread of Nationalism*. London: Verso, 1983.

Appadurai, Arjun. "Introduction: Commodities and the Politics of Value." In *The Social Life of Things: Commodities in Cultural Perspective*, edited by Arjun Appadurai, 3–63. Cambridge: Cambridge University Press, 1986.

Argudiaeva, Iuliia. "Russkoe naselenie v Trekhrech'e." *Rossiia i ATR* 4 (2006): 121–134.

Ascher, Abraham. *P. A. Stolypin: The Search for Stability in Late Imperial Russia*. Stanford: Stanford University Press, 2001.

Atwood, Christopher. "Sino-Soviet Diplomacy and the Second Partition of Mongolia, 1945–1946." In *Mongolia in the Twentieth Century: Landlocked Cosmopolitan*, edited by Stephen Kotkin and Bruce A. Elleman, 137–161. Armonk, N.Y.: M. E. Sharpe, 1999.

————. "State Service, Lineage and Locality in Hulun Buir." *East Asian History* 30 (2005): 5–22.

————. *Young Mongols and Vigilantes in Inner Mongolia's Interregnum Decades 1911–1931*. Vols. 1–2. Leiden: Brill, 2002.

Baberowski, Jörg. *Der Feind ist überall: Stalinismus im Kaukasus*. Munich: Deutsche Verlags-Anstalt, 2003.

————. *Der rote Terror: Die Geschichte des Stalinismus*. Munich: Deutsche Verlags-Anstalt, 2003.

Bakich, Olga. "Charbin: 'Rußland jenseits der Grenzen' in Fernost." In *Der große Exodus: Die russische Emigration und ihre Zentren, 1917 bis 1941*, edited by Karl Schlögel, 304–328. Munich: C.H. Beck, 1994.

Baldano, Marina. "People of the Border: The Destiny of the Shenehen Buryats." In *Frontier Encounters: Knowledge and Practice at the Russian, Chinese and Mongolian Border*, edited by Franck Billé, Grégory Delaplace, and Caroline Humphrey, 183–198. Cambridge: Open Book, 2012.

Baldano, Marina, and Viktor Diatlov. "Shenekhenskie Buriaty: Iz diaspory v diasporu?" *Diaspory* 1 (2008): 164–192.

Ball, Alan. "Private Trade and Traders during NEP." In *Russia in the Era of NEP: Explorations in Soviet Society and Culture*, edited by Sheila Fitzpatrick, Alexander Rabinowitch, and Richard Stites, 89–105. Bloomington: Indiana University Press, 1991.

Bassin, Mark. *Imperial Visions: Nationalist Imagination and Geographical Expansion in the Russian Far East, 1840–1865*. Cambridge: Cambridge University Press, 1999.

Baud, Michiel, and Willem van Schendel. "Toward a Comparative History of Borderlands." *Journal of World History* 8, no. 2 (Fall 1997): 211–242.

Beckwith, Christopher I. *Empires of the Silk Road: A History of Central Eurasia from the Bronze Age to the Present*. Princeton: Princeton University Press, 2009.

Beliaeva, Natal'ia. *Ot porto-franko k tamozhne: Ocherk regional'noi istorii rossiiskogo protektsion-izma*. Vladivostok, Dal'nauka, 2003.

Bernstein, Anya. "Pilgrims, Fieldworkers, and Secret Agents: Buryat Buddhologists and the History of an Eurasian Imaginary," *Inner Asia* 11, no. 1 (2009): 23–45.

Billé, Franck. "On Ideas of the Border in the Russian and Chinese Social Imaginaries." In *Frontier Encounters: Knowledge and Practice at the Russian, Chinese and Mongolian Border*, edited by Franck Billé, Grégory Delaplace, and Caroline Humphrey, 19–32. Cambridge: Open Book, 2012.

Billé, Franck, Grégory Delaplace, and Caroline Humphrey, eds. *Frontier Encounters: Knowledge and Practice at the Russian, Chinese and Mongolian Border*. Cambridge: Open Book, 2012.

Boeck, Brian J. *Imperial Boundaries: Cossack Communities and Empire-Building in the Age of Peter the Great*. Cambridge: Cambridge University Press, 2009.

Boikova, Elena. "Aspects of Soviet-Mongolian Relations, 1929–1939." In *Mongolia in the Twentieth Century: Landlocked Cosmopolitan*, edited by Stephen Kotkin and Bruce A. Elleman, 107–121. Armonk, N.Y.: M. E. Sharpe, 1999.

Bol'shaia Sovetskaia Entsiklopediia. Vol. 9. Moscow: Sovetskaia Entsiklopediia, 1972.

Bolton, Herbert E. *The Spanish Borderlands: A Chronicle of Old Florida and the Southwest*. New Haven, Conn.: Yale University Press, 1921.

Breuillard, Sabine. "General V. A. Kislitsin: From Russian Monarchism to the Spirit of Bushido." *South Atlantic Quarterly* 99 (2000): 121–141.

Brophy, David. *Uyghur Nation: Reform and Revolution on the Russia-China Frontier*. Cambridge, Mass.: Harvard University Press, 2016.

Brunero, Donna. *Britain's Imperial Cornerstone in China: The Chinese Maritime Customs Service, 1854–1949*. London: Routledge, 2006.

Bulag, Uradyn E. "Clashes of Administrative Nationalisms: Banners and Leagues vs. Counties and Provinces in Inner Mongolia." In *Managing Frontiers in Qing China: The Lifanyuan and Libu Revisited*, edited by Dittmar Schorkowitz and Chia Ning, 349–388. Leiden: Brill, 2017.

———. *Collaborative Nationalism: The Politics of Friendship on China's Mongolian Frontier*. Lanham, Md.: Rowman & Littlefield, 2010.

———. "Inner Mongolia: The Dialectics of Colonization and Ethnicity Building." In *Governing China's Multiethnic Frontiers*, edited by Morris Rossabi, 84–116. Seattle: University of Washington Press, 2005.

———. *The Mongols at China's Edge: History and the Politics of National Unity*. Lanham, Md.: Rowman & Littlefield, 2002.

Burbank, Jane, and Frederick Cooper. *Empires in World History: Power and the Politics of Difference*. Princeton: Princeton University Press, 2010.

Burds, Jeffrey. "The Soviet War against 'Fifth Columnists': The Case of Chechnya, 1942–1944." *Journal of Contemporary History* 42, no. 2 (2007): 267–314.

Bushueva, Tat'iana. "Khalkhin-Gol: Vzgliad cherez 70 let: Maloizvestnye stranitsy predistorii vtoroj mirovoi voiny." *Rossiiskaia Istoriia* 5 (2009): 34–51.

Chandler, Andrea. *Institutions of Isolation: Border Controls in the Soviet Union and Its Successor States, 1917–1993*. Montreal: McGill-Queen's University Press, 1998.

Chen Jian. *Mao's China and the Cold War*. Chapel Hill: University of North Carolina Press, 2001.

Chernolutskaia, Elena. "Vytesnenie kitaitsev s Dal'nego Vostoka i deportatsiia 1938 g." *Problemy Dal'nego Vostoka* 4 (2008): 133–145.

Chiasson, Blaine R. *Administering the Colonizer: Manchuria's Russians under Chinese Rule, 1918–29.* Vancouver: University of British Columbia Press, 2010.

Clubb, O. Edmund. *Chinese Communist Development Programs in Manchuria: With a Supplement on Inner Mongolia.* New York: Institute of Pacific Relations, 1954.

Coox, Alvin D. *Nomonhan: Japan against Russia, 1939.* Vols. 1–2. Stanford: Stanford University Press, 1985.

Coquin, François-Xavier. *La Sibérie: Peuplement et immigration paysanne en XIXe siècle.* Paris: Institut d'études slaves, 1969.

Crossley, Pamela Kyle. *The Manchus.* Cambridge, Mass.: Blackwell, 1997.

Cui Guangyu, ed. *Haila'er fengyun lu (1732–1932 nian).* Vol. 1. Hailar: Neimenggu wenhua chubanshe, 2000.

———, ed. *Haila'er fengyun lu (1932–1945 nian).* Vol. 2. Hailar: Neimenggu wenhua chubanshe, 2003.

Dabringhaus, Sabine. "Grenzzone im Gleichgewicht: China und Rußland im 18. Jahrhundert." In *Frieden und Krieg in der Frühen Neuzeit: Die europäische Staatenordnung und die außereuropäische Welt*, edited by Ronald G. Asch, Wulf Eckart Voß, and Martin Wrede, 577–597. Munich: Fink, 1999.

Dobrenko, Evgeny. "The Art of Social Navigation: The Cultural Topography of the Stalin Era." In *The Landscape of Stalinism: The Art and Ideology of Soviet Space*, edited by Evgeny Dobrenko and Eric Naiman, 163–200. Seattle: University of Washington Press, 2003.

Duara, Prasenjit. "Nationalism, Imperialism, Federalism, and the Case of Manchukuo: A Response to Anthony Pagden." *Common Knowledge* 12, no. 1 (2006): 47–65.

———. *Sovereignty and Authenticity: Manchukuo and the East Asian Modern.* Lanham, Md.: Rowman & Littlefield, 2003.

Dvornichenko, N. E. *Na strazhe vostochnoi granitsy rodiny: Ocherki o boevom puti voisk Zabaikal'skogo pogranichnogo okruga.* Kyzyl: Tuvinskoe kn. izd-vo, 1978.

Echenberg, Myron. *Plague Ports: The Global Urban Impact of Bubonic Plague, 1894–1901.* New York: New York University Press, 2007.

E'erguna youqi zhi. Edited by E'erguna youqi shi zhi bianzuan weiyuanhui. Hailar: Neimenggu wenhua chubanshe, 1993.

Elleman, Bruce A. "The Final Consolidation of the USSR's Sphere of Interest in Outer Mongolia." In *Mongolia in the Twentieth Century: Landlocked Cosmopolitan*, edited by Stephen Kotkin and Bruce A. Elleman, 123–136. Armonk, N.Y.: M. E. Sharpe, 1999.

———. *Moscow and the Emergence of Communist Power in China, 1925–30: The Nanchang Uprising and the Birth of the Red Army.* London: Routledge, 2010.

———. "Secret Sino-Soviet Negotiations on Outer Mongolia, 1918–1925." *Pacific Affairs* 68, no. 4 (Winter 1993–1994): 539–563.

———. "Sino-Soviet Tensions and Soviet Administrative Control over the Chinese Eastern Railway, 1917–25." In *Manchurian Railways and the Opening of China: An International History*, edited by Bruce A. Elleman and Stephen Kotkin, 59–80. Armonk, N.Y.: M. E. Sharpe, 2009.

Elliott, Mark C. "The Limits of Tartary: Manchuria in Imperial and National Geographies." *Journal of Asian Studies* 59, no. 3 (2000): 603–646.

––––––. *The Manchu Way: The Eight Banners and Ethnic Identity in Late Imperial China*. Stanford: Stanford: Stanford University Press 2001.

Entsiklopediia Zabaikal'ia: Chitinskaia oblast'. Vols. 1, 4. Novosibirsk: Nauka, 2000, 2006.

Erickson, John. *The Soviet High Command: A Military-Political History 1918–1941*. London: Macmillan, 1962.

Esherick, Joseph W. "How the Qing Became China." In *Empire to Nation: Historical Perspectives on the Making of the Modern World*, edited by Joseph W. Esherick, Hasan Kayali, and Eric Van Young, 229–259. Lanham, Md.: Rowman & Littlefield, 2006.

Federal'naia Sluzhba Bezopasnosti Rossiiskoi Federatsii, ed. *Pogranichnaia Sluzhba Rossii: Entsiklopedia*. Moscow: Voennaia kniga, 2009.

Fedorovna, Kapitolina. "Transborder Trade on the Russian-Chinese Border: Problems of Interethnic Communication." In *Subverting Borders: Doing Research on Smuggling and Small-Scale Trade*, edited by Bettina Bruns and Judith Miggelbrink, 107–128. Wiesbaden: VS Verlag für Sozialwissenschaften, 2012.

Fisher, Carney T. "Bubonic Plague in Modern China: An Overview." *Journal of the Oriental Society of Australia* 27–28 (1995–1996): 57–104.

Fitzpatrick, Sheila. *Everyday Stalinism: Ordinary Life in Extraordinary Times: Soviet Russia in the 1930s*. Oxford: Oxford University Press, 1999.

––––––. *Stalin's Peasants: Resistance and Survival in the Russian Village after Collectivization*. New York: Oxford University Press, 1994.

Foust, Clifford M. *Muscovite and Mandarin: Russia's Trade with China and Its Setting, 1727–1805*. Chapel Hill: University of North Carolina Press, 1969.

Frolov, Aleksandr. "Razvitie sovetsko-kitaiskikh prigranichnykh otnoshenii na Dal'nem Vostoke SSSR (1949–1969 gg.)." Dissertation, Khabarovskii pogranichnyi institut FSB Rossii, 2007.

Gamsa, Mark. "California on the Amur, or the 'Zheltuga Republic' in Manchuria (1883–86)." *Slavonic and East European Review* 81, no. 2 (April 2003): 236–266.

––––––. "The Epidemic of Pneumonic Plague in Manchuria 1910–1911." *Past & Present* 190 (February 2006): 147–183.

Gessen, Masha. *Two Babushkas: How My Grandmothers Survived Hitler's War and Stalin's Peace*. London: Bloomsbury, 2005.

Geyer, Dietrich. *Der russische Imperialismus: Studien über den Zusammenhang von innerer und auswärtiger Politik 1860–1914*. Göttingen: Vandenhoeck & Ruprecht, 1977.

Giersch, C. Patterson. *Asian Borderlands: The Transformation of Qing China's Yunnan Frontier*. Cambridge, Mass.: Harvard University Press, 2006.

Glantz, David M. *Soviet Operational and Tactical Combat in Manchuria, 1945*. London: Frank Cass, 2003.

––––––. *The Soviet Strategic Offensive in Manchuria, 1945*. London: Frank Cass, 2003.

Goldman, Stuart. *Nomonhan, 1939: The Red Army's Victory That Shaped World War II*. Annapolis, Md.: Naval Institute Press, 2012.

Goldstein, Lyle J. "Return to Zhenbao Island: Who Started Shooting and Why It Matters." *China Quarterly* 168 (December 2001): 985–997.

Gottschang, Thomas R., and Diana Lary. *Swallows and Settlers: The Great Migration from North China to Manchuria*. Ann Arbor: University of Michigan, Center for Chinese Studies, 2000.

Günther, Hans. "Broad Is My Motherland: The Mother Archetype and Space in the Soviet Mass Song." In *The Landscape of Stalinism: The Art and Ideology of Soviet Space*, edited by Evgeny Dobrenko and Eric Naiman, 77–95. Seattle: University of Washington Press, 2003.

Guseinov, Gasan. *Karta Nashei Rodiny: Ideologema mezhdu Slovom i Telom*. Helsinki: Institute for Russian and East European Studies, 2000.

Haila'er tielu fenju zhi. Edited by Haila'er tielu fenju zhi bianzuan weiyuanhui. Beijing: Zhongguo tiedao chubanshe, 1997.

Hämäläinen, Pekka, and Samuel Truett. "On Borderlands." *Journal of American History* 98, no. 2 (September 2011): 338–361.

Herlihy, Patricia. *The Alcoholic Empire: Vodka and Politics in Late Imperial Russia*. Oxford: Oxford University Press, 2002.

Hess, Christian A. "Big Brother Is Watching: Local Sino-Soviet Relations and the Building of New Dalian, 1945–1955." In *Dilemmas of Victory: The Early Years of the People's Republic of China*, edited by Jeremy Brown and Paul G. Pickowicz, 160–183. Cambridge, Mass.: Harvard University Press, 2007.

Hobsbawm, Eric, and Terence Ranger, eds. *The Invention of Tradition*. Cambridge: Cambridge University Press, 1983.

Hosking, Geoffrey A. *Russia and the Russians: A History*. Cambridge, Mass.: Belknap, 2001.

Hsu, Chia Yin. "The Chinese Eastern Railroad and the Making of Russian Imperial Orders in the Far East." PhD dissertation, New York University, 2006.

Hughes, James. *Stalin, Siberia, and the Crisis of the New Economic Policy*. Cambridge: Cambridge University Press, 1991.

———. *Stalinism in a Russian Province: A Study of Collectivization and Dekulakization in Siberia*. Basingstoke: Macmillan, 1996.

Hulunbei'er gong'an bianfang zhilüe. Edited by Hulunbei'er meng gong'an chu bianfang ju. Hailar: Neimenggu zizhiqu xinwen chubanju, 1991.

Hulunbei'er meng waishi zhi. Edited by Hulunbei'er meng waishi zhi bangongshi. Hailar: n.p., 1994.

Hulunbei'er meng zhi. Vol. 1. Edited by Hulunbei'er meng shizhi bianzuan weiyuanhui. Hailar: Neimenggu wenhua chubanshe, 1999.

Humphrey, Caroline. "Detachable Groups and Kinship Tensions: The Tsongol at the Russian-Qing Border." *Inner Asia* 16, no. 1 (2014): 34–63.

———, ed. *Trust and Mistrust in the Economies of the China-Russia Borderlands*. Amsterdam: Amsterdam University Press, 2018.

Humphrey, Caroline, and Urgunge Onon. *Shamans and Elders: Experience, Knowledge, and Power among the Daur Mongols*. Oxford: Clarendon, 1996.

Hurelbaatar, A. "Survey of the Mongols in Present-Day China: Perspectives on Demography and Culture Change." In *Mongolia in the Twentieth Century: Landlocked Cosmopolitan*, edited by Stephen Kotkin and Bruce A. Elleman, 191–222. Armonk, N.Y.: M. E. Sharpe, 1999.

Ichiko, Chuzo. "Political and Institutional Reform, 1901–11." In *The Cambridge History of China*, vol. 11, pt. 2, edited by Denis Twitchett and John K. Fairbank, 375–415. Cambridge: Cambridge University Press, 1980.

Iwashita, Akihiro. *A 4,000 Kilometer Journey along the Sino-Russian Border*. Sapporo: Slavic Research Center, Hokkaido University, 2004.

Janhunen, Juha. *Manchuria: An Ethnic History*. Helsinki: Finno-Ugrian Society, 1996.

Jansen, Marc, and Nikita Petrov. *Stalin's Loyal Executioner: People's Commissar Nikolai Ezhov, 1895–1940*. Stanford: Hoover Institution Press, 2002.

Jersild, Austin. *Sino-Soviet Alliance: An International History*. Chapel Hill: University of North Carolina Press, 2014.

Kaplonski, Christopher. "Prelude to Violence: Show Trials and State Power in 1930s Mongolia." *American Ethnologist* 35, no. 2 (2008): 321–337.

Kappeler, Andreas. *Rußland als Vielvölkerreich: Entstehung—Geschichte—Zerfall*. Munich: C.H. Beck, 1992.

Khinganskii Krasnoznamennyi pogranichnyi otriad, ed. *80 let na strazhe granits Otechestva*. Chita: Ekspress izdatel'stvo, 2004.

Khitin, Maksim. "Pogranichnaia okhrana Dal'nevostochnoi Respubliki." *Rossiia i ATR* 4 (2006): 5–15.

Kim, Loretta Eumie. "Marginal Constituencies: Qing Borderland Policies and Vernacular Histories of Five Tribes on the Sino-Russian Frontier." PhD dissertation: Harvard University, 2009.

Kindler, Robert. *Stalins Nomaden: Herrschaft und Hunger in Kasachstan*. Hamburg: Hamburger Edition, 2014.

Kirby, E. Stuart. "The Soviet Far East: A Broad View." *International Affairs* 47, no. 1 (January 1971): 63–78.

Kireeev, Aleksei. *Dal'nevostochnaia granitsa Rossii: Tendentsii formirovaniia i funktsionirovaniia (seredina XIX–nachalo XXI vv.)*. Vladivostok: Izdatel'stvo Dal'nevostochnogo federal'nogo universiteta, 2011.

König, Helmut. "Der sowjetisch-chinesische Rundfunkkrieg." *Osteuropa* 19, no. 8 (August 1969): 560–574.

Kravchuk, S., and E. Motrich. "Demograficheskii potentsial kak faktor sotsial'no-ekonomicheskogo razvitiia i pogranichnoi bezopasnosti SSSR na Dal'nem Vostoke v 1950–1970 gody." *Problemy Dal'nego Vostoka* 4 (2008): 80–89.

Krebs, Gerhard. "Japan and the German-Soviet War, 1941." In *From Peace to War: Germany, Soviet Russia and the World, 1939–1941*, edited by Bernd Wegner, 541–560. Providence: Berghahn Books, 1997.

Kuromiya, Hiroaki. *The Voices of the Dead: Stalin's Great Terror in the 1930s*. New Haven, Conn.: Yale University Press, 2007.

Ladds, Catherine. *Empire Careers: Working for the Chinese Customs Service, 1854–1949*. Manchester: Manchester University Press, 2013.

Lahusen, Thomas. "A Place Called Harbin: Reflections on a Centennial." *China Quarterly* 154 (June 1998): 400–410.

Lamar, Howard, and Leonard Thompson, eds. *The Frontier in History: North America and Southern Africa Compared*. New Haven, Conn.: Yale University Press, 1981.

Lan, Mei-hua. "China's 'New Administration' in Mongolia." In *Mongolia in the Twentieth Century: Landlocked Cosmopolitan*, edited by Stephen Kotkin and Bruce A. Elleman, 39–58. Armonk, N.Y.: M. E. Sharpe, 1999.

———. "The Mongolian Independence Movement of 1911: A Pan-Mongolian Endeavor." PhD dissertation, Harvard University, 1996.

Larin, Aleksandr. *Kitaiskie migranty v Rossii: Istoriia i sovremennost'.* Moscow: Vostochnaia kniga, 2009.

Larin, Viktor. *Rossiisko-kitaiskie otnosheniia v regional'nykh izmereniiakh (80-e gody xx–nachalo xxi v.).* Moscow: Vostok-Zapad, 2005.

Lary, Diana. *China's Civil War: A Social History, 1945–1949.* Cambridge: Cambridge University Press, 2015.

Lattimore, Owen. "The Historical Setting of Inner Mongolian Nationalism." *Pacific Affairs* 9, no. 3 (September 1936): 388–405.

———. *Manchuria: Cradle of Conflict.* New York: Macmillan, 1932.

———. *The Mongols of Manchuria: Their Tribal Divisions, Geographical Distribution, Historical Relations with Manchus and Chinese, and Present Political Problems.* New York: Howard Fertig, 1969.

———. *Studies in Frontier History: Collected Papers 1928–1958.* Paris: Mouton, 1962.

Lee, Robert H. G. *The Manchurian Frontier in Ch'ing History.* Cambridge, Mass.: Harvard University Press, 1970.

Lensen, George Alexander. *The Damned Inheritance: The Soviet Union and the Manchurian Crises, 1924–1935.* Tallahassee, Fla.: Diplomatic Press, 1974.

———. *The Strange Neutrality: Soviet-Japanese Relations during the Second World War, 1941–1945.* Tallahassee, Fla.: Diplomatic Press, 1972.

Li Danhui. "The Sino-Soviet Dispute over Assistance for Vietnam's Anti-American War, 1965–1972." In *Behind the Bamboo Curtain: China, Vietnam, and the World beyond Asia,* edited by Priscilla Roberts, 289–318. Stanford: Stanford University Press, 2006.

Li, Rose Maria. "Migration to China's Northern Frontier, 1953–82." *Population and Development Review* 15, no. 3 (September 1989): 503–538.

Lieven, Dominic. *Empire: The Russian Empire and Its Rivals from the Sixteenth Century to the Present.* London: John Murray, 2000.

Limerick, Patricia Nelson. *The Legacy of Conquest: The Unbroken Past of the American West.* New York: Norton, 1987.

Lindgren, Ethel John. "An Example of Culture Contact without Conflict: Reindeer Tungus and Cossacks of Northwestern Manchuria." *American Anthropologist* 40, no. 4 (October–December 1938): 605–621.

———. "North-Western Manchuria and the Reindeer-Tungus." *Geographical Journal* 75, no. 6 (June 1930): 518–534.

Little, L. K. "Introduction." In *The I. G. in Peking: Letters of Robert Hart, Chinese Maritime Customs, 1868–1907 (Letters Written to J. D. Campbell),* edited by John King Fairbank et al., 3–34. Cambridge, Mass.: Belknap, 1975.

Lo, Bobo. *How the Chinese See Russia.* Russie.Nei Reports, no. 6. Paris: Institut français des relations internationales, 2010.

Lohr, Eric. *Nationalizing the Russian Empire: The Campaign against Enemy Aliens during World War I.* Cambridge, Mass.: Harvard University Press, 2003.

Lü Yiran, ed. *Zhongguo jindai bianjie shi.* Vol. 1. Chengdu: Sichuan renmin chubanshe, 2007.

Ludden, David. "Presidential Address: Maps in the Minds and the Mobility of Asia." *Journal of Asian Studies* 62, no. 4 (November 2003): 1057–1078.

Lull, James. *China Turned On: Television, Reform, and Resistance*. London: Routledge, 1991.

Lüthi, Lorenz M. *The Sino-Soviet Split: Cold War in the Communist World*. Princeton: Princeton University Press, 2008.

Luzianin, S. "Diplomaticheskaia istoriia sobytii na Khalkhin-Gole, 1932–1939 gg." *Novaia i Noveishaia istoriia* 2 (2001): 41–51.

Lynteris, Christos. *Ethnographic Plague: Configuring Disease on the Chinese-Russian Frontier*. London: Palgrave Macmillan, 2016.

———. "Skilled Natives, Inept Coolies: Marmot Hunting and the Great Manchurian Pneumonic Plague (1910–1911)." *History and Anthropology* 24, no. 3 (2013): 303–321.

Maier, Charles S. *Once within Borders: Territories of Power, Wealth, and Belonging since 1500*. Cambridge, Mass.: Belknap, 2016.

Mancall, Mark. *Russia and China: Their Diplomatic Relations to 1728*. Cambridge, Mass.: Harvard University Press, 1971.

Manzhouli haiguan zhi. 1949–1999. Edited by Manzhouli haiguan zhi bianweihui. Huhehaote: Yuanfang chubanshe, 1999.

Manzhouli shi zhi. Edited by Manzhouli shi bianzuan weiyuanhui. Huhehaote: Neimenggu renmin chubanshe, 1998.

Manzhouli zhan zhi. 1901–2001. Edited by "Manzhouli zhan zhi" bianweihui. Beijing: Zhongguo tiedao chubanshe, 2002.

Marks, Steven G. *Road to Power: The Trans-Siberian Railroad and the Colonization of Asian Russia, 1850–1917*. Ithaca, N.Y.: Cornell University Press, 1991.

Martin, Terry. *The Affirmative Action Empire: Nations and Nationalism in the Soviet Union, 1923–1939*. Ithaca, N.Y.: Cornell University Press, 2001.

Matsusaka, Yoshihisa Tak. *The Making of Japanese Manchuria, 1904–1932*. Cambridge, Mass.: Harvard University Asia Center, 2001.

Matsuzato, Kimikata. "The Creation of the Priamur Governor Generalship in 1884 and the Reconfiguration of Asiatic Russia." *Russian Review* 71 (July 2012): 365–390.

Matthews, Mervyn. *The Passport Society: Controlling Movement in Russia and the USSR*. Boulder, Colo.: Westview, 1993.

McClain, Charles J. *In Search of Equality: The Chinese Struggle against Discrimination in Nineteenth-Century America*. Berkeley: University of California Press, 1994.

McKeown, Adam M. *Melancholy Order: Asian Migration and the Globalization of Borders*. New York: Columbia University Press, 2008.

Mehnert, Klaus. "Die Schüsse am Ussuri und ihr Echo." *Osteuropa* 19, no. 8 (August 1969): 549–559.

Meng Ssu-ming. "The E-lo-ssu Kuan (Russian Hostel) in Peking." *Harvard Journal of Asiatic Studies* 23 (1960): 19–46.

Miasnikov, Vladimir, and Evgenii Stepanov, eds. *Granitsy Kitaia: Istoriia formirovaniia*. Moscow: Pamiatniki istoricheskoi mysli, 2001.

Mitter, Rana. *The Manchurian Myth: Nationalism, Resistance, and Collaboration in Modern China*. Berkeley: University of California Press, 2000.

Murphy, David E. *What Stalin Knew: The Enigma of Barbarossa*. New Haven, Conn.: Yale University Press, 2005.

Nakami Tatsuo. "On Babujab and His Troops: Inner Mongolia and the Politics of Imperial Collapse, 1911–21." In *Russia's Great War and Revolution in the Far East: Re-imagining the Northeast Asian Theater, 1914–22*, edited by David Wolff, Yokote Shinji, and Willard Sunderland, 352–368. Bloomington, Ind.: Slavica, 2018.

———. "Russian Diplomats and Mongol Independence, 1911–1915." In *Mongolia in the Twentieth Century: Landlocked Cosmopolitan*, edited by Stephen Kotkin and Bruce A. Elleman, 69–78. Armonk, N.Y.: M. E. Sharpe, 1999.

Namsaraeva, Sayana. "Caught between States: Urjin Garmaev and the Conflicting Loyalties of Trans-border Buryats." *History and Anthropology* 28, no. 4 (2017): 406–428.

Nathan, Carl F. *Plague Prevention and Politics in Manchuria 1910–1931*. Cambridge, Mass.: East Asian Research Center, Harvard University, 1967.

Natsagdorzh, Tsongool B. "O prichine podpisaniia 'mezhdunarodnogo protokola' mezhdu Tsinskoi i Rossiiskoi imperiiami v 1792 godu v Kyakhte." In *Transgranichnye migratsii v prostranstve mongol'skogo mira: Istoriya i sovremennost'*, vol. 2, edited by Bair Nanzatov, 73–101. Ulan-Ude: Izdatel'stvo Buriatskogo Nauchnogo Tsentra SO RAN, 2012.

Naumov, Igor V. *The History of Siberia*. Edited by David N. Collins. London: Routledge, 2006.

Niu Jun. "The Origins of the Sino-Soviet Alliance." In *Brothers in Arms: The Rise and Fall of the Sino-Soviet Alliance, 1945–1963*, edited by Odd Arne Westad, 47–89. Washington, D.C.: Woodrow Wilson Center Press, 1998.

Ocherki istorii Vostochnogo Zabaikal'ia: Chitinskaia oblast'. Vol. 2. Chita: Ekspress izdatel'stvo, 2007.

O'Rourke, Shane. *The Cossacks*. Manchester: Manchester University Press, 2007.

Osterhammel, Jürgen. *Die Verwandlung der Welt: Eine Geschichte des 19. Jahrhunderts*. Munich: C.H. Beck, 2009.

Paine, Sarah C. M. "The Chinese Eastern Railway: From the First Sino-Japanese War until the Russo-Japanese War." In *Manchurian Railways and the Opening of China: An International History*, edited by Bruce A. Elleman and Stephen Kotkin, 13–36. Armonk, N.Y.: M. E. Sharpe, 2009.

———. *Imperial Rivals: China, Russia, and Their Disputed Frontier*. Armonk, N.Y.: M. E. Sharpe, 1996.

Pallot, Judith. *Land Reform in Russia, 1906–1917: Peasant Responses to Stolypin's Project of Rural Transformation*. Oxford: Clarendon, 1999.

Park, Alyssa. *Sovereignty Experiments: Korean Migrants and the Building of Borders in Northeast Asia, 1860–1945*. Ithaca, N.Y.: Cornell University Press, 2019.

Pasternak, Burton, and Janet W. Salaff. *Cowboys and Cultivators: The Chinese of Inner Mongolia*. Boulder, Colo.: Westview, 1993.

Patrikeeff, Felix. *Russian Politics in Exile: The Northeast Asian Balance of Power, 1924–1931*, Basingstoke: Palgrave, 2002.

Perdue, Peter C. *China Marches West: The Qing Conquest of Central Eurasia*. Cambridge, Mass.: Belknap, 2005.

Peshkov, Ivan. "In the Shadow of 'Frontier Disloyalty' at Russia-China-Mongolia Border Zones." *History and Anthropology* 28, no. 4 (2017): 429–444.

———. "Politicisation of Quasi-Indigenousness on the Russo-Chinese Frontier." In *Frontier Encounters: Knowledge and Practice at the Russian, Chinese and Mongolian Border*, edited by Franck Billé, Grégory Delaplace, and Caroline Humphrey, 165–181. Cambridge: Open Book, 2012.

———. "The Trade Town of Manzhouli: Trust Created and Undermined." In *Trust and Mistrust in the Economies of the China-Russia Borderlands*, edited by Caroline Humphrey, 121–142. Amsterdam: Amsterdam University Press, 2018.

Petrov, Victor. "New Railway Links between China and the Soviet Union." *Geographical Journal* 122, no. 4 (December 1956): 471–477.

Polian, Pavel. *Against Their Will: The History and Geography of Forced Migrations in the USSR*. Budapest: Central European University Press, 2004.

Popenko, Aleksandr. "Deiatel'nost' Dal'revkoma po organizatsii bor'by s kontrabandoi na sovetskom Dal'nem Vostoke (1922–1925 gg.)." *Problemy Dal'nego Vostoka* 6 (2007): 112–120.

———. "Opyt bor'by s kontrabandoi na Dal'nem Vostoke Rossii (1884-konets 20-kh gg. XX v.)." Dissertation, Khabarovskii pogranichnyi institut FSB Rossii, 2009.

Prescott, John R. V. *Political Frontiers and Boundaries*. London: Allen & Unwin, 1987.

Prokhorov, A. *K voprosu o sovetsko-kitaiskoi granitse*. Moscow: Izd-vo "Mezhdunar. otnosheniia," 1975.

Quested, R. K. I. *"Matey" Imperialists? The Tsarist Russians in Manchuria, 1895–1917*. Hong Kong: Centre of Asian Studies, University of Hong Kong, 1982.

Radchenko, Sergey. "Soviet Withdrawal from Mongolia, 1986–1992: A Reassessment." *Journal of Slavic Military Studies* 25, no. 2 (2012): 183–203.

———. *Two Suns in the Heavens: The Sino-Soviet Struggle for Supremacy, 1962–1967*. Washington, D.C.: Woodrow Wilson Center Press, 2009.

Reardon-Anderson, James. *Reluctant Pioneers: China's Expansion Northward, 1644–1937*. Stanford: Stanford University Press, 2005.

Remnev, Anatolii, ed. *Sibir' v sostave Rossiiskoi imperii*. Moscow: Novoe literaturnoe obozrenie, 2007.

Ren Guofang. "1945 nian Su, Ri zai Haila'er shi de jizhan." In *Haila'er wenshi ziliao*, vol. 5, edited by Zhongguorenmin zhengzhi xieshang huiyi Haila'er shi weiyuanhui wenshi ziliao weiyuanhui, 54–61. Hailar: Haila'er shi chubanshe, 1995.

Rieber, Alfred J. *Stalin and the Struggle for Supremacy in Eurasia*. Cambridge: Cambridge University Press, 2015.

———. *The Struggle for the Eurasian Borderlands: From the Rise of Early Modern Empires to the End of the First World War*. Cambridge: Cambridge University Press, 2014.

Ristaino, Marcia R. "Shanghai: Russische Flüchtlinge im 'gelben Babylon.'" In *Der große Exodus: Die russische Emigration und ihre Zentren, 1917 bis 1941*, edited by Karl Schlögel, 329–345. Munich: C.H. Beck, 1994.

Robinson, Thomas. "China Confronts the Soviet Union: Warfare and Diplomacy on China's Inner Asian Frontiers." In *Cambridge History of China*, vol. 15, edited by Roderick MacFarquhar and John K. Fairbank, 218–301. Cambridge: Cambridge University Press, 1991.

Rossabi, Morris, ed. *Governing China's Multiethnic Frontiers*. Seattle: University of Washington Press, 2005.

Roth-Ey, Kristin. "Finding a Home for Television in the USSR, 1950–1970." *Slavic Review* 66, no. 2 (2007): 278–306.

Rupen, Robert A. "The Buriat Intelligentsia." *Far Eastern Quarterly* 15, no. 3 (May 1956): 383–398.

———. "Mongolia in the Sino-Soviet Dispute." *China Quarterly* 16 (October–December 1963): 75–85.

Sablin, Ivan. "National Autonomies in the Far Eastern Republic: Post-imperial Diversity Management in Pacific Russia, 1920–1922." *History and Anthropology* 28, no. 4 (2017): 445–460.

Sahlins, Peter. *Boundaries: The Making of France and Spain in the Pyrenees.* Berkeley: University of California Press, 1989.

Sanders, Alan J. K. "Mongolia 1975: 'One Crew in Battle, One Brigade in Labour' with the USSR." *Asian Survey* 16, no. 1 (January 1976): 66–71.

Sanjdorj, M. *Manchu Chinese Colonial Rule in Northern Mongolia.* Translated by Urgunge Onon. London: Hurst, 1980.

Sassen, Saskia. *Territory, Authority, Rights: From Medieval to Global Assemblages.* Princeton: Princeton University Press, 2006.

Schivelbusch, Wolfgang. *The Railroad Journey: The Industrialization of Time and Space in the 19th Century.* Berkeley: University of California Press, 1986.

Schlögel, Karl. "Polenmarkt." In *Das Wunder von Nishnij oder die Rückkehr der Städte: Berichte und Essays*, 259–266. Frankfurt a. M.: Eichborn, 1991.

———. *Terror und Traum: Moskau 1937.* Munich: Hanser, 2008.

Scott, N. B. "Sino-Soviet Trade." *Soviet Studies* 10, no. 2 (October 1958): 151–161.

Shan, Patrick Fuliang. *Taming China's Wilderness: Immigration, Settlement and the Shaping of the Heilongjiang Frontier, 1900–1931.* London: Routledge, 2014.

Shao Dan. *Remote Homeland, Recovered Borderland: Manchus, Manchoukuo, and Manchuria, 1907–1985.* Honolulu: University of Hawai'i Press, 2011.

Shaw, Charles. "Friendship under Lock and Key: The Soviet Central Asian Border, 1918–34." *Central Asian Survey* 30, nos. 3–4 (2011): 331–348.

Shen Zhihua and Li Danhui. *After Leaning to One Side: China and Its Allies in the Cold War.* Washington, D.C.: Woodrow Wilson Center Press, 2011.

Shi Fang, Liu Shuang, and Gao Ling. *Ha'erbin E qiao shi.* Harbin: Heilongjiang renmin chubanshe, 2003.

Shu Guang Zhang. "Sino-Soviet Economic Cooperation." In *Brothers in Arms: The Rise and Fall of the Sino-Soviet Alliance, 1945–1963*, edited by Odd Arne Westad, 189–225. Washington, D.C.: Woodrow Wilson Center Press, 1998.

Shulman, Elena. *Stalinism on the Frontier of Empire: Women and State Formation in the Soviet Far East.* Cambridge: Cambridge University Press, 2008.

Sibiriakov, N. S. "Konets Zabaikal'skogo kazach'ego voiska (Primechaniia B. Trofimova)." In *Minuvshee: Istoricheskii al'manakh*, 193–254. Moscow: Progress, 1990.

Siegelbaum, Lewis H. "Another 'Yellow Peril': Chinese Migrants in the Russian Far East and the Russian Reaction before 1917." *Modern Asian Studies* 12, no. 2 (1978): 307–330.

Siri Sentai. "Minguo, weiman shidai yihou de Hulunbei'er." In *Hulunbei'er wenshi ziliao*, vol. 5, edited by Zhongguorenmin zhengzhi xieshang huiyi Hulunbei'er meng weiyuanhui wenshi ziliao weiyuanhui, 89–107. Hailar: Neimenggu wenhua chubanshe, 1994.

Skrynnikova, Tat'iana. "Pogranichnye identichnosti: Buriaty mezhdu Mongoliei i Rossiei." *Ab Imperio* 1 (2003): 395–420.

Sneath, David. *Changing Inner Mongolia: Pastoral Mongolian Society and the Chinese State.* Oxford: Oxford University Press, 2000.

Snow, Russell E. "The Russian Revolution of 1917–1918 in Transbaikalia." *Soviet Studies* 23 (1971–1972): 201–215.

Song Nianshen. *Making Borders in Modern East Asia: The Tumen River Demarcation, 1881–1919.* Cambridge: Cambridge University Press, 2018.

Sontag, John P. "The Soviet War Scare of 1926–27." *Russian Review* 34, no. 1 (January 1975): 66–77.

Sorokina, Tat'iana. "'Vzaimnoe soglashenie o spirte i opiume': Opyt sovmestnoi bor'by Rossii i Kitaia s kontrabandoi v nachale XX v." In *Migratsii i diaspory v sotsiokul'turnom, politicheskom i ekonomicheskom prostranstve Sibiri: Rubezhi XIX–XX i XX–XXI vekov*, edited by Viktor Diatlov, 229–251. Irkutsk: Ottisk, 2010.

Steinberg, John W., David Wolff, et al., eds. *The Russo-Japanese War in Global Perspective: World War Zero.* Vols. 1–2. Leiden: Brill, 2005, 2007.

Stephan, John J. *The Russian Far East: A History.* Stanford: Stanford University Press, 1994.

Suleski, Ronald. *Civil Government in Warlord China: Tradition, Modernization and Manchuria.* New York: Peter Lang, 2002.

Summers, William C. *The Great Manchurian Plague of 1910–1911: The Geopolitics of an Epidemic Disease.* New Haven, Conn.: Yale University Press, 2012.

Sunderland, Willard. *The Baron's Cloak: A History of the Russian Empire in War and Revolution.* Ithaca, N.Y.: Cornell University Press, 2014.

———. "Empire without Imperialism? Ambiguities of Colonization in Tsarist Russia." *Ab Imperio* 2 (2003): 101–114.

———. *Taming the Wild Field: Colonization and Empire on the Russian Steppe.* Ithaca, N.Y.: Cornell University Press, 2004.

Suny, Ronald Grigor. *The Revenge of the Past: Nationalism, Revolution, and the Collapse of the Soviet Union.* Stanford: Stanford University Press, 1993.

Tagliacozzo, Eric. *Secret Trades, Porous Borders: Smuggling and States along a Southeast Asian Frontier, 1865–1915.* New Haven, Conn.: Yale University Press, 2005.

Tang, Peter S. H. *Russian and Soviet Policy in Manchuria and Outer Mongolia.* Durham, N.C.: Duke University Press, 1959.

Tarasov, Alexander. "The Chinese in the Transbaikal." *Far Eastern Affairs* 32, no. 1 (January 2004): 93–114.

Taskina, E., ed. *Russkii Kharbin.* Moscow: Izd-vo Moskovskogo universiteta "CheRo," 1998.

Tolmacheva, Marina. "The Early Russian Exploration and Mapping of the Chinese Frontier." *Cahiers du Monde russe* 41, no. 1 (January–March 2000): 41–56.

Treadgold, Donald W. *The Great Siberian Migration: Government and Peasant in Resettlement from Emancipation to the First World War.* Princeton: Princeton University Press, 1957.

Tsybin, Andrei. "Rol' organov OGPU v bor'be s kontrabandoi na Dal'nem Vostoke Rossii v 20–30-e gody XX v." *Tamozhennaia politika Rossii na Dal'nem Vostoke* 3, no. 44 (2008): 114–124.

Turner, Frederick Jackson. *The Frontier in American History.* 1893. New York: Henry Holt, 1920.

Urbansky, Sören. "Challenges of Subalternity on the Northeast Asian Frontier." *Kritika: Explorations in Russian and Eurasian History* 19, no. 4 (Fall 2018): 867–876.

———. "Der betrunkene Kosake: Schmuggel im sino-russischen Grenzland (circa 1860–1930)." In *Globalisierung imperial und sozialistisch: Russland und die Sowjetunion in der Globalgeschichte 1851–1991*, edited by Martin Aust, 301–329. Frankfurt a. M.: Campus, 2013.

———. "Der Kosake als Lehrer oder Exot? Fragen an einen Mandschukuo-Dokumentarfilm über die bäuerliche russische Diaspora am Grenzfluss Argun." In *Osteuropäische Geschichte und Globalgeschichte*, edited by Martin Aust and Julia Obertreis, 103–127. Stuttgart: Steiner, 2014.

———. "Diplomacy of Shunters: The Sino-Soviet Split Seen from a Provincial Archive in Russia." *PRC History Review* 2, no. 3 (June 2017): 16–18.

———. "Ebbe statt Sturmflut: Chinesen in Russlands Fernem Osten." *Osteuropa* 62, no. 3 (2012): 21–40.

———. *Kolonialer Wettstreit: Russland, China, Japan und die Ostchinesische Eisenbahn.* Frankfurt a. M.: Campus, 2008.

———. "Tokhtogo's Mission Impossible: Russia, China, and the Quasi-independence of Hulunbeir." *Inner Asia* 16, no. 1 (2014): 64–94.

———. "The Unfathomable Foe: Constructing the Enemy in the Sino-Soviet Borderlands, ca. 1969–1982." *Journal of Modern European History* 10, no. 2 (2012): 255–277.

Vámos, Péter. "'Only a Handshake but No Embrace': Sino-Soviet Normalization in the 1980s." In *China Learns from the Soviet Union, 1949–Present*, edited by Thomas Bernstein and Li Hua-yu, 79–104. Lanham, Md.: Rowman & Littlefield, 2009.

van de Ven, Hans. *Breaking with the Past: The Maritime Customs Service and the Global Origins of Modernity in China.* New York: Columbia University Press, 2014.

Varnavskii, Pavel. "Granitsy Sovetskoi Buriatskoi Natsii: 'Natsional'no-kul'turnoe stroitel'stvo' v Buriatii v 1926–1929 gg. v proektakh natsional'noi intelligentsii i natsional-bol'shevikov." *Ab Imperio* 1 (2003): 149–176.

Walker, Edward W. "The Long Road from Empire: Legacies of Nation Building in the Soviet Successor States." In *Empire to Nation: Historical Perspectives on the Making of the Modern World*, edited by Joseph W. Esherick, Hasan Kayali, and Eric Van Young, 299–339. Lanham, Md.: Rowman & Littlefield, 2006.

Walker, Michael. *The 1929 Sino-Soviet War: The War Nobody Knew.* Lawrence: University Press of Kansas, 2017.

Wemheuer, Felix. *Famine Politics in Maoist China and the Soviet Union.* New Haven, Conn.: Yale University Press, 2014.

Westad, Odd Arne. "Introduction." In *Brothers in Arms: The Rise and Fall of the Sino-Soviet Alliance, 1945–1963*, edited by Odd Arne Westad, 1–46. Washington, D.C.: Woodrow Wilson Center Press, 1998.

———. "Struggles for Modernity: The Golden Years of the Sino-Soviet Alliance." In *The Cold War in East Asia 1945–1991*, edited by Tsuyoshi Hasegawa, 35–62. Washington, D.C.: Woodrow Wilson Center Press, 2011.

White, Richard. *Middle Ground: Indians, Empires, and Republics in the Great Lakes Region, 1650–1815.* Cambridge: Cambridge University Press, 1991.

Widmer, Eric. *The Russian Ecclesiastical Mission in Peking during the Eighteenth Century.* Cambridge, Mass.: Harvard University Press, 1976.

Wilson, Jeanne L. *Strategic Partners: Russian-Chinese Relations in the Post-Soviet Era*. Armonk, N.Y.: M. E. Sharpe, 2004.

Wishnick, Elizabeth. *Mending Fences: The Evolution of Moscow's China Policy, from Brezhnev to Yeltsin*. Seattle: University of Washington Press, 2001.

Wolff, David. "Stalin's Postwar Border-Making Tactics: East and West." *Cahiers du Monde russe* 52, nos. 2–3 (April–September 2011): 273–291.

———. *To the Harbin Station: The Liberal Alternative in Russian Manchuria, 1898–1914*. Stanford: Stanford University Press, 1999.

Worster, Donald. *Under Western Skies: Nature and History in the American West*. New York: Oxford University Press, 1992.

Wu Tieying. "'Manzhouli jieyue' zhi xingcheng jiqi qianyin houguo zai tan." In *Manzhouli wenshi ziliao*, vol. 5, edited by Zhengxie Manzhouli shi weiyuanhui wenshi ziliao yanjiu weiyuanhui, 1–17. N.p., 1995.

Xu Zhanxin. "Canjia Aotebao'er chezhan lüke zhanshe luocheng yishi jingguo." In *Manzhouli wenshi ziliao*, vol. 9, edited by Zhongguorenmin zhengzhi xieshang huiyi Manzhouli shi weiyuanhui, 133–134. Hulunbeir: n.p., 2003.

———. "Zhong Su renmin youyi gong jianshe shimo." In *Manzhouli wenshi ziliao*, edited by Zhongguorenmin zhengzhi xieshang huiyi Manzhouli shi weiyuanhui, vol. 9, 217–219. Hulunbeir: n.p., 2003.

Yamamuro, Shin'ichi. *Manchuria under Japanese Dominion*. Philadelphia: University of Pennsylvania Press, 2006.

Yang Kuisong. "The Sino-Soviet Border Clash of 1969: From Zhenbao Island to Sino-American Rapprochement." *Cold War History* 1, no. 1 (2000): 21–52.

Young, Louise. *Japan's Total Empire: Manchuria and the Culture of Wartime Imperialism*. Berkeley: University of California Press, 1998.

Zalesskaia, Ol'ga. "Gosudarstvennaia torgovlia sovetskogo Dal'nego Vostoka s Severo-Vostochnym Kitaem v 1920-e gg." *Problemy Dal'nego Vostoka* 3 (2008): 43–57.

Zatsepine, Victor. *Beyond the Amur: Frontier Encounters between China and Russia, 1850–1930*. Vancouver: University of British Columbia Press, 2017.

Zhamtsarano, Ts. Zh. "Kollektivizatsiia sel'skogo khoziaistva v Aginskom okruge." In *Novosti Aginskikh Kraevedov*, no. 1, 36–44. Chita: RIS Zabaikal'skogo Filiala Geogr. ob-va SSSR, 1971.

Zhang Shengfa. "The Main Causes for the Return of the Changchun Railway to China and Its Impact on Sino-Soviet Relations." In *China Learns from the Soviet Union, 1949-Present*, edited by Thomas Bernstein and Li Hua-yu, 61–78. Lanham, Md.: Rowman & Littlefield, 2010.

———. "Return of the Chinese Changchun Railway to China by the USSR." In *Manchurian Railways and the Opening of China: An International History*, edited by Bruce A. Elleman and Stephen Kotkin, 171–194. Armonk, N.Y.: M. E. Sharpe, 2009.

Zherebtsov, Gennadii A. *Krest'ianskie vosstaniia v Zabaikal'e (1930–1931 gody)*. Chita: n.p., 1996.

Zhonggong Manzhouli shi difang jian shi. Edited by Zhonggong Manzhouli shiwei "jian shi" bianxie zu. Beijing: Zhonggong dang shi chubanshe, 1997.

Zubkova, Elena. *Russia after the War: Hopes, Illusions, and Disappointments, 1945–1957.* Armonk, N.Y.: M. E. Sharpe, 1998.

Zubok, Vladislav. "Gorbachev's Policy toward East Asia, 1985–1991." In *The Cold War in East Asia 1945–1991,* edited by Tsuyoshi Hasegawa, 265–288. Washington, D.C.: Woodrow Wilson Center Press, 2011.

———. "The Soviet Union and China in the 1980s: Reconciliation and Divorce." *Cold War History* 17, no. 2 (2017): 121–141.

ILLUSTRATION CREDITS

0.1, 0.2, and 3.2   Maps by Cox Cartographic Ltd.

1.1   Photo album *Amur: Ot reki Arguni do sg. Pokrovskoi*, n.p., n.d. Courtesy of the Far East State Scientific Library, Khabarovsk.

1.2, and 3.3   Courtesy of the Library of Congress (LOT 13251 and LOT 2444).

2.1   Courtesy of Russian State Historical Archive of the Far East, Vladivostok (RGIA DV/702/1/312/9).

2.2   Courtesy of Olga Bakich, Toronto.

2.3   Courtesy of Russian State Historical Archive, Saint Petersburg (RGIA 323/1/1026/9).

2.4   *Okeanskii Vestnik*, 18 October 1912 (31 October 1912), 3.

2.5, 5.2, and 5.5   Images courtesy of the East Asia Image Collections (http://digital.lafayette.edu/collections/eastasia), from the Gerald & Rella Warner Collection, Special Collections and College Archives, Skillman Library, © Lafayette College.

2.6   E. L. Tesler, "Gan'chzhurskaia iarmarka 1933 goda," *Vestnik Man'chzhurii* 18–19 (15 October 1933): 85.

2.7, 4.2, and 4.3   Reproduced by permission of University of Cambridge Museum of Archaeology & Anthropology (N.21287.LIN, N.22060.LIN, and N.81225.LIN).

3.1   Courtesy of the British Library (EAP264/1/8).

4.1   Ekonomicheskoe biuro KVZhD, *Man'chzhuriia: Ekonomichesko-geograficheskoe opisanie*, pt. 1 (Harbin: Tipo-litografiia KVZhD, 1934), 92.

5.1   Author's private collection.

5.3   Courtesy of State Archive of Chita Region, Chita (GAChO/R-1077/1/273).

5.4   *National Geographic* 82, no. 5 (November 1942): 630.

5.6   Nikolai Kostarev, *Granitsa na zamke* (Moscow: Molodaia gvardiia, 1930).

5.7   *Otpor*, 1 August 1934, 3.

6.1   Moscow: Izobrazitel'noe iskusstvo, 6 September 1954.

6.2, 6.3, 7.1, 9.1, and 9.2   Photographs by the author.

7.2   *Doloi novykh tsarei! Antikitaiskie zlodeianiia sovetskogo revizionizma na rekakh Kheiluntszian i Usulitszian* (Beijing: Izdatel'stvo literatury na inostrannykh iazykakh, 1969), no pagination.

7.3   *Zabaikal'ets*, 15 July 1978, 4.

8.1   Courtesy *Zabaikal'skaia Magistral'* editorial archive.

8.2   Courtesy of Aleksandr P. Tarasov, Chita.

8.3   Photo by Phillip Partridge, London.

INDEX

Abagaitui, 12, 33–37, 77–80, 82, 86, 124, 143,
    159, 165–166, 170, 172, 212–214, 221,
    226–227, 245, 285n58
Abagaitui Island, 268
Ablov, Vasilii I., 114
Afansev, Mikhail E., 113
Afghanistan, 219, 251, 253
Aga Steppe, 11, 24–25, 92–93, 99, 138–142,
    280n27, 291n5, 299n78, 310n4, 314n31
agriculture, 29, 63–68, 74–75, 93, 120,
    142–145, 181, 198, 213, 215, 227, 229, 257,
    269, 306n117, 314n31; and animal
    husbandry, 1, 13, 16, 21, 65, 68, 74, 93,
    140–141, 143, 158, 180, 183–184, 213, 269,
    299n72
Aigun, 27, 32
Aksha, 15, 23, 93, 281n33
Albazin, 19
alcohol: impact on public health and safety,
    127–128; such as khanshin, 57, 58, 59, 63;
    such as vodka, 15, 46, 57, 59, 63, 68, 203,
    263, 311n40. See also smuggling
Aleshin, Vasilii V., 203
American Committee for the Aid to the
    People of Trekhreche, 158
Amur region, 17–19, 30, 32–33, 37, 52–53, 57,
    62, 65–66, 174, 207, 268–270, 279nn8 and
    22, 290n155
Amur River, 8–9, 11, 18–19, 27, 44, 62, 66,
    166, 188, 268–269; steamship operations
    on the, 44
Andropov, Yuri, 252
Anti-Comintern: day, 183; Pact, 164. See also
    Comintern

architecture, 35, 146, 181, 300n88; in
    Manzhouli, 48, 127, 233, 266
Argun basin, 7–14, 20, 37, 44, 64, 88, 94, 117,
    132, 149, 207, 264, 270–272; demographics
    in the, 8–9, 19, 65, 174, 226–230, 268, 270
Argun River, 1–2, 7–17, 62, 66, 188, 269;
    topography of, 11, 65, 75–77, 207;
    transport on the, 3, 12–13, 16, 32, 167, 207,
    272
Argunsk, 55, 65, 156
arms race, 164, 167, 193, 219
Asiatic Mounted Division, 117
Association of Russian (Soviet) Émigrés,
    212
asylum, 97, 100, 222
Australia, 212, 275
Averchenko, Arkadii T., 126

Babuzhab, 109, 293n67
Badmazhabe, Namsarai B., 305n108
Baikal Lake, 8, 18, 24, 30, 40, 53, 164
Baikov, Fedor I., 18
Baksheev, Aleksei P., 184
banner system, 25–27, 72–73, 91, 107–110,
    138, 179, 281nn35 and 37
Barguts. See indigenous peoples
Batuev, Dair, 92, 143
bazaar, 35, 38, 48, 112, 121, 261, 262, 271,
    321n39
Beijing: Chinese merchants from, 33;
    Orthodox Diocese of 156; Red Guards in,
    241; Russian mission to 18–20; Russian-
    Orthodox Mission in, 48; See also
    diplomatic relations; railroads